82

TROUBLE-SHOOTING MATHEMATICS SKILLS

BASIC COMPETENCY EDITION

Allen L. Bernstein

David W. Wells

TROUBLE-SHOOTING MATHEMATICS SKILLS

BASIC COMPETENCY EDITION

HOLT, RINEHART AND WINSTON, PUBLISHERS
New York • Toronto • London • Sydney

ABOUT THE AUTHORS

ALLEN L. BERNSTEIN is Curriculum and Research Consultant, Wayne County Intermediate School District, Wayne, Michigan.

DAVID W. WELLS is Assistant Superintendent for Instruction and Director of Mathematics Education, Oakland Schools, Pontiac, Michigan.

Photo credits appear on page 385.

ISBN: 0-03-041686-8

8 9 0 1 2 3 4 5 6 7 039 9 8 7 6 5 4 3 2 1

Contents

UNIT 1
Addition of Whole Numbers

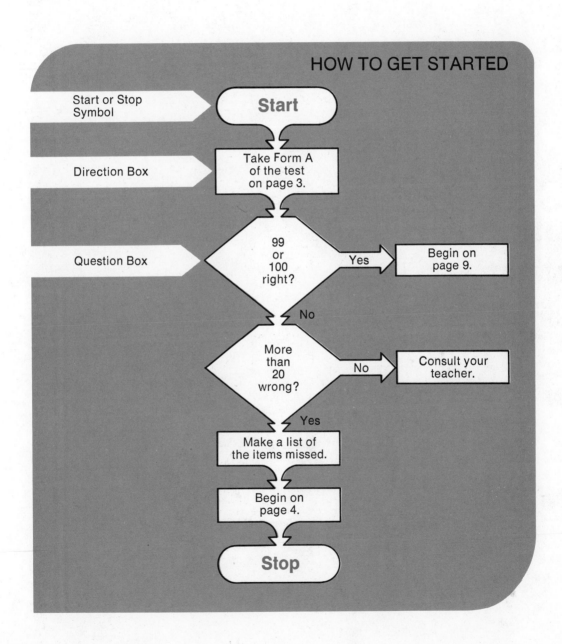

HOW TO GET STARTED

Start or Stop Symbol

Start

Direction Box

Take Form A of the test on page 3.

Question Box

99 or 100 right? — Yes → Begin on page 9.

No

More than 20 wrong? — No → Consult your teacher.

Yes

Make a list of the items missed.

Begin on page 4.

Stop

ADDITION FACTS TEST FORM A—4 MINUTES

1.	0 +2	9 +2	1 +1	7 +2	0 +1	7 +3	5 +2	8 +3	4 +2	2 +1
2.	3 +2	2 +0	0 +0	2 +3	1 +2	8 +2	6 +3	1 +0	6 +2	9 +3
3.	6 +4	4 +1	3 +4	2 +2	7 +4	1 +3	2 +4	5 +3	8 +4	3 +0
4.	0 +4	4 +3	1 +4	3 +3	5 +4	3 +1	4 +4	0 +3	9 +4	4 +0
5.	2 +5	9 +6	5 +5	7 +6	1 +5	6 +6	6 +5	8 +6	5 +0	4 +5
6.	3 +6	9 +5	2 +6	5 +1	3 +5	4 +6	7 +5	0 +5	5 +6	8 +5
7.	2 +7	6 +8	7 +1	7 +8	6 +1	5 +7	1 +7	1 +6	0 +7	8 +8
8.	4 +7	7 +7	6 +0	6 +7	9 +7	3 +7	0 +6	9 +8	8 +7	7 +0
9.	5 +9	1 +8	4 +9	3 +8	9 +1	6 +9	0 +8	2 +8	1 +9	8 +0
10.	4 +8	2 +9	0 +9	7 +9	3 +9	5 +8	8 +9	9 +0	8 +1	9 +9

ADDITION FACTS TEST FORM B—3 MINUTES

1.	6 +6	9 +6	4 +5	2 +5	5 +0	7 +6	1 +5	6 +5	5 +5	8 +6
2.	2 +6	8 +5	3 +6	7 +5	5 +1	4 +6	5 +6	9 +5	0 +5	3 +5
3.	7 +1	8 +8	1 +6	7 +8	5 +7	0 +7	6 +8	2 +7	6 +1	1 +7
4.	0 +6	7 +7	7 +0	6 +7	6 +0	8 +7	4 +7	9 +7	9 +8	3 +7
5.	6 +9	8 +0	5 +9	2 +8	4 +9	9 +1	1 +8	0 +8	1 +9	3 +8
6.	7 +9	9 +9	9 +0	4 +8	8 +1	3 +9	0 +9	8 +9	5 +8	2 +9

Addition Facts

THINK OF MONEY

EXAMPLE 1   Add.   6
                          +9

SOLUTION

Think of 6 as 1 nickel
and 1 cent.

Think of 9 as 1 nickel
and 4 cents.

2 nickels, 5 cents is 15¢. So,   6
                                +9
                                15

Add. Think of money.

1. 6	**2.** 6	**3.** 5	**4.** 4	**5.** 8
+7	+8	+7	+8	+9

THINK OF MAKING DOUBLES

These facts are called doubles.

5	6	7	8	9	10
+5	+6	+7	+8	+9	+10
10	12	14	16	18	20

EXAMPLE 2   Add.
$$\begin{array}{r} 8 \\ +9 \end{array}$$

SOLUTION

8 and 8 is 16. 8 and 9
must be 1 more than 16.

$$\begin{array}{r} 8 \\ +9 \end{array} \longrightarrow \left\{\begin{array}{r} 8 \\ 8 \\ 1 \end{array}\right. \qquad \left.\begin{array}{r} 8 \\ 8 \end{array}\right\} \longrightarrow 16$$
$$\begin{array}{r} 1 \qquad \qquad 1 \\ \hline 17 \end{array}$$

EXAMPLE 3   Add.
$$\begin{array}{r} 7 \\ +8 \end{array}$$

SOLUTION   7 and 7 is 14. 7 and 8 must be 1 more than 14, or 15.

Add. Think of making doubles.

6.	**7.**	**8.**	**9.**	**10.**
5 +6	6 +7	8 +6	8 +9	10 +11

THINK OF MAKING A TEN

These are facts that make ten.

9	8	7	6	5	4
+1	+2	+3	+4	+5	+6
10	10	10	10	10	10

EXAMPLE 4   Add.
$$\begin{array}{r} 9 \\ +7 \end{array}$$

SOLUTION   Think of a dot strip.

Put 1 colored dot with the
9 black dots to make a ten.

9   **7**   **10**   **6**

$$\begin{array}{r} 10 \\ +6 \\ \hline 16 \end{array} \qquad \text{So,} \begin{array}{r} 9 \\ +7 \\ \hline 16 \end{array}$$

Add. Think of making a ten.

11.	**12.**	**13.**	**14.**	**15.**
9 +6	8 +7	8 +9	8 +5	9 +5

PRACTICE SET 1
Practice the facts that you missed on Form A of the test until you know them.

Return to Form B on page 3.

Using the Addition Facts

OBJECTIVE To find sums such as $\begin{array}{r}67\\+\ 8\end{array}$ by using the addition facts

To find each of these sums, you use this one fact:
$$\begin{array}{r}8\\+5\\\hline13\end{array}$$

$$\begin{array}{r}18\\+\ 5\\\hline23\end{array}\qquad\begin{array}{r}28\\+\ 5\\\hline33\end{array}\qquad\begin{array}{r}38\\+\ 5\\\hline43\end{array}\qquad\begin{array}{r}48\\+\ 5\\\hline53\end{array}$$

EXAMPLE 1 Add. $\begin{array}{r}58\\+\ 5\end{array}$

SOLUTION

Use $\begin{array}{r}8\\+5\\\hline13\end{array}$

$$58\longrightarrow\begin{cases}50\\8\\5\end{cases}\qquad\begin{matrix}50\\8\\5\end{matrix}\Big\}\longrightarrow\begin{array}{r}50\\+13\\\hline63\end{array}$$

EXAMPLE 2 Add. Use the same addition fact.

$$\begin{array}{r}27\\+\ 8\end{array}\qquad\qquad\begin{array}{r}57\\+\ 8\end{array}$$

SOLUTION

Use $\begin{array}{r}7\\+8\\\hline15\end{array}$

$$27\longrightarrow\begin{cases}20\\7\\8\end{cases}\longrightarrow\begin{array}{r}20\\+15\\\hline35\end{array}\qquad57\longrightarrow\begin{cases}50\\7\\8\end{cases}\longrightarrow\begin{array}{r}50\\+15\\\hline65\end{array}$$

- -

Add. Use the same addition fact.

1. $\begin{array}{r}29\\+\ 7\end{array}$ $\begin{array}{r}39\\+\ 7\end{array}$ **2.** $\begin{array}{r}37\\+\ 5\end{array}$ $\begin{array}{r}67\\+\ 5\end{array}$ **3.** $\begin{array}{r}48\\+\ 9\end{array}$ $\begin{array}{r}88\\+\ 9\end{array}$

4. $\begin{array}{r}78\\+\ 5\end{array}$ $\begin{array}{r}88\\+\ 5\end{array}$ **5.** $\begin{array}{r}29\\+\ 4\end{array}$ $\begin{array}{r}69\\+\ 4\end{array}$ **6.** $\begin{array}{r}76\\+\ 7\end{array}$ $\begin{array}{r}46\\+\ 7\end{array}$

PRACTICE SET 2

Add.

1. 34 + 8	**2.** 44 + 8	**3.** 94 + 8	**4.** 49 + 8	**5.** 29 + 8	**6.** 79 + 8
7. 69 + 5	**8.** 49 + 5	**9.** 89 + 5	**10.** 97 + 4	**11.** 37 + 4	**12.** 57 + 4
13. 79 + 4	**14.** 29 + 4	**15.** 69 + 4	**16.** 86 + 7	**17.** 26 + 7	**18.** 56 + 7
19. 46 + 8	**20.** 56 + 8	**21.** 96 + 8	**22.** 67 + 8	**23.** 87 + 8	**24.** 27 + 8

PRACTICE SET 3

Add.

1. 56 + 1	**2.** 81 + 3	**3.** 80 + 3	**4.** 73 + 6	**5.** 33 + 7	**6.** 54 + 4
7. 72 + 3	**8.** 53 + 7	**9.** 62 + 7	**10.** 68 + 3	**11.** 79 + 3	**12.** 96 + 6
13. 77 + 9	**14.** 95 + 6	**15.** 77 + 7	**16.** 22 + 8	**17.** 50 + 6	**18.** 59 + 3
19. 19 + 9	**20.** 33 + 8	**21.** 47 + 5	**22.** 41 + 9	**23.** 23 + 9	**24.** 50 + 7

PRACTICE SET 4

Add.

1. 58 + 4	**2.** 98 + 2	**3.** 23 + 9	**4.** 15 + 8	**5.** 44 + 9	**6.** 48 + 8
7. 67 + 5	**8.** 77 + 6	**9.** 87 + 3	**10.** 64 + 7	**11.** 72 + 7	**12.** 35 + 8
13. 38 + 6	**14.** 62 + 9	**15.** 49 + 3	**16.** 63 + 4	**17.** 27 + 8	**18.** 15 + 8
19. 39 + 6	**20.** 38 + 7	**21.** 17 + 9	**22.** 51 + 5	**23.** 22 + 7	**24.** 63 + 8

Tens, Hundreds, and Thousands

OBJECTIVE To find sums such as $\begin{array}{r}90\\+60\end{array}$, $\begin{array}{r}900\\+600\end{array}$, and $\begin{array}{r}9,000\\+6,000\end{array}$

You can use the addition facts to add tens, hundreds, or thousands.

EXAMPLE

Use 9 + 6 = 15.

90	900	9,000
+60	+600	+6,000
150	1,500	15,000

Add.

1. 40   2. 400   3. 4,000
   +70   +700   +7,000

PRACTICE SET 5

Add.

1. 60   2. 80   3. 30   4. 40   5. 70   6. 30
   +70   +90   +80   +50   +10   +70

7. 10   8. 90   9. 60   10. 40   11. 50   12. 80
   +90   +70   +80   +20   +40   +60

13. 20   14. 70   15. 90   16. 80   17. 60   18. 80
    +70   +60   +90   +10   +90   +50

PRACTICE SET 6

Add.

1. 300   2. 400   3. 500   4. 700   5. 800
   +900   +600   +500   +200   +400

6. 600   7. 300   8. 500   9. 700   10. 900
   +900   +500   +900   +900   +200

11. 700   12. 900   13. 900   14. 600   15. 700
    +400   +800   +700   +700   +700

16. 1,000   17. 1,100   18. 1,400   19. 3,200   20. 4,100
    +6,000   +3,000   +2,300   +1,000   +2,200

DIAGNOSTIC TEST: ADDITION FORM A—20 MINUTES

Add and check.

1.	**2.**	**3.**	**4.**	**5.**	**6.**	**7.**
23	15	75	59	18	599	376
5	54	55	43	105	350	890
14	87	16	50	324	622	350
38	97	67	51	940	585	378
97	31	26	18	997	87	94
11	74	26	81	443	87	232

8.	**9.**	**10.**	**11.**	**12.**	**13.**	**14.**
249	7	25	23	92	246	271
611	43	28	10	81	448	638
51	61	88	63	60	61	736
805	31	34	37	99	107	791
251	57	53	65	26	277	959
797	9	25	42	18	687	210
	97	11	50	70	408	948
	93	7	95	25	437	819

Did You Have

More than 11 right?
Begin on page 17.

9, 10, or 11 right?
Begin on page 15.

Less than 9 right?
Begin on page 10.

DIAGNOSTIC TEST: ADDITION FORM B—20 MINUTES

Add and check.

1.	**2.**	**3.**	**4.**	**5.**	**6.**	**7.**
32	51	57	95	23	789	736
4	45	75	34	206	530	908
18	78	26	63	423	262	503
28	79	76	15	940	855	873
87	13	62	81	998	87	96
31	96	62	76	446	93	323

8.	**9.**	**10.**	**11.**	**12.**	**13.**	**14.**
347	6	36	24	82	246	127
610	34	24	11	91	844	836
71	72	87	36	70	16	637
508	43	43	38	99	701	971
152	58	56	76	37	772	599
896	8	52	24	19	786	102
	79	10	70	80	804	937
	98	8	98	34	347	806

More than 11 right? Begin on page 17. Less than 12 right? Consult your teacher.

Adding More Than Two Numbers

OBJECTIVE   To find the sum of several numbers, each less than 10

Sometimes, you can use the facts that make 10 to help find the sum of several numbers.

EXAMPLE   Find the sum.

Look for facts that make 10.

The facts that make 10 are on page 5.

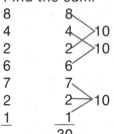

```
8        8
4        4  >10
2        2  >10
6        6
7        7
2        2  >10
1        1
        ___
         30
```

- -

Add.

1.	**2.**	**3.**	**4.**	**5.**
8	7	9	8	5
2	3	1	1	5
5	8	5	1	3
5	4	4	4	2
4	2	1	1	5
6	6	5	5	4
		5	7	7

PRACTICE SET 7
Add and check.

1.	**2.**	**3.**	**4.**	**5.**	**6.**	**7.**	**8.**	**9.**
5	6	3	1	6	7	6	7	6
6	8	4	3	8	8	5	5	7
7	5	2	2	9	9	7	6	5
9	3	1	5	5	5	4	8	4
1	4	5	4	7	5	3	1	3
3	7	7	7	3	6	1	1	3
5	9	9	8	1	7	2	7	8
9	1	6	5	2	7	7	9	1
3	6	5	2	1	9	8	5	4
7	4	5	8	9	1	2	5	6

PRACTICE SET 8
Add and check.

1.	2.	3.	4.	5.	6.	7.	8.	9.
9	7	8	2	6	8	1	1	5
8	6	9	9	8	9	5	9	6
3	4	3	7	5	1	9	4	4
7	2	7	5	2	5	6	6	3
5	9	8	6	4	6	4	8	9
2	8	6	4	8	4	3	2	8
1	2	5	2	9	2	7	3	7
5	7	4	9	1	3	8	4	2

10.	11.	12.	13.	14.	15.	16.	17.	18.
3	3	7	4	9	8	3	5	9
5	8	5	9	2	7	6	4	3
4	4	8	2	5	3	2	7	9
8	1	4	7	1	1	5	2	8
7	6	8	8	9	8	6	3	2
1	3	1	4	2	6	8	7	6
3	7	4	5	8	4	3	6	7
9	5	6	2	4	2	9	1	5

PRACTICE SET 9
Add and check.

1.	2.	3.	4.	5.	6.	7.	8.	9.
8	4	4	2	9	6	9	5	4
2	7	2	1	5	3	1	6	7
8	1	9	8	1	4	9	4	1
5	5	7	1	3	7	7	9	6
8	4	8	5	6	8	6	5	4
4	8	3	4	8	6	5	3	8
9	8	3	8	5	4	1	2	4
9	7	5	7	7	5	2	7	9
7	1	6	6	2	1	8	8	2
7	3	3	8	4	2	3	3	6

10.	11.	12.	13.	14.	15.	16.	17.	18.
2	8	7	3	5	1	6	7	4
1	2	5	5	2	4	2	9	6
9	8	7	1	7	8	8	3	3
3	8	5	1	4	4	4	9	3
7	5	1	8	6	2	7	9	2
8	4	1	7	6	1	1	9	8
6	9	4	2	8	2	9	8	1
4	9	7	7	7	9	5	7	9
2	1	8	1	2	7	7	7	5
1								

Adding Larger Numbers

OBJECTIVE To find the sum of larger numbers

Here are two ways of thinking about adding larger numbers.

EXPANDED FORM

EXAMPLE 1 Find the sum.
```
42
29
18
```

SOLUTION

Write each numeral in expanded form.

$19 = 10 + 9$
$70 + 10 = 80$

$42 = 40 + 2$
$29 = 20 + 9$
$\underline{18 = 10 + 8}$
$\quad = 70 + 19$
$\quad = 80 + 9$
$\quad = 89$

Add ones: 19
Add tens: 70
Sum: 89

EXAMPLE 2 Find the sum.
```
195
327
486
```

SOLUTION

Write each numeral in expanded form.

$18 = 10 + 8$
$190 + 10 = 200$
$800 + 200 = 1,000$

$195 = 100 + 90 + 5$
$327 = 300 + 20 + 7$
$\underline{486 = 400 + 80 + 6}$
$\quad = 800 + 190 + 18$
$\quad = 800 + 200 + 8$
$\quad = 1,000 + 8$
$\quad = 1,008$

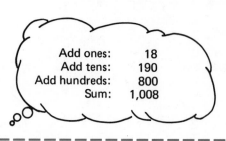

Add ones: 18
Add tens: 190
Add hundreds: 800
Sum: 1,008

Add. Use expanded form.

1. 38	**2.** 76	**3.** 87
53	21	49
<u>42</u>	<u>38</u>	<u>56</u>

4. 144	**5.** 235	**6.** 440
281	463	576
<u>352</u>	<u>598</u>	<u>729</u>

NUMBER PUZZLES

To add 23 and 46, write them in a box like this.

23 = 20 + 3
46 = 40 + 6

20	3	23
40	6	46

Now find the sums in each column.

```
  20        3        23
+40       +6       +46
 60        9        69
```

20	3	23
40	6	46
60	9	69

To check, add across the bottom: 60 + 9 = 69.

- -

Copy and complete these number puzzles.

7.

70	8	78
90	7	97

8.

25	36	
37	49	

PRACTICE SET 10
Add. Use expanded form.

```
 1. 23      2. 47      3. 28      4. 37      5. 34
    42         72         45         63         59
    34         95         55         85         82


 6. 54      7. 39      8. 31      9. 32     10. 23
    20         61         19         19         19
    97         11         61         62         26


11. 323    12. 247    13. 528    14. 637    15. 934
    342        372        445        163        153
    434        195        555        385        482


16. 754    17. 839    18. 631    19. 532    20. 723
    720        261        619        519        419
    197        311        561        562        326
```

PRACTICE SET 11
Add.

1. 38	2. 37	3. 33	4. 103	5. 105	6. 108
97	93	98	28	23	25
3	8	7	15	18	13

7. 49	8. 41	9. 48	10. 63	11. 67	12. 64
78	78	71	44	43	47
21	29	29	57	54	53

13. 74	14. 78	15. 75	16. 185	17. 189	18. 186
55	54	58	366	365	369
68	65	64	579	576	575

PRACTICE SET 12
Copy and complete these number puzzles.

1.

10	3	
50	6	

2.

40	8	
50	1	

3.

40	4	
70	7	

4.

30	6	
80	7	

5.

80	7	
50	8	

6.

50	6	
70	6	

7.

30	9	
90	9	

8.

80	3	
80	8	

9.

54	7	
63	4	

10.

45	7	
36	5	

11.

90	14	
53	47	

12.

29	63	
47	29	

13.

80	3	
40	8	

14.

20		23
	6	36

15.

	8	46
50		
	9	

16.

40		44
	7	
110		

17.

	6	36
50	7	

18.

80	7	
	8	
		145

19.

	6	93
100		111

20.

50		
	9	
	17	168

Regrouping in Addition

EXAMPLE 1 Add.
```
          384
          567
          249
          382
```

SOLUTION

As you add, write the regrouped numeral at the top of the next column.

```
       22     ←——— Regrouped numerals
      384
      567
      249
      382
    1,582
```

EXAMPLE 2 Add.
```
        1,689
          578
          367
          249
            3
           47
```

SOLUTION

As you add, write the regrouped numeral at the top of the next column.

```
     1 34     ←——— Regrouped numerals
    1,689
      578
      367
      249
        3
       47
    2,933
```

- -

Add.

1.	**2.**	**3.**
483	1,869	2,354
765	785	968
942	376	79
283	942	9
	4	456
	73	87
		1,003
		224
		999

Add and check.

1.	2.	3.	4.	5.	6.
44	67	3	235	886	401
43	13	22	960	744	367
34	8	38	541	322	637
95	16	87	422	194	19
13	5	21	884	841	363
50	68	77	642	118	23
37	40	46	128	902	835
	29				

7.	8.	9.	10.	11.	12.
20	53	84	733	446	1,596
47	46	29	974	488	469
93	69	74	501	233	292
19	69	48	258	486	399
54	22	53	506	463	673
50	76	82	929	560	731
87	15	26	253	212	223
69	45	64	599	269	333
58	54	92	601	330	246

Check the following sums. Correct those that are wrong.

1.	2.	3.	4.	5.
12	22	59	201	769
43	63	44	303	811
30	85	3	746	659
41	3	48	797	965
16	14	28	24	827
59	11	22	736	62
16	78	5	783	932
56	48	43	783	666
272	326	252	4,373	5,691

6.	7.	8.	9.	10.
64	75	58	358	584
10	30	25	228	977
71	1	79	849	551
60	33	25	560	588
37	86	9	465	649
47	54	98	701	131
279	278	294	3,161	4,270

Return to Form B on page 9.

Not Enough Information

What else do you need to know before you can solve the problem?

1. A dozen golf balls are marked down $2.50. What is the cost per dozen?

2. A youth group washed 23 cars to earn money. How much did they earn?

3. Dog food is sold in 6-can packages. How much would 15 cans cost?

4. Wool material was on sale for $4.25 a meter. How much did it cost Dee to make a skirt?

5. A scout group needs $16.00 to go on a camping trip. How much will each scout have to give?

6. Doug's plane ticket cost $97. How much per kilometer did his trip cost?

7. Ms. Gomez drives 60 kilometers from her business to her vacation home. How long does it take?

8. Betty bought eggs for 87¢ and a bag of potatoes for $1.39. How much change did she get?

Rounding

OBJECTIVE To round numbers to the nearest 10 or 100

About 40¢   About 90¢   About $14.00   About $20.00

NEAREST 10

To round to the nearest 10, use the digit in the ones place.

EXAMPLE 1 Round 35 to the nearest 10.
SOLUTION

30	
35	
40	35 ⟵ 5

35 is between 30 and 40. The digit in the ones place is 5.

So, 35 is 40 to the nearest 10.

EXAMPLE 2 Round 296 to the nearest 10.
SOLUTION

290	
296	
300	296 ⟵ 5 or more

296 is between 290 and 300. The digit in the ones place is 6.

So, 296 is 300 to the nearest 10.

EXAMPLE 3 Round 124 to the nearest 10.
SOLUTION

120	
124	
130	124 ⟵ less than 5

124 is between 120 and 130. The digit in the ones place is 4.

So, 124 is 120 to the nearest 10.

- -

Round to the nearest 10.

1. 38   **2.** 76   **3.** 94   **4.** 133   **5.** 158

NEAREST 100

To round to the nearest 100, use the digit in the tens place.

EXAMPLE 4 Round 388 to the nearest 100.

SOLUTION

388 is between 300 and 400. The digit in the tens place is 8.

$$
\begin{array}{l}
300 \\
388 \\
400
\end{array}
\qquad
\begin{array}{l}
388 \\
\;\;\uparrow\!\!-\!5 \text{ or more}
\end{array}
$$

So, 388 is 400 to the nearest 100.

EXAMPLE 5 Round 747 to the nearest 100.

SOLUTION

747 is between 700 and 800. The digit in the tens place is 4.

$$
\begin{array}{l}
700 \\
747 \\
800
\end{array}
\qquad
\begin{array}{l}
747 \\
\;\;\uparrow\!\!-\!\text{less than 5}
\end{array}
$$

So, 747 is 700 to the nearest 100.

- -

Round to the nearest 100.

6. 486 **7.** 761 **8.** 975 **9.** 816 **10.** 203

EXERCISES
Round to the nearest 10.

1. 28 **2.** 74 **3.** 77 **4.** 362 **5.** 471 **6.** 179

7. 455 **8.** 991 **9.** 563 **10.** 895 **11.** 2,472 **12.** 404

Round to the nearest 100.

13. 147 **14.** 231 **15.** 866 **16.** 575 **17.** 251

18. 687 **19.** 809 **20.** 722 **21.** 1,567 **22.** 456

23. 8,199 **24.** 647 **25.** 2,844 **26.** 1,448 **27.** 3,383

Fun Corner

Which do you think has the greater sum? Check by adding.

```
1 2 3 4 5 6 7 8 9                           1
1 2 3 4 5 6 7 8                           2 1
1 2 3 4 5 6 7                           3 2 1
1 2 3 4 5 6                           4 3 2 1
1 2 3 4 5                           5 4 3 2 1
1 2 3 4                           6 5 4 3 2 1
1 2 3                           7 6 5 4 3 2 1
1 2                           8 7 6 5 4 3 2 1
1                           9 8 7 6 5 4 3 2 1
```

Estimating Sums

OBJECTIVE   To estimate sums by rounding

EXAMPLE 1   Estimate the sum to the nearest 10.

Round each number to the nearest 10.

79 ⟶ 80
91 ⟶ 90
27 ⟶ 30
       200

The sum is about 200.

EXAMPLE 2   Estimate the sum to the nearest 10.

Round each number to the nearest 10.
Look for combinations that make 100.
The sum is about 250.

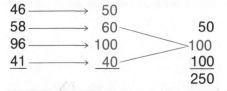

46 ⟶ 50
58 ⟶ 60   50
96 ⟶ 100   100
41 ⟶ 40   100
              250

Estimate the sum to the nearest 10.

1. 38	**2.** 22	**3.** 19	**4.** 136
55	77	31	49
72	89	63	8
		29	224

EXAMPLE 3   Estimate the sum to the nearest 100.

Round each number to the nearest 100.
Look for combinations that make 1,000.

The sum is about 2,100.

96 ⟶ 100
363 ⟶ 400   100
628 ⟶ 600   1,000
729 ⟶ 700
288 ⟶ 300   1,000
              2,100

Estimate the sum to the nearest 100.

5. 172	**6.** 737	**7.** 233	**8.** 309
387	547	96	760
213	458	681	58
		576	834

EXAMPLE 4

Round each price to the nearest 10 cents.

Estimate the total cost to the nearest 10 cents.

Chicken	$1.81	⟶	$1.80
Peaches	.59	⟶	.60
Milk	.72	⟶	.70
Bread	.68	⟶	.70
			$3.80

Estimate the total cost to the nearest 10 cents.

9. Shirt	$8.95	**10.** Cloth	$9.70
Tie	6.50	Lining	3.79
Socks	1.29	Pattern	2.35
Cuff links	5.50	Buckle	1.70

EXERCISES

Estimate the sum to the nearest 10.

1. 58	**2.** 93	**3.** 94	**4.** 67	**5.** 6	**6.** 142
34	95	70	8	260	37
72	82	86	43	943	43
51	20	42	63	56	530
		78	5	41	35

7. 65	**8.** 8	**9.** 22	**10.** 708	**11.** 181	**12.** 441
82	95	79	331	183	442
15	70	63	800	190	109
18	77	14	53	330	920
	24	84	260	433	47

Estimate the sum to the nearest 100.

13. 147	**14.** 830	**15.** 836	**16.** 928	**17.** 128	**18.** 574
62	441	765	452	148	327
155	182	353	130	936	890
218	77	95	805	67	424
191	51	96	819	636	74
318	192	199	138	792	722

19. 209	**20.** 470	**21.** 797	**22.** 972	**23.** 165	**24.** 241
191	121	984	416	424	251
115	325	764	262	211	83
978	764	676	824	219	127
506	303	780	149	226	175
68	354	819	696		

Estimate the total cost to the nearest 10 cents.

25. Light fixture $8.95
    Wire   .65
    Wall plug   .39
    Switch   .89
    Pliers   1.25

26. Paint $5.85
    Brush   2.95
    Drop cloth   .98
    Thinner   1.19
    Sandpaper   .40

27.
S-4095

JEAN'S DEPARTMENT STORE

Sold to *Mr. R. Burns*   6/5/78

1 Rug	$22.95
1 Blouse	4.59
2 pr. Stockings	3.85
1 Vacuum Cleaner	82.50
1 Handkerchief	.98
Tax	5.74
Total	

28.
936-25

BILL'S SERVICE CENTER

Sold to *Ms. C. Leland*   7/1/78

2 Used tires	$22.95
40 liters gas	7.24
Lubrication	1.75
8 liters oil	3.20
Brake repair	7.50
Tax	1.97
Total	

29. Estimate the total number of points scored to the nearest 10.

KICKOFFS RECORD	
Game	Points Scored
1	56
2	31
3	14
4	41
5	28
6	6

30. Estimate the total number of votes cast to the nearest 100.

VOTE TALLY	
Candidate	Votes
Mayor Eve Coleman	2,384
James Mason	1,194
Polly James	322
John Paulson	191
Marvin Stone	84

31. Estimate the total number of units to the nearest 100.

Monday   283 units
Tuesday   292 units
Wednesday   208 units
Thursday   326 units
Friday   342 units

32. Estimate the total number of square meters (m^2) of plaster to the nearest 10.

Bedrooms   335 m^2
Bathroom   18 m^2
Closet   36 m^2
Living room   112 m^2
Kitchen   110 m^2

Mental Arithmetic

$5.15 AND $.80 MAKES $5.95; $3.33 IS $3.30 PLUS $.03; $5.95 + $3.30 = $9.25; ANOTHER $.03 IS A TOTAL OF $9.28

$ 5.15

Oil 80¢
ANTIFREEZE $3.33

EXAMPLE   Find the sum mentally. $4.65
                                               .40
                                               .67

SOLUTION   Think: $4.65 and $.40 make $5.05; add $.67 (or $.65 and $.02) for a total of $5.72.

Another way   Think: $.40 and $.67 is $1.07; $1.00 and $4.65 is $5.65 plus another $.07 is $5.72.

Find the sum mentally.

1. $3.29	**2.** $2.60	**3.** $8.70	**4.** $5.50
.50	.55	.55	.99
.12	.60	.45	.21

EXERCISES
Find the sum mentally. Check by adding the columns.

1. $2.28	**2.** $3.19	**3.** $4.81	**4.** $4.27	**5.** $3.60
.40	.55	.21	1.28	.65
.12	1.09	.74	.36	.60

6. $ .57	**7.** $ .98	**8.** $7.50	**9.** $7.02	**10.** $ .91
9.70	.42	.99	2.11	5.15
.43	1.50	.08	.97	.75

Coin Problems

To find the number of each kind of coin in a collection

3 quarters   75¢

2 dimes   20¢

3 nickels   15¢

8 coins   110¢

8 coins make $1.10

EXAMPLE   How many of each kind of coin are in the collection?

7 coins make $1.00

SOLUTION

Look for 3 numbers that add to 7 until you find the combination whose value is the same as that of the collection.

$$
\begin{array}{lll}
4 & 4 \times 5¢ & = 20¢ \\
2 & 2 \times 10¢ & = 20¢ \\
\underline{1} & \underline{1 \times 25¢} & = \underline{25¢} \\
7 & & 65¢
\end{array}
$$

Doesn't work

$$
\begin{array}{lll}
3 & 3 \times 5¢ & = 15¢ \\
1 & 1 \times 10¢ & = 10¢ \\
\underline{3} & \underline{3 \times 25¢} & = \underline{75¢} \\
7 & & 100¢
\end{array}
$$

Works

There are 3 nickels, 1 dime, and 3 quarters.

How many of each kind of coin are in the collection?
More than one answer is possible for Exercises 8–10.

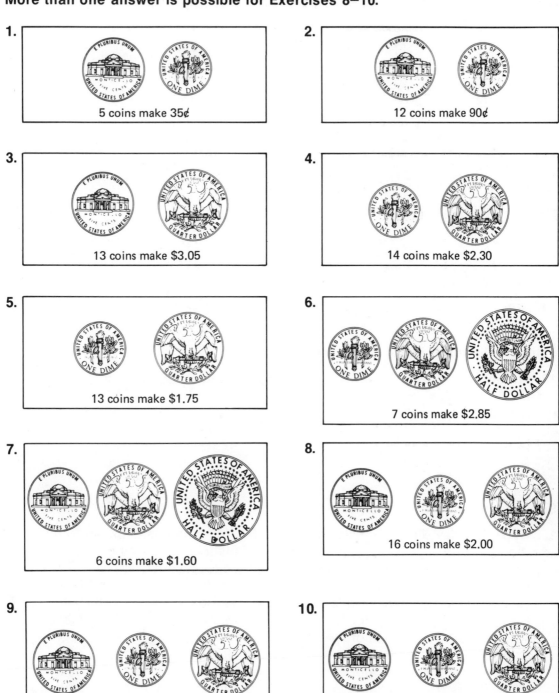

1. 5 coins make 35¢

2. 12 coins make 90¢

3. 13 coins make $3.05

4. 14 coins make $2.30

5. 13 coins make $1.75

6. 7 coins make $2.85

7. 6 coins make $1.60

8. 16 coins make $2.00

9. 20 coins make $2.20

10. 80 coins make $14.00

COIN PROBLEMS **25**

Test: Unit 1

Add and check.

1.	2.	3.	4.
235	48	503	720
341	665	190	819
880	404	963	704
390	220	757	388
257	45	444	791
588	651	62	211
		377	492
		77	388

Round to the nearest 10.

5. 47   6. 23   7. 142   8. 896

Round to the nearest 100.

9. 238   10. 483   11. 1,984   12. 2,429

Estimate the total cost to the nearest 10 cents.

13.		14.	
Turkey	$12.33	Sweater	$14.98
Milk	.67	Shirt	7.87
Bread	.68	Tie	3.49
Eggs	.93	Socks	1.69
Potatoes	1.29	Shoes	20.43
Butter	1.08	Umbrella	5.64

Solve each problem.

15. Bob's Sunday dinner consisted of the following:

Tomato juice	45 calories
Broiled steak	330 calories
Baked potato	90 calories
Butter	100 calories
Asparagus	10 calories
Carrots	45 calories
Apple pie	350 calories
Milk	160 calories

Find the total number of calories in Bob's dinner.

16. To the nearest thousand, state populations according to a recent census were:

California	19,954,000
Florida	6,789,000
Michigan	8,875,000
New Jersey	7,168,000
New York	18,191,000
Texas	11,197,000

What was the total population of these states?

UNIT 2
Subtraction of Whole Numbers

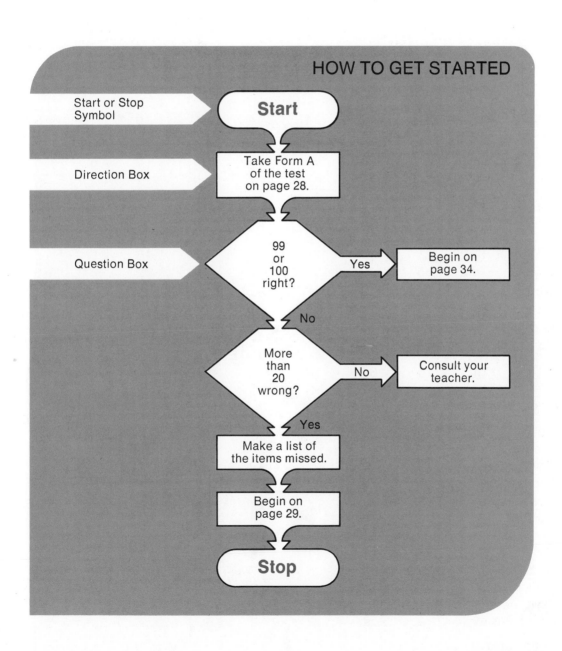

HOW TO GET STARTED

Start or Stop Symbol → **Start**

Direction Box → Take Form A of the test on page 28.

Question Box → 99 or 100 right? — Yes → Begin on page 34.

No

More than 20 wrong? — No → Consult your teacher.

Yes

Make a list of the items missed.

Begin on page 29.

Stop

SUBTRACTION FACTS TEST FORM A—4 MINUTES

1. $10-1$	$1-1$	$1-0$	$6-6$	$9-9$	$3-1$	$8-0$	$3-3$	$4-3$	$6-5$
2. $5-2$	$8-8$	$7-0$	$10-9$	$0-0$	$8-2$	$2-1$	$9-8$	$4-4$	$4-0$
3. $5-1$	$3-2$	$6-0$	$5-5$	$4-1$	$7-6$	$6-1$	$2-0$	$8-1$	$2-2$
4. $5-4$	$9-0$	$9-1$	$7-7$	$5-0$	$4-2$	$7-1$	$3-0$	$8-7$	$6-2$
5. $10-3$	$10-5$	$14-9$	$6-3$	$10-4$	$11-9$	$7-2$	$6-4$	$12-9$	$10-2$
6. $9-2$	$18-9$	$10-7$	$12-6$	$11-2$	$14-7$	$10-6$	$10-8$	$16-8$	$8-4$
7. $12-4$	$15-8$	$9-4$	$9-7$	$7-5$	$13-7$	$12-8$	$13-8$	$9-5$	$9-3$
8. $15-9$	$7-4$	$11-4$	$11-6$	$14-6$	$8-5$	$12-5$	$13-9$	$7-3$	$14-8$
9. $17-8$	$11-8$	$11-5$	$13-4$	$8-3$	$15-7$	$15-6$	$16-7$	$9-6$	$5-3$
10. $12-7$	$17-9$	$13-5$	$11-3$	$8-6$	$13-6$	$11-7$	$16-9$	$14-5$	$12-3$

SUBTRACTION FACTS TEST FORM B—3 MINUTES

1. $10-4$	$14-9$	$10-2$	$6-4$	$10-3$	$11-9$	$6-3$	$12-9$	$7-2$	$10-5$
2. $11-2$	$16-8$	$18-9$	$10-8$	$9-2$	$12-6$	$8-4$	$10-6$	$14-7$	$10-7$
3. $9-7$	$9-3$	$12-4$	$13-8$	$9-5$	$15-8$	$12-8$	$9-4$	$13-7$	$7-5$
4. $13-9$	$11-4$	$8-5$	$15-9$	$14-8$	$7-3$	$12-5$	$11-6$	$7-4$	$14-6$
5. $15-7$	$5-3$	$17-8$	$15-6$	$11-5$	$16-7$	$8-3$	$11-8$	$9-6$	$13-4$
6. $13-6$	$12-7$	$11-3$	$14-5$	$16-9$	$17-9$	$8-6$	$12-3$	$11-7$	$13-5$

Subtraction Facts

THINK OF RELATED ADDITION FACTS

EXAMPLE 1   Subtract.
$$\begin{array}{r} 15 \\ -\ 6 \\ \hline \end{array}$$

SOLUTION   Think: What do I add to 6 to get 15?   6 So,

The related addition is
6 + 9 = 15.

$$\begin{array}{r} 6 \\ +9 \\ \hline 15 \end{array} \qquad \begin{array}{r} 15 \\ -\ 6 \\ \hline 9 \end{array}$$

Subtract. Think of related addition facts.

1.	**2.**	**3.**	**4.**
9	11	17	12
−7	− 4	− 9	− 8

THINK OF BRIDGING TENS

Learn these facts.

$$\begin{array}{r} 10 \\ -\ 1 \\ \hline 9 \end{array} \quad \begin{array}{r} 10 \\ -\ 2 \\ \hline 8 \end{array} \quad \begin{array}{r} 10 \\ -\ 3 \\ \hline 7 \end{array} \quad \begin{array}{r} 10 \\ -\ 4 \\ \hline 6 \end{array} \quad \begin{array}{r} 10 \\ -\ 5 \\ \hline 5 \end{array} \quad \begin{array}{r} 10 \\ -\ 6 \\ \hline 4 \end{array} \quad \begin{array}{r} 10 \\ -\ 7 \\ \hline 3 \end{array} \quad \begin{array}{r} 10 \\ -\ 8 \\ \hline 2 \end{array} \quad \begin{array}{r} 10 \\ -\ 9 \\ \hline 1 \end{array}$$

EXAMPLE 2   Subtract.
$$\begin{array}{r} 13 \\ -\ 7 \\ \hline \end{array}$$

SOLUTION

Think: 7 from 10 is 3
and 3 more is 6.

$$\begin{array}{r} 13 \\ -\ 7 \\ \hline \end{array} \longrightarrow \begin{array}{r} 10 + 3 \\ -\ 7 \\ \hline 3 + 3 = 6 \end{array} \qquad \text{So,} \begin{array}{r} 13 \\ -\ 7 \\ \hline 6 \end{array}$$

EXAMPLE 3   Subtract.
$$\begin{array}{r} 17 \\ -\ 9 \\ \hline \end{array}$$

SOLUTION   Think: 9 from 10 is 1 and 7 more is 8.

Subtract. Think of bridging tens.

5.	**6.**	**7.**	**8.**
16	12	15	14
− 9	− 5	− 9	− 6

PRACTICE SET 1
Practice the facts that you missed on Form A of the test until you know them.

Return to Form B on page 28.

Using the Subtraction Facts

OBJECTIVE   To find differences such as $\begin{array}{r} 66 \\ -\ 8 \\ \hline \end{array}$

To do these subtractions, you use this one fact: $\begin{array}{r} 13 \\ -\ 7 \\ \hline \end{array}$

$\begin{array}{r} 23 \\ -\ 7 \\ \hline 16 \end{array}$ $\begin{array}{r} 33 \\ -\ 7 \\ \hline 26 \end{array}$ $\begin{array}{r} 43 \\ -\ 7 \\ \hline 36 \end{array}$ $\begin{array}{r} 63 \\ -\ 7 \\ \hline 56 \end{array}$ $\begin{array}{r} 83 \\ -\ 7 \\ \hline 76 \end{array}$ $\begin{array}{r} 93 \\ -\ 7 \\ \hline 86 \end{array}$

EXAMPLE 1   Subtract and check. $\begin{array}{r} 52 \\ -\ 7 \\ \hline \end{array}$

SOLUTION

Think of 52 as 40 + 12.

Add the answer to the number subtracted.

$52 \longrightarrow \begin{array}{r} 40 + 12 \\ -\ 7 \\ \hline 40 + \ 5 = 45 \end{array}$ So, $\begin{array}{r} 52 \\ -\ 7 \\ \hline 45 \end{array}$

Check: $\begin{array}{r} 7 \\ +45 \\ \hline 52 \end{array}$ ⟵——— Number subtracted
⟵——— Answer
⟵——— Number started with

EXAMPLE 2   Subtract and check. $\begin{array}{r} 76 \\ -\ 9 \\ \hline \end{array}$

SOLUTION   Think: 76 is 60 + 16; 16 − 9 is 7 and 60 more is 67.
Check: 67 + 9 is 76, so 67 is correct.

- -

Subtract. Use the same subtraction fact.

1. $\begin{array}{r} 66 \\ -\ 9 \\ \hline \end{array}$ $\begin{array}{r} 96 \\ -\ 9 \\ \hline \end{array}$ **2.** $\begin{array}{r} 27 \\ -\ 8 \\ \hline \end{array}$ $\begin{array}{r} 37 \\ -\ 8 \\ \hline \end{array}$

PRACTICE SET 2
Subtract and check.

1. $\begin{array}{r} 26 \\ -\ 2 \\ \hline \end{array}$ **2.** $\begin{array}{r} 36 \\ -\ 2 \\ \hline \end{array}$ **3.** $\begin{array}{r} 46 \\ -\ 2 \\ \hline \end{array}$ **4.** $\begin{array}{r} 56 \\ -\ 2 \\ \hline \end{array}$ **5.** $\begin{array}{r} 66 \\ -\ 9 \\ \hline \end{array}$ **6.** $\begin{array}{r} 76 \\ -\ 9 \\ \hline \end{array}$

7. $\begin{array}{r} 80 \\ -\ 4 \\ \hline \end{array}$ **8.** $\begin{array}{r} 90 \\ -\ 4 \\ \hline \end{array}$ **9.** $\begin{array}{r} 60 \\ -\ 4 \\ \hline \end{array}$ **10.** $\begin{array}{r} 50 \\ -\ 4 \\ \hline \end{array}$ **11.** $\begin{array}{r} 40 \\ -\ 4 \\ \hline \end{array}$ **12.** $\begin{array}{r} 30 \\ -\ 4 \\ \hline \end{array}$

13. $\begin{array}{r} 91 \\ -\ 3 \\ \hline \end{array}$ **14.** $\begin{array}{r} 31 \\ -\ 3 \\ \hline \end{array}$ **15.** $\begin{array}{r} 21 \\ -\ 3 \\ \hline \end{array}$ **16.** $\begin{array}{r} 52 \\ -\ 8 \\ \hline \end{array}$ **17.** $\begin{array}{r} 72 \\ -\ 8 \\ \hline \end{array}$ **18.** $\begin{array}{r} 82 \\ -\ 8 \\ \hline \end{array}$

PRACTICE SET 3
Subtract and check.

1. 43 $-\ 6$	**2.** 33 $-\ 6$	**3.** 34 $-\ 5$	**4.** 24 $-\ 5$	**5.** 94 $-\ 7$	**6.** 84 $-\ 7$
7. 27 $-\ 8$	**8.** 37 $-\ 8$	**9.** 47 $-\ 8$	**10.** 22 $-\ 6$	**11.** 32 $-\ 6$	**12.** 42 $-\ 6$
13. 53 $-\ 9$	**14.** 52 $-\ 5$	**15.** 48 $-\ 6$	**16.** 44 $-\ 5$	**17.** 61 $-\ 6$	**18.** 71 $-\ 4$
19. 37 $-\ 4$	**20.** 25 $-\ 9$	**21.** 29 $-\ 3$	**22.** 79 $-\ 5$	**23.** 36 $-\ 9$	**24.** 44 $-\ 7$

PRACTICE SET 4
Subtract and check.

1. 23 $-\ 8$	**2.** 45 $-\ 6$	**3.** 69 $-\ 4$	**4.** 35 $-\ 8$	**5.** 71 $-\ 9$	**6.** 52 $-\ 3$
7. 43 $-\ 8$	**8.** 44 $-\ 6$	**9.** 71 $-\ 7$	**10.** 79 $-\ 7$	**11.** 83 $-\ 6$	**12.** 90 $-\ 3$
13. 56 $-\ 8$	**14.** 72 $-\ 5$	**15.** 25 $-\ 8$	**16.** 53 $-\ 9$	**17.** 32 $-\ 9$	**18.** 35 $-\ 7$
19. 84 $-\ 5$	**20.** 100 $-\ 2$	**21.** 105 $-\ 8$	**22.** 107 $-\ 9$	**23.** 108 $-\ 9$	**24.** 103 $-\ 5$

PRACTICE SET 5
Subtract and check.

1. 83 $-\ 8$	**2.** 42 $-\ 8$	**3.** 33 $-\ 7$	**4.** 32 $-\ 7$	**5.** 85 $-\ 3$	**6.** 99 $-\ 6$
7. 56 $-\ 7$	**8.** 45 $-\ 6$	**9.** 45 $-\ 7$	**10.** 98 $-\ 3$	**11.** 72 $-\ 9$	**12.** 82 $-\ 8$
13. 114 $-\ 5$	**14.** 124 $-\ 5$	**15.** 134 $-\ 5$	**16.** 132 $-\ 6$	**17.** 122 $-\ 6$	**18.** 112 $-\ 6$
19. 215 $-\ 7$	**20.** 432 $-\ 8$	**21.** 685 $-\ 7$	**22.** 987 $-\ 7$	**23.** 421 $-\ 6$	**24.** 212 $-\ 9$

Tens, Hundreds, and Thousands

OBJECTIVE To find differences such as $\begin{array}{r} 130 \\ -\ 70 \\ \hline \end{array}$ and $\begin{array}{r} 1{,}300 \\ -\ 700 \\ \hline \end{array}$ by using the subtraction facts

You can use the subtraction facts to subtract tens, hundreds, and thousands.

EXAMPLE 1

Use 18 − 9 = 9.
Bring down the 0's.

Subtract.

180	1,800	18,000
− 90	− 900	− 9,000
90	900	9,000

Subtract.

1. 11	**2.** 110	**3.** 1,100	**4.** 11,000
− 3	− 30	− 300	− 3,000

EXAMPLE 2

Add 5,000 to 7,000. The missing number is 12,000.

Find the missing number.

☐	12,000
− 7,000	− 7,000
5,000	5,000

Find the missing number.

5. ☐	**6.** ☐	**7.** ☐
−700	−8,000	−4,000
500	7,000	11,000

PRACTICE SET 6

Subtract.

1. 40	**2.** 30	**3.** 60	**4.** 120	**5.** 110	**6.** 150
−30	−20	−40	− 40	− 60	− 60

7. 160	**8.** 110	**9.** 150	**10.** 110	**11.** 110	**12.** 160
− 90	− 70	− 70	− 40	− 90	− 80

13. 70	**14.** 80	**15.** 130	**16.** 140	**17.** 120	**18.** 150
−40	−30	− 60	− 90	− 60	− 90

PRACTICE SET 7
Subtract and check.

1.	2.	3.	4.	5.	6.
90 −50	130 − 70	70 −30	140 − 80	120 − 80	120 − 60

7.	8.	9.	10.	11.	12.
100 − 30	80 −20	100 − 50	110 − 20	130 − 80	170 − 80

13.	14.	15.	16.	17.	18.
170 − 90	130 − 50	110 − 80	150 − 80	160 − 90	140 − 60

PRACTICE SET 8
Subtract and check.

1.	2.	3.	4.
1,300 − 400	1,500 − 900	1,000 − 800	1,000 − 400

5.	6.	7.	8.
1,100 − 900	1,600 − 800	700 −400	800 −300

9.	10.	11.	12.
1,400 − 900	200 −200	900 −800	600 −300

13.	14.	15.	16.
900 −300	1,100 − 500	1,100 − 300	800 −600

17.	18.	19.	20.
9,000 −3,000	11,000 − 5,000	11,000 − 3,000	8,000 −6,000

21.	22.	23.	24.
16,000 − 7,000	18,000 − 9,000	15,000 − 6,000	15,000 − 9,000

PRACTICE SET 9
Find the missing number.

1.	2.	3.	4.	5.
☐ −800 400	☐ −600 500	☐ −700 600	☐ −400 800	☐ −9,000 4,000

6.	7.	8.	9.	10.
☐ −70 30	☐ −80 60	☐ −90 30	☐ −70 80	☐ −4,000 9,000

11.	12.	13.	14.	15.
☐ −5,000 9,000	☐ −8,000 4,000	☐ −6,000 7,000	☐ −8,000 0	☐ −7,000 8,000

DIAGNOSTIC TEST: SUBTRACTION FORM A—20 MINUTES
Subtract and check.

1. 63 − 5	**2.** 48 − 6	**3.** 72 − 9	**4.** 87 −23
5. 831 − 84	**6.** 831 −645	**7.** 947 −899	**8.** 84,596 − 9,824
9. 69,844 −18,249	**10.** 71,117 − 5,555	**11.** 54,792 −32,895	**12.** 78,905 −18,737
13. 60,801 − 3,625	**14.** 402,302 − 91,559	**15.** 503,504 −113,486	**16.** 40,050 − 8,512
17. 40,000 − 129	**18.** 700,000 − 1,086	**19.** 20,000 − 98	**20.** 27,342 − 7,407

Did You Have

More than 18 right? Begin on page 39.

16, 17, or 18 right? Begin on page 37.

Less than 16 right? Begin on page 35.

DIAGNOSTIC TEST: SUBTRACTION FORM B—20 MINUTES
Subtract and check.

1. 83 − 7	**2.** 38 − 5	**3.** 82 − 8	**4.** 77 −32
5. 841 − 76	**6.** 751 −546	**7.** 947 −889	**8.** 76,584 − 9,742
9. 89,733 −28,439	**10.** 82,227 − 6,666	**11.** 45,684 −32,785	**12.** 68,804 −28,646
13. 50,702 − 4,435	**14.** 802,406 − 80,667	**15.** 602,405 −222,376	**16.** 30,080 − 7,463

More than 13 right? Begin on page 39. Less than 14 right? Consult your teacher.

Regrouping

EXAMPLE 1 Subtract.
$$506$$
$$-317$$

SOLUTION

Think of money.

| 5 dollars + | 0 dimes + | 6 cents | $5.06 |
| 3 dollars + | 1 dime + | 7 cents | −3.17 |

Change $1 for 10 dimes.

$$\begin{array}{r} 4\ 10 \\ \$5.\cancel{0}6 \\ -3.17 \end{array}$$

| 4 dollars + | 10 dimes + | 6 cents |
| 3 dollars + | 1 dime + | 7 cents |

Change 1 dime for 10 cents.

$$\begin{array}{r} 9 \\ 4\ \cancel{10}\ 16 \\ \$5.\cancel{0}\cancel{6} \\ -3.17 \end{array}$$

| 4 dollars + | 9 dimes + | 16 cents | $5.06 |
| 3 dollars + | 1 dime + | 7 cents | −3.17 |

Subtract.

| 1 dollar + | 8 dimes + | 9 cents | $1.89 |

To check, add the number subtracted to the answer.

So, $\begin{array}{r} 506 \\ -317 \\ \hline 189 \end{array}$ Check. $\begin{array}{r} 317 \\ +189 \\ \hline 506 \end{array}$ ← Number subtracted
← Answer
← Number started with

EXAMPLE 2 Subtract.
$$78,005$$
$$-14,737$$

SOLUTION

Think of money.

$$\begin{array}{r} \$780.05 \\ -147.37 \end{array}$$

Change 1 $10 for 10 $1.

$$\begin{array}{r} 7\ 10 \\ \$7\,\cancel{8}\,0.05 \\ -147.37 \end{array}$$

Change $1 for 10 dimes.
Change 1 dime for 10 cents.
Subtract.

$$\begin{array}{r} 9 \\ 7\ \cancel{10}\ 10 \\ \$78\cancel{0}.05 \\ -147.37 \end{array}$$

$$\begin{array}{r} 9\ \ 9 \\ 7\ 10\ \cancel{10}\ 15 \\ \$7\,\cancel{8}\,0.0\cancel{5} \\ -147.37 \\ \hline \$632.68 \end{array}$$

To check, add the number subtracted to the answer.

So, $\begin{array}{r} 78,005 \\ -14,737 \\ \hline 63,268 \end{array}$ Check: $\begin{array}{r} 14,737 \\ 63,268 \\ \hline 78,005 \end{array}$

- -

Subtract. Think of money.

| 1. | 807 | 2. | 5,348 | 3. | 86,491 |
| | − 38 | | − 139 | | − 5,693 |

EXAMPLE 3 Subtract. 700
                        -184

SOLUTION

Think of money.
Change $1 for 10 dimes
and 1 dime for 10 cents.

$$\begin{array}{r} \$7.00 \\ 1.84 \\ \hline \end{array} \qquad \begin{array}{r} 9 \\ 6\ 10\ 10 \\ \$7.0\ 0 \\ -\ 1.8\ 4 \\ \hline \$5.1\ 6 \end{array} \qquad \begin{array}{r} 700 \\ \text{So,} -184 \\ \hline 516 \end{array}$$

Subtract. Think of money.

4.	600	5.	5,000	6.	20,000
	-157		$-\ 279$		$-\ 853$

PRACTICE SET 10
Subtract and check.

1.	504	2.	808	3.	718	4.	1,406	5.	2,811
	$-\ 39$		-329		-578		$-\ 568$		$-\ 734$

6.	703	7.	846	8.	792	9.	111	10.	222
	$-\ 46$		$-\ 97$		$-\ 99$		$-\ 88$		$-\ 77$

11.	4,906	12.	9,472	13.	8,111	14.	5,736	15.	8,777
	$-\ 788$		$-9,466$		$-7,222$		$-1,999$		$-5,987$

PRACTICE SET 11
Subtract and check.

1.	58,567	2.	32,351	3.	53,854	4.	87,279
	$-51,419$		$-\ 5,470$		$-\ 9,208$		$-66,652$

5.	83,006	6.	66,858	7.	15,877	8.	94,160
	$-\ 5,053$		$-\ 8,763$		$-\ 9,393$		$-12,932$

9.	19,514	10.	51,673	11.	65,347	12.	13,460
	$-\ 5,052$		$-\ 8,043$		$-28,939$		$-\ 7,923$

PRACTICE SET 12
Subtract and check.

1.	$6.00	2.	$60.00	3.	$600.00	4.	$90.00
	$-\ .08$		$-\ .08$		$-\ .08$		$-\ .65$

5.	$900.00	6.	90,000	7.	800	8.	8,000
	$-\ .65$		$-\ 65$		-384		$-\ 384$

9.	80,000	10.	40,000	11.	400,000	12.	4,000,000
	$-\ 384$		$-\ 937$		$-\ 937$		$-\ 9,370$

Showing Regrouping

OBJECTIVE To subtract with regrouping

Many people make errors in subtraction because they do not show the regrouping. Always show the regrouping in writing.

EXAMPLE 1 Subtract.
$$\begin{array}{r} 1{,}874 \\ -\quad 58 \\ \hline \end{array}$$

SOLUTION

Change 1 ten to 10 ones to give 14 ones.

$$\begin{array}{r} 1{,}874 \\ -\quad 58 \\ \hline \end{array} \longrightarrow \begin{array}{r} {}^{6\,14} \\ 1{,}8\,7\,4 \\ -\quad 5\,8 \\ \hline 1{,}8\,1\,6 \end{array}$$ ←——— Regrouped numerals

EXAMPLE 2 Subtract and check.
$$\begin{array}{r} 43{,}456 \\ -21{,}285 \\ \hline \end{array}$$

SOLUTION

Change 1 hundred to 10 tens to give 15 tens.

$$\begin{array}{r} 43{,}456 \\ -21{,}285 \\ \hline \end{array} \longrightarrow \begin{array}{r} {}^{3\,15} \\ 4\,3{,}4\,5\,6 \\ -2\,1{,}2\,8\,5 \\ \hline 2\,2{,}1\,7\,1 \end{array}$$

Check: $$\begin{array}{r} 21{,}285 \\ +22{,}171 \\ \hline 43{,}456 \end{array}$$

- -

Subtract and check.

1. 5,614 – 408	**2.** 9,372 – 186	**3.** 16,352 – 7,441	**4.** 23,386 – 4,487

PRACTICE SET 13
Subtract and check.

1. 73,380
−13,503

2. 46,638
– 3,318

3. 83,708
−59,920

4. 33,573
– 8,850

5. 23,478
−18,382

6. 88,352
– 5,811

7. 49,324
– 8,206

8. 47,197
– 6,930

9. 93,935
−65,231

10. 33,828
−15,364

11. 98,526
−58,649

12. 16,396
– 2,201

PRACTICE SET 14
Subtract and check.

1. 59,060
   −27,493

2. 90,602
   −73,766

3. 50,105
   −23,137

4. 80,090
   − 8,341

5. 90,080
   − 9,961

6. 70,405
   −26,738

7. 10,030
   − 8,879

8. 20,407
   − 5,659

9. 30,307
   − 5,718

10. 80,302
    −46,783

11. 90,907
    −82,657

12. 89,806
    −18,657

PRACTICE SET 15
Subtract and check.

1. 58,567
   −51,419

2. 32,351
   − 5,470

3. 53,854
   − 9,208

4. 87,279
   −66,652

5. 83,006
   −61,747

6. 66,858
   − 8,763

7. 15,877
   − 9,392

8. 94,160
   −12,932

9. 19,514
   − 5,053

10. 51,673
    − 8,043

11. 65,347
    −28,939

12. 13,460
    − 7,923

PRACTICE SET 16
Subtract and check.

1. 50,000
   −   8

2. 50,000
   −   80

3. 50,000
   −   800

4. 50,000
   − 8,000

5. 50,000
   −   83

6. 50,000
   −   833

7. 50,000
   − 8,333

8. 50,000
   −   803

9. 50,000
   − 8,003

10. 50,000
    − 3,008

11. 50,000
    − 8,300

12. 50,000
    − 7,000

13. 70,000
    −   988

14. 50,000
    −   788

15. 40,000
    −   681

16. 60,000
    − 2,569

17. 40,000
    − 9,106

18. 70,000
    − 9,106

19. 80,000
    − 9,106

20. 90,000
    − 9,601

Return to Form B on page 34.

The Solar System

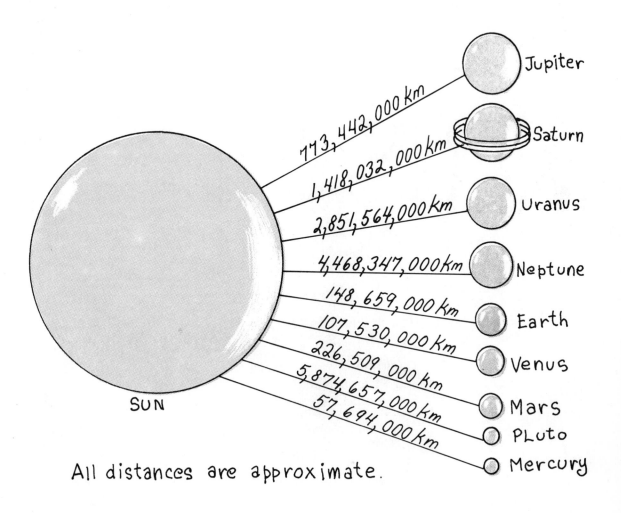

773,442,000 Km — Jupiter
1,418,032,000 Km — Saturn
2,851,564,000 Km — Uranus
4,468,347,000 Km — Neptune
148,659,000 Km — Earth
107,530,000 Km — Venus
226,509,000 Km — Mars
5,874,657,000 Km — Pluto
57,694,000 Km — Mercury

SUN

All distances are approximate.

1. Which planet is farthest from the sun?

2. Which planet is nearest to the sun?

3. List the planets in order from farthest to nearest.

4. Round each distance to the nearest million kilometers.

5. Which planet do you think has the highest temperature? the lowest temperature?

6. Traveling from the sun at 1,000,000 kilometers per hour (km/h), how long would it take to reach each planet?

Making Change

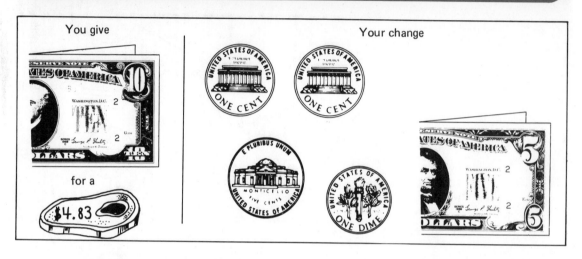

You give   Your change

for a

$4.83

EXAMPLE 1   How much change would you give from $5?

SOLUTION   Think: 69¢ and 31¢ make $1;
Start at 69¢ and count to   and $4 more make $5.
$1. Then count on to $5.   So, I would give $4.31 change.

How much change would you give?
  1. Change for $2.50 out of $5

  2. Change for $3.15 out of $10

  3. Change for $8.27 out of $20

EXAMPLE 2   How much change would you give for $1.49 out of $5.04?

SOLUTION   Think: $1.45 and 55¢ make $2 and $3 more make $5.
4¢ from $1.49 is $1.45.   So, I would give $3.55 change.

How much change would you give?
  4. Change for $1.73 out of $10.73

  5. Change for $13.43 out of $20.03

EXERCISES
How much change would you give from $5?

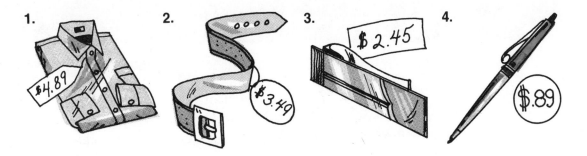

1. $4.89
2. $3.49
3. $2.45
4. $.89

How much change would you give from $10?

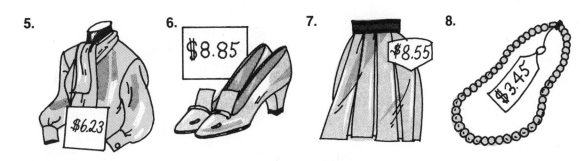

5. $6.23
6. $8.85
7. $8.55
8. $3.45

How much change would you give from $20?

9. $13.50
10. $9.95
11. $16.50
12. $19.35

How much change would you give?
13. Change for $6.83 out of $10.03
14. Change for $3.58 out of $10.58
15. Change for $2.86 out of $10.01
16. Change for $2.13 out of $10.03
17. Change for 78¢ out of $10.03
18. Change for $4.31 out of $20.06
19. Change for $1.65 out of $20.15
20. Change for $1.26 out of $5.01
21. Change for 88¢ out of $1.03
22. Change for $1.88 out of $2.03

Multi-Step Problems

EXAMPLE 1 Mr. Narita has 153 students in his math classes. How much will it cost to supply each of his students with a book and a work book?

SOLUTION

Step 1: Add.

$5.75 ←———— Cost of book
+1.93 ←———— Cost of work book
$7.68 ←———— Cost per student

Step 2: Multiply.

$7.68 ←———— Cost per student
×153 ←———— Number of students

3 × 768   23 04
50 × 768   384 0
100 × 768   768
$1,175.04 ←———— Cost for 153 students

EXAMPLE 2 Joyce bought 3 packages of film and had them developed. She also ordered 25 prints. How much did Joyce spend?

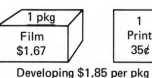

Developing $1.85 per pkg

SOLUTION

Step 1: Add.

$1.67 ←———— Film cost per package
+1.85 ←———— Developing cost per package
$3.52 ←———— Total cost per package

Step 2: Multiply.

$3.52 ←———— Total cost per package
×3 ←———— Number of packages
$10.56 ←———— Total cost for 3 packages

Step 3: Multiply.

$ .35 ←———— Cost per print
×25 ←———— Number of prints
1 75
7 0
$8.75 ←———— Total cost for prints

Step 4: Add.

$10.56 ←———— Film and developing
+8.75 ←———— Prints
$19.31 ←———— Amount Joyce spent

Solve these problems.

1.

Jorge paid for these items with two $20 bills. How much change did he get?

2.

Ono has $20. How much more does she need to buy 4 A albums and 2 B albums?

3.

How much can Joe save?

4.

How much did Pearl earn?

5. Marie had $5.55. She lost 2 coins. Now she has $5.20. Which 2 coins did she lose?

6. Mr. Sloan had $13.00. He lost 5 coins. Now he has $11.60. Which 5 coins did he lose?

Estimating in Subtraction

OBJECTIVE To estimate differences by using rounding

EXAMPLE 1 Estimate the difference to the nearest 100.

1,846
− 254

SOLUTION

Round to the nearest 100.
Then subtract.

1,846 ⟶ 1,800
− 254 ⟶ − 300
          1,500

Estimate to the nearest 100.

1. 748	**2.** 2,692	**3.** 4,347
−473	− 963	−2,546

EXAMPLE 2 Estimate to the nearest dollar.

$32.73
− 3.28

SOLUTION

Round to the nearest $1.
Then subtract.

$32.73 ⟶ $33.00
− 3.28 ⟶ − 3.00
          $30.00, or $30

Estimate to the nearest dollar.

4. $162.50	**5.** $872.46	**6.** $384.37
− 44.00	− 57.62	−299.98

EXAMPLE 3 Estimate to the nearest 1,000.

56,342
− 7,931

SOLUTION

Round to the nearest 1,000.
Then subtract.

56,342 ⟶ 56,000
− 7,931 ⟶ − 8,000
          48,000

Estimate to the nearest 1,000.

7. 63,527	**8.** 49,999	**9.** 18,483
− 8,489	−27,498	− 8,768

EXERCISES

Estimate the difference to the nearest 100.

1. 328 − 74	**2.** 298 − 97	**3.** 919 − 76	**4.** 7,752 − 786	**5.** 8,289 − 224

Estimate the difference to the nearest dollar.

6. $50.00 −39.98	**7.** $10.00 − 3.97	**8.** $23.57 −13.48	**9.** $14.06 − 9.23

10. 20.00 −14.95	**11.** $24.83 −12.84	**12.** $46.22 −16.53	**13.** $75.08 −57.80

Estimate the difference to the nearest 1,000.

14. 6,617 −1,404	**15.** 4,772 − 889	**16.** 28,438 − 1,833	**17.** 53,883 − 2,747

18. 81,004 − 1,695	**19.** 92,458 −17,233	**20.** 10,000 − 4,999	**21.** 55,927 −19,489

Estimate the answer to the nearest dollar.

22. Joe owed Lisa $52.50. He sent her a check for $27.84. How much more does he owe?

23. Ms. Allen owes Spotless, Inc., $181.00. She paid $44.25. How much more does she owe?

24. Mrs. Brew got $1,150 for her old car in trade.

25. Angelo got $35 for his old TV set in trade.

How much more did she have to pay?

How much more did he have to pay?

Estimate the answer to the nearest 1,000.

26. Mae's gas tank holds 12,500 liters of gasoline. She pumped out 2,827 liters of gas. How much is left?

27. On Saturday, 32,158 people attended a baseball game. 5,642 of them had free tickets. How many paid?

Estimate the answer to the nearest 100.

28. Dales had 1,128 shirts in stock on Friday. On Saturday, 272 shirts were sold. How many were left?

29. Mac's had 2,483 skirts in stock on Monday. On Tuesday, 342 skirts were sold. How many were left?

30. Miss Wong is on a motor trip of 1,946 kilometers. She drove 1,515 kilometers in three days. How far must she drive on the fourth day?

31. Bob is on a motor trip of 2,153 kilometers. He drove 1,847 kilometers in three days. How far must he drive on the fourth day?

Estimate the answer to the nearest dollar.

32. Jim had $219.86. He paid two bills: one for $22.75 and one for $64.40. How much did he have left?

33. Mary had $367.22. She spent $32.50 for groceries and $19.33 for car repairs. How much did she have left?

34. Mr. Tompkins earned $856.73 last month. He had these deductions.

Deduction	Amount
Federal tax	$102.73
State tax	29.50
Retirement	24.50
Insurance	32.02

What was his take-home pay?

35. Here is Jane's earning record for one week.

Tuesday	$13.55
Wednesday	14.75
Thursday	12.02
Friday	
Total	$48.87

How much did Jane earn on Friday?

Fun Corner

1. 42 × 38 = 1,596. What number do you add to 1,596 to find the answer to 43 × 38?

2. 70 × 52 = 3,640. What number do you subtract from 3,640 to find the answer to 69 × 52?

3. 178 × 1,001 = 178,178. What number do you subtract from 178,178 to find the answer to 178 × 1,000?

4. 1,000 × 876 = 876,000. What number do you subtract from 876,000 to find the answer to 999 × 876?

Choosing the Correct Operation

OBJECTIVE To decide which operation to use to solve a problem

Tell whether you would add, subtract, multiply, or divide to solve the problem.

1. Ruby, Britt, Lisa, Sean, Joan, and Bill shared the expenses of a party. The party cost $24.72. How much was each one's share?

2. Jim bought a steak for $3.59, a bag of potatoes for $.79, and a loaf of bread for $.43. How much did he spend?

3. Joe bought a sweater for $12.99. He gave the cashier a $20 bill and 4 pennies. He received $7.05 change. Did Joe get the right change?

4. Mrs. Ling bought a 1-kilogram can of coffee at a 25¢ off sale. The regular price was $6.14. How much did she pay?

5. Maria bought 5 kilograms of butter to make cookies. Butter was selling for $1.48 per kilogram. How much did Maria pay?

6. Apples were selling at 3 kilograms for $1.00. Mr. O'Neill bought 1 kilogram of apples. How much did he pay?

Test: Unit 2

Subtract and check.

1. 736	2. 1,122	3. 90,609	4. 22,346	5. 70,000
−378	− 805	−10,501	− 4,884	− 9,633

How much change would you give?

6. Change for $2.87 out of $5

7. Change for $3.45 out of $10

8. Change for $8.88 out of $20

9. Change for $7.84 out of $20.04

Estimate the answer to the nearest dollar.

10. Linda earned $137.83. Her deductions amounted to $15.37. What was her take-home pay?

11. Manuel owes Ruby $171.86. He paid $53.98. How much more does he owe?

Estimate the answer to the nearest 100.

12. The Diaz family used 8,093 kilowatt hours of electricity in December. In January, the Diaz family used 7,689 kilowatt hours. How much more electricity did the family use in December?

13. The Drake family used 6,207 cubic units of gas in February. In March, the Drakes used 4,450 cubic units. How much less gas did the Drakes use in March?

Solve each problem.

14. Mt. McKinley is about 6,096 meters high. Pikes Peak is about 4,233 meters high. How much higher is Mt. McKinley?

15. Jupiter's diameter is about 140,800 kilometers. Mercury's diameter is about 4,960 kilometers. How much longer is Jupiter's diameter?

Fun Corner

Harry had $50 in the bank and wrote checks as shown below. Explain where the extra dollar came from.

Checks		Balance
$20	→	$30
15	→	15
9	→	6
6	→	0
$50		$51

UNIT 3

Multiplication of Whole Numbers

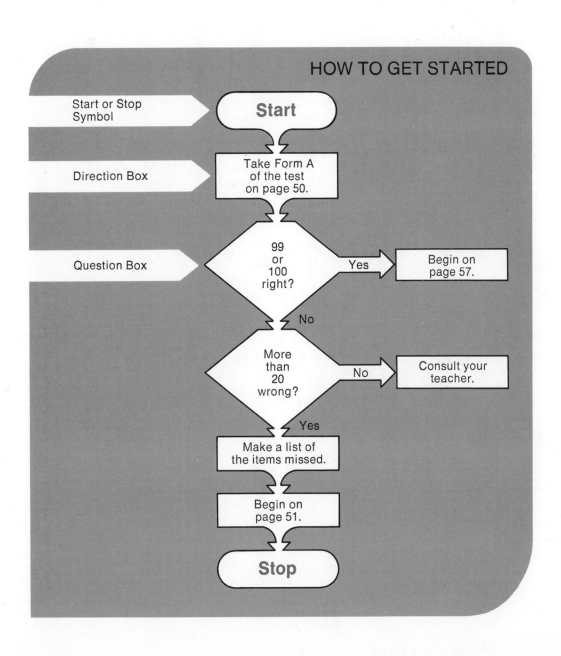

HOW TO GET STARTED

Start or Stop Symbol → **Start**

Direction Box → Take Form A of the test on page 50.

Question Box → 99 or 100 right? — Yes → Begin on page 57.

No

More than 20 wrong? — No → Consult your teacher.

Yes

Make a list of the items missed.

Begin on page 51.

Stop

MULTIPLICATION FACTS TEST FORM A – 4 MINUTES

1.	8 ×3	4 ×2	2 ×1	3 ×2	2 ×0	0 ×0	2 ×2	1 ×2	8 ×2	6 ×3
2.	5 ×2	7 ×3	0 ×1	7 ×2	1 ×1	9 ×2	0 ×2	1 ×0	6 ×2	9 ×3
3.	2 ×4	1 ×3	7 ×4	2 ×3	3 ×4	4 ×1	6 ×4	5 ×4	3 ×1	4 ×4
4.	5 ×3	8 ×4	3 ×0	0 ×4	4 ×3	1 ×4	4 ×0	3 ×3	0 ×3	9 ×4
5.	5 ×1	2 ×6	9 ×5	3 ×6	4 ×5	5 ×0	8 ×6	7 ×5	4 ×6	3 ×5
6.	6 ×5	6 ×6	1 ×5	7 ×6	5 ×5	9 ×6	2 ×5	0 ×5	5 ×6	8 ×5
7.	2 ×7	6 ×8	7 ×1	7 ×8	6 ×1	5 ×7	1 ×7	9 ×8	8 ×7	7 ×0
8.	6 ×7	6 ×0	7 ×7	4 ×7	8 ×8	0 ×7	1 ×6	9 ×7	3 ×7	0 ×6
9.	7 ×9	0 ×9	2 ×9	4 ×8	8 ×0	1 ×9	2 ×8	8 ×9	5 ×8	3 ×9
10.	9 ×0	8 ×1	9 ×9	5 ×9	1 ×8	4 ×9	3 ×8	9 ×1	6 ×9	0 ×8

MULTIPLICATION FACTS TEST FORM B – 3 MINUTES

1.	9 ×0	7 ×9	8 ×1	6 ×7	0 ×9	9 ×9	2 ×7	6 ×0	2 ×9	5 ×9
2.	6 ×5	6 ×8	7 ×7	4 ×8	1 ×8	5 ×1	6 ×6	7 ×1	4 ×7	8 ×0
3.	4 ×9	2 ×6	1 ×5	7 ×8	8 ×8	1 ×9	3 ×8	9 ×5	7 ×6	6 ×1
4.	0 ×7	2 ×8	9 ×1	3 ×6	5 ×5	5 ×7	1 ×6	8 ×9	6 ×9	4 ×5
5.	9 ×6	1 ×7	9 ×7	5 ×8	0 ×8	5 ×0	2 ×5	9 ×8	3 ×7	3 ×9
6.	8 ×6	0 ×5	8 ×7	0 ×6	7 ×5	5 ×6	7 ×0	4 ×6	8 ×5	3 ×5

Multiplication Facts

OBJECTIVE To do at least 59 multiplication facts correctly

Here are several ways to help you learn the multiplication facts.

THINK OF AN ARRAY

Each group of facts can be thought of as an array.

EXAMPLE 1 Make an array that shows all the 5's facts.

SOLUTION

1 row of 5 is 5.

4 rows of 5 is 20.

7 rows of 5 is 35.

If you can count by 5's, you know the 5's facts.

$$(1)(2)(3)(4)(5) \longrightarrow 1 \times 5 = 5$$
$$(6)(7)(8)(9)(10) \longrightarrow 2 \times 5 = 10$$
$$(11)(12)(13)(14)(15) \longrightarrow 3 \times 5 = 15$$
$$(16)(17)(18)(19)(20) \longrightarrow 4 \times 5 = 20$$
$$(21)(22)(23)(24)(25) \longrightarrow 5 \times 5 = 25$$
$$(26)(27)(28)(29)(30) \longrightarrow 6 \times 5 = 30$$
$$(31)(32)(33)(34)(35) \longrightarrow 7 \times 5 = 35$$
$$(36)(37)(38)(39)(40) \longrightarrow 8 \times 5 = 40$$
$$(41)(42)(43)(44)(45) \longrightarrow 9 \times 5 = 45$$
$$(46)(47)(48)(49)(50) \longrightarrow 10 \times 5 = 50$$

- -

Make an array to show each group of facts.

1. 2's   **2.** 3's   **3.** 4's   **4.** 6's

5. 7's   **6.** 8's   **7.** 9's   **8.** 10's

This array shows all the facts.

1	2	3	4	5	6	7	8	9	10
2	4	6	8	10	12	14	16	18	20
3	6	9	12	15	18	21	24	27	30
4	8	12	16	20	24	28	32	36	40
5	10	15	20	25	30	35	40	45	50
6	12	18	24	30	36	42	48	54	60
7	14	21	28	35	42	49	56	63	70
8	16	24	32	40	48	56	64	72	80
9	18	27	36	45	54	63	72	81	90
10	20	30	40	50	60	70	80	90	100

To place the numbers in the 2's column, count by 2's.

To place the numbers in the 3's column, count by 3's.

EXAMPLE 2 Use the array to find 9×6.

SOLUTION

Use a piece of cardboard cut in an L shape to cover the array as shown.

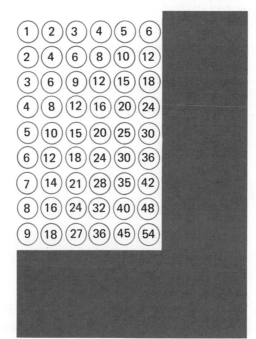

The array shows 9 rows of 6 is 54.
So, $9 \times 6 = 54$.

- -

Multiply. Use the array and your cardboard.

9. 6×7 **10.** 4×5 **11.** 8×8 **12.** 9×9

THINK OF MONEY

EXAMPLE 3   Multiply 4 × 8.
SOLUTION   Think of 4 × 8 as 4 × 8¢.

8¢ can be thought of as
1 nickel and 3 pennies.

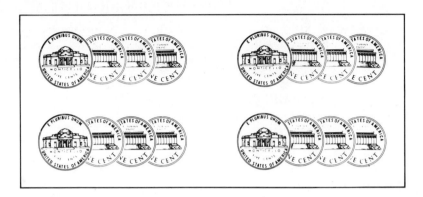

4 nickels is 4 × 5¢.

$4 \times 5¢ = 20¢$
$4 \times 3¢ = \underline{12¢}$
$32¢$ So, 4 × 8 = 32

Multiply. Think of money.
13. 3 × 7   **14.** 4 × 9   **15.** 6 × 6   **16.** 7 × 8

THINK OF NINES

These are the 9's facts.

The sum of the digits of
each answer is 9.
The first digit of each
answer is 1 less than
the multiplier.

1 × 9 = 9	4 × 9 = 36	7 × 9 = 63
2 × 9 = 18	5 × 9 = 45	8 × 9 = 72
3 × 9 = 27	6 × 9 = 54	9 × 9 = 81

EXAMPLE 4   Multiply 8 × 9.
SOLUTION   Think: One less than 8 is 7, and 7 and 2 is 9.
So, 8 × 9 = 72

Multiply.
17. 5 × 9   **18.** 6 × 9   **19.** 9 × 9   **20.** 7 × 9

PRACTICE SET 1
Practice the facts that you missed on Form A of the test until you know them.

Return to Form B on page 50.

Using the Facts

EXAMPLE Use the same fact to find each product.

SOLUTION

Use the fact $2 \times 6 = 12$.

$$\begin{array}{r} 20 \\ \times 6 \\ \hline 120 \end{array} \qquad \begin{array}{r} 200 \\ \times 6 \\ \hline 1,200 \end{array} \qquad \begin{array}{r} 2,000 \\ \times 6 \\ \hline 12,000 \end{array}$$

Multiply.

1. $\begin{array}{r} 30 \\ \times 6 \end{array}$
2. $\begin{array}{r} 3,000 \\ \times 6 \end{array}$
3. $\begin{array}{r} 40 \\ \times 5 \end{array}$
4. $\begin{array}{r} 400 \\ \times 5 \end{array}$

PRACTICE SET 2
Multiply.

1. $\begin{array}{r} 40 \\ \times 6 \end{array}$
2. $\begin{array}{r} 400 \\ \times 6 \end{array}$
3. $\begin{array}{r} 4,000 \\ \times 6 \end{array}$
4. $\begin{array}{r} 40 \\ \times 7 \end{array}$
5. $\begin{array}{r} 4,000 \\ \times 7 \end{array}$

6. $\begin{array}{r} 40 \\ \times 8 \end{array}$
7. $\begin{array}{r} 400 \\ \times 8 \end{array}$
8. $\begin{array}{r} 4,000 \\ \times 8 \end{array}$
9. $\begin{array}{r} 80 \\ \times 5 \end{array}$
10. $\begin{array}{r} 8,000 \\ \times 5 \end{array}$

11. $\begin{array}{r} 80 \\ \times 7 \end{array}$
12. $\begin{array}{r} 800 \\ \times 7 \end{array}$
13. $\begin{array}{r} 8,000 \\ \times 7 \end{array}$
14. $\begin{array}{r} 70 \\ \times 9 \end{array}$
15. $\begin{array}{r} 7,000 \\ \times 9 \end{array}$

16. $\begin{array}{r} 10 \\ \times 4 \end{array}$
17. $\begin{array}{r} 100 \\ \times 4 \end{array}$
18. $\begin{array}{r} 1,000 \\ \times 4 \end{array}$
19. $\begin{array}{r} 10 \\ \times 6 \end{array}$
20. $\begin{array}{r} 1,000 \\ \times 6 \end{array}$

21. $\begin{array}{r} 60 \\ \times 5 \end{array}$
22. $\begin{array}{r} 600 \\ \times 5 \end{array}$
23. $\begin{array}{r} 6,000 \\ \times 5 \end{array}$
24. $\begin{array}{r} 600 \\ \times 3 \end{array}$
25. $\begin{array}{r} 6,000 \\ \times 3 \end{array}$

Multiplying by a One-Digit Number

Recall the meaning of
each digit in 7,825.

$$7{,}825 = 7{,}000 + 800 + 20 + 5$$

7 Thousands 8 Hundreds 2 Tens 5 Units

EXAMPLE 1 Multiply.

$$\begin{matrix}43\\ \times 4\end{matrix}$$

SOLUTION

The 4 stands for 40.

$$\begin{matrix}43\\ \times 4\end{matrix}$$

$4 \times 3 = \quad 12$
$4 \times 40 = \underline{160}$
$\qquad\qquad 172$

Short way

$\overset{1}{4}3$
$\underline{\times 4}$
172

Multiply.

1. 53	**2.** 82	**3.** 48	**4.** 74	**5.** 95
×6	×5	×6	×8	×9

EXAMPLE 2 Multiply.

$$\begin{matrix}436\\ \times 3\end{matrix}$$

SOLUTION

$$\begin{matrix}436\\ \times 3\end{matrix}$$

$3 \times 6 = \quad 18$

The 3 stands for 30. $3 \times 30 = \quad 90$
The 4 stands for 400. $3 \times 400 = \underline{1{,}200}$
$\qquad\qquad\quad 1{,}308$

Short way

$\overset{11}{4}36$
$\underline{\times 3}$
$1{,}308$

Multiply.

6. 412	**7.** 561	**8.** 834	**9.** 705
×4	×5	×6	×7

EXAMPLE 3 Multiply.   4,356
                                  ×2

SOLUTION   4,356   Short way
                                  ×2   11
In 4,356,   2 × 6 =   12   4,356
the 5 stands for 50;   2 × 50 =   100   ×2
the 3 stands for 300; 2 × 300 =   600   8,712
the 4 stands for 4,000. 2 × 4,000 = 8,000
                                  8,712

Multiply.

10. 2,341   **11.** 4,523   **12.** 5,723   **13.** 1,474
          ×3   ×4   ×5   ×6

PRACTICE SET 3
Multiply.

1. 48   **2.** 37   **3.** 69   **4.** 76   **5.** 84
       ×5   ×5   ×5   ×6   ×6

6. 135   **7.** 243   **8.** 351   **9.** 342   **10.** 366
       ×4   ×4   ×4   ×5   ×5

11. 451   **12.** 506   **13.** 714   **14.** 328   **15.** 622
        ×7   ×7   ×7   ×3   ×6

16. 4,321   **17.** 4,321   **18.** 4,321   **19.** 6,543   **20.** 6,543
         ×4   ×5   ×6   ×6   ×7

21. 6,543   **22.** 6,543   **23.** 5,674   **24.** 6,786   **25.** 8,763
         ×8   ×9   ×9   ×9   ×5

26. 7,890   **27.** 8,904   **28.** 9,008   **29.** 7,068   **30.** 6,807
         ×8   ×8   ×7   ×5   ×4

31. 5,145   **32.** 3,406   **33.** 7,605   **34.** 2,999   **35.** 9,210
         ×4   ×3   ×5   ×9   ×2

DIAGNOSTIC TEST: MULTIPLICATION FORM A—30 MINUTES

Multiply.

1. 427 ×26	2. 415 ×35	3. 595 ×41	4. 118 ×37
5. 275 ×93	6. 493 ×76	7. 7,617 ×17	8. 5,292 ×21
9. 9,115 ×75	10. 7,460 ×89	11. 803 ×204	12. 102 ×415
13. 439 ×727	14. 813 ×240	15. 409 ×770	16. 490 ×701
17. 612 ×151	18. 7,939 ×168	19. 5,675 ×916	20. 8,300 ×245
21. 691 ×10	22. 326 ×100	23. 9,432 ×100	24. 8,342 ×1,000

Did You Have

More than 23 right? Begin on page 62.	21, 22, or 23 right? Begin on page 60.	Less than 21 right? Begin on page 58.

DIAGNOSTIC TEST: MULTIPLICATION FORM B—30 MINUTES

Multiply.

1. 274 ×62	2. 543 ×53	3. 955 ×14	4. 566 ×44
5. 334 ×23	6. 493 ×76	7. 706 ×89	8. 5,423 ×21
9. 6,804 ×32	10. 7,946 ×54	11. 157 ×123	12. 843 ×486
13. 924 ×850	14. 209 ×104	15. 803 ×501	16. 107 ×145
17. 803 ×240	18. 5,675 ×912	19. 6,072 ×516	20. 5,109 ×307
21. 782 ×10	22. 457 ×100	23. 8,960 ×100	24. 7,643 ×1,000

23 or more right? Begin on page 62. Less than 23 right? Consult your teacher.

Multiplying by a Two-Digit Number

OBJECTIVE   To multiply a whole number by a two-digit number

EXAMPLE 1   Multiply.   26
                                 ×43

SOLUTION   Short way

                                26
                               ×43   26
            3 × 6 =   18   ×43
            3 × 20 =   60   3 × 26 =   78
            40 × 6 = 240   40 × 26 = 1,040
The 2 in 26 stands for 20.   40 × 20 = 800   1,118
The 4 in 43 stands for 40.   1,118

- -

Multiply.

1.	24	2.	38	3.	57	4.	88
	×34		×26		×32		×42

EXAMPLE 2   Multiply.   301
                                 ×34

SOLUTION   301   Short way
                                 ×34
                 4 × 1 =   4   301
                 4 × 0 =   0   ×34
                 4 × 300 = 1,200   4 × 301 = 1,204
                 30 × 1 =   30   30 × 301 = 9,030
Remember: 30 × 0 =   0   10,234
4 × 0 = 0   30 × 300 = 9,000
30 × 0 = 0   10,234
Any number times 0
equals 0.

- -

Multiply.

5.	402	6.	703	7.	804	8.	666
	×24		×35		×27		×44

EXAMPLE 3 Multiply.   5,642
                            ×45

SOLUTION   Short way
The problem can also   5,642
be done the long way.   ×45
                            5 × 5,642 = 28,210
                           40 × 5,642 = 225,680
                                        253,890
— —
                            Multiply.
                            9. 1,234   **10.** 1,234   **11.** 3,456   **12.** 4,206
                                    ×31   ×52   ×67   ×95

PRACTICE SET 4
Multiply.

1. 48	**2.** 76	**3.** 89	**4.** 59	**5.** 64	**6.** 21
×22	×98	×21	×39	×28	×26

7. 56	**8.** 80	**9.** 90	**10.** 82	**11.** 67	**12.** 70
×37	×42	×73	×40	×30	×44

13. 92	**14.** 87	**15.** 28	**16.** 39	**17.** 88	**18.** 15
×28	×78	×37	×93	×77	×16

PRACTICE SET 5
Multiply.

1. 423	**2.** 416	**3.** 234	**4.** 561	**5.** 824	**6.** 923
×32	×42	×45	×26	×74	×62

7. 801	**8.** 903	**9.** 704	**10.** 600	**11.** 731	**12.** 942
×17	×24	×77	×82	×59	×97

13. 888	**14.** 777	**15.** 666	**16.** 808	**17.** 406	**18.** 902
×33	×54	×67	×80	×70	×80

PRACTICE SET 6
Multiply.

1. 5,641	**2.** 3,456	**3.** 5,947	**4.** 8,721	**5.** 8,642
×52	×21	×31	×64	×72

6. 7,438	**7.** 8,246	**8.** 1,907	**9.** 1,039	**10.** 6,043
×73	×37	×16	×82	×77

Multiplying by a Three-Digit Number

OBJECTIVE To multiply a whole number by a three-digit number

EXAMPLE 1 Multiply.
$$\begin{array}{r} 408 \\ \times 276 \end{array}$$

SOLUTION

Remember $6 \times 0 = 0$.

The 7 in 276 stands for
7 tens; the 2 stands for
2 hundreds.

$$\begin{array}{r} 408 \\ \times 276 \\ \hline \end{array}$$
$6 \times 408 = \quad 2,448$
$70 \times 408 = \quad 28,560$
$200 \times 408 = \quad 81,600$
$\overline{\quad\quad\quad 112,608}$

EXAMPLE 2 Multiply.
$$\begin{array}{r} 5,376 \\ \times 234 \end{array}$$

SOLUTION

In 234, the 3 stands
for 3 tens; the 2 stands
for 2 hundreds.

$$\begin{array}{r} 5,376 \\ \times 234 \\ \hline \end{array}$$
$4 \times 5,376 = \quad 21,504$
$30 \times 5,376 = \quad 161,280$
$200 \times 5,376 = 1,075,200$
$\overline{\quad\quad\quad 1,257,984}$

EXAMPLE 3 Multiply.
$$\begin{array}{r} 831 \\ \times 407 \end{array}$$

SOLUTION

A short cut is to not
multiply by 0. But,
remember that the 4 in
407 stands for 4 hundreds.

$$\begin{array}{r} 831 \\ \times 407 \\ \hline \end{array}$$
$7 \times 831 = \quad 5,817$
$0 \times 831 = \quad\quad 0$
$400 \times 831 = 332,400$
$\overline{\quad\quad 338,217}$

Short way
$$\begin{array}{r} 831 \\ \times 407 \\ \hline \end{array}$$
$7 \times 831 = \quad 5,817$
$400 \times 831 = 332,400$
$\overline{\quad\quad 338,217}$

Multiply.

1. $\begin{array}{r} 706 \\ \times 534 \end{array}$ 2. $\begin{array}{r} 209 \\ \times 916 \end{array}$ 3. $\begin{array}{r} 871 \\ \times 542 \end{array}$ 4. $\begin{array}{r} 561 \\ \times 371 \end{array}$

5. $\begin{array}{r} 4,732 \\ \times 481 \end{array}$ 6. $\begin{array}{r} 6,285 \\ \times 175 \end{array}$ 7. $\begin{array}{r} 7,193 \\ \times 201 \end{array}$

PRACTICE SET 7
Multiply.

1. 695 ×212	2. 384 ×209	3. 349 ×407	4. 327 ×234	5. 723 ×243
6. 616 ×727	7. 604 ×254	8. 641 ×452	9. 653 ×245	10. 602 ×354
11. 432 ×211	12. 819 ×536	13. 901 ×438	14. 712 ×206	15. 875 ×193

PRACTICE SET 8
Multiply.

1. 2,207 ×234	2. 3,408 ×243	3. 4,509 ×342	4. 5,610 ×432	5. 6,721 ×423
6. 7,832 ×345	7. 8,943 ×453	8. 9,054 ×534	9. 9,163 ×567	10. 7,943 ×675
11. 1,704 ×214	12. 5,351 ×798	13. 7,022 ×106	14. 3,296 ×615	15. 4,791 ×267

PRACTICE SET 9
Multiply.

1. 4,256 ×78	2. 5,367 ×87	3. 5,145 ×68	4. 6,034 ×86	5. 5,076 ×147
6. 878 ×9	7. 4,649 ×9	8. 3,147 ×328	9. 3,008 ×823	10. 2,130 ×98
11. 403 ×702	12. 1,786 ×901	13. 2,469 ×793	14. 749 ×287	15. 910 ×47
16. 78 ×327	17. 49 ×402	18. 6,905 ×218	19. 7,732 ×84	20. 4,070 ×67
21. 646 ×13	22. 1,279 ×107	23. 3,721 ×24	24. 3,457 ×123	25. 6,923 ×123

Return to Form B on page 57.

Number Problems

EXAMPLE 1 Sum: 8   Difference: 4
Find the two numbers.

SOLUTION

List the combinations that add to 8.

$$
\begin{array}{ccccc}
8 & 7 & 6 & 5 & 4 \\
+0 & +1 & +2 & +3 & +4 \\
\hline
8 & 8 & 8 & 8 & 8
\end{array}
$$

Use the same combinations, but subtract.

$$
\begin{array}{ccccc}
8 & 7 & 6 & 5 & 4 \\
-0 & -1 & -2 & -3 & -4 \\
\hline
8 & 6 & 4 & 2 & 0
\end{array}
$$

$6 + 2 = 8$

$6 - 2 = 4$

This combination works.

So, the numbers are 6 and 2.

EXAMPLE 2 Sum: 8   Product: 15
Find the two numbers.

SOLUTION

List the combinations that add to 8.

$$
\begin{array}{ccccc}
8 & 7 & 6 & 5 & 4 \\
+0 & +1 & +2 & +3 & +4 \\
\hline
8 & 8 & 8 & 8 & 8
\end{array}
$$

Use the same combinations, but multiply.

$$
\begin{array}{ccccc}
8 & 7 & 6 & 5 & 4 \\
\times 0 & \times 1 & \times 2 & \times 3 & \times 4 \\
\hline
0 & 7 & 12 & 15 & 16
\end{array}
$$

$5 + 3 = 8$

$5 \times 3 = 15$

This combination works.

So, the numbers are 5 and 3.

Find the two numbers.

1. Sum: 20
Difference: 8

2. Product: 50
Difference: 5

3. Product: 100
Difference: 15

4. Product: 100
Difference: 0

5. Sum: 17
Difference: 1

6. Sum: 17
Product: 72

7. Sum: 5
Product: 0

8. Sum: 20
Product: 75

9. Sum: 21
Product: 110

10. Difference: 1
Product: 90

11. Difference: 10
Product: 600

12. Sum: 80
Product: 700

Multiples of 10, 100, or 1,000

OBJECTIVE To multiply multiples of 10, 100, and 1,000

EXAMPLE 1 Multiply.

$$40$$
$$\times 20$$

SOLUTION

Use the fact $2 \times 4 = 8$.

40 ⟵——— 1 zero
×20 ⟵——— 1 zero
800 ⟵——— 2 zeros

Multiply.

1. 30	2. 30	3. 50	4. 60	5. 80
×20	×30	×20	×10	×40

EXAMPLE 2 Multiply.

$$300$$
$$\times 40$$

SOLUTION

Use the fact $3 \times 4 = 12$.

300 ⟵——— 2 zeros
×40 ⟵——— 1 zero
12,000 ⟵——— 3 zeros

Multiply.

6. 400	7. 500	8. 600	9. 800
×30	×70	×50	×90

EXAMPLE 3 Multiply.

$$600$$
$$\times 200$$

SOLUTION

Use the fact $2 \times 6 = 12$.

600 ⟵——— 2 zeros
×200 ⟵——— 2 zeros
120,000 ——— 4 zeros

Multiply.

10. 700	11. 800	12. 900	13. 600
×200	×300	×400	×900

EXERCISES
Multiply.

1. 20
    ×20

2. 20
    ×30

3. 20
    ×60

4. 70
    ×20

5. 70
    ×30

6. 70
    ×40

7. 30
    ×30

8. 30
    ×40

9. 30
    ×50

10. 40
    ×50

11. 40
    ×60

12. 40
    ×80

13. 90
    ×90

14. 90
    ×80

15. 90
    ×70

16. 200
    ×20

17. 200
    ×30

18. 200
    ×40

19. 700
    ×20

20. 700
    ×40

21. 700
    ×30

22. 800
    ×40

23. 400
    ×60

24. 400
    ×50

25. 300
    ×50

26. 300
    ×40

27. 500
    ×70

28. 500
    ×60

29. 700
    ×70

30. 700
    ×90

31. 700
    ×900

32. 600
    ×700

33. 300
    ×500

34. 700
    ×300

35. 700
    ×700

36. 600
    ×800

37. 400
    ×500

38. 700
    ×200

39. 200
    ×300

40. 700
    ×600

41. 600
    ×900

42. 500
    ×600

43. 300
    ×300

44. 900
    ×900

45. 800
    ×800

46. 2,000
    ×30

47. 2,000
    ×300

48. 2,000
    ×3,000

49. 3,000
    ×90

50. 3,000
    ×900

51. 3,000
    ×9,000

52. 6,000
    ×50

53. 6,000
    ×500

54. 6,000
    ×5,000

55. 7,000
    ×70

56. 7,000
    ×700

57. 7,000
    ×7,000

58. 9,000
    ×80

59. 9,000
    ×800

60. 9,000
    ×8,000

Estimating Products

EXAMPLE 1   Estimate the product.

SOLUTION

Round each number.
Then multiply.

$$113 \longrightarrow 100$$
$$\underline{\times 88} \longrightarrow \underline{\quad 90}$$
$$9,000$$

So, 113 × 88 is about 9,000.

EXAMPLE 2   Estimate the product.

SOLUTION

Round each number.
Then multiply.

$$210 \longrightarrow 200$$
$$\underline{\times 208} \longrightarrow \underline{\quad 200}$$
$$40,000$$

So, 210 × 208 is about 40,000.

- -

Estimate.

1. 205 ×42	2. 115 ×97	3. 459 ×11
4. 13 ×90	5. 302 ×78	6. 105 ×102

EXERCISES
Estimate.

1. 89 ×11	2. 312 ×4	3. 32 ×6	4. 273 ×12	5. 28 ×41
6. 69 ×36	7. 18 ×31	8. 112 ×29	9. 185 ×119	10. 58 ×5
11. 79 ×19	12. 63 ×25	13. 97 ×8	14. 39 ×85	15. 47 ×43
16. 130 ×55	17. 22 ×35	18. 162 ×213	19. 337 ×108	20. 118 ×321

Estimating Costs

EXAMPLE 1 Estimate the cost of 8 liters of gasoline at 18.2¢ per liter.

SOLUTION
Round to the nearest ten cents.

$$18.2¢ \longrightarrow 20¢$$
$$\underline{\times 8} \qquad \underline{\times 8}$$
$$160¢, \text{ or } \$1.60$$

EXAMPLE 2 Estimate the cost of 9 shirts at $7.75 per shirt.

SOLUTION
Round to the nearest dollar.

$$\$7.75 \longrightarrow \$8$$
$$\underline{\times 9} \qquad \underline{\times 9}$$
$$\$72$$

EXAMPLE 3 Estimate the cost of 7 tires at $22.10 per tire.

SOLUTION
Round to the nearest ten dollars.

$$\$22.10 \longrightarrow \$20$$
$$\underline{\times 7} \qquad \underline{\times 7}$$
$$\$140$$

Estimate the cost.

1. 3 kilograms of meat at $2.62 per kilogram
2. 2 pairs of shoes at $14.95 a pair
3. 8 dozen pencils at 88¢ per dozen
4. 5 bags of apples at $1.12 a bag

EXERCISES

Estimate the cost.

1. 3 blouses at $8.55 each

2. 6 chairs at $19.75 each

3. 2 kilograms of margarine at $1.38 per kilogram

4. 5 sofas at $521.78 each

Estimate the answer.

5. Lulu sold tickets at the school play. She sold 250 tickets at 75¢ each. How much money did she collect?

6. An art club bought jackets for 8 members. Each jacket cost $16.93. How much did the club spend?

7.

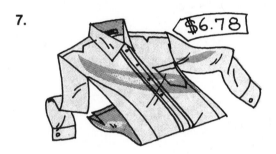

How much do 11 shirts cost?

8.

How much do 3 dozen eggs cost?

9. Bob spends 44¢ each day to ride the bus. He rides 5 days each week. How much does he spend in a year?

10. José bought 3 shirts for $4.95 each, 2 pairs of pants at $6.95 each, and a pair of shoes at $11.95 a pair. How much was his bill?

11.

How much will it cost to buy 15 ties and 13 pairs of socks?

12.

How much will it cost to buy 3 dozen school sweaters?

Using a Diagram

EXAMPLE 1   Mrs. Garcia wants to panel a wall with mahogany plywood. The wall is 18 feet wide and 8 feet long. A sheet of plywood is 4 feet wide and 8 feet long and costs $8.00 a sheet. How much will it cost?

SOLUTION

Draw a diagram to show how the plywood sheets fit on the wall. The diagram shows about 4.5 sheets.
Multiply.
```
 $ 8
 ×5
$40
```

1 Sheet	1 Sheet	1 Sheet	1 Sheet	

8′   8′   8′   8′   8′

4′   4′   4′   4′   2′

|←———— 18′ ————→|

Mrs. Garcia needs 5 sheets of plywood. So, it will cost her $40.

EXAMPLE 2   Shirts are packed 3 to a box. A box of shirts sells for $12.95. How much will 15 shirts cost?

SOLUTION

Draw a diagram.

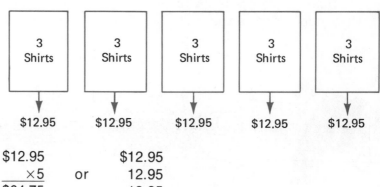

3 Shirts	3 Shirts	3 Shirts	3 Shirts	3 Shirts
↓	↓	↓	↓	↓
$12.95	$12.95	$12.95	$12.95	$12.95

Solve by multiplying or by adding.

```
$12.95              $12.95
  ×5      or         12.95
$64.75              12.95
                    12.95
                    12.95
                   $64.75
```

So, 15 shirts will cost $64.75.

Draw a diagram. Then solve.

1. Mrs. Kurella was hired to paint a house whose area was about 288 square meters. She used a paint with a coverage of 54 square meters per liter. How many liters of paint did she use?

2. Frank is paid 66¢ per 100 boxes stamped by his machine. One day he stamped 2,500 boxes. How much did he earn?

3. A brand of soap comes in packages of 4 bars and is priced at 25¢ per package. How much would you pay for 20 bars?

4. In an auditorium 200 people were seated, 20 people per row. How many rows of people were there?

5. A taxi company charges 70¢ for the first .2 kilometer and 20¢ for each additional .2 kilometer. Anita's fare was $2.30. How far did she ride?

6. Bob's TV set has a square viewing screen, 38 cm by 38 cm. Robin's model has a square viewing screen 53 cm by 53 cm. How much more viewing area does Robin have?

7. Mr. Hiner's bank balance was $82.50 at the beginning of May. He deposited $63.00 and made withdrawals of $28.75 and $18.22 in the first week. What was his balance then?

8. Mrs. Fisher is putting a fence around her garden. The garden is 14 m by 18 m. The fencing comes in 2-m sections. How many sections should she buy?

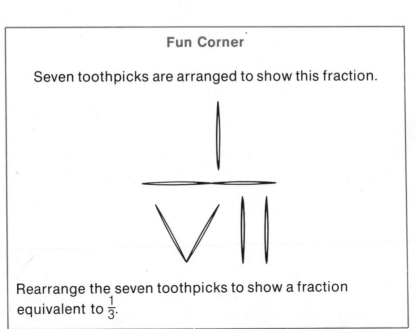

Fun Corner

Seven toothpicks are arranged to show this fraction.

Rearrange the seven toothpicks to show a fraction equivalent to $\frac{1}{3}$.

Mental Multiplication

EXAMPLE Multiply 42 by 10, 100, 1,000, and 10,000.

42	42	42	42
×10	×100	×1,000	×10,000
420	4,200	42,000	420,000

The number of 0's after 42 is the same as the number of 0's in the multiplier.

1 zero   2 zeros   3 zeros   4 zeros

Multiply.

1. 88
   ×10

2. 88
   ×1,000

3. 94
   ×100

4. 764
   ×100

5. 9
   ×10,000

6. 546
   ×1,000

EXERCISES
Multiply.

1. 94
   ×10

2. 52
   ×100

3. 477
   ×1,000

4. 273
   ×100

5. 852
   ×10

6. 676
   ×1,000

7. 59
   ×100

8. 325
   ×1,000

9. 78
   ×10,000

10. 598
   ×10

11. 150
   ×10

12. 4,879
   ×100

13. 29
   ×1,000

14. 810
   ×100

15. 960
   ×100

16. 24
   ×100

17. 666
   ×100

18. 74
   ×10,000

19. 306
   ×1,000

20. 460
   ×10

Fun Corner

Six chickens lay 6 eggs in 6 minutes. How many chickens will lay 100 eggs in 100 minutes?

Best Batter of Them All

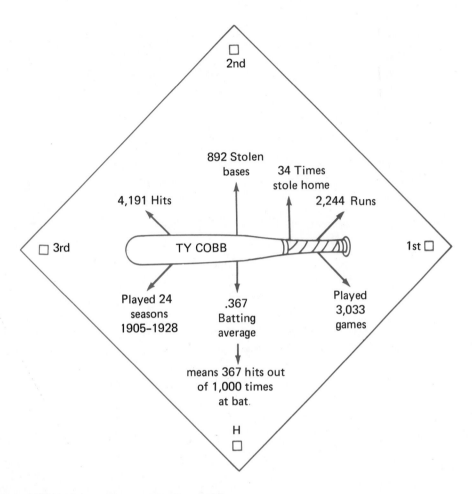

892 Stolen bases

34 Times stole home

4,191 Hits

2,244 Runs

TY COBB

3rd

1st

2nd

Played 24 seasons 1905–1928

.367 Batting average

Played 3,033 games

means 367 hits out of 1,000 times at bat.

H

True or false? Show that you are right.

1. Cobb averaged more than 1 hit per game during his lifetime.

2. Cobb scored 7 runs for each 10 games he played.

3. Cobb stole about 3 bases for each 10 games he played.

4. Cobb was at bat more than 11,000 times.

5. Cobb played an average of 126 games per season.

6. Cobb stole a base or home base about 38 times per season.

7. Cobb stole home base about 1 time for each 65 games he played.

8. Cobb stole home base about 1 time out of each 28 bases he stole.

Test: Unit 3

Multiply and check.

1. 39
  ×4

2. 54
  ×3

3. 26
  ×7

4. 121
  ×92

5. 348
  ×41

6. 742
  ×75

7. 6,561
  ×894

8. 7,522
  ×360

9. 2,087
  ×706

10. 8,101
  ×500

11. 7,040
  ×650

12. 5,091
  ×302

Estimate the answer.

13. How much will 7 portable fans cost at $28.95 each?

14. How much will 11 oranges cost at 23¢ apiece?

15. If the paper service charges $2.27 per week, what is the cost per year?

16. How much will a dozen pairs of socks cost if one pair costs 89¢?

Fun Corner

Sarah asked Otto to mark any 3 by 3 array of numbers on a calendar.

Sun	Mon	Tues	Wed	Thurs	Fri	Sat
		1	2	3	4	5
6	7	8	9	10	11	12
13	14	15	16	17	18	19
20	21	22	23	24	25	26
27	28	29	30	31		

$7 + 8 = 15$ and
$15 \times 9 = 135$

She asked Otto to give her the smallest number in the array. Sarah said the sum was 135.

1. Mark a different 3 by 3 array. Find the sum of the 9 numbers in the same way.

2. Mark some 2 by 2 arrays. Try to invent a similar method for finding the sum of the 4 numbers.

3. Try some 4 by 4 arrays.

UNIT 4
Division of Whole Numbers

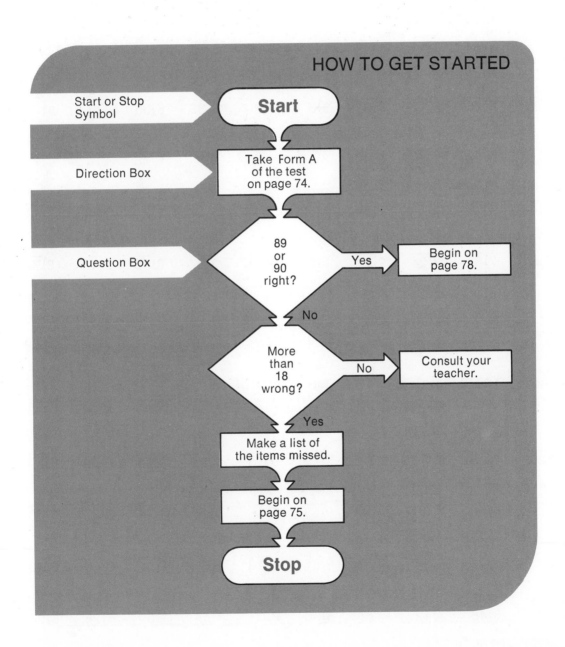

HOW TO GET STARTED

Start or Stop Symbol

Direction Box

Question Box

Start

Take Form A of the test on page 74.

89 or 90 right? — Yes → Begin on page 78.

No

More than 18 wrong? — No → Consult your teacher.

Yes

Make a list of the items missed.

Begin on page 75.

Stop

DIVISION FACTS TEST FORM A–4 MINUTES

1. 2)16   2)2   2)14   2)8   1)0   2)4   3)0   2)18   2)10   1)1

2. 2)6   2)12   1)2   3)3   3)9   1)3   3)6   2)0   3)12   4)32

3. 4)8   4)16   3)27   4)24   4)36   3)24   4)12   3)15   4)4   3)21

4. 3)18   1)4   4)20   5)45   4)0   4)28   6)0   5)35   6)24   5)5

5. 6)12   5)15   5)10   5)0   6)6   5)20   6)36   5)30   1)6   5)25

6. 6)30   6)18   1)5   5)40   8)16   7)21   8)8   6)48   8)0   7)28

7. 6)42   7)56   7)7   7)35   7)0   7)49   6)54   1)7   7)42   7)14

8. 1)8   7)63   8)24   9)72   8)64   9)54   9)27   8)56   9)0   8)72

9. 1)9   8)32   9)9   9)36   9)45   8)40   9)63   9)18   9)81   8)48

DIVISION FACTS TEST FORM B–3 MINUTES

1. 1)9   1)8   8)32   6)42   7)63   9)9   6)30   7)56   8)24   9)36

2. 6)12   6)18   7)7   9)72   9)45   5)15   1)5   7)35   8)64   8)40

3. 5)10   5)40   7)0   9)54   9)63   5)0   8)16   7)49   9)27   9)18

4. 6)6   7)21   6)54   8)56   9)81   5)20   8)8   1)7   9)0   8)48

5. 6)36   6)48   7)42   8)72   5)30   8)0   7)14   1)6   7)28   5)25

Division Facts

OBJECTIVE   To do at least 49 division facts correctly

THINK OF RELATED MULTIPLICATION FACTS

EXAMPLE 1   Complete.

$$\begin{array}{r} \boxed{} \\ \times 5 \\ \hline 30 \end{array}$$

SOLUTION

Think of the multiplication fact.

$$\begin{array}{r} 6 \\ \times 5 \\ \hline 30 \end{array}$$ So, 6 is the answer.

EXAMPLE 2   Divide. $6\overline{)54}$

SOLUTION

The related fact is $6 \times 9 = 54$.

Think: 6 times what number is 54?

$$\begin{array}{r} 9 \\ \times 6 \\ \hline 54 \end{array}$$ So, $6\overline{)\overset{9}{54}}$

- -

Divide. Think of a related fact.

1. $8\overline{)32}$ **2.** $9\overline{)36}$ **3.** $7\overline{)35}$ **4.** $6\overline{)42}$

EXAMPLE 3   Divide. $7\overline{)56}$

SOLUTION

The related fact is $7 \times 8 = 56$.

Think: 7 times what number is 56?

$$\begin{array}{r} 8 \\ \times 7 \\ \hline 56 \end{array}$$ So, $7\overline{)\overset{8}{56}}$

- -

Divide.

5. $8\overline{)64}$ **6.** $5\overline{)45}$ **7.** $4\overline{)24}$

PRACTICE SET 1
Practice the facts that you missed on Form A of the test until you know them.

Return to Form B on page 74.

Using the Division Facts

OBJECTIVE To divide multiples of 10, 100, and 1,000

$$5 \longleftarrow \text{Quotient}$$

Divisor $\longrightarrow 3\overline{)15} \longleftarrow$ Dividend

EXAMPLE 1 Divide. $2\overline{)60}$

SOLUTION

Use the fact $3 \times 2 = 6$.

$$2\overline{)60}^{\,30}$$

Dividend: 1 zero
Divisor: no zeros
Quotient: 1 zero

EXAMPLE 2 Divide and check. $40\overline{)1,200}$

SOLUTION

Use the fact $3 \times 4 = 12$.
To check, multiply the
answer, 30, by the divisor,
40. The product must be
the dividend, 1,200.

$$40\overline{)1,200}^{\,30}$$

Check: 30
       $\times 40$
       $\overline{1,200}$

Dividend: 2 zeros
Divisor: 1 zero
Quotient: 1 zero

- -

Divide and check.

1. $3\overline{)90}$ **2.** $3\overline{)900}$ **3.** $30\overline{)180}$

EXAMPLE 3 Divide. $50\overline{)45,000}$

SOLUTION

Use the fact $9 \times 5 = 45$.

$$50\overline{)45,000}^{\,900}$$

Dividend: 3 zeros
Divisor   1 zero
Quotient 2 zeros

- -

Divide.

4. $5\overline{)50}$ **5.** $50\overline{)50,000}$ **6.** $900\overline{)2,700}$

PRACTICE SET 2
Divide.

1. $8\overline{)80}$
2. $8\overline{)800}$
3. $8\overline{)8,000}$
4. $7\overline{)70}$

5. $7\overline{)7,000}$
6. $7\overline{)700}$
7. $6\overline{)60}$
8. $6\overline{)600}$

9. $6\overline{)6,000}$
10. $8\overline{)160}$
11. $8\overline{)1,600}$
12. $8\overline{)2,400}$

13. $8\overline{)240}$
14. $8\overline{)560}$
15. $8\overline{)5,600}$
16. $7\overline{)560}$

17. $7\overline{)5,600}$
18. $3\overline{)240}$
19. $3\overline{)2,400}$
20. $8\overline{)720}$

21. $8\overline{)7,200}$
22. $9\overline{)7,200}$
23. $60\overline{)360}$
24. $60\overline{)540}$

25. $60\overline{)240}$
26. $70\overline{)4,900}$
27. $70\overline{)350}$
28. $70\overline{)2,100}$

29. $5\overline{)150}$
30. $9\overline{)2,700}$
31. $90\overline{)4,500}$
32. $90\overline{)3,600}$

33. $70\overline{)4,200}$
34. $9\overline{)450}$
35. $9\overline{)1,800}$
36. $60\overline{)420}$

PRACTICE SET 3
Divide.

1. $800\overline{)8,000}$
2. $800\overline{)2,400}$
3. $800\overline{)4,000}$
4. $700\overline{)1,400}$

5. $700\overline{)2,800}$
6. $700\overline{)6,300}$
7. $900\overline{)7,200}$
8. $900\overline{)2,700}$

9. $600\overline{)4,200}$
10. $600\overline{)5,400}$
11. $400\overline{)3,200}$
12. $300\overline{)2,100}$

PRACTICE SET 4
Divide.

1. $80\overline{)7,200}$
2. $30\overline{)1,500}$
3. $3\overline{)1,800}$
4. $900\overline{)5,400}$

5. $800\overline{)3,200}$
6. $40\overline{)3,600}$
7. $80\overline{)1,600}$
8. $5\overline{)4,500}$

DIAGNOSTIC TEST: DIVISION FORM A—35 MINUTES
Divide.

1. 7)427 **2.** 6)3,552 **3.** 8)4,968 **4.** 4)2,664

5. 3)21,435 **6.** 8)83,512 **7.** 34)5,950 **8.** 43)10,965

9. 92)30,084 **10.** 29)8,507 **11.** 62)7,739 **12.** 28)5,212

13. 15)24,090 **14.** 15)4,530 **15.** 26)52,260 **16.** 17)53,040

17. 34)17,238 **18.** 12)12,093 **19.** 21)110,424 **20.** 13)161,149

Did You Have

More than 15 right?
Begin on page 85.

13, 14, or 15 right?
Begin on page 84.

Less than 13 right?
Begin on page 79.

DIAGNOSTIC TEST: DIVISION FORM B—35 MINUTES
Divide.

1. 9)459 **2.** 8)4,736 **3.** 6)3,492 **4.** 8)2,776

5. 7)20,657 **6.** 9)70,911 **7.** 28)5,348 **8.** 34)6,290

9. 17)7,004 **10.** 37)27,049 **11.** 34)6,295 **12.** 42)7,813

13. 15)39,090 **14.** 15)6,030 **15.** 13)91,299 **16.** 36)10,080

17. 14)91,099 **18.** 17)190,152 **19.** 31)110,424 **20.** 17)291,669

More than 15 right? Begin on page 85. Less than 16 right? Consult your teacher.

Remainders

OBJECTIVE To do divisions such as $9\overline{)74}$ by using the facts

EXAMPLE Divide. $6\overline{)51}$

SOLUTION

6×8 is 48, and
3 more is 51.

$$\begin{array}{r} 8 \text{ r3} \\ 6\overline{)51} \\ 48 \\ \hline 3 \end{array} \text{ remainder} \qquad \text{or } \begin{array}{r} 8 \text{ r3} \\ 6\overline{)51} \end{array}$$

To check, multiply the
divisor 6 by the answer 8.
Then add the remainder 3.
The sum must be the
dividend, 51.

Check:

$$\begin{array}{r} 6 \longleftarrow \text{ divisor} \\ \times 8 \longleftarrow \text{ answer} \\ \hline 48 \\ + \ 3 \longleftarrow \text{ remainder} \\ \hline 51 \longleftarrow \text{ dividend} \end{array}$$

Divide and check.

1. $8\overline{)73}$ 2. $5\overline{)6}$ 3. $3\overline{)44}$ 4. $5\overline{)14}$

5. $9\overline{)18}$ 6. $8\overline{)9}$ 7. $9\overline{)78}$ 8. $4\overline{)7}$

PRACTICE SET 5
Divide and check.

1. $5\overline{)22}$ 2. $5\overline{)32}$ 3. $9\overline{)15}$ 4. $8\overline{)67}$ 5. $5\overline{)49}$

6. $5\overline{)29}$ 7. $7\overline{)65}$ 8. $9\overline{)49}$ 9. $8\overline{)46}$ 10. $8\overline{)23}$

11. $9\overline{)38}$ 12. $3\overline{)8}$ 13. $9\overline{)33}$ 14. $7\overline{)48}$ 15. $9\overline{)13}$

16. $8\overline{)71}$ 17. $7\overline{)33}$ 18. $5\overline{)28}$ 19. $7\overline{)45}$ 20. $8\overline{)34}$

21. $8\overline{)14}$ 22. $5\overline{)21}$ 23. $4\overline{)11}$ 24. $9\overline{)70}$ 25. $6\overline{)23}$

26. $6\overline{)40}$ 27. $6\overline{)13}$ 28. $3\overline{)22}$ 29. $8\overline{)31}$ 30. $8\overline{)16}$

31. $7\overline{)19}$ 32. $6\overline{)28}$ 33. $7\overline{)64}$ 34. $5\overline{)35}$ 35. $6\overline{)47}$

36. $9\overline{)56}$ 37. $7\overline{)69}$ 38. $6\overline{)26}$ 39. $8\overline{)25}$ 40. $6\overline{)17}$

One-Digit Divisors

EXAMPLE   Divide and check.   6)5,056

SOLUTION

Use the facts 6 × 8 = 48 and 6 × 9 = 54.

1. Estimate. 6 × 800 = 4,800
                6 × 900 = 5,400
So, the answer is between 800 and 900.

6)5,056

The 50 in 5,056 stands for 50 hundreds. So, 8 stands for 800.

2. Divide 6)50. Write the 8 in the hundreds place.

$$\begin{array}{r} 8 \\ 6\overline{)5{,}056} \end{array}$$

Now, the remainder 256 must be divided by 6.

3. Multiply. 6 × 800 = 4,800 ⟶
Then subtract.

$$\begin{array}{r} 8 \\ 6\overline{)5{,}056} \\ -4{,}800 \\ \hline 256 \end{array}$$

The 25 in 256 stands for 25 tens. So, 4 stands for 40.

4. Divide 6)25. Write the 4 in the tens place.

$$\begin{array}{r} 84 \\ 6\overline{)5{,}056} \\ -4{,}800 \\ \hline 256 \end{array}$$

The remainder 16 must be divided by 6.

5. Multiply. 6 × 40 = 240 ⟶
Then subtract.

$$\begin{array}{r} 84 \\ 6\overline{)5{,}056} \\ -4{,}800 \\ \hline 256 \\ -240 \\ \hline 16 \end{array}$$

6. Divide 6)16. Write the 2 in the ones place.

$$\begin{array}{r} 842 \\ 6\overline{)5{,}056} \\ -4{,}800 \\ \hline 256 \\ -240 \\ \hline 16 \end{array}$$

The remainder 4 is less than 6. So, the division stops.

7. Multiply. 6 × 2 = 12 ⟶
Then subtract. 4 is the remainder.

$$\begin{array}{r} -12 \\ \hline 4 \end{array}$$

The answer is multiplied
by the divisor 6. Then
the remainder 4 is added.
The result is the dividend.

Check: 842
         ×6
       5,052
      +   4
       5,056

           842 r4
So, 6)5,056

- -

Divide and check.

1. 6)432   **2.** 8)2,576   **3.** 7)2,407

4. 9)721   **5.** 4)1,026   **6.** 4)2,054

PRACTICE SET 6
Divide and check.

1. 3)2,823   **2.** 4)1,332   **3.** 5)1,408   **4.** 7)2,938

5. 4)164   **6.** 6)3,666   **7.** 8)408   **8.** 8)4,008

9. 5)1,565   **10.** 5)1,505   **11.** 5)1,000   **12.** 9)478

13. 9)3,789   **14.** 9)270   **15.** 9)5,598   **16.** 7)4,354

17. 7)4,802   **18.** 8)3,456   **19.** 6)6,512   **20.** 7)8,477

21. 5)625   **22.** 5)7,660   **23.** 8)976   **24.** 8)8,184

25. 6)793   **26.** 6)8,832   **27.** 6)4,416   **28.** 4)6,532

29. 5)4,666   **30.** 8)1,141   **31.** 7)3,924   **32.** 6)4,629

33. 4)2,643   **34.** 5)3,118   **35.** 9)7,416   **36.** 7)6,825

37. 2)3,617   **38.** 3)2,299   **39.** 8)4,934   **40.** 6)3,527

41. 5)78,193   **42.** 7)20,684   **43.** 9)37,189   **44.** 4)13,519

Two-Digit Divisors

EXAMPLE   Divide.   26)‾5‾6‾,‾9‾3‾2‾

SOLUTION   **1.** Estimate. 26 × 2,000 = 52,000
Use 26 × 2 = 52 and   26 × 3,000 = 78,000   26)‾5‾6‾,‾9‾3‾2‾
26 × 3 = 78.   So, the answer is between
2,000 and 3,000.

The 56 in 56,932 stands   **2.** Divide 26)‾5‾6‾. Write the 2   2
for 56 thousands. So,   above the 6 in the thousands   26)‾5‾6‾,‾9‾3‾2‾
the 2 stands for 2,000.   place.

                                                                                        2
                                                                              26)‾5‾6‾,‾9‾3‾2‾
                            3. Multiply. 26 × 2,000 = 52,000   52,000
                                Then subtract.   4,932

Now, the remainder 4,932   2,1
must be divided by 26.   26)‾5‾6‾,‾9‾3‾2‾
The 49 in 4,932 stands for   **4.** Divide 26)‾4‾9‾. Write the 1   52,000
49 hundreds. So, the 1   above the 9 in the hundreds   4,932
stands for 100.   place.

                                                                                      2,1
                                                                              26)‾5‾6‾,‾9‾3‾2‾
                                                                                  52,000
                                                                                    4,932
                            5. Multiply. 26 × 100 = 2,600   2,600
                                Then subtract.   2,332

Now, the remainder 2,332   2,18
must be divided by 26.   26)‾5‾6‾,‾9‾3‾2‾
The 233 in 2,332 stands   **6.** Divide 26)‾2‾3‾3‾. Write the 8   52,000
for 233 tens. So, the 8   above the 3 in the tens place.   4,932
stands for 80.   2,600
                                                                                    2,332

$$
\begin{array}{r}
2{,}18 \\
26\overline{)56{,}932} \\
52{,}000 \\
\hline
4{,}932 \\
2{,}600 \\
\hline
2{,}332 \\
2{,}080 \\
\hline
252
\end{array}
$$

7. Multiply. $26 \times 80 = 2{,}080$
Then subtract.

$$
\begin{array}{r}
2{,}189 \\
26\overline{)56{,}932} \\
52{,}000 \\
\hline
4{,}932 \\
2{,}600 \\
\hline
2{,}332 \\
2{,}080 \\
\hline
252 \\
234 \\
\hline
18
\end{array}
$$

Now divide the remainder by 26. The remainder is less than 26. So, the division stops.

8. Divide $26\overline{)252}$. Write the 9 in the ones place. Then multiply. $26 \times 9 = 234$ The remainder is 18.

Divide.

1. $12\overline{)3{,}874}$ **2.** $24\overline{)102{,}270}$ **3.** $45\overline{)28{,}349}$

PRACTICE SET 7
Divide and check.

1. $14\overline{)3{,}168}$ **2.** $34\overline{)17{,}238}$ **3.** $26\overline{)157{,}664}$ **4.** $18\overline{)55{,}044}$

5. $17\overline{)52{,}020}$ **6.** $13\overline{)91{,}169}$ **7.** $15\overline{)24{,}090}$ **8.** $15\overline{)4{,}530}$

9. $27\overline{)24{,}462}$ **10.** $39\overline{)11{,}973}$ **11.** $26\overline{)17{,}680}$ **12.** $36\overline{)10{,}080}$

PRACTICE SET 8
Divide and check.

1. $13\overline{)65{,}845}$ **2.** $28\overline{)61{,}740}$ **3.** $44\overline{)13{,}244}$ **4.** $15\overline{)39{,}135}$

5. $46\overline{)27{,}738}$ **6.** $59\overline{)29{,}795}$ **7.** $23\overline{)13{,}984}$ **8.** $12\overline{)8{,}436}$

9. $29\overline{)20{,}880}$ **10.** $38\overline{)50{,}666}$ **11.** $29\overline{)15{,}370}$ **12.** $18\overline{)4{,}448}$

A Shortcut

EXAMPLE   Divide.   12)3,456

SOLUTION

Use the facts $2 \times 12 = 24$
and $3 \times 12 = 36$.

1. Estimate. The answer is
between 200 and 300.

$$12\overline{)3,456}$$

2. Divide 12)34. Write the 2
over the 4 in 3,456. Multiply.
$2 \times 12 = 24$. Write the 24
under the 34. Subtract to get
10. Then bring down the 5.

$$
\begin{array}{r}
2 \\
12\overline{)3,456} \\
2\,4 \\
\hline
1\,05
\end{array}
$$

3. Divide 12)105. Write the 8
over the 5 in 3,456. Multiply.
$8 \times 12 = 96$. Write the 96
under the 105. Subtract to
get 9. Bring down the 6.

$$
\begin{array}{r}
28 \\
12\overline{)3,456} \\
2\,4 \\
\hline
1\,05 \\
96 \\
\hline
96
\end{array}
$$

Check the answer by
multiplying.
Do the problem the long
way and compare it with
this example. Use either
way in the future.

4. Divide 12)96. Write the 8
over the 6 in 3,456. Multiply.
$8 \times 12 = 96$. Write the 96
under the 96. Subtract to get
0.

$$
\begin{array}{r}
288 \\
12\overline{)3,456} \\
2\,4 \\
\hline
1\,05 \\
96 \\
\hline
96 \\
96 \\
\hline
0
\end{array}
$$

PRACTICE SET 9
Divide and check.

1. 21)5,523   2. 34)8,942   3. 23)4,738   4. 51)1,989

5. 18)6,500   6. 28)19,880   7. 62)3,472   8. 25)3,125

9. 31)2,883   10. 41)4,018   11. 52)3,328   12. 67)12,663

13. 35)1,225   14. 48)14,888   15. 93)11,442   16. 98)25,186

Return to Form B on page 78.

Using an Array

EXAMPLE Akiko uses only 1 kind of ice cream and 1 topping in her sundaes. How many different sundaes can she make?

SOLUTION Draw an array.

Kinds of ice cream

Toppings

Vh means a sundae with vanilla ice cream and hot fudge topping.

	V	C	S	M	R	P	B
h	Vh	Ch	Sh	Mh	Rh	Ph	Bh
b	Vb	Cb	Sb	Mb	Rb	Pb	Bb
p	Vp	Cp	Sp	Mp	Rp	Pp	Bp

The array shows 3 rows of 7 sundaes each. So, Akiko can make 3×7, or 21 sundaes.

Draw an array. Then solve the problem.

1. Al's menu lists 5 dinners: chopped steak, roast beef, bluefish, shrimp, and veal cutlet. The menu lists 6 desserts: ice cream, apple pie, layer cake, jello, custard pudding, and coffee cake. How many different combinations of 1 dinner and 1 dessert can he make?

2. Lula has 6 colors of skirt material: brown, rust, green, gray, red, and purple. She has 8 colors of blouse material: white, pink, blue, yellow, lavender, gold, orange, and tan. How many different skirt and blouse outfits can she make?

Average

EXAMPLE 1 The height of each player on the Rushville Falcon's basketball team is shown. What is the average height?

Player	Height
Pat	144 cm
Lee	152 cm
Sandy	140 cm
Ray	142 cm
Mel	132 cm

SOLUTION

To find the average height, add the 5 heights, then divide the total by the number of players.

```
144          142
152        5) 710
140
142
132
710
```

So, the average height is 142 centimeters.

Find the average.

1. 48, 52, 46, 54   **2.** 90, 110, 106, 94, 95

EXAMPLE 2 Ida's average score on three tests was 80. Her first two scores were 72 and 94. What was her score on the third test?

SOLUTION

Scores	72	94	?

To find the total points scored on the 3 tests, multiply 80 by 3. Then find the sum of the points scored on the 2 tests. Then subtract.

```
  80          72          240
  ×3         +94         −166
 240         166           74
```

So, the score on the third test was 74.

The average of six numbers is 21. Find the sixth number.

3. 23, 19, 17, 24, 27   **4.** 13, 31, 24, 11, 20

EXERCISES

1. Sara got the following scores on her science tests: 76, 78, 60, and 66. Her average must be at least 70 to get credit. Will she get credit?

2. Each of four runners ran 400 meters in a relay race. Their times were 56 sec, 54 sec, 58 sec, and 52 sec. What was their average time?

3. Jill saved the money she earned each week. What was the average amount saved each week?

4. Eiko's record shows her lunch expense for a work week. What is the average daily cost?

Week	Amount
Nov. 1	$3.50
Nov. 8	2.98
Nov. 15	4.02
Nov. 22	5.70

Monday	$1.15
Tuesday	1.35
Wednesday	.95
Thursday	.63
Friday	1.17

5. Ola's average on four tests was 85. What was his score on the fourth test?

6. The DeKalb School paper was torn. The number of students in grade 12 could not be read. Find the missing number.

Test	Score
1	81
2	89
3	79
4	?

Students in each class	
Grade	Number
10	1,383
11	1,251
12	

Average per class: 1,269

Fun Corner

1. Choose a number between 0 and 10.
2. Multiply by 9.
3. Then multiply by 12,345,679.
4. Choose another number and repeat the process.
5. What do you notice about your answers?

Size Records

1. The tallest living adult is about 249 cm tall. The shortest living adult is about 71 cm tall. What is the difference in their heights?

2. The smallest bone in the human body, the stirrup bone in the ear, is about 3 mm long. The longest bone, the thighbone, is about 501 mm long in a person who is 2 meters tall. About how many times longer is the thighbone than the stirrup bone?

3. The longest river in the world is about 6,632,000 meters long. The shortest river is about 134 meters long. What is the difference in their lengths?

4. The largest guitar in the world is about 270 cm tall. The price of this guitar is $15,000. What is the price for each centimeter of length?

5. The smallest playing record is about 35 mm in diameter. If 250 of these records are placed next to each other, how long would all the records be?

6. The longest suspension bridge in the world has a span of about 1,410 meters. The longest steel-arch bridge has a span of about 518 meters. What is the total length of the two bridge spans?

7. It took 36 weeks to carve the tallest totem pole in the world. About 146 cm were carved each week. How tall is this totem pole?

8. The smallest bicycle in the world weighs about 909 grams. The largest tricycle in the world weighs about 1,212,091 grams. What is the total weight of the bicycle and the tricycle?

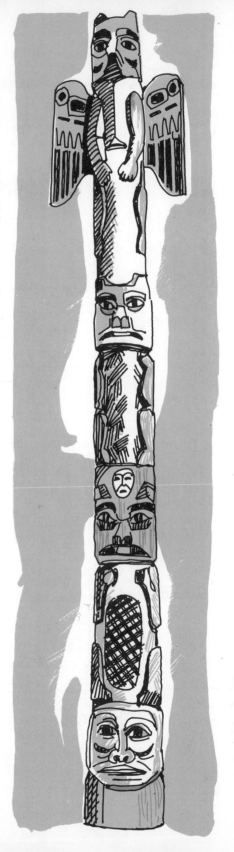

Estimating in Division

OBJECTIVE To estimate answers to division problems

EXAMPLE 1 Estimate. $58\overline{)3{,}174}$

SOLUTION $58\overline{)3{,}174} \longrightarrow 60\overline{)3{,}000}$
Round the divisor and
the dividend.
$60 \times 50 = 3{,}000$
So, a good estimate is 50.

EXAMPLE 2 Estimate. $87\overline{)45{,}863}$
SOLUTION $87\overline{)45{,}863} \longrightarrow 90\overline{)46{,}000}$
Round the divisor and
the dividend.
$90 \times 500 = 45{,}000$
So, a good estimate is 500.

Estimate the answer.

1. $8\overline{)960}$ **2.** $14\overline{)79}$ **3.** $115\overline{)393}$ **4.** $102\overline{)35{,}876}$

EXERCISES
Estimate the answer.

1. $46\overline{)51{,}732}$ **2.** $44\overline{)13{,}172}$ **3.** $84\overline{)72{,}710}$ **4.** $84\overline{)48{,}970}$

5. $59\overline{)61{,}281}$ **6.** $51\overline{)68{,}001}$ **7.** $56\overline{)63{,}819}$ **8.** $44\overline{)40{,}261}$

9. $95\overline{)460}$ **10.** $25\overline{)40{,}133}$ **11.** $924\overline{)49{,}217}$ **12.** $94\overline{)560}$

13. $40\overline{)8{,}495}$ **14.** $51\overline{)25{,}016}$ **15.** $568\overline{)704}$ **16.** $75\overline{)4{,}414}$

17. $43\overline{)686}$ **18.** $64\overline{)296}$ **19.** $445\overline{)648}$ **20.** $51\overline{)7{,}099}$

21. A bolt of cloth 20 meters long cost $67.95. What was the price per meter?

22. Jane saved $31.50 for her Christmas Club in 13 weeks. How much did she save each week?

23. Six baseballs cost $12.54. How much did each ball cost?

24. Three shirts cost $21.95. How much did one shirt cost?

25. Twelve T-shirts sold for $12.95. How much did each cost?

26. Six pairs of stockings sold for $7.13. What was the price per pair?

A Traveling Sales Representative

1. Ms. Hurst travels the route shown each week. How many kilometers does she travel?

2. How much farther is it from Rushville to DeKalb than from Rushville to Atchison?

3. The company paid Ms. Hurst 7¢ per kilometer for car expenses. How much was she paid each week? each year?

4. Ms. Hurst uses about 129 liters of fuel going from Rushville to DeKalb. About how many liters should she use going from DeKalb to Faucett?

5. How much fuel should Ms. Hurst use per week? Use the information from Exercise 4.

6. How much fuel should Ms. Hurst use per year?

7. Fuel costs 14¢ per liter. How much per week does Ms. Hurst spend on fuel?

8. How much per year does Ms. Hurst spend on fuel?

9. Ms. Hurst's company pays her $120 per 5-day work week for living expenses. She spends $16 per night for a motel room. How much does she have left for food each week?

10. Ms. Hurst spends an average of $9.25 each day of her 5-day week. Does her pay of $120 cover both room and food expenses for the week?

11. Ms. Hurst's company made a profit of $49,105 on her sales. The company paid Ms. Hurst a salary of $18,500 per year plus her total living expenses. How much profit was left?

12. Ms. Hurst earned a bonus of $100 on each $1,000 of sales over $30,000. How much was her bonus?

Fun Corner

Beth and Rob were each asked to choose the container which had the most money in it. Beth chose the one with the dimes. Rob chose the quarters. The containers were the same size. Who got more money? How do you know?

Mental Division

OBJECTIVE To do divisions such as $3\overline{)6,912}$ mentally

EXAMPLE 1 Divide mentally. $2\overline{)8,462}$

SOLUTION $8 \div 2 = 4$ $\qquad 4 \div 2 = 2$ $\qquad 6 \div 2 = 3$ $\qquad 2 \div 2 = 1$

Do 4 divisions, using the basic facts.

$$\begin{array}{r} 4,231 \\ 2\overline{)8,462} \end{array}$$

EXAMPLE 2 Divide mentally. $7\overline{)49,637}$

SOLUTION $49 \div 7 = 7$

$4 \div 7$ is not a whole number, so start with $49 \div 7$.

$6 \div 7$ is not a whole number.
Write 0; carry 6.
$63 \div 7 = 9$
$7 \div 7 = 1$

$$\begin{array}{r} 7,0\,9\,1 \\ {}^{6} \\ 7\overline{)49,6\,37} \end{array}$$

- -

Divide mentally.

1. $4\overline{)844}$ **2.** $8\overline{)248}$ **3.** $6\overline{)318}$ **4.** $7\overline{)35,000}$

EXERCISES
Divide mentally.

1. $3\overline{)597}$ **2.** $6\overline{)858}$ **3.** $9\overline{)144}$ **4.** $5\overline{)655}$

5. $4\overline{)840}$ **6.** $5\overline{)975}$ **7.** $2\overline{)1,050}$ **8.** $7\overline{)6,461}$

9. $8\overline{)1,608}$ **10.** $9\overline{)7,398}$ **11.** $3\overline{)3,912}$ **12.** $15\overline{)4,560}$

13. A group of 15 scout troops shared $165 in banquet expenses. How much did each troop owe?

14. A woman drove 480 kilometers and used 80 liters of gasoline. Find the number of kilometers she drove per liter.

15. At a garage sale, $150 worth of $25 dresses were sold. How many dresses were sold?

16. You owe $48 on a radio. How many monthly payments of $4 will you have to make?

Record Sales

1. In about 10 years the Beatles sold the equivalent of 545,000,000 single records. What was the average number sold per year?

2. Suppose the Beatles earned a royalty of 5¢ per single. How much did they get in royalties for the 10 years?

3. The Johnny Mathis album *Johnny's Greatest Hits* was put on the best-seller list in December of 1958. It stayed on the list for 490 weeks. When was it taken off the list?

4. The record album *Sound of Music* was released in March, 1965, and as of December, 1972, had sold about 19,000,000 copies. What were the average sales per month?

5. The fastest selling record was *John Fitzgerald Kennedy*, a memorial album, which sold about 4 million copies in 6 days at $1 per copy. What were the average daily sales?

6. The Carole King recording of *Tapestry* was among the top 100 records for 5 years. Total sales during that period were $65,000,000. What were the average sales per month?

Making an Easier Problem

EXAMPLE   Rewrite the problem in easier form.

A plane averaged 380 kilometers per hour on a flight from New York to Detroit. The trip took $2\frac{3}{4}$ hours. How far is it from New York to Detroit?

SOLUTION
380 is about 400.
$2\frac{3}{4}$ is about 3.

A plane averaged 400 kilometers per hour on a flight from New York to Detroit. The trip took 3 hours. How far is it from New York to Detroit?

Rewrite the problem in easier form.

1. Mrs. Spencer traveled 320 kilometers and used 94.2 liters of gasoline. Find the average number of kilometers traveled per liter of gasoline.

2. A bottle contains 125 milliliters of cough syrup. The cough syrup is .4 alcohol. How many milliliters of alcohol are there?

3. A union contract called for $3.25 per hour. It was replaced with a new contract which called for $3.42 per hour. The contract applied to a 40-hour work week. How much of a weekly raise was this?

4. A football game must get "off the air" by 4:30 pm. The game should take 2 hours and 15 minutes. What time should the game start?

5. Mr. Owens averaged 10.3 kilometers per liter of fuel. He made a round trip from Detroit to Chicago, which is 337.5 kilometers. How much fuel did he use for the trip?

6. What is the average of these lengths?
.8 meter, 1.3 meters, .9 meter, .4 meter, and .7 meter

7. Mr. Bond had the following expenses during the month of May:

Transportation, 670 kilometers at 11¢ per kilometer
Entertaining customers, $28
Bills, $32
Mailing expenses, $2.30
What were Mr. Bond's total expenses for the month?

8. Ms. Malone's corporation owned $256,000 worth of shares of stock. Her corporation made a quarterly profit of $382,123. What was the quarterly dividend rate?

9. Joan wants to make curtains for 2 windows. Each window requires 2 standard width panels $138\frac{1}{2}$ cm long with $3\frac{1}{2}$ cm extra for the hems. How many meters of material will she need?

10. Paul drove from New York to Los Angeles in 8 days and 8 hours. He could have made the trip by plane in 5 hours and 28 minutes. How many times as long as the plane trip was the car trip?

Fun Corner

USED CARS

I SOLD TWO CARS TODAY FOR $1,500 EACH. ON ONE I MADE 25%. ON THE OTHER I LOST 25%.

THAT'S OKAY. YOU BROKE EVEN FOR THE DAY.

Is the man right or wrong?
Show that your answer is correct.

Test: Unit 4

Estimate. Then divide and check with your estimate.

1. $3\overline{)99}$
2. $6\overline{)192}$
3. $12\overline{)264}$
4. $15\overline{)330}$
5. $21\overline{)315}$
6. $65\overline{)21,060}$
7. $37\overline{)20,646}$
8. $29\overline{)20,880}$
9. $18\overline{)5,504}$
10. $4\overline{)7,604}$
11. $24\overline{)217,200}$
12. $56\overline{)39,450}$
13. $26\overline{)61,750}$
14. $36\overline{)34,416}$
15. $37\overline{)46,212}$
16. $54\overline{)96,481}$

17. Joanna kept a record of her math test scores. What is her average?

18. How much does this carpeting cost per meter?

Test	Score
1	88
2	73
3	62
4	93
5	94

SALE !

36 m²
for
$366.16

Fun Corner

To square a number means to multiply the number by itself.

Read 8^2 as the square of 8.

$8^2 = 8 \times 8$, or 64	$3^2 = 3 \times 3$, or 9
$10^2 = 10 \times 10$, or 100	$25^2 = 25 \times 25$, or 625

Here's a new way to square numbers near 100.

EXAMPLE 1 Find 108^2.

SOLUTION Think: 108 is 8 more than 100 and $8^2 = 64$.

Write the 64 to the right of 116.

$$108 + 8 = 116$$
$$\text{So, } 108^2 = 11,664$$

EXAMPLE 2 Find 96^2.

SOLUTION Think: 96 is 4 less than 100 and $4^2 = 16$.

Subtract, since 96 is less than 100.

$$96 - 4 = 92$$
$$\text{So, } 96^2 = 9,216$$

EXAMPLE 3 Find 112^2.

SOLUTION Think: 112 is 12 more than 100 and $12^2 = 144$.

Think of 124 as 12,400. Then add 144.

$$112 + 12 = 124$$
$$144$$
$$\text{So, } 112^2 = 12,544$$

Square each number from 85 through 115.

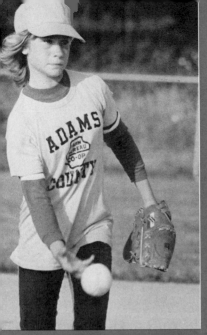

UNIT 5

Addition and Subtraction
of Decimals

DIAGNOSTIC TEST: ADDITION AND SUBTRACTION FORM A—25 MINUTES

Add.

1. 0.3 + 2.04

2. 4.1 + 7.83 + 19

3. 29.2 + 3.07 + 589 + .04

4. 64.09 + 0.85 + 0.017 + 10

5. 6.71 + .8074 + 10.1 + 7

6. 37.63 + 0.56 + 0.54 + 26

7. 8,151 + 65.52 + .015 + 71.75

8. $555.61 + $7.83 + $19

Subtract.

9. 32 − 5.8

10. 27 − 8.6

11. 329 − 6.01

12. 632 − 2.79

13. 62.52 − 5.4

14. 42.5 − 23.97

15. 9.08 − 4.173

16. 68.45 − 8.3

17. 72.519 − 2.36

18. 482 − 2.64

19. 36.212 − 2.16

20. 56 − 1.3

Did You Have

| More than 17 right?
Begin on page 109. | 15, 16, or 17 right?
Begin on page 104. | Less than 15 right?
Begin on page 100. |

DIAGNOSTIC TEST: ADDITION AND SUBTRACTION FORM B—25 MINUTES

Add.

1. 0.6 + 3.02

2. 6.2 + 5.73 + 16

3. 18.7 + 6.07 + 476 + .05

4. 58.02 + 0.76 + 0.023

5. 4.63 + 0.7084 + 20.1 + 8

6. 36.37 + 0.42 + 0.22

7. 5,463 + 85.25 + 0.029 + 64.35

8. $456.39 + $7.83 + $19

Subtract.

9. 43 − 5.8

10. 32 − 6.8

11. 418 − 7.02

12. 722 − 2.79

13. 48.32 − 9.4

14. 33.87 − 32.5

15. 8.03 − 4.217

16. 78.54 − 7.4

17. 63.329 − 3.21

18. 348 − 3.62

19. 84.323 − 3.14

20. 78 − 3.4

More than 17 right? Begin on page 109. Less than 18 right? Consult your teacher.

Writing Decimals

Our system for writing numbers uses place value. The decimal point is used to locate the ones place. The place values are symmetrical about the ones place.

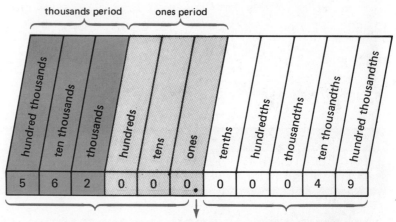

Five hundred sixty–two thousand and forty–nine hundred thousandths

EXAMPLE 1 Read 174.8.

SOLUTION

The decimal point is read *and*.

$$\underline{174} . \underline{8}$$

one hundred seventy-four   and eight tenths

EXAMPLE 2 Read 476,814.76.

SOLUTION

476 is in the thousands period. 814 is in the ones period.

$$\underline{476}, \underline{814} . \underline{76}$$

four hundred seventy-six thousand   eight hundred fourteen   and seventy-six hundredths

EXAMPLE 3 Read 987,634.156.

SOLUTION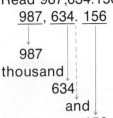

Read.
1. 78.3　　　　2. 7.83　　　　3. 0.783　　　　4. 1.078

EXAMPLE 4 Write the decimal for seventeen thousand, six hundred eighty-one and forty-four hundredths.

SOLUTION

Seventeen thousand,	six hundred and eighty one	forty-four hundredths
17 ,	681 .	44

Write a decimal.
5. Eight hundred forty-six and seventy-eight hundredths

6. Five hundred seventy-four and fifteen hundredths

PRACTICE SET 1
Read.

1. 34.263　　　2. 3.4263　　　3. 3,426.3　　　4. 1,789.43

5. 17,894.37　　6. 17,894.371　　7. 642,431.07　　8. 64,243.107

PRACTICE SET 2
Write a decimal.

1. Six thousand nine hundred and twenty-four hundredths

2. Seven hundred forty-three and forty-four hundredths

3. Nine hundred sixty-three and thirty-five hundredths

4. Nine hundred ninety-nine and ninety-nine hundredths

5. Two hundred thirty-two and four tenths

6. One hundred thirty-four and two tenths

7. One hundred ninety-two and twenty-five hundredths

8. Six hundred ninety-three and five hundred fifty-one thousandths

Placing the Decimal Point

> **OBJECTIVE** To place the decimal point in a sum or difference by estimation

EXAMPLE 1 Place the decimal point in the sum.
45.6 + 12.9 + 23.28 = 8178

SOLUTION

Round each number to the nearest whole number.

Think: 45.6 $\longrightarrow$ 46
　　　12.9 $\longrightarrow$ 13
　　　23.28 $\longrightarrow$ 23
　　　　　　　　　　　82

So, 81.78 is the right answer.

EXAMPLE 2 Place the decimal point in the difference.
376.4 − 218.5 = 1579

SOLUTION

A difference is the answer to a subtraction.

Think:　376.4 $\longrightarrow$ 　376
　　　 −218.5 $\longrightarrow$ −219
　　　　　　　　　　　 157

So, 157.9 is the right answer.

EXAMPLE 3 Place the decimal point in the difference.
8,437.56 − 2,869.23 = 556833

SOLUTION

Think:　8,437.56 $\longrightarrow$ 　8,438
　　　 −2,869.23 $\longrightarrow$ −2,869
　　　　　　　　　　　　 5,569

So, 5,568.33 is the right answer.

Place the decimal point in each answer to make it correct.

1. 73.5 + 86.83 + 117.1 = 27743

2. 438.7 + 58.63 + 9.231 = 506561

3. 743.19 − 292.4 = 45079

4. 8,001.1 − 7,999.9 = 12

PRACTICE SET 3

Place the decimal point in each answer to make it correct.

1. $78.3 + 17.2 = 955$

2. $38.12 + 5.6 = 4372$

3. $298.5 + 17.63 + 8.1 = 32423$

4. $0.87 + 1.96 + 8.2 = 1103$

5. $0.39 + 117 + 23.8 = 14119$

6. $878.4 + 352 + 1.6 = 1232$

7. $880 - 380.16 = 49984$

8. $3 - 1.563 = 1437$

9. $156.83 - 57.9 = 9893$

10. $5,000 - 4,992.53 = 747$

11. $178.06 + 8.04 + 0.9 = 187$

12. $8.732 + 5.148 + 0.120 = 14$

13. $186.01 - 87.009 = 99001$

14. $5.926 - 0.947 = 4979$

15. $8.92 + 0.07 + 21.01 = 30$

16. $7,469.1 + 6.8 + 8.5 = 74844$

17. $328.09 - 233 = 9509$

18. $3.235 + 1.42 + 0.07 = 4725$

19. $8,005 + 3,826.54 = 1183154$

20. $27.1 + 2.71 + 0.271 = 30081$

21. $2,351.78 - 1,286.9 = 106488$

22. $158.1 - 62.35 = 9575$

23. $9,123 + 8,888.57 = 1801157$

24. $4,783.16 - 4,175.932 = 607228$

25. $6,243.5 + 708.46 = 695196$

26. $0.973 - 0.810 = 163$

27. $234.57 - 38.6 = 19597$

28. $1,348.1 - 216.7 = 11314$

Adding Decimals

EXAMPLE 1 Find the sum of 9.8, 16.3, and 106.7.

SOLUTION
```
  9.8 Check:     9.8 ──────→   10
 16.3           16.3 ──────→   16
106.7          106.7 ──────→  107
132.8                         133
```
To check, round each number to the nearest whole number.

└─Line up decimal points.

EXAMPLE 2 Find the sum of 18, 19.7, and 188.62.

SOLUTION
```
 18.00 Check:   18
 19.70          20
188.62         189
226.32         227
```
You can use zeros to make the number of decimal places the same.

└─Line up decimal points.

- -

Find the sum.

1. 6.46, 88.07, and 326.01

2. 878.6, 432.35, and 786

3. 588.5, 58.85, 5.885, and 0.5885

PRACTICE SET 4
Add.

1. 28.32 + 0.58 + 0.057 + 5

2. 8.07 + 0.0047 + 9.6 + 83

3. 57.91 + 0.87 + 5 + 17.05

4. 937.44 + 0.56 + 0.0051 + 52

5. 2,744 + 27.73 + 0.02642

6. 20.13 + 0.87 + 9 + 98.29

7. 5.84 + 0.062 + 5.9 + 65

8. 25.35 + 0.85 + 0.047 + 3

9. 463.14 + 0.28 + 0.0073 + 13

10. 36.92 + 0.76 + 8 + 56.67

11. 5,469 + 61.32 + 0.02368

12. 92.36 + 0.72 + 13 + 56.67

PRACTICE SET 5
Add.

1. 28.88 + 0.95 + 159.29 + 8

2. 421.06 + 0.0713 + 12.95

3. 28.79 + 4 + 841.54 + 0.46

4. 6.53 + 0.0508 + 9.7 + 73

5. 442.18 + 0.47 + 0.0093 + 77

6. 78.75 + 0.33 + 0.045 + 47

7. 28 + 9.7 + 0.0868 + 4.14

8. 39.63 + 1.359 + 3,471 + 0.7

9. 91.46 + 0.32 + 0.003 + 37

10. 82.97 + 0.39 + 2 + 558.46

11. 19.51 + 1.654 + 0.07143

12. 8.87 + 0.0887 + 0.00887

PRACTICE SET 6
Solve these problems.

1. Mrs. Smith bought shoes for her 4 children. How much did she spend?

2. Four boys each ran 50 meters in the 200-meter relay race. How many seconds did it take to run the race?

Will's Shoe Salon	Receipt
shoes " " "	$ 5.71 5.32 6.75 7.95

Relay Race Time Sheet	
José: 8.4	Frank: 7.3
Juma: 9.7	Sam : 6.8

3. How much did Marie spend?

$11.25

$5.85

$5.00

$2.35

4. How long did it take Jeff to finish the test?

Part	Time in minutes
I	7.6
II	8.5
III	10.2
IV	10.3
V	9.0
VI	7.4

5. Julie listed her expenses for the week. How much did she spend?

Weekly Expenses	
Books	$4.78
Supplies	.75
Lunches	3.50

6. How much does Mr. Craig need to pay his July business expenses?

July Expenses	
Salaries	$11,552.37
Rent	3,100.50
Other	2,256.07

7. How far is it around the lot?

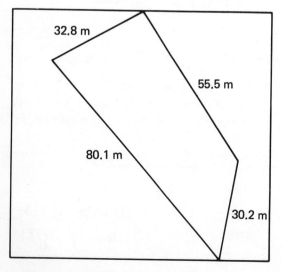

32.8 m

55.5 m

80.1 m

30.2 m

8. How many kilometers (km) is it from St. Joseph to St. Louis?

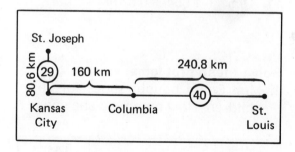

St. Joseph

80.6 km

(29) 160 km 240.8 km

Kansas City   Columbia   (40)   St. Louis

Subtracting Decimals

OBJECTIVE To subtract decimals

EXAMPLE 1 Subtract 87.6 from 196.4.

SOLUTION

Remember to put the
decimal point in the answer.

$$\begin{array}{r} 196.4 \\ -\ 87.6 \\ \hline 108.8 \end{array}$$

Check:
$$\begin{array}{r} 196 \\ -\ 88 \\ \hline 108 \end{array}$$

└─Line up decimal points.

EXAMPLE 2 Subtract 47.54 from 60.

SOLUTION

Use zeros to make the
number of decimal places
the same.

$$\begin{array}{r} 60.00 \\ -47.54 \\ \hline 12.46 \end{array}$$

Check:
$$\begin{array}{r} 60 \\ -48 \\ \hline 12 \end{array}$$

└─Line up decimal points.

1. Subtract 47.08 from 934.20.

2. Subtract 647.4 from 650.

3. Subtract 327.931 from 926.854.

4. Subtract 876.6 from 2,801.5.

5. Subtract 1,738.63 from 4,007.54.

PRACTICE SET 7
Subtract.

1. 198 − 56.987

2. $20 − $8.98

3. 615.98 − 88.78

4. 567 − 19.856

5. 868.87 − 516.89

6. 986 − .650

7. 156 − .068

8. 567.94 − 59.78

9. $20.03 − $15.88

10. $815.23 − $65.98

11. 650 − .986

12. 9,578.26 − 657.84

PRACTICE SET 8

Subtract.

1. 10 − .084

2. 53 − 6.116

3. 694.7 − 24.3

4. 21.93 − .0085

5. $15 − $12.53

6. 5,000 − 892.66

7. 35 − 1.661

8. 78.1 − .017

9. 469.7 − 2.43

10. 50,000 − 8,926.6

11. 219.3 − .085

12. 50,000 − 892.66

PRACTICE SET 9

Solve these problems.

1. How far is it from Willis to Flint?

```
|←————— 895 kilometers ——————→|
|←-372.8 km-→|
| Prescott    Willis              Flint |
```

2. How many meters (m) long is pipe z?

```
| 3.7 m   |   5.9 m   |        |
|    x    |     y     |    z   |
|←——————-15.1 m—————————→|
```

3. Joe bought the shirt and tie. How much change did he get from $20.00?

4. How much more does the skirt cost than the blouse?

5. Sara used 37.5 liters (L) of gas in November. How much gas did she use on November 30?

November 1	1 L
November 10	7.91 L
November 17	12.21 L
November 24	1.31 L
November 30	

6. Together the 4 packages of meat weigh 14 kilograms (kg). How much does package D weigh?

Package	Weight
A	2.4 kg
B	5.9 kg
C	3 kg
D	

Return to Form B on page 99.

Odometer Readings

OBJECTIVE To use odometer readings to compute distances

An odometer measures distance in miles or in kilometers.

The odometer shows that the car was driven 14,015.6 kilometers.

1	4	0	1	5	6

EXAMPLE The same odometer is shown before and after a trip. How many kilometers was the car driven?

1	4	0	1	5	6
1	5	2	5	7	8

SOLUTION

$$\begin{array}{r} 15{,}257.8 \\ -14{,}015.6 \\ \hline 1{,}242.2 \end{array}$$

So, the car was driven 1,242.2 kilometers.

Find the distance in kilometers.

Before:	1	6	6	5	3	1
After:	1	6	8	4	7	2

EXERCISES

The same car traveled to different cities. The odometer readings are shown below. Find each distance in kilometers.

1. Cleveland to Detroit
2. Detroit to Toledo
3. Toledo to Chicago
4. Chicago to Madison
5. Madison to Milwaukee
6. Cleveland to Chicago

Cleveland	2	9	0	8	3	8
Detroit	2	9	3	5	0	2
Toledo	2	9	4	4	5	0
Chicago	2	9	8	2	5	6
Madison	3	0	0	6	6	1
Milwaukee	3	0	1	8	5	8

Too Much Information

EXAMPLE What information is not needed to solve this problem?

A bag of 5 grapefruit sold for 89¢. A bag of 6 oranges sold for 79¢. How much did Willie pay for 3 bags of oranges?

SOLUTION Think: The cost of the oranges is 3 × 79¢.
So, I don't need the cost of the grapefruit.

What information is not needed to solve the problem?

1. Mrs. Basso's electric bill was $31.45. Her heating bill was $63.78, and her phone bill was $18.27. How much did Mrs. Basso spend on heat and electricity?

2. Carl left his home at 8:00 am. He averaged 30 kilometers per hour and arrived at the ski lodge at 1:00 pm. How long did the trip take?

3. Rose left her house at 9:00 am. She averaged 25 kilometers per hour and drove for 8 hours. How far did she drive?

4. Amir is 1.6 meters tall and weighs 60.7 kilograms. Bill is 1.5 meters tall and weighs 80.6 kilograms. How much more does Bill weigh than Amir?

5. Debbie weighs 54.3 kilograms. She bought 5 kilograms of potatoes, 1.5 kilograms of meat, and .5 of a kilogram of butter. What was the total weight of the potatoes, meat, and butter?

6. Mr. Wolf's rent is $250 per month. His food bill averages $135 per month, and his commuting expenses amount to $30 per month. How much are his monthly rent and food expenses?

The Pony Express

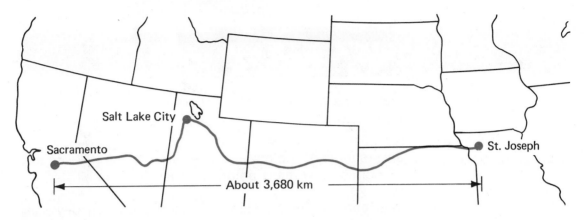

Salt Lake City

Sacramento

St. Joseph

About 3,680 km

1. Between St. Joseph and Sacramento, there were 190 stations. What was the average distance between stations?

2. Riders covered about 400 kilometers per 24-hour day. About how many days did the trip take?

3. Riders covered 400 kilometers in 24 hours. What was the average speed?

4. Each rider covered about 200 kilometers. About how long did he ride?

5. About how many riders were used to make the entire trip?

6. A stage coach covering the same route covered 200 kilometers per 24-hour day. How many days did it take the coach to make the trip?

7. The trip from St. Joseph to Salt Lake City took about 6 days by the Pony Express. About how far is it between the two cities?

8. About how far is it from Salt Lake City to Sacramento?

9. The charge for carrying a letter by the Pony Express was about $5 per 15 grams. How much did it cost to send 150 grams?

10. The Pony Express was started on April 3, 1860. It ended October 24, 1861. How long was it in operation?

Making Up Problems

EXAMPLE 1   Make up a problem for this operation.
Add 16 to 18.

Mary's solution   Jack scored 16 points in a basketball game. Rita scored 18 points. How many points did they score in all?

Bill's solution   Kali earned $16 on Monday and $18 on Tuesday. How much did he earn in all?

EXAMPLE 2   Make up a problem for these operations.
Add 18 to 20, then subtract 5.

Beth's solution   Linda had 20 stamps in her collection. Pedro gave her 18 more stamps. Linda gave 5 stamps to Judy. How many stamps did Linda have left?

Rob's solution   Dave had 20 white shirts and 18 blue shirts in his store. He sold 5 white shirts. How many shirts did he have left?

Make up a problem for the operation(s).

1. Subtract 298 from 1,000.

2. Multiply 12 by 25.

3. Add 125, 153, and 142.

4. Divide 420 by 3.

5. Add 95 to 80, then divide by 25.

6. Add 245 to 79, then divide by 18.

7. Subtract 76 from 124, then divide by 12.

8. Subtract 155 from 285, then divide by 5.

9. Multiply 8 by 12, then add 15.

10. Multiply 25 by 32, then subtract 10.

11. Add $5.25 and $1.90, then subtract from $10.

12. Add 72, 88, 94, and 66, then divide by 4.

Rare Coins

Value
1967: $ 46,000
1977: $113,000

Value of Proof Coin
1972: $4,900
1977: $8,250

Value of Proof Coin
1975: $50,000

1. How much more was the 1913 Liberty head nickel worth in 1977 than in 1967?

2. What was the average yearly increase in value of the nickel?

3. There are 5 known 1913 Liberty head nickels. How much are all 5 nickels worth?

4. How much did the 1895 silver dollar increase in value from 1972 to 1977?

5. What was the average yearly increase in value of the silver dollar?

6. Suppose you had 3 of the nickels, 2 of the silver dollars, and 4 of the half dollars. How much would they be worth?

7. How many of the half dollars would it take so that the value of the half dollars will be more than the 1977 value of the nickel?

8. How many of the silver dollars would it take so that the value of the silver dollars will be more than the half dollar?

9. How many of the silver dollars would it take so that the value of the silver dollars will be worth more than the 1977 value of the nickel?

10. The last known sale of an 1838 half dollar was in 1975. Suppose its value increases at a rate of $1,800 per year. How much will it be worth in 1979?

Test: Unit 5

1. 5.89 + 0.273 + 6.4 + 52

2. $49.10 + $27 + $5 + $1.25

3. 92.1 + 3.15 + 5.524 + 8

4. 6.7 + 2.18 + 3.5 + 7.984

5. 4.023 − 2.7

6. 40,812 − 246.93

7. 4.08 − 1.006

8. 78.6 − 5.046

9. Mr. Blue Spruce bought a chair, a table, and a sofa. How much did he spend?

10. Beth bought an umbrella as a gift for her sister. How much change did she receive from $10.00?

$137.95
$18.95
$119.95
$6.23

Fun Corner

Gil told Isaac that he knew a short cut for finding the sum of the whole numbers from 1 through 101.

The 3 dots mean and so on.
$$1 + 2 + 3 + 4 + 5 + 6 + 7 + 8 + . . . + 101$$

He gave Isaac this hint.
$$1 + 2 + 3 + 4 + 5 + 6$$

Write the numbers in reverse order and add. Divide by 2 since each number was used twice.

$$\underline{6 + 5 + 4 + 3 + 2 + 1}$$

$$7 + 7 + 7 + 7 + 7 + 7 = 6 \times 7, \text{ or } 42$$

$$42 \div 2 = 21$$

So, 1 + 2 + 3 + 4 + 5 + 6 = 21

Find the sum of the numbers. Use Gil's method.

1. 1 through 15

2. 1 through 40

3. 1 through 65

4. 1 through 101

UNIT 6

Multiplication of Decimals

DIAGNOSTIC TEST: MULTIPLICATION FORM A—30 MINUTES
Multiply.

1. 62.7 ×6.4	2. 22.3 ×0.3	3. 2.6 ×0.007	4. .71 ×6.64
5. 8.08 ×7.98	6. 92.6 ×.007	7. 0.4 ×0.05	8. 4.9 ×.723
9. 26 ×.79	10. .04 ×.6	11. .824 ×.019	12. 5.45 ×7.53

Did You Have

More than 10 right? Begin on page 122.	8, 9, or 10 right? Begin on page 119.	Less than 8 right? Begin on page 117.

DIAGNOSTIC TEST: MULTIPLICATION FORM B—30 MINUTES
Multiply.

1. 37.2 ×6.4	2. 32.4 ×0.4	3. 4.2 ×0.005	4. 0.73 ×7.74
5. 7.07 ×8.97	6. 83.5 ×0.004	7. 0.6 ×0.07	8. 6.7 ×0.923
9. 38 ×0.73	10. 0.854 ×0.028	11. 0.06 ×.4	12. 4.55 ×8.35

More than 10 right? Begin on page 122. Less than 11 right? Consult your teacher.

Estimating Products

EXAMPLE 1   Place the decimal point in the product.

$$
\begin{array}{r}
3.43 \\
\times 2.2 \\
\hline
686 \\
686 \\
\hline
7546
\end{array}
$$

SOLUTION

Round each number to the nearest whole number.

$$
\begin{array}{r}
3.43 \\
\times 2.2 \\
\hline
\end{array}
\qquad
\begin{array}{r}
3 \\
\times 2 \\
\hline
6
\end{array}
$$

So, the answer is 7.546.

EXAMPLE 2   Place the decimal point in the product.

$$
\begin{array}{r}
197.86 \\
\times 4.01 \\
\hline
19786 \\
79144 \\
\hline
7934186
\end{array}
$$

SOLUTION

$$
\begin{array}{r}
197.86 \\
\times 4.01 \\
\hline
\end{array}
\qquad
\begin{array}{r}
198 \\
\times 4 \\
\hline
792
\end{array}
$$

So, the answer is 793.4186

EXAMPLE 3   Place the decimal point in the product.

$$
\begin{array}{r}
827 \\
\times .9 \\
\hline
7443
\end{array}
$$

SOLUTION

$$
\begin{array}{r}
827 \\
\times .9 \\
\hline
\end{array}
\qquad
\begin{array}{r}
827 \\
\times 1 \\
\hline
827
\end{array}
$$

So, the answer is 744.3

Place the decimal point in each product to make it correct.

1. 7.99
 $\times 6.2$
 49538

2. 108.75
 $\times 12.3$
 1337625

3. 888.73
 $\times 9.86$
 87628778

PRACTICE SET 1
Place the decimal point in each product to make it correct.

1. 4.75
 $\times 3.8$
 18050

2. 7.33
 $\times 8.76$
 642108

3. 9.01
 $\times 7.06$
 636106

4. 6.66
 $\times 1.07$
 71262

5. 18.35
 $\times 7.24$
 1328540

6. 39.47
 $\times 6.93$
 2735271

7. 55.83
 $\times 9.87$
 5510421

8. 94.44
 $\times 8.91$
 8414604

9. 476.5
 $\times 9.97$
 4750705

10. 647.6
 $\times 3.87$
 2506212

11. 978.6
 $\times 4.09$
 4002474

12. 1,020.9
 $\times 16.7$
 1704903

13. 428.2
 $\times 12.5$
 535250

14. 208.7
 $\times 4.07$
 849409

15. 869.3
 $\times 2.01$
 1747293

16. 674
 $\times 5.83$
 392942

17. 67.4
 $\times 5.83$
 392942

18. 6.74
 $\times 5.83$
 392942

19. 674
 $\times 58.3$
 392942

20. 5.73
 $\times 2.08$
 119184

21. 69.5
 $\times 0.93$
 64635

22. 4,376
 $\times .0089$
 389464

23. 8,001
 $\times 1.9$
 152019

24. 7,111
 $\times 5.09$
 3619499

Multiplying Decimals

EXAMPLE   Find the product.

$$486.73$$
$$\times 2.035$$

SOLUTION

Add the number of decimal places in each factor to find the number of decimal places in the product.

486.73 ⟵ 2 decimal places
×2.035 ⟵ 3 decimal places
243365
146019
97346
990.49555 ⟵ 5 decimal places

Check by estimating.

Check: 487
    ×2
    974

So, the answer is 990.49555.

- -

Multiply.

1.   7.52
    ×3.01

2. 10.52
    ×.54

3.   7.3
    ×46

PRACTICE SET 2

Multiply.

1. 7.02
   ×.51

2. 120
   ×.33

3. .043
   ×2.4

4. .168
   ×12

5. 26.4
   ×3.8

6. .83
   ×.55

7. 7.02
   ×.92

8. .069
   ×.01

9. 9.06
   ×4.3

10. 2.64
   ×3.1

11. 28.2
   ×.9

12. 574
   ×.34

13.   9.1
   ×.78

14.   32.1
   ×29.9

15.   8.5
   ×.35

16. 69.3
   ×.75

PRACTICE SET 3
Multiply.

1. 8.03
×9.2

2. 593
×.77

3. 53.2
×.09

4. 2.6
×4.7

5. 20.6
×20.7

6. .119
×.05

7. .39
×.25

8. .141
×49

9. 21.6
×.3

10. 1.25
×.23

11. 60.1
×8.2

12. 939
×.06

13. .091
×8.2

14. 1.472
×3.07

15. 1.472
×30.7

16. 1.472
×307

17. 10.72
×.39

18. 1,472
×.307

19. 987.6
×56.7

20. 98.76
×56.7

21. 9.1
×8.2

22. 987.6
×.567

23. 6.432
×.0008

24. 6.432
×0.007

25. 1.472
×.307

26. 50.07
×10.1

27. 50.07
×1.01

28. 3.456
×7.21

29. 147.2
×.307

30. 636.2
×0.36

31. 7,642
×.406

32. 1.737
×.373

33. 987.6
×5.67

34. 345.6
×12.7

35. 34.56
×21.7

36. 50.42
×6.32

37. 50.07
×101

38. 14.72
×.307

39. 6.432
×0.07

40. 9.876
×56.7

41. 26.57
×.03

42. 7.149
×2.0161

43. 300.1
×5.6

44. 5,128
×.97

PRACTICE SET 4
Solve these problems.

1. The Hold-Up Book Company pays Ms. Fernandez to use her car. How much is she paid for driving 2,356 kilometers in one month?

First 1,000 km	14¢ a km
Second 1,000 km	12¢ a km
Third 1,000 km	10¢ a km

2. Mrs. Bonk went shopping for the family. She bought 4 jackets, 3 flashlights, and a tent. How much did she spend?

3. One week Frank worked 37.5 hours at $2.65 an hour and 12.5 hours at $3.85 an hour. How much did he earn?

4. Mr. Bonk earns $4.93 per hour. His wife May earns $5.05 per hour. How much more does May make for working 40 hours than Mr. Bonk?

5. In the lab, Faye has 7 dishes, each weighing 30.65 grams. Each dish is filled with 14.45 grams of water. What is the total weight of the 7 filled dishes?

6. Suppose carpeting costs $12.95 per m² and padding costs $3.05 per m². What would be the cost of 50 m² of each?

PRACTICE SET 5
Find the cost.

1. 120 meters of pine at 48¢ a meter

2. 60 meters of fir at 38¢ a meter

3. 2 chairs at $15.95 each

4. 6 cushions at $1.85 each

5. 5 shirts at $7.69 each

6. 4 pairs of socks at 88¢ a pair

7. 2 dresses at $16.50 each

8. 2 blouses at $4.90 each

9. 6 meters of cloth at $4.60 a meter

10. 4 meters of ribbon at 80¢ a meter

11. 5 tires at $8.95 each

12. 8 spark plugs at 69¢ each

13. 3 boxes of stationery at $2.25 a box

14. 2 packages of razor blades at 98¢ a package

Return to Form B on page 116.

Multiplying by 10, 100, or 1,000

The number of zeros after 67 is the same as the number of zeros in the multiplier.

67	67
×10 ←——— 1 zero	×1,000 ←——— 3 zeros
670 ←——— 1 zero	67,000 ←——— 3 zeros

EXAMPLE 1 Multiply.

6.7　　6.7　　6.7
×10　×100　×1,000

SOLUTION

Multiply as if 6.7 were 67. Then mark off the number of decimal places in 6.7.

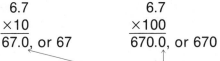

6.7	6.7	6.7
×10	×100	×1,000
67.0, or 67	670.0, or 670	6700.0, or 6,700

1 decimal place

A short cut for multiplying by 10, 100, or 1,000 involves "moving" the decimal point.

EXAMPLE 2 Multiply.

2.64
×10

SOLUTION

Check the answer by multiplying as in Example 1.

Think: 10 has 1 zero, so "move" the decimal point 1 place to the right.

2.64 × 10 = 2.6ᴧ4

So, the answer is 26.4.

EXAMPLE 3 Multiply.

342.18
×100

SOLUTION

The number of zeros in the multiplier tells how many decimal places to "move."

Think: 100 has 2 zeros, so "move" the decimal point 2 places to the right.

342.18 × 100 = 342.18ᴧ

So, the answer is 34,218.

EXAMPLE 4 Multiply.   0.4
                                 $\times 1{,}000$

SOLUTION   Think: 1,000 has 3 zeros, so "move" the decimal
Zeros are used to fill in   point 3 places to the right.
the correct number of
decimal places. $0.4 \times 1{,}000 = .400_\wedge$

                          So, the answer is 400.
- -
Multiply.

1. 247.76	**2.** 3.75	**3.** 0.147	**4.** 0.16
$\times 100$	$\times 10$	$\times 1{,}000$	$\times 100$

EXERCISES
Multiply.

1. 7,099
$\times 100$

2. 61.75
$\times 10$

3.   4.45
$\times 1{,}000$

4. 64.8
$\times 10$

5.   .0187
$\times 10{,}000$

6.   47.3
$\times 100$

7.   287
$\times 100$

8.   6.69
$\times 1{,}000$

9. 8.16
$\times 100$

10.   37.8
$\times 100$

11. .3686
$\times 10$

12. .0064
$\times 100$

13.   81.6
$\times 100$

14. 8.108
$\times 100$

15. .892
$\times 10$

16. 2,801
$\times 10$

17. .0351
$\times 10$

18. .0064
$\times 10$

19. 69.239
$\times 100$

20. 64.25
$\times 10$

21. .3967
$\times 100$

Enough, Too Much, or Too Little

OBJECTIVE   To decide if a problem has enough, too much, or not enough information

Enough, too much, or not enough?

1. Who had the higher bowling score?

E   *NE*

Game	Rob	Beth
1	97	108
2	132	128
3	148	156

2. How much profit did the Bad Food Diner make?

Day	Receipts
Monday	$1,611.28
Tuesday	1,247.55
Wednesday	982.00

3. A piece of drill rod is 46 centimeters long. How many pins can be cut from it?

NE

4. Ms. Regis used 200 liters of gasoline in July. She charged these amounts: $8.75, $10.50, $8.42, $3.58, and $7.24. What was the total cost of the gasoline?   *TM,*

5. Earth's diameter measures about twice as long as Pluto's diameter. What is the measure of Pluto's diameter?   *NE.*

6. Mrs. Brown died after paying 13 premiums of $65 each on an $8,000 life insurance policy. Mr. Brown received $8,000. The Browns had 3 children. How much more did he receive than the amount paid out?

T0M

7. Dora averages 19.2 kilometers on 3.8 liters of gasoline. How far can she travel on a full tank of gas?

NE

8. Alex traveled 144 kilometers and used 19 liters of gasoline. How many kilometers per liter did he average?

E

Rounding Products

EXAMPLE 1 Multiply and round to the nearest tenth.

$$32.41$$
$$\times.76$$

SOLUTION

To round to tenths, check the digit to the right of the tenth's place.

$$
\begin{array}{r}
32.41 \\
\times.76 \\
\hline
19446 \\
22687 \\
\hline
24.6316
\end{array}
$$

Less than 5

So, the answer to the nearest tenth is 24.6.

EXAMPLE 2 Multiply and round to the nearest hundredth.

$$675.5$$
$$\times.009$$

SOLUTION

To round to hundredths, check the digit to the right of the hundredth's place.

$$
\begin{array}{r}
675.5 \\
\times.009 \\
\hline
6.0795
\end{array}
$$

5 or greater

So, the answer to the nearest hundredth is 6.08.

EXERCISES

Multiply. Round the answer to the nearest tenth.

1. 7.19
   ×.3

2. 14.3
   ×7.6

3. 1,543
   ×.005

4. 342.8
   ×21.8

5. 72.9
   ×.34

6. 5.268
   ×.07

Multiply. Round the answer to the nearest hundredth.

7. 4.216
   ×.83

8. 8.25
   ×.12

9. 77.1
   ×.302

Cost of Electricity in the Home

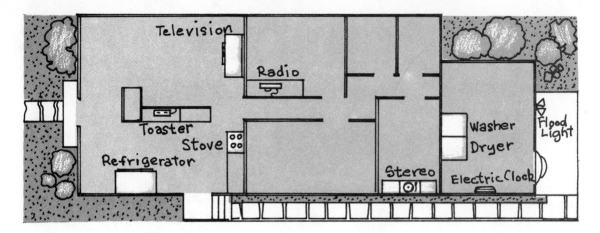

1,000 watts = 1 kilowatt

To find the number of kilowatt-hours (kwh), multiply the number of kilowatts (kw) by the number of hours (h): kilowatts × hours = kilowatt-hours.

For all exercises, the cost of 1 kilowatt hour is 8.5¢.

1. A washer used .82 kw. It takes .5 h to wash a load of clothes. What is the cost per load?

2. A dryer uses 5.5 kw. It takes .6 h to dry a load of clothes. What is the cost per load?

3. A television set uses 150 watts. The Viewer family uses the TV set 6.5 hours per day. What is the cost of using the set per week?

4. A toaster uses 1,020 watts. It takes .03 hour to toast 8 slices of bread. How much does it cost to toast 8 slices?

5. An electric stove, using all 4 burners, requires 14.1 kilowatts. How much does it cost to use the stove 45 minutes (45 minutes is .75 hour)?

6. A 500-watt yard light is used each night for about 9 hours. How much does it cost per year?

7. The Viewer family agreed to cut the time spent watching TV from 6.5 h to 4.25 h per day. How many kwh would be saved per week? How much money would be saved per week?

8. The total electric bill for the Martinez house for 1 month was $24.75. How many kilowatt hours were used that month?

Speed Records

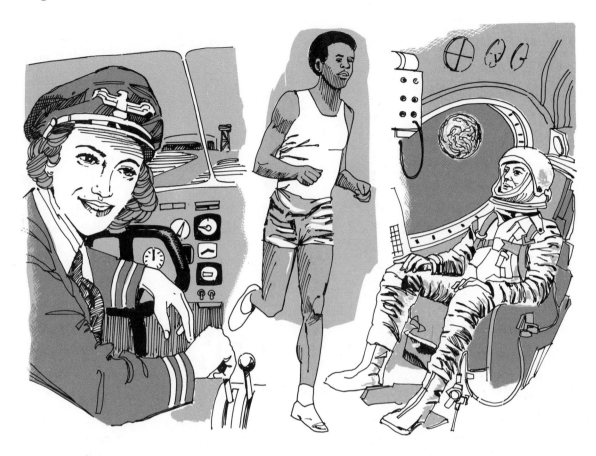

1. Tom Stafford traveled 39,665.6 kilometers per hour during an Apollo X flight. How far did he travel in 10 hours?

2. Donald M. Campbell traveled 524.8 kilometers per hour on water in the Bluebird K7. How far did he travel in .75 hour?

3. During a flight of Vostok VI, a Russian woman traveled at about 27,960 km/h. About how many km did she travel in .02 h?

4. The greatest speed achieved by a woman in an airplane is 2,671.8 km/h. How many km did she travel in .5 h?

5. Gary Gabelich traveled .288 kilometer per second in a race car. How far did he travel in 3.354 seconds? (Round your answer to the nearest kilometer.)

6. During a transcontinental race, Johnny Salo averaged 11.15 kilometers per hour. He ran for 525.9 hours. How far did he run?

Test: Unit 6

Multiply.

1. 3.8
  ×.4

2. 500
  ×.48

3. 3.14
  ×1.57

4. 876.4
  ×.12

5. 7.91
  ×5.6

6. .235
  ×42.3

7. 63.7
  ×100

8. 9.24
  ×1,000

9. 6.327
  ×10

10. Joan bought 12 m² of carpet and 12 m² of padding. How much did she pay?

11. Mrs. Smith bought 4 chairs and 1 table. How much did she spend, to the nearest dollar?

CARPET
$8.55 per m²

PADDING
$3.45 per m²

$24.95

$119.95

Multiply. Round the answer to the nearest tenth.

12. 54.1
  ×3.6

13. 12.46
  ×2.17

14. 47.9
  ×.11

Multiply. Round the answer to the nearest hundredth.

15. 245.8
  ×.015

16. 7.98
  ×.006

17. 13.1
  ×.24

Fun Corner

Rules of the game:
Use exactly four 4's.
Use only these signs:
+, −, ×, ÷, ( ).

Jill named some whole numbers like this.
$0 = (4 + 4) − (4 + 4)$ or $(4 ÷ 4) − (4 ÷ 4)$
$1 = (4 ÷ 4) ÷ (4 ÷ 4)$ or $(4 + 4) ÷ (4 + 4)$
$2 = (4 ÷ 4) + (4 ÷ 4)$ or $(4 × 4) ÷ (4 + 4)$
$10 = (44 − 4) ÷ 4$
$11 = (4 ÷ .4) + (4 ÷ 4)$

Rename the numbers 3 through 9 in this way.

Rename the numbers 12 through 20 in this way.

UNIT 7

Division of Decimals

DIAGNOSTIC TEST: DIVISION FORM A — 25 MINUTES
Divide.

1. $.05\overline{)12.5}$

2. $5\overline{)12.5}$

3. $.09\overline{)2.7}$

4. $.5\overline{)12.5}$

5. $2.65\overline{)294.68}$

6. $.3\overline{)81}$

7. $3.14\overline{)62.8}$

8. $12.5\overline{)5}$

9. $.07\overline{)630}$

10. $.17\overline{)3,468}$

11. $.22\overline{)330}$

12. $.64\overline{)1,236.4}$

Did You Have

| More than 10 right? Begin on page 138. | 8, 9, or 10 right? Begin on page 136. | Less than 8 right? Begin on page 131. |

DIAGNOSTIC TEST: DIVISION FORM B — 25 MINUTES

Divide.

1. $.05\overline{)14.5}$

2. $5\overline{)14.5}$

3. $.09\overline{)4.5}$

4. $.5\overline{)14.5}$

5. $3.63\overline{)36.3}$

6. $.9\overline{)4.5}$

7. $.24\overline{)5.4}$

8. $8.5\overline{)1.70}$

9. $.07\overline{)6.3}$

10. $.105\overline{).42}$

11. $.33\overline{)660}$

12. $.24\overline{)3,132}$

More than 10 right? Begin on page 138. Less than 11 right? Consult your teacher.

Estimating Quotients

EXAMPLE 1   Place the decimal point in the quotient.
$$209.04 \div 31.2 = 67$$

SOLUTION

Round each number to the nearest whole number.

$$
\begin{array}{r}
6 \\
31\overline{)209} \\
186 \\
\hline
23
\end{array}
$$

So, the answer is 6.7.

EXAMPLE 2   Place the decimal point in the quotient.
$$31.5798 \div 4.38 = 721$$

SOLUTION

Round each number to the nearest whole number.

$$
\begin{array}{r}
8 \\
4\overline{)32} \\
32 \\
\hline
0
\end{array}
$$

So, the answer is 7.21.

Place the decimal point in the quotient to make it correct.

1. $5.82 \div .97 = 60$

2. $297.54 \div 51.3 = 580$

3. $71.4 \div 3.4 = 210$

PRACTICE SET 1

Place the decimal point in the quotient to make it correct.

1. $237.8 \div 5.2 = 457307$

2. $9.12 \div 3.7 = 24648$

3. $4,325.67 \div 16.3 = 26538$

4. $59.3 \div 6.8 = 872$

5. $726.11 \div .92 = 78925$

6. $68.4 \div 4.12 = 16602$

Dividing by a Whole Number

OBJECTIVE To divide any decimal by a whole number

EXAMPLE 1 Divide. $12\overline{)17.28}$

SOLUTION

Divide as if 17.28
were 1,728.
Then place the decimal
point over the decimal
point in 17.28.
Estimate to check if
the decimal point is in
the correct place.

```
        1.44
  12)17.28
      12
       5 2
       4 8
         48
         48
          0
```

Check by multiplying.

Check:
```
      1.44
     ×12
     2 88
    14 4
    17.28
```
So, 1.44 is correct.

EXAMPLE 2 Divide. $26\overline{)1,034.8}$

SOLUTION

Divide as if 1,034.8
were 10,348. Then
place the decimal
point over the decimal
point in 1,034.8.
Estimate to check if
the decimal point is in
the correct place.

```
         39.8
  26)1,034.8
      78
      254
      234
       20 8
       20 8
          0
```

Check by multiplying.

Check:
```
       39.8
      ×26
      238 8
      796
     1,034.8
```
So, 39.8 is correct.

Divide and check.
1. $24\overline{)34.56}$ **2.** $36\overline{)5.184}$ **3.** $16\overline{)5,284.8}$

PRACTICE SET 2
Divide and check.
1. $9\overline{)6.3}$ **2.** $8\overline{)60.08}$ **3.** $15\overline{)1.1370}$

4. $47\overline{)6.909}$ **5.** $45\overline{)283.545}$ **6.** $82\overline{)15.990}$

7. $83\overline{)4,158.3}$ **8.** $24\overline{)156.24}$ **9.** $88\overline{)5,024.8}$

10. $59\overline{)0.15281}$ **11.** $36\overline{)36.3636}$ **12.** $65\overline{)39.4615}$

PRACTICE SET 3
Write only the answer.
1. $5\overline{).35}$ **2.** $4\overline{)8.4}$ **3.** $4\overline{)1.6}$ **4.** $2\overline{).8}$

5. $5\overline{)7.5}$ **6.** $3\overline{)3.75}$ **7.** $6\overline{).36}$ **8.** $5\overline{)9.5}$

9. $8\overline{)8.32}$ **10.** $3\overline{).9}$ **11.** $4\overline{).28}$ **12.** $8\overline{).48}$

13. $2\overline{).60}$ **14.** $3\overline{)4.5}$ **15.** $9\overline{)8.1}$ **16.** $21\overline{)10.5}$

PRACTICE SET 4
Solve these problems.
1. Janine bought 3 skirts for $35.94. What was the average cost per skirt?

2. Mr. Sachs paid $632.40 for gas last year. What was his average monthly bill?

3. Tom bought 12 tickets for a game. He paid $9 for the tickets. How much did Tom pay per ticket?

4. Ms. Kosednar drove 6,708 km last year. Find the average number of km Ms. Kosednar drove each week.

Multiplying To Get a Whole Number

OBJECTIVE To multiply a decimal by 10, 100, or 1,000 to find the smallest whole-number product

EXAMPLE 1 Multiply 6.8 to find the smallest whole-number product.

SOLUTION

10 has 1 zero.
6.8 has 1 decimal place.

$$\begin{array}{r} 6.8 \\ \times 10 \\ \hline 68.0 \end{array} \qquad \begin{array}{r} 6.8 \\ \times 100 \\ \hline 680.0 \end{array} \qquad \begin{array}{r} 6.8 \\ \times 1,000 \\ \hline 6,800.0 \end{array}$$

└─ Smallest whole-number product

EXAMPLE 2 Multiply .43 to find the smallest whole-number product.

SOLUTION

Multiply by 100.

.43 ←──── 2 decimal places
×100 ←──── Think: 100 has 2 zeros.
43.00 ←──── Smallest whole-number product

EXAMPLE 3 Multiply .036 to find the smallest whole-number product.

SOLUTION

Multiply by 1,000.

.036 ←──── 3 decimal places
×1,000 ←──── Think: 1,000 has 3 zeros.
36.000 ←──── Smallest whole-number product

Find the smallest whole-number product.

1. 8.8   **2.** 5.06   **3.** .57   **4.** .043

PRACTICE SET 5
Find the smallest whole-number product.

1. 3.22   **2.** 5.77   **3.** 15.63   **4.** 6.03

5. 8.01   **6.** 68.12   **7.** 4.2   **8.** 8.9

9. 6.6   **10.** .4   **11.** .7   **12.** .3

13. .142   **14.** .765   **15.** .111   **16.** .690

Keeping the Quotient the Same

OBJECTIVE To use the idea that both dividend and divisor can be multiplied by the same number, except 0

EXAMPLE 1 Divide $2\overline{)4}$. Multiply both dividend and divisor by 2, and divide again. Compare the answers.

SOLUTION $2\overline{)4}^{\,2}$ $\longleftarrow$ Same answer $\longrightarrow$ $2 \times 2\overline{)4 \times 2}$ $\longrightarrow$ $4\overline{)8}^{\,2}$

EXAMPLE 2 Divide $2\overline{)18}$. Multiply both dividend and divisor by 10, and divide again. Repeat this for 100 and 1,000. Compare all answers.

SOLUTION

Multiply 18 and 2 by 10. $2\overline{)18}^{\,9}$ $2 \times 10\overline{)18 \times 10}$ $\longrightarrow$ $20\overline{)180}^{\,9}$

Multiply 18 and 2 by 100. $2 \times 100\overline{)18 \times 100}$ $\longrightarrow$ $200\overline{)1{,}800}^{\,9}$

Multiply 18 and 2 by 1,000. $2 \times 1{,}000\overline{)18 \times 1{,}000}$ $\longrightarrow$ $2{,}000\overline{)18{,}000}^{\,9}$

The quotient stays the same. The answer is 9 each time.

Divide. Multiply both dividend and divisor by 10, and divide again. Repeat this for 100 and 1,000.

1. $2\overline{)36}$ **2.** $3\overline{)3.6}$ **3.** $4\overline{).48}$

PRACTICE SET 6
Divide. Multiply both dividend and divisor by 10, and divide again.

1. $8\overline{)8.8}$ **2.** $12\overline{)24}$ **3.** $4\overline{)3.6}$ **4.** $16\overline{)4.8}$ **5.** $6\overline{)9.6}$

Divide. Multiply both dividend and divisor by 100, and divide again.

6. $2\overline{)8}$ **7.** $2\overline{)16}$ **8.** $5\overline{)50}$ **9.** $10\overline{)20}$ **10.** $1\overline{)10}$

Divide. Multiply both dividend and divisor by 1,000, and divide again.

11. $8\overline{)24}$ **12.** $6\overline{)60}$ **13.** $9\overline{)9}$ **14.** $12\overline{)102}$ **15.** $7\overline{)21}$

Dividing by a Decimal

EXAMPLE 1 Divide. $.12\overline{)1.728}$

SOLUTION

$.12 \times 100 = 12$
$17.28 \times 100 = 172.8$
Now the divisor is a
whole number.

$.12\overline{)1.728}$ has the same answer as

$$12\overline{)172.8}$$

```
      14.4
12)172.8
      12
       52
       48
        48
        48
```

So, $.12\overline{)17.28}$ gives 14.4

Check:
```
       14.4
      ×.12
       288
      1 44
      1.728
```
So, 14.4 is correct.

EXAMPLE 2 Divide. $.125\overline{)37.5}$

SOLUTION

$.125 \times 1,000 = 125$
$37.5 \times 1,000 = 37,500$
Now the divisor is a
whole number.

$.125\overline{)37.5}$ has the same answer as

$$125\overline{)37,500}$$

```
        300
125)37,500
     37 5
        0
```

So, $.125\overline{)37.500}$ gives 300

Check:
```
        .125
       ×300
      37.500
```
So, 300 is correct.

- -

Divide and check.

1. $.12\overline{)34.56}$ **2.** $2.4\overline{)4.56}$ **3.** $.064\overline{)1.024}$

PRACTICE SET 7
Divide and check.

1. $.25\overline{)164.50}$

2. $.36\overline{)9,108}$

3. $.52\overline{)36.088}$

4. $.29\overline{)8.41}$

5. $.68\overline{)165.24}$

6. $.68\overline{)16.524}$

7. $.68\overline{)1,652.4}$

8. $.46\overline{)1.4950}$

9. $.8\overline{)87.2}$

10. $.9\overline{)9.09}$

11. $.7\overline{)5.67}$

12. $.6\overline{)9,666}$

13. $1.8\overline{)114.12}$

14. $2.6\overline{)68.64}$

15. $13.5\overline{)27}$

16. $40.5\overline{)810}$

PRACTICE SET 8
Write only the answer.

1. $.8\overline{)2.4}$

2. $.6\overline{)3.6}$

3. $.8\overline{)4.8}$

4. $.4\overline{)16}$

5. $2.2\overline{)6.6}$

6. $2.3\overline{)6.9}$

7. $.5\overline{).025}$

8. $.6\overline{)42}$

9. $.08\overline{).56}$

10. $.09\overline{)4.5}$

11. $.08\overline{).064}$

12. $.09\overline{)45}$

PRACTICE SET 9
Solve these problems.

1. Mr. Allen drove 1,835.98 kilometers on 223.9 liters of gasoline. How many kilometers to the liter did he average?

2. A club needs $186 to break even on a dance. Tickets sell for $1.50. How many tickets must the club sell to break even?

3. A train traveled 600.6 kilometers in 6.5 hours. What was its average speed in kilometers per hour?

4. Mrs. Schwartz gave each of her employees $25.50. She gave away a total of $1,071. How many employees does she have?

5. Mr. Firth pays $.048 per unit of electrical power. For one month his bill was $39.12. How many units did he use?

6. Mrs. Juarez paid $21.17 for natural gas for one month. The cost per unit was $.365. How many units did she use?

7. Ms. Carbone owes $2,251.20 on her new car. She makes monthly payments of $75.04. How many months will it take her to pay off the car?

8. A class sold greeting cards to earn money for a field trip. They sold each card for $.12. Their total sales were $37.44. How many cards did they sell?

Return to Form B on page 130.

Didiving by 10, 100, or 1,000

OBJECTIVE To divide a decimal by 10, 100, or 1,000

10 has 1 zero.

$$\begin{array}{r} 12.34 \\ 10\overline{)123.40} \end{array}$$ ←——— decimal places increased by 1

100 has 2 zeros.

$$\begin{array}{r} 1.234 \\ 100\overline{)123.400} \end{array}$$ ←——— decimal places increased by 2

1,000 has 3 zeros.

$$\begin{array}{r} .1234 \\ 1,000\overline{)123.4000} \end{array}$$ ←——— decimal places increased by 3

A short cut for dividing by 10, 100, or 1,000 involves "moving" the decimal point.

EXAMPLE 1 Divide. $7.63 \div 10$

SOLUTION Think: There is 1 zero in 10, so "move" the decimal point 1 place to the left.
$7.63 \div 10 = \lefthalfcap 7.63$

So, the answer is .763.

EXAMPLE 2 Divide. $8 \div 100$

SOLUTION Think: There are 2 zeros in 100, so "move" the decimal point 2 places to the left.

Use zeros to fill in the right number of decimal places.

$8 \div 100 = \lefthalfcap 8.$
So, the answer is .08.

EXAMPLE 3 Divide. $6,326.4 \div 1,000$

Move the decimal point 3 places to the left.

$6,326.4 \div 1,000 = 6 \lefthalfcap 326.4$

So, the answer is 6.3264.

- -

Divide.

1. $849 \div 100$ **2.** $7.65 \div 1,000$ **3.** $45.6 \div 10$

EXERCISES

Divide.

1. 729 ÷ 100

2. .865 ÷ 10

3. 46.5 ÷ 10

4. 583 ÷ 1,000

5. 1.68 ÷ 100

6. 3.68 ÷ 10

7. 54.2 ÷ 10

8. 9.02 ÷ 1,000

9. 6.38 ÷ 10

10. 5.7 ÷ 100

11. 7.5 ÷ 1,000

12. 4.08 ÷ 10

13. .944 ÷ 100

14. 17.68 ÷ 1,000

15. 3.52 ÷ 1,000

16. 640 ÷ 1,000

17. 4,828 ÷ 1,000

18. .658 ÷ 100

19. 792 ÷ 1,000

20. $35 ÷ 100

21. 6.004 ÷ 100

22. 4.006 ÷ 100

23. 6,000 ÷ 10

24. 6,000 ÷ 1,000

25. 75.8 ÷ 10

26. 2,848 ÷ 100

27. $35 ÷ 1,000

28. 2,424 ÷ 100

29. 4,242 ÷ 1,000

30. 64 ÷ 1,000

Fun Corner

Find the 5 numbers that meet these conditions.
Their sum is 91.

Four of them are even numbers, and the other is odd.

Arrange the numbers in order from smallest to largest.

The third number is the sum of the first 2 numbers.

The fifth number is 3.5 times the second number.

Divide the fifth number by 2: the remainder is 1.

A Shortcut

EXAMPLE 1 Divide. $3.2\overline{)73.28}$

In the divisor, "move" the decimal point to get a whole number.
"Move" the same number of decimal places in the dividend. Now divide.

$3.2_\wedge\overline{)73.2_\wedge 8}$

1 decimal place to the right

$$\begin{array}{r} 22.9 \\ 32\overline{)732.8} \\ \underline{64} \\ 92 \\ \underline{64} \\ 28\ 8 \\ \underline{28\ 8} \end{array}$$

So, the answer is 22.9.

EXAMPLE 2 Divide. $2.65\overline{)42.4}$

In the divisor, "move" the decimal point to get a whole number.
"Move" the same number of decimal places in the dividend. Now divide.

$2.65_\wedge\overline{)42.40_\wedge}$

2 decimal places to the right

$$\begin{array}{r} 16. \\ 265\overline{)4240.} \\ \underline{265} \\ 1590 \\ \underline{1590} \\ 0 \end{array}$$

So, the answer is 16.

- -

Divide.

1. $1.9\overline{)33.44}$

2. $0.71\overline{)6.2125}$

EXERCISES
Divide.

1. $3.4\overline{).782}$

2. $1.2\overline{)48}$

3. $6.7\overline{)81.472}$

4. $.98\overline{)364.168}$

5. $5.5\overline{)4.9225}$

6. $.42\overline{).35826}$

7. $12.1\overline{)7.3447}$

8. $34.9\overline{)268.032}$

9. $.216\overline{)5.36112}$

Write only the answer.

10. $.02\overline{).27}$

11. $1.2\overline{)7.2}$

12. $.004\overline{)8}$

13. $.9\overline{).81}$

14. $.07\overline{)4.9}$

15. $1.1\overline{)330}$

16. $.008\overline{)3.4816}$

17. $.5\overline{)3,786}$

18. $.06\overline{)32.7}$

Fun Corner

Here is another way to multiply. You need only to know how to divide by 2, multiply by 2, and add.
Multiply. 17×24

Ignore any remainders.
If the number in the left-hand column is even, cross out both numbers.
Add the right-hand column.

	17	×	24	
$17 ÷ 2 \longrightarrow$	8	×	48	$\longleftarrow$ 24 × 2
$8 ÷ 2 \longrightarrow$	4	×	96	$\longleftarrow$ 48 × 2
$4 ÷ 2 \longrightarrow$	2	×	192	$\longleftarrow$ 96 × 2
$2 ÷ 2 \longrightarrow$	1	×	384	$\longleftarrow$ 192 × 2
			408	

So, $17 \times 24 = 408$.

Use this method to find these products.

1. 44×26 **2.** 52×21 **3.** 11×38

Women in Sports

Give approximate answers.

1. Monica Zehrt of East Germany completed the 400-meter run in 51.08 seconds. How many meters per second was this?

2. Maureen Carid of Australia completed the 80-meter hurdles in 10.3 seconds. How many meters per second was this?

3. Debbie Meyer of the United States swam 400 meters in 4 minutes 31.8 seconds. She swam 800 meters in 9 minutes 24 seconds. How many times as long did it take her to swim 800 meters than to swim 400 meters?

4. Mrs. V. Brown caught a thresher shark at Mayor Island, New Zealand. The shark weighed 331.4 kilograms. Its length was 2.6 meters. What was the average weight of the shark for each meter of length?

5. In cross-country skiing, Martha Rockwell skied 5 kilometers in 18 minutes 3 seconds. She skied 10 kilometers in 37 minutes 9 seconds. How many kilometers per second did she average?

6. Sue Berning received the first prize of $6,000 in a U. S. golf tournament. She scored 290 points. How much did she earn per point?

7. In a speed ice-skating tournament, Sheila Young skated 500 meters in 43.56 seconds. Mrs. Keulen Deelstra skated 1,000 meters in 1 minute 30.41 seconds. Who had the better record?

8. Marisa Danisi of West Germany holds the record for roller skating. She skated 35.19 kilometers in 1 hour. What was her average speed per minute?

Rounding Quotients

EXAMPLE 1 Divide and round the answer to the nearest tenth.

$$22\overline{)72.4}$$

SOLUTION

To find the answer to the nearest tenth, carry the division to hundredths. You may use any number of zeros to the right of the decimal point.

```
      3.29
22)72.40
   66
    6 4
    4 4
    2 00
    1 98
       2
```

3.29
⌐5 or more

So, the answer is 3.3 to the nearest tenth.

EXAMPLE 2 Divide and round the answer to the nearest hundredth.

$$19.8\overline{)4.36}$$

SOLUTION

To find the answer to the nearest hundredth, carry the division to thousandths.

```
        .220
19.8)4.3 600
     3 96
      4 00
      3 96
        40
```

.220
⌐less than 5

So, the answer is .22 to the nearest hundredth.

EXERCISES

Divide and round the answer to the nearest tenth.

1. $1.3\overline{)42.9}$ **2.** $.72\overline{)1.764}$ **3.** $5.6\overline{)32.19}$

4. $.02\overline{).7931}$ **5.** $16.5\overline{)234.8}$ **6.** $9.11\overline{).823}$

Divide and round the answer to the nearest hundredth.

7. $2.3\overline{)5.128}$ **8.** $1.42\overline{)798.3}$ **9.** $51.8\overline{)36.72}$

What's the Question?

I MISSED THE PUNCH LINE!

EXAMPLE What question could be asked about this information?

Mr. Overdraw wrote checks for these amounts:
$192.50, $64.50, $18.53, $80.00,
$13.64, and $83.50.

PEG'S SOLUTION How much did Mr. Overdraw pay out?

DON'S SOLUTION How much more than $400 did he pay out?

BETH'S SOLUTION What is the difference between the largest amount and the smallest amount?

What question can be asked? More than 1 question is possible in each case.

1. The "Know It All Newspaper" has a daily circulation of 250,000 papers and a Sunday circulation of 325,000 papers.

2. Ms. Gray Eagle sold some clothing for $925. The clothing cost $560. Ms. Gray Eagle's overhead was $305.

3. The distance from the fulcrum to one end of a lever is 1 meter. The distance from the fulcrum to the other end of the lever is 15 centimeters.

4. Dot and Joe left Little Falls at the same time. Dot traveled north and averaged 72 kilometers per hour. Joe traveled south and averaged 64 kilometers per hour.

5. Mr. Kanelos paid for these items with a $10 bill.

Meat	$3.15
Canned beans	.50
Sugar	.42
Cereal	.60
Bread (2 loaves)	.33 each

6. A mail carrier stops at 15 houses on a block. She walks 4 meters from the corner to the mailbox of the first house. She then walks 18 meters between the mailboxes of each house thereafter.

Fun Corner 1

Find the 5 numbers that meet these conditions.
Each is an even number.

Their sum is 36.

The largest number is 6 times the smallest number.

Fun Corner 2

Find the 5 numbers that meet these conditions.
Each is an odd number.

Their sum is 53.

The difference between the largest number and the smallest number is 14.

The second largest number is 5 times the smallest number.

Test: Unit 7

Divide.

1. $2.4\overline{)9.6}$

2. $.04\overline{)484}$

3. $.65\overline{)93.925}$

4. $5.5\overline{)\ .00847}$

5. $7 \div 10$

6. $9.43 \div 10$

7. $1.34 \div 100$

8. $2{,}103.6 \div 10$

9. $25 \div 1{,}000$

10. $45.6 \div 1{,}000$

Divide and round the answer to the nearest tenth.

11. $16.3\overline{)324.8}$

12. $.03\overline{)\ .7854}$

Divide and round the answer to the nearest hundredth.

13. $2.4\overline{)6.237}$

14. $42.4\overline{)36.88}$

Solve these problems.

15. Ed traveled 463 kilometers and used 47.4 liters of gasoline. How many kilometers per liter of gas did he average? Round your answer to the nearest kilometer.

16. Inez traveled 935.8 kilometers (km) and used 50 liters (L) of gasoline. How many kilometers per liter of gas did she average? Round your answer to the nearest kilometer.

Fun Corner

Can you complete this pattern? Try.

$$0 \times 9 + 1 = 1$$
$$1 \times 9 + 2 = 11$$
$$12 \times 9 + 3 = 111$$
$$123 \times 9 + 4 = 1{,}111$$
$$\underline{\ ?\ } \times 9 + \underline{\ ?\ } = \underline{\ ?\ }$$
$$\underline{\ ?\ } \times 9 + \underline{\ ?\ } = \underline{\ ?\ }$$
$$\underline{\ ?\ } \times 9 + \underline{\ ?\ } = \underline{\ ?\ }$$
$$\underline{\ ?\ } \times 9 + \underline{\ ?\ } = \underline{\ ?\ }$$

UNIT 8
Metric System

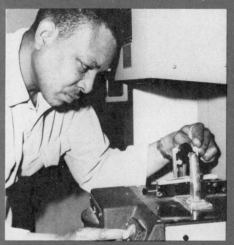

Lengths in Centimeters

EXAMPLE 1 What is the length of the pencil to the nearest centimeter (cm)?

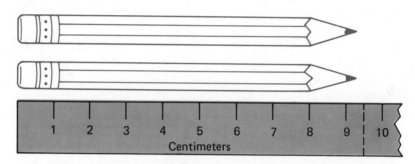

SOLUTION

Place the ruler so that the endpoint or zero point of the ruler and an endpoint of the pencil line up. Imagine a mark halfway between 9 and 10 cm.

The pencil is between 9 and 10 cm long. It is nearer 9 cm. So, the pencil is 9 cm long to the nearest cm.

EXAMPLE 2 Find the length to the nearest cm.

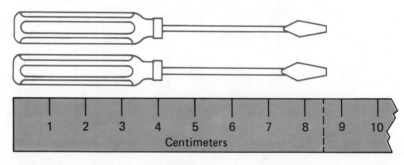

SOLUTION

Imagine a mark halfway between 8 and 9 cm.

The length is between 8 and 9 cm. It is nearer 9 cm. So, the length is 9 cm to the nearest cm.

- -

Measure each segment to the nearest cm.

1. _____

2. _____

3. _____   4. ___   5. _____

EXERCISES
Measure to the nearest centimeter (cm).

1. _____

2. _____

3. _____

4. _____

5. _____

6. _____

7. _____

8. _____

9. _____

10. _____

11. _____

12. _____

13. _____

14. _____

15. _____

16. _____

17. _____

18. _____

19. _____

20. _____

Lengths in Millimeters

EXAMPLE   What is the length of the paper clip to the nearest millimeter (mm)?

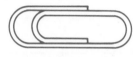

SOLUTION

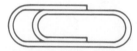

This ruler shows that each centimeter contains 10 mm. So, 10 mm = 1 cm.

1 Millimeter

The paper clip is 34 mm long to the nearest mm.

Measure the length of each object to the nearest mm.

1.

2.

3.

4.

EXERCISES

Measure to the nearest millimeter (mm).

1. _____   2. _____   3. ____

4. _____   5. _____

6. _____   7. _____

8. _____

Metric Units of Length

OBJECTIVE To recognize and use the relationships among the measures millimeter, centimeter, meter, and kilometer

EXAMPLE 1 Measure a diameter of a quarter in both mm and cm.

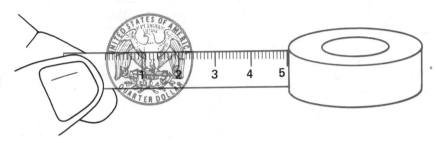

SOLUTION

Use a metric tape measure.
1 cm = 10 mm;
1 mm = .1 cm

A diameter of a quarter measures about
24 mm, or 2.4 cm.

- -

Measure in both mm and cm.

1. _____

2. _____

3. _____

EXAMPLE 2 How many cm are there in 1 meter (m)?

An actual meter stick is
10 times as long as this
picture.
Try making one.

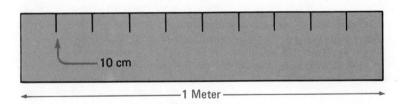

SOLUTION Think: $10 \times 10 = 100$

Each length is 10 cm.

There are 100 cm in 1 meter.

1 cent = .01 dollar.
The prefix *centi* means
one hundredth.

1 <u>centi</u>meter = .01 meter
↓
one hundredth

EXAMPLE 3	Make the sentence true.
	1 millimeter (mm) = __?__ meter(s)
SOLUTION	1 mm = .1 cm and 1 cm = .01 m
Milli means .001.	So, 1 mm = .1 × .01, or .001 m.

EXAMPLE 4	*Kilo* means 1,000. What is a kilometer(km)?
SOLUTION	kilometer

1,000   So, a kilometer is 1,000 meters.

LENGTH COMPARISONS	
1 kilometer (km) = 1,000 meters (m)	1 meter = .001 kilometer
1 meter (m) = 100 centimeters (cm)	1 centimeter = .01 meter
1 centimeter (cm) = 10 millimeters (mm)	1 millimeter = .1 centimeter
1,000 millimeters (mm) = 1 meter(m)	1 millimeter = .001 meter

EXAMPLE 5   How many meters to Toledo?

TOLEDO   3.5 km

SOLUTION	3.5 km = 3.5 × 1 km Think: 1 km = 1,000 m
Think: A meter is smaller than a km. Multiply to find the answer.	= 3.5 × 1,000 m
	= 3,500
	So, it is 3,500 meters to Toledo.

EXAMPLE 6   How many centimeters high?

SOLUTION   Think: 10 mm = 1 cm

Think: A cm is larger than a mm, so divide.   180 ÷ 10 = 18
So, it is 18 cm high.

180 mm

Make true sentences.

4. 4.5 m = __?__ cm   5. .5 m = __?__ cm

6. 240 mm = __?__ cm   7. 560 mm = __?__ cm

8. 60 cm = __?__ m   9. 120 cm = __?__ m

10. 1,850 m = __?__ km   11. 3.6 m = __?__ mm

EXERCISES

Measure the length of the segment in both mm and cm.

1. *AB*

2. *BC*

3. *CD*

4. *DE*

5. *EA*

6. *AC*

7. *AD*

8. *BE*

9. *BD*

10. *CE*

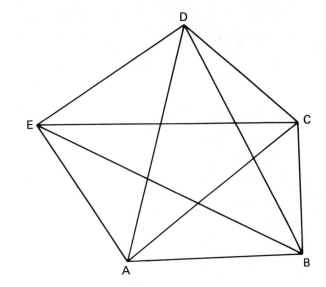

Make true sentences.

11. 1 km = ___?___ m

12. 2 km = ___?___ m

13. 6 km = ___?___ m

14. 9.6 km = ___?___ m

15. 1,000 m = ___?___ km

16. 2,500 m = ___?___ km

17. 700 cm = ___?___ m

18. 100 cm = ___?___ m

19. 100 m = ___?___ cm

20. 500 cm = ___?___ m

21. 50 cm = ___?___ m

22. 10 cm = ___?___ m

23. 1.5 m = ___?___ cm

24. 8.7 m = ___?___ cm

25. .75 m = ___?___ cm

26. .9 m = ___?___ cm

27. 1,000 mm = ___?___ m

28. 800 mm = ___?___ m

29. 450 mm = ___?___ m

30. 8 mm = ___?___ m

31. 15 mm = ___?___ cm

32. 78 mm = ___?___ cm

33. 128 mm = ___?___ cm

34. 2 mm = ___?___ cm

35. 8 cm = ___?___ mm

36. 7.6 cm = ___?___ mm

37. 4.65 mm = ___?___ cm

38. 3 mm = ___?___ cm

Estimating Measures

REFERENCE MEASURES USED FOR ESTIMATING

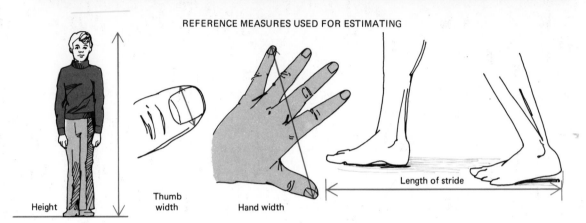

Height   Thumb width   Hand width   Length of stride

EXAMPLE 1 Rob knew that his thumb width was about 1.5 cm. He used this to estimate the length of a bolt. How long is the bolt?

He marked off thumb widths.

The bolt is a little more than 4 thumb widths.

So, the length is about 4 × 1.5, or about 6 cm.

EXAMPLE 2 Denise knew that she was about 120 cm tall. She used this to estimate the height of a pipe. How high is it?

She thought, "The pipe is about half as tall as I."

So, the pipe is about 120 ÷ 2, or 60 cm high.

- -

Complete these measures about yourself.

1. Height about __?__ cm, or __?__ m

2. Waist about __?__ cm

3. Width of hand about __?__ cm

4. Width of thumb about __?__ cm, or __?__ mm

5. Distance from tip of left hand to tip of right hand with arms outstretched about __?__ m

6. Length of stride __?__ m

EXERCISES
Estimate. Use your reference measures.

1. Width of your desk

2. Width of a window

3. Height of a window

4. Length of your room

5. Width of your room

6. Height of ceiling

7. Width of door

8. Height of door

9. Height of chalkboard

10. Length of a new pencil

11. Length of hallway

12. Height of your desk

13. Length of a paper clip

14. Width of a paper clip

15. Diameter of a dime

16. Diameter of a half dollar

17. Length of your foot

18. Length of a dollar bill

Fun Corner

1. Sam Fetchwater needed exactly 4 liters of water from a spring. How did he use the containers to get it?

3 Liters

5 Liters

2. Place four + signs in the left side of the equation to make it true.   1 2 3 4 5 6 7 = 100

Perimeter

The perimeter of an object is the distance around it.
To find the perimeter, add the lengths of the sides.

EXAMPLE 1   Find the perimeter of the bulletin board.

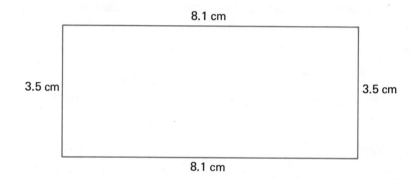

8.1 cm

3.5 cm   3.5 cm

8.1 cm

SOLUTION

Think: Find the distance
all the way around. Add the
lengths of the sides.

3.5 cm
8.1 cm
3.5 cm
8.1 cm
_____
23.2 cm   So, the perimeter is 23.2 cm.

EXAMPLE 2   Find the perimeter.

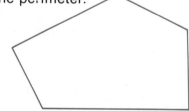

SOLUTION

Measure the length of
each side. Then add.

4   cm
2.1 cm
2.1 cm
3.2 cm
1.9 cm
_____
13.3 cm   So, the perimeter is 13.3 cm.

Find the perimeter. Use your ruler where necessary.

1.

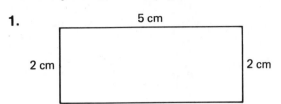

5 cm

2 cm   2 cm

5 cm

2.

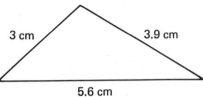

3 cm   3.9 cm

5.6 cm

3.

4.

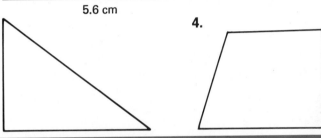

EXERCISES
Find the perimeter.

1.

6 cm

3 cm   3 cm

6 cm

2.

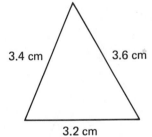

3.4 cm   3.6 cm

3.2 cm

3.

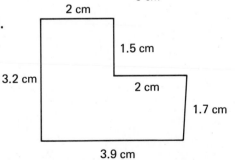

2 cm

1.5 cm

3.2 cm

2 cm

1.7 cm

3.9 cm

4.

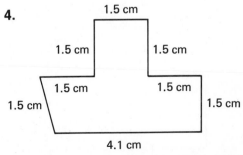

1.5 cm

1.5 cm   1.5 cm

1.5 cm   1.5 cm

1.5 cm   1.5 cm

4.1 cm

Measure the length of each side. Then find the perimeter.

5.

6.

7.

8.

9.

Solve these problems.

10. How much aluminum molding is needed to cover the edge of the table?

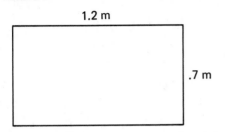

1.2 m

.7 m

11. The perimeter of the rock garden is 127.5 m. What is the length of side *a*?

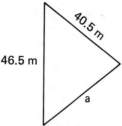

40.5 m

46.5 m

a

12. Mr. Kickingbird fenced his chicken yard. Fencing was $1.50 a meter. How much did he spend?

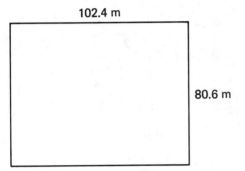

102.4 m

80.6 m

13. A yard is shaped like a diamond. How much fencing is needed to enclose the yard?

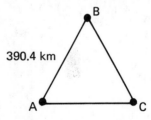

27.432 m

27.432 m

14. Weatherstripping costs $.28 a meter. How much will it cost to weather-strip the door?

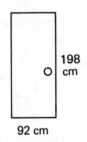

198 cm

O

92 cm

15. A plane flies from *A* to *B* to *C* to *A*. *ABC* is an equilateral triangle. (Each side has the same length.) How far does the plane travel?

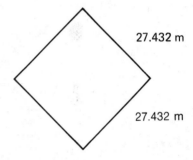

B

390.4 km

A   C

16. The perimeter of a court is 238 m. What is its length?

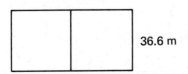

36.6 m

17. A classroom is shaped like a square. Find the length of side *a*.

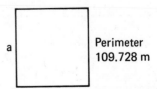

a

Perimeter
109.728 m

Area

1 cm
1 cm

The square centimeter (cm²) is a commonly used unit of area in the metric system.

To find the area of a region in square centimeters, find the number of square centimeters needed to cover it.

EXAMPLE 1   Find the area of the rectangle.

SOLUTION

Use a clear plastic surface or a piece of tracing paper marked off in cm². Use it to cover the rectangle.

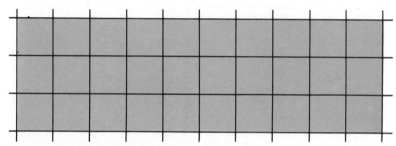

Count the number of cm² needed to cover the region.

The area is 30 square centimeters.

EXAMPLE 2   Find the area of the shaded region.

SOLUTION

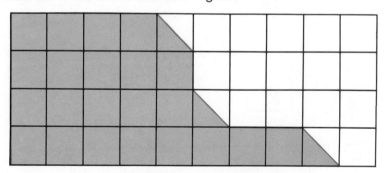

Count the number of cm² in each row.
Be sure to count the halves.
A half is the same as .5.

Add.

Top row	→	4.5 cm²
2nd row	→	5 cm²
3rd row	→	5.5 cm²
4th row	→	8.5 cm²
Area	→	23.5 cm²

EXAMPLE 3 Find the area of △ABC. (△ABC is read *triangle ABC*.)

SOLUTION

Complete the rectangle.
Think: The area of △ABC
is half the area of the
rectangle.
The area of the rectangle
is 32 cm².

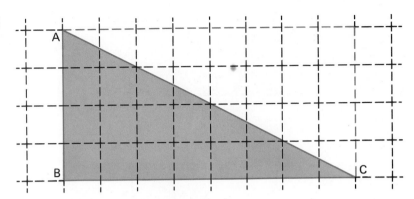

$$\begin{array}{r} 16 \\ 2\overline{)32} \end{array}$$

The area of △ABC is 32 ÷ 2, or 16 cm².

Find the area of the shaded region.

1.

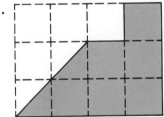

2.

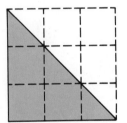

EXERCISES
Find the area of the shaded region.

1.

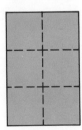

2.

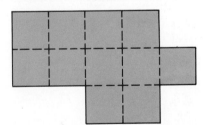

3.

4.

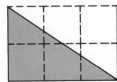

5.

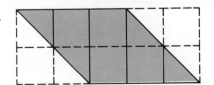

6.

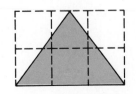

Find the area.

7.

8.

9.

10.

11.

12.

13.

14.

15.

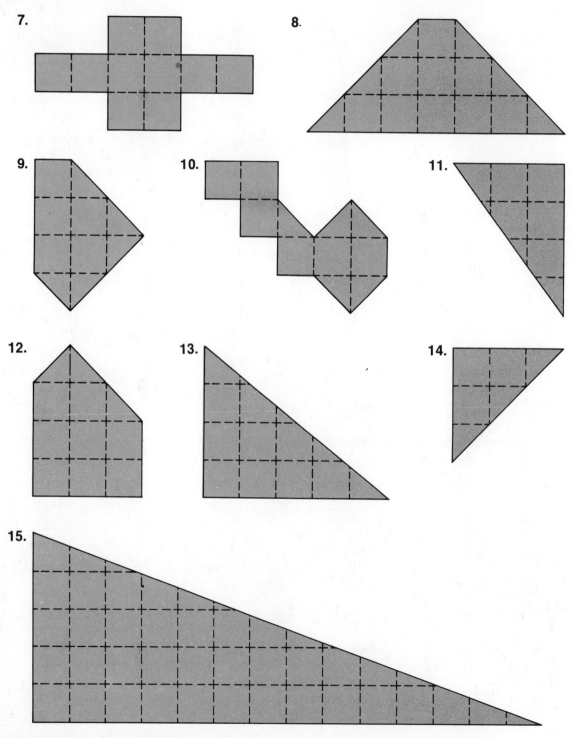

Computing Areas

EXAMPLE 1   Find the area of a rectangle 8 cm long and 4 cm wide.

SOLUTION

Think of a rectangle 8 cm long and 4 cm wide.
Think of it as covered with cm².
There are 4 rows of 8 cm² each, or 32 cm².

Example 1 suggests this.

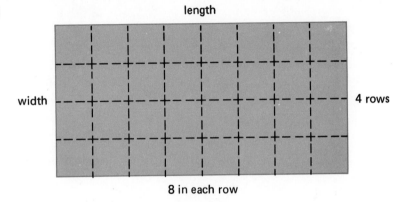

length

width

4 rows

8 in each row

The area of the rectangle is 32 cm².

To find the area of a rectangle, multiply:
length × width.

EXAMPLE 2   Find the area of a rectangle with dimensions 46 mm by 23 mm.

SOLUTION

Length, width, height are dimensions.

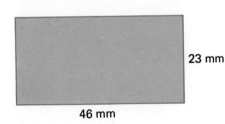

23 mm

46 mm

$$\begin{array}{r} 46 \\ \times 23 \\ \hline 138 \\ 92 \\ \hline 1{,}058 \end{array}$$

23 rows of 46 mm² each.

The area is 1,058 square millimeters (mm²).

- -

Find the area of each rectangle.

1. Length: 46 cm
Width: 13 cm

2. Length: 41 cm
Width: 10 cm

3. Length: 34 mm
Width: 12 mm

4. Length: 5.6 m
Width: 8 m

EXAMPLE 3   Find the area of a right triangle whose height is 3 cm and whose base is 8 cm long.

SOLUTION

Think of a right triangle and completing the rectangle.
Think of covering the rectangle with cm².

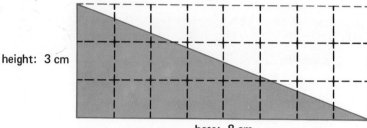

height: 3 cm

base: 8 cm

The area of the right triangle is half the area of the rectangle.

The area of the rectangle is 3 × 8, or 24 cm².
So, the area of the triangle is 2)‾2‾4‾, or 12 cm².

Example 3 suggests this.

To find the area of a right triangle, multiply:
length of the base × height. Then divide by 2.

Find the area of the right triangle.

5. Base: 8 cm
   Height: 13 cm

6. Base: 24 mm
   Height: 10 mm

EXERCISES

Find the area of the rectangle.

1. Length: 9 cm
   Width: 5 cm

2. Length: 38 cm
   Width: 24 cm

3. Length: 42.4 cm
   Width: 12.5 cm

4. Length: 10.6 cm
   Width: 11.7 cm

5. Length: 107 cm
   Width: .5 cm

6. Length: 88 cm
   Width: 14.8 cm

7. Length: 37 mm
   Width: 12 mm

8. Length: 100 mm
   Width: 73 mm

9. Length: 44 mm
   Width: 11.7 mm

10. Length: 14.5 m
    Width: 10.6 m

11. Length: 786 m
    Width: 101 m

12. Length: 7 km
    Width: 4 km

Find the area of the right triangle.

13. Base: 11 cm
    Height: 5 cm

14. Base: 38 cm
    Height: 42 cm

15. Base: 88 cm
    Height: 78 cm

16. Base: 5 mm
    Height: 4 mm

17. Base: 8 mm
    Height: 22 mm

18. Base: 102 mm
    Height: 12 mm

19. Base: 4 m
    Height: 8 m

20. Base: 204 m
    Height: 106 m

21. Base: 792 m
    Height: 238 m

Measure the sides of each figure. Then find the area.

22.

23.
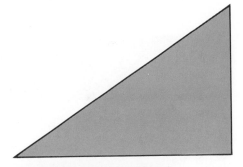

24.
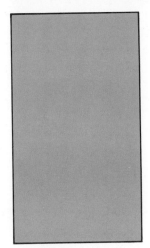

25.
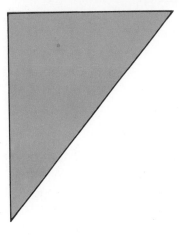

Areas of Other Figures

EXAMPLE 1   Find the area.

Divide the figure into two rectangles.
Find the area of the smaller rectangle.
Find the area of the larger rectangle.
Add the areas.

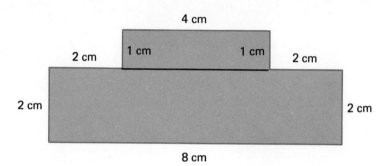

Length: 4 cm
Width: 1 cm 4×1, or   4 cm²
Length: 8 cm
Width: 2 cm 8×2, or 16 cm²

So, the area of the figure is 20 cm².

EXAMPLE 2   Find the area.

Divide the figure into a rectangle and two right triangles.
Area of rectangle

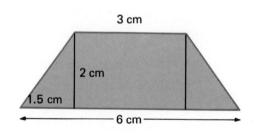

Area of each triangle

Area of both triangles
Add the areas.

6×2, or 12 cm²

$\begin{array}{l} 1.5 \\ \underline{\times 2} \\ 3.0 \end{array}$ $\begin{array}{r} 1.5 \\ 2\overline{)3.0} \end{array}$ 1.5 cm²

$\begin{array}{l} 1.5 \\ \underline{\times 2} \\ 3.0, \text{ or 3 cm}^2 \end{array}$

$12 \text{ cm}^2 + 3 \text{ cm}^2 = 15 \text{ cm}^2$

So, the area of the figure is 15 cm².

EXAMPLE 3 Find the area of the shaded region.

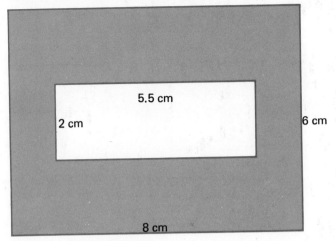

Area of larger   8 × 6,   or 48 cm²
Area of smaller   5.5
                  ×2
                  11.0,   or 11 cm²

Subtract.   So, the area is 37 cm².

— —

Find the area of the shaded region.

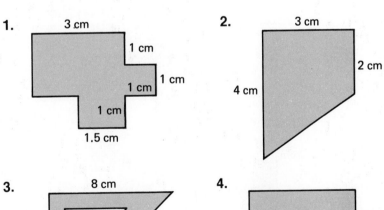

1.

2.

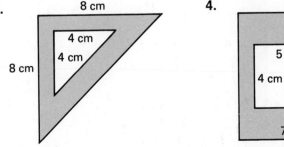

3.

4.

EXERCISES
Find the area of the shaded region.

1.

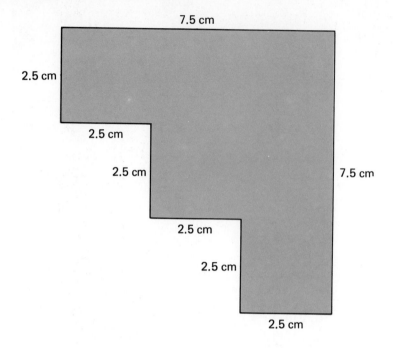

2.

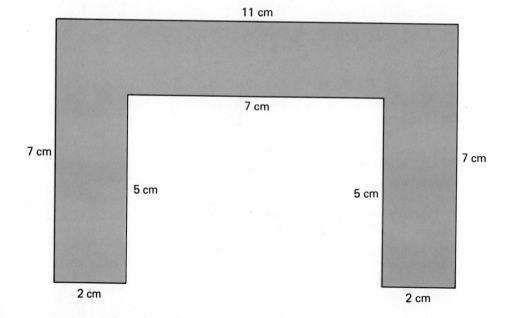

Find the area of the shaded region.

3.

5 cm

5 cm

3 cm

8 cm

4.

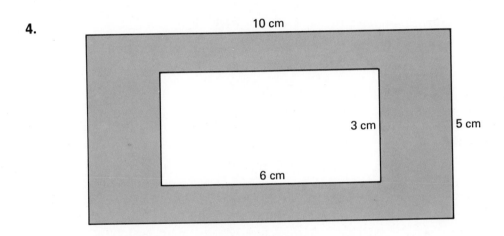

10 cm

3 cm

5 cm

6 cm

5.

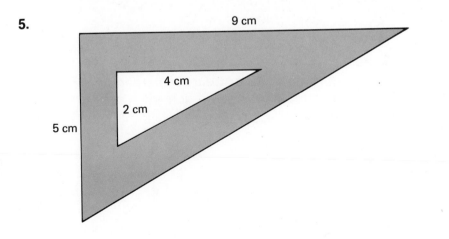

9 cm

4 cm

2 cm

5 cm

Area Problems

EXAMPLE

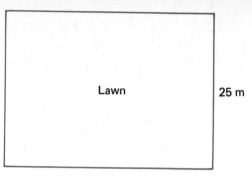

Lawn

25 m

35 m

Sod costs $1.25 a square meter. How much will it cost to cover the lawn?

SOLUTION

Multiply: length × width to find the area of the lawn.

```
  35 ←——— Length
 ×25 ←——— Width
 175 ←——— 5 × 35
 70  ←——— 20 × 35
 875      The area of the lawn is 875 m².
```

Multiply to find the cost.

```
   $1.25 ←——— Cost for 1 m²
   ×875  ←——— Number of m²
   6 25  ←——— 5 × 125
   875   ←——— 70 × 125
  1000   ←——— 800 × 125
$1,093.75      It will cost $1,093.75 to cover the lawn.
```

Solve.

Carpeting costs $8.75 a square meter, and padding costs $2.25 a square meter. How much will it cost to cover the floor with both?

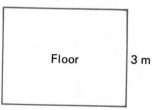

Floor

3 m

4 m

EXERCISES

Solve these problems.

1. A basement ceiling is 7 m wide and 8 m long. How many boxes of tiles are needed to cover the ceiling?

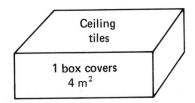

Ceiling tiles

1 box covers 4 m²

2. A kitchen floor is 570 cm long and 480 cm wide. How many tiles are needed to cover the floor?

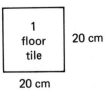

1 floor tile

20 cm

20 cm

3. The area of the playground is about 5,760 m². What is its width?

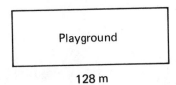

Playground

128 m

4. The area of the stamp is about 550 mm². What is its length?

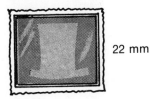

22 mm

Answer these questions about the bedroom in the picture.

5. How many m² of ceiling?

6. How many m² of walls?

7. Windows and doors cover 5 m². What is the total area to be painted?

8. How much paint will be needed?

9. How much will the paint cost?

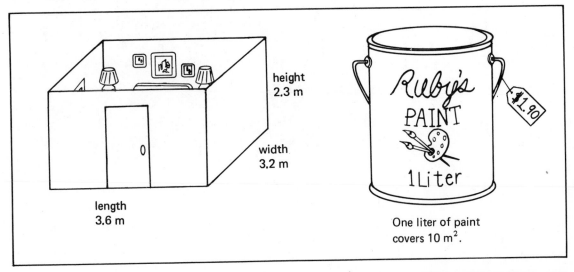

height 2.3 m

width 3.2 m

length 3.6 m

Ruby's PAINT 1 Liter

$1.90

One liter of paint covers 10 m².

Irregular Areas

EXAMPLE Estimate the area.

SOLUTION

Cover it with a piece of clear plastic or tracing paper marked off in cm².

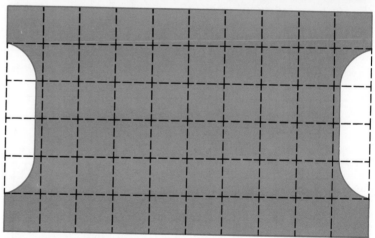

Count the number of cm² in each row.

Add.   27
      +27
      ─────
       54

1st row: 10   cm²   2nd row: 8.6 cm²
3rd row: 8.4 cm²   4th row: 8.4 cm²
5th row: 8.6 cm²   6th row: 10   cm²
         ─────────   ─────────
         27.0 cm²   27.0 cm²

So, the area is about 54 cm².

EXERCISES

Estimate the area.

1.

2.

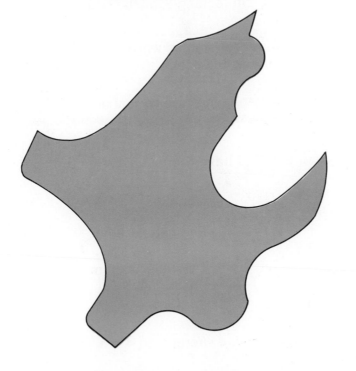

Comparing Areas

EXAMPLE Draw 3 different rectangles whose perimeter is 12 cm.
Find the area of each rectangle.
Which rectangle has the largest area?

SOLUTION

Add the lengths of the sides to find the perimeter.

Multiply the length and width to find the area.

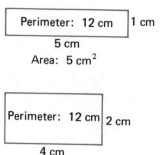

Perimeter: 12 cm | 1 cm
5 cm
Area: 5 cm^2

Perimeter: 12 cm | 2 cm
4 cm
Area: 8 cm^2

Perimeter: 12 cm | 3 cm
3 cm
Area: 9 cm^2

The 3 cm by 3 cm rectangle, or the square, has the largest area.

Use square-ruled paper.

Draw 4 different rectangles whose perimeter is 16 cm.
   1. Find the areas of each.

   2. Which rectangle has the largest area?

EXERCISES

Draw as many rectangles as you can that have the given perimeter.

Find the area of each.

Tell which rectangle has the largest area.

1. Perimeter: 8 cm

2. Perimeter: 40 cm

3. Perimeter: 24 cm

4. Perimeter: 36 cm

5. Perimeter: 32 cm

6. Perimeter: 28 cm

7. Perimeter: 20 cm

8. Perimeter: 4 cm

Comparing Perimeters

EXAMPLE   Draw 3 different rectangles whose area is 16 cm².
Find the perimeter of each.
Which rectangle has the smallest perimeter?

SOLUTION

Area: 16 cm²   1 cm
16 cm
Perimeter: 34 cm

Multiply the length and
width to find the area.

Area: 16 cm²   2 cm
8 cm
Perimeter: 20 cm

Add the lengths of the
sides to find the perimeter.

Area: 16 cm²   4 cm
4 cm
Perimeter: 16 cm

The 4-cm by 4-cm square has the smallest perimeter.

- -

Use square-ruled paper.
Don't try to draw a 1-cm
by 36-cm rectangle.

Draw 4 different rectangles whose area is 36 cm².
  1. Find the perimeter of each.

  2. Which rectangle has the smallest perimeter?

EXERCISES
Draw as many rectangles as you can that have the given area.
Find the area of each.
Tell which rectangle has the smallest perimeter.

1. Area: 4 cm²

2. Area: 9 cm²

3. Area: 25 cm²

4. Area: 100 cm²

5. Area: 49 cm²

6. Area: 64 cm²

7. Area: 81 cm²

8. Area: 400 cm²

Volume

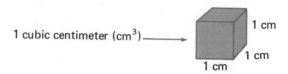

Volume is the amount of space inside an object.

The cubic centimeter (cm^3) is a commonly used unit of volume in the metric system.

1 cubic centimeter (cm^3) ⟶

1 cm
1 cm
1 cm

To find the volume of a container in cubic centimeters, find the number of cubic centimeters needed to fill it.

EXAMPLE   Find the volume of the container.

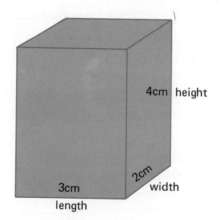

4cm height
3cm length
2cm width

The dimensions of the container are length, width, and height.

The container is 3 cm long by 2 cm wide by 4 cm high.

SOLUTION

There are 2 rows of 3 cm³ each in the bottom layer. There are 2 × 3, or 6 cm³ in the layer.

Think of cm³ covering the bottom.

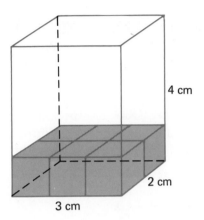

To fill it, 4 layers of 6 cm³ are needed.

Think of cm³ filling the container.

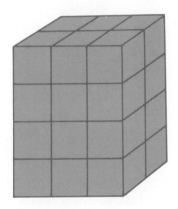

The volume is 2 × 3 × 4, or 24 cm³.

To find the volume of a rectangular solid, multiply: length × width × height.

- -

Find the volume.

1. Length: 1 cm
   Width: 3 cm
   Height: 4 cm

2. Length: 4 cm
   Width: 4 cm
   Height: 5 cm

EXERCISES
Find the volume.
1. Length: 4 cm
   Width: 6 cm
   Height: 10 cm

2. Length: 5 cm
   Width: 5 cm
   Height: 12 cm

3. Length: 8 cm
   Width: 8 cm
   Height: 8 cm

4. Length: 3.5 cm
   Width: 3.5 cm
   Height: 4 cm

5. Length: 7.6 cm
   Width: 7.4 cm
   Height: 5 cm

6. Length: 15 cm
   Width: 4.2 cm
   Height: 20 cm

Solve these problems.

7.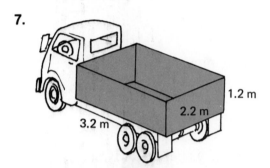

How many cubic meters (m³) of sand will the truck hold?

8.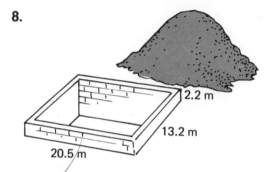

How many m³ of dirt were removed to make the basement?

9. A truck can carry 10 m³ of dirt. How many truckloads of dirt were removed in Exercise **8**?

10. A fish tank is 30 cm long, 70 cm wide, and 35 cm high. How much space is there in the tank?

11.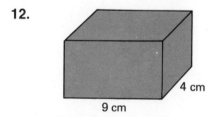

Before the brick was placed in the tank, the depth of the water was 10 cm. What is the volume of the brick?

12.

The volume of the box is 216 cm³. What is the height of the box?

Capacity

The prefix *milli* means one thousandth.
1 L = 1,000 mL

The liter (L) and milliliter (mL) are two commonly used units of capacity in the metric system.

A 1,000-cm³ container will hold 1 liter of water.
A 1-cm³ container will hold 1 mL of water.

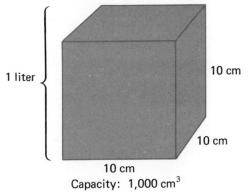

1 liter

10 cm

10 cm

10 cm

Capacity: 1,000 cm³

1 milliliter

1 cm

1 cm

1 cm

Capacity: 1 cm³

EXAMPLE 1   How many milliliters are there in 6.23 liters?

SOLUTION   Think: A liter is larger than a milliliter.

To change liters to milliliters, multiply by 1,000.
"Move" the decimal point.

6.23 × 1,000   6.230   6,230

So, there are 6,230 mL in 6.23 L.

EXAMPLE 2   How many liters are there in 3,450 milliliters?

SOLUTION   Think: A milliliter is smaller than a liter.

To change milliliters to liters, divide by 1,000.
"Move" the decimal point.

3,450 ÷ 1,000   3,450.   3.45

So, there are 3.45 L in 3,450 mL.

Make true sentences.

1. 2.45 L = __?__ mL

2. .76 L = __?__ mL

3. 7.256 mL = __?__ L

4. 825 mL = __?__ L

EXAMPLE 3 How much water will the tank hold?

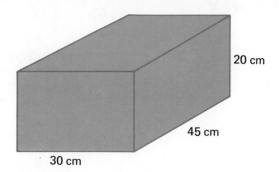

20 cm

45 cm

30 cm

SOLUTION The volume is $30 \times 45 \times 20$, or 27,000 cm³.

45
×30
1,350

1,350
×20
27,000

27,000 ÷ 1 = 27,000

1,000 cm³ holds 1 liter, and 1 cm³ holds 1 mL.

27,000 ÷ 1,000   27,000   27.000

So the tank holds 27 L or 27,000 mL of liquid.

- -

How much liquid will each container hold?

5.

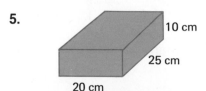

10 cm

25 cm

20 cm

6.

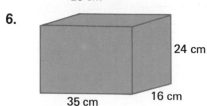

24 cm

35 cm   16 cm

EXERCISES

Make true sentences.

1. 3L = __?__ mL

2. 8 L = __?__ mL

3. 12 L = __?__ mL

4. 12.5 L = __?__ mL

5. 1.46 L = __?__ mL

6. .47 L = __?__ mL

7. 185 mL = __?__ L

8. 2,450 mL = __?__ L

9. 18,453 mL = __?__ L

10. 373 mL = __?__ L

11. 1 mL = __?__ L

12. 88 mL = __?__ L

Solve these problems.

13. What is the volume of the tank in cubic centimeters?

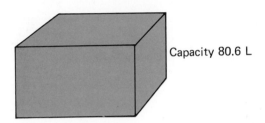

Capacity 80.6 L

14. How many liters of gasoline will the can hold?

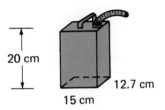

20 cm

12.7 cm

15 cm

15. How many mL of milk are there in the container? How many L?

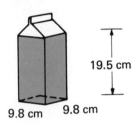

19.5 cm

9.8 cm 9.8 cm

16. What is the volume of the can in cubic centimeters?

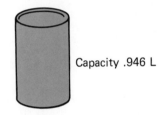

Capacity .946 L

17. How many liters of vaccine are there in the 2 boxes?

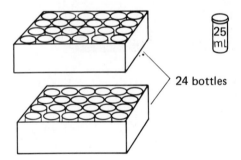

25 mL

24 bottles

18. Hy-Jinx costs 85¢ per 500 mL. How much should Peg pay?

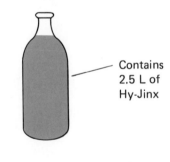

Contains 2.5 L of Hy-Jinx

Fun Corner

How much does the brick weigh?

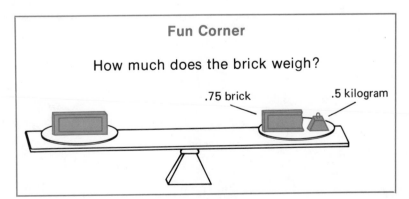

.75 brick   .5 kilogram

Weight

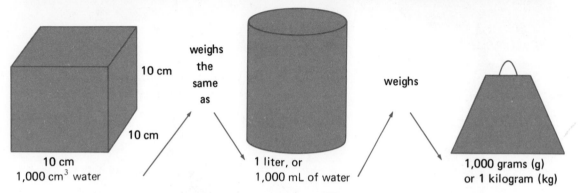

10 cm
10 cm
10 cm
1,000 cm³ water

weighs
the
same
as

1 liter, or
1,000 mL of water

weighs

1,000 grams (g)
or 1 kilogram (kg)

EXAMPLE   What is the weight of the bread in kilograms (kg)?
in milligrams (mg)?

BREAD
Weight: 636 grams

SOLUTION   Think: 1,000 g = 1 kg   1,000 mg = 1g

To change g to kg, divide.
To change g to mg, multiply.

$$1{,}000\overline{)636.000}\ \ ^{.636}$$

$$1{,}000 \times 636 = 636{,}000$$

So, the bread weighs .636 kg, or 636,000 mg.

- -

Find the weight.

1.

weight: 566 g

How many kg?

2.

weight:
1.2 kg

How many g?

EXERCISES
How many kilograms?

1.

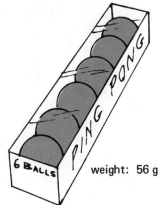

weight: 56 g

2.

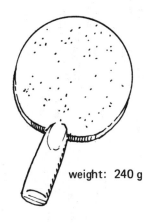

weight: 240 g

3.

weight: 289 g

4.

weight: 100 g

5.

weight: 304,500 g

6.

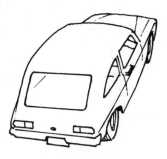

weight: 1,000,000 g

7.

weight: 562 g

8.

weight: 475 g

9.

weight: 61 g

How many grams?

10.

weight: 23 kg

11.

weight: 3.5 kg

12.

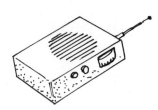

weight: 3.4 kg

13.

weight: 20 kg

14.

weight: 4.1 kg

15.

weight: 845,000 mg

16.

weight: 810 mg

17.

weight: 342 mg

18.

weight: 28,400 mg

Make true sentences.

19. 1 kg = ___?___ g

20. 2 kg = ___?___ g

21. 3 kg = ___?___ g

22. 6.2 kg = ___?___ g

23. 1,473 kg = ___?___ g

24. 2,260 kg = ___?___ g

25. .148 kg = ___?___ g

26. .001 kg = ___?___ g

27. .007 kg = ___?___ g

28. 1,000 g = ___?___ kg

29. 800 g = ___?___ kg

30. 100 g = ___?___ kg

31. 10 g = ___?___ kg

32. 1 g = ___?___ kg

33. 3,460 g = ___?___ kg

34. 1,742 g = ___?___ kg

35. 1,000 mg = ___?___ g

36. 1,543 mg = ___?___ g

37. 286 mg = ___?___ g

38. 28 mg = ___?___ g

39. 6 g = ___?___ mg

Deci, Deka, and Hecto

Deci (d) means .1.
Deka (da) means 10.
Hecto (h) means 100.

The prefixes that are used in the metric system have the same meanings as the place-value names that are used in our number system.

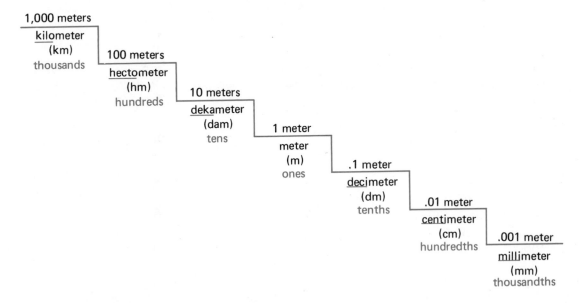

1,000 meters
kilometer (km)
thousands

100 meters
hectometer (hm)
hundreds

10 meters
dekameter (dam)
tens

1 meter
meter (m)
ones

.1 meter
decimeter (dm)
tenths

.01 meter
centimeter (cm)
hundredths

.001 meter
millimeter (mm)
thousandths

EXAMPLE 1   Make true sentences.

28 m = __?__ dam   28 g = __?__ dag

SOLUTION

Use dam for dekameter.
Use dag for dekagram.

Think: 10 m = 1 dam   Think: 10 g = 1 dag
      28 ÷ 10 = 2.8   28 ÷ 10 = 2.8
So, 28 m = 2.8 dam and 28 g = 2.8 dag.

EXAMPLE 2   Make true sentences.

.5g = __?__ dg   .5L = __?__ dL

SOLUTION

Use dg for decigram.
Use dL for deciliter.

Think: 1g = 10 dg   Think: 1L = 10 dL
      .5 × 10 = 5   .5 × 10 = 5
So, .5 g = 5 dg and .5 L = 5 dL.

Make true sentences.

1.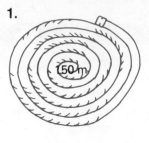

Coil of rope

——?—— dam

——?—— hm

2.

1.2 kg

Butter

——?—— hg

——?—— dag

3.

3.45 L

Cider

——?—— dL

——?—— daL

EXERCISES

Make true sentences.

1. 5.6 m = ——?—— dam

2. 20.6 m = ——?—— dam

3. 28 cm = ——?—— dm

4. 842 m = ——?—— km

5. 842 m = ——?—— hm

6. 842 cm = ——?—— dam

7. 880 g = ——?—— kg

8. 880 g = ——?—— hg

9. 880 g = ——?—— dag

10. 165 L = ——?—— kL

11. 165 L = ——?—— hL

12. 165 L = ——?—— daL

Fun Corner

SELL WIDGETS

SALARY: $10,000 per day

SELL GIDGETS!

SALARY: 1st day 1¢
2nd day 2¢
3rd day 4¢
and doubled each
day thereafter

Pat got the job selling widgets. Ramos got the job selling gidgets. Who will make more money in 31 days? How much more?

Metric Tables

LENGTH

1 millimeter (mm) = .001 meter (m)	1,000 millimeters = 1 meter
1 centimeter (cm) = .01 meter	100 centimeters = 1 meter
1 decimeter (dm) = .1 meter	10 decimeters = 1 meter
1 dekameter (dam) = 10 meters	.1 dekameter = 1 meter
1 hectometer (hm) = 100 meters	.01 hectometer = 1 meter
1 kilometer (km) = 1,000 meters	.001 kilometer = 1 meter

CAPACITY

1 milliliter (mL) = .001 liter (L)	1,000 milliliters = 1 liter
1 centiliter (cL) = .01 liter	100 centiliters = 1 liter
1 deciliter (dL) = .1 liter	10 deciliters = 1 liter
1 dekaliter (daL) = 10 liters	.1 dekaliter = 1 liter
1 hectoliter (hL) = 100 liters	.01 hectoliter = 1 liter
1 kiloliter (kL) = 1,000 liters	.001 kiloliter = 1 liter

WEIGHT OR MASS

1 milligram (mg) = .001 gram (g)	1,000 milligrams = 1 gram
1 centigram (cg) = .01 gram	100 centigrams = 1 gram
1 decigram (dg) = .1 gram	10 decigrams = 1 gram
1 dekagram (dag) = 10 grams	.1 dekagram = 1 gram
1 hectogram (hg) = 100 grams	.01 hectogram = 1 gram
1 kilogram (kg) = 1,000 grams	.001 kilogram = 1 gram
1 ton (t) = 1,000 kilograms	

AREA

$1 \ mm^2 = .000001 \ m^2$
$1 \ cm^2 = .0001 \ m^2$
$1 \ dm^2 = .01 \ m^2$
$1 \ dam^2 = 100 \ m^2$
$1 \ hm^2 = 10,000 \ m^2$
$1 \ km^2 = 1,000,000 \ m^2$

VOLUME

$1 \ mm^3 = .000000001 \ m^3$
$1 \ cm^3 = .000001 \ m^3$
$1 \ dm^3 = .001 \ m^3$
$1 \ dam^3 = 1,000 \ m^3$
$1 \ hm^3 = 1,000,000 \ m^3$
$1 \ km^3 = 1,000,000,000 \ m^3$

Temperature

Temperature is measured in degrees Celsius (formerly called Centigrade) in the metric system.

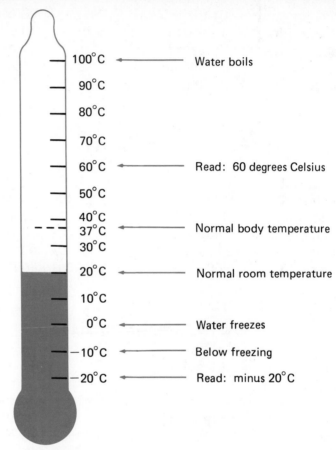

— 100°C ← Water boils

— 90°C

— 80°C

— 70°C

— 60°C ← Read: 60 degrees Celsius

— 50°C

— 40°C
- - 37°C ← Normal body temperature
— 30°C

— 20°C ← Normal room temperature

— 10°C

— 0°C ← Water freezes

— -10°C ← Below freezing

— -20°C ← Read: minus 20°C

Celsius Thermometer

The thermometer shows a temperature of 20°C. Read 20°C as 20 degrees Celsius.

EXAMPLE 1 Is it too cold, too hot, or comfortable at the given room temperature: 35°C, 22°C, 5°C?

SOLUTION Think: Normal room temperature is 20°C.

$$\begin{array}{r} 35 \\ -20 \\ \hline 15 \end{array} \quad \begin{array}{r} 22 \\ -20 \\ \hline 2 \end{array} \quad \begin{array}{r} 20 \\ -\ 5 \\ \hline 15 \end{array}$$

35°C: 15° above normal   22°C: 2° above normal   5°C: 15° below normal

The room is too hot at 35°C, comfortable at 22°C, and too cold at 5°C.

EXAMPLE 2 What temperature is suggested by the picture?

212°C or 100°C   37.5°C or 100°C

SOLUTION   212°C: 112° above   37.5°C: .5° above
                                boiling   normal

212	37.5	100.0
−100	−37.0	− 37.5
112	.5	62.5

100°C: boiling   100°C: 62.5° above
        point   normal

So, the suggested temperatures are 100°C and 37.5°C.

- -

Is it too cold, too hot, or comfortable?
  1. 5°C   **2.** 50°C   **3.** 25°C   **4.** 0°C

EXAMPLE 3 At noon the temperature was 15°C. At midnight it was
−5°C. How many degrees did the temperature drop?

SOLUTION   From 15°C to 0°C is a drop of 15°.

−5°C means 5° below 0°.
Add 15° and 5°.   From 0°C to −5°C is a drop of 5°.

So, the temperature dropped 20°.

- -

Solve these problems.
  5. At dawn the temperature was 5°C. At 3:00 pm it was
     15°C. How many degrees did the temperature rise?

  6. At 9:00 am the temperature was 20°C. At 9:00 pm it
     was 0°C. How many degrees did the temperature
     drop?

  7. At 8:00 am the temperature was 10°C. By noon it
     dropped 20°. What was the temperature then?

Is it too cold, too hot, or comfortable?

1. 15°C **2.** 40°C **3.** 21°C **4.** 10°C **5.** 30°C

6. −10°C **7.** 45°C **8.** −5°C **9.** 38°C **10.** 20°C

What temperature is suggested?

11. A cake of ice

0°C or 32°C

12. A tub of bath water

120°C or 50°C

13. A blizzard

18°C or 1°C

Solve these problems.

14. At noon the temperature was 10°C. At 7:00 pm it was 30°C. How many degrees did the temperature rise?

15. At 8:00 am the temperature was 20°C. At 8:00 pm it was 40°C. How many degrees did the temperature rise?

16. At dawn the temperature was 0°C. At noon it was −10°C. How many degrees did the temperature drop?

17. At noon the temperature was 10°C. At 9:00 pm it was −15°C. How many degrees did the temperature drop?

18. At 7:00 am the temperature was 15°C. By 7:00 pm it dropped 20°. What was the temperature then?

19. At 2:00 am the temperature was 40°C. By noon it dropped 15°. What was the temperature then?

20. At dawn the temperature was 20°C. By noon it rose 10°. What was the temperature then?

21. At 8:00 am the temperature was −10°C. By noon it rose 15°. What was the temperature then?

Fun Corner

Find the number that meets these conditions.

Divide it by 2; the remainder is 0.

Divide it by 3; the remainder is 0.

Divide it by 13; the remainder is 0.

The sum of its digits is 15.

Test: Unit 8

Measure to the nearest centimeter.

1. _____

Measure to the nearest millimeter.

2. _____

Make true sentences.

3. 124 cm = __?__ m

4. 8.8 m = __?__ cm

5. 56 mm = __?__ cm

6. 3.2 cm = __?__ mm

7. 3,400 m = __?__ km

8. 5.1 km = __?__ m

Find the perimeter. Use a ruler marked in centimeters.

9.

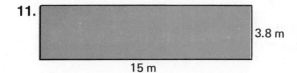

Find the perimeter.

10.

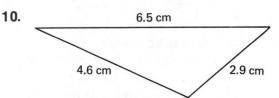

6.5 cm

4.6 cm

2.9 cm

Find the area of the shaded region.

11.

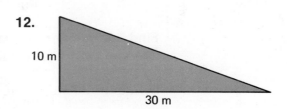

3.8 m

15 m

12.

10 m

30 m

13.

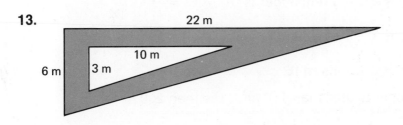

22 m

10 m

6 m

3 m

Answer these questions about the tank.

14. What is the volume?

15. How many milliliters of water does the tank hold?

16. How many kilograms does the water weigh?

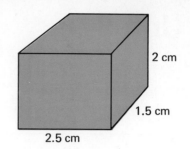

2 cm

1.5 cm

2.5 cm

Make true sentences.

17. 3 L = _?_ mL

18. 3,460 mL = _?_ L

19. 566 g = _?_ kg

20. .04 kg = _?_ g

21. 2,000 mg = _?_ g

22. 2.5 g = _?_ mg

23. 2.3 m = _?_ dam

24. 870 g = _?_ kg

25. 12 L = _?_ hL

26. 25 cg = _?_ dg

Solve these problems.

27. At dawn the temperature was 40°C. At noon it was 25°C. How many degrees did the temperature drop?

28. At 7:00 am the temperature was 15°C. At noon it rose 7°. What was the temperature then?

Fun Corner

Find the number that meets these conditions.
Divide it by 2; the remainder is 0

Divide it by 7; the remainder is 0.

Divide it by 28; the remainder is 0.

Divide it by 98; the remainder is 0.

The sum of its digits is 16.

Is the number more than 150 and less than 200?

UNIT 9

Meaning of Fractions

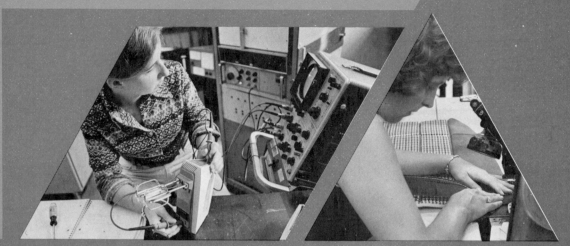

DIAGNOSTIC TEST: FRACTIONS FORM A—40 MINUTES

Write a fraction for the part of the set that is shaded.

1.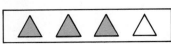

2.

3.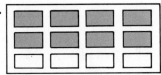

Write three fractions for the portion that is shaded. The unit is shown by solid lines.

4.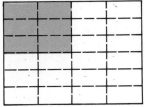

5.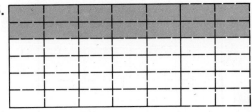

Make true sentences.

6. $\frac{3}{4} = \frac{?}{12}$

7. $\frac{7}{10} = \frac{?}{30}$

8. $\frac{?}{8} = \frac{15}{24}$

9. $\frac{?}{3} = \frac{12}{18}$

Simplify each fraction.

10. $\frac{8}{10}$

11. $\frac{16}{20}$

12. $\frac{20}{100}$

13. $\frac{12}{16}$

14. $\frac{10}{6}$

Which fraction in each pair is greater?

15. $\frac{5}{8}, \frac{1}{2}$

16. $\frac{3}{16}, \frac{1}{4}$

17. $\frac{4}{3}, \frac{13}{12}$

18. $\frac{5}{8}, \frac{7}{12}$

Did You Have

More than 15 right?
Begin on page 208.

13–15 right?
Begin on page 200.

Less than 13 right?
Begin on page 197.

DIAGNOSTIC TEST FORM A **195**

DIAGNOSTIC TEST: FRACTIONS FORM B—40 MINUTES

Write a fraction for the part of the set that is shaded.

1.
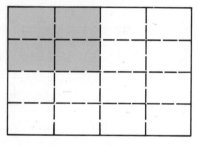

2.
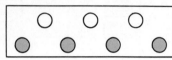
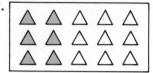

3.

Write three fractions for the portion that is shaded. The unit is shown by solid lines.

4.
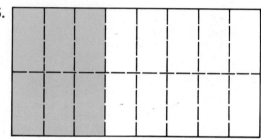

5.

Make true sentences.

6. $\frac{1}{4} = \frac{?}{12}$

7. $\frac{3}{10} = \frac{?}{30}$

8. $\frac{?}{8} = \frac{16}{32}$

9. $\frac{7}{5} = \frac{?}{15}$

Simplify each fraction.

10. $\frac{6}{10}$

11. $\frac{12}{20}$

12. $\frac{40}{100}$

13. $\frac{4}{16}$

14. $\frac{12}{10}$

Which fraction in each pair is greater?

15. $\frac{3}{4}, \frac{7}{8}$

16. $\frac{1}{3}, \frac{1}{2}$

17. $\frac{5}{3}, \frac{11}{6}$

18. $\frac{3}{5}, \frac{8}{15}$

More than 14 right? Begin on page 208. Less than 15 right? Consult your teacher.

Meaning of Fractions

Fractions are used to answer questions such as

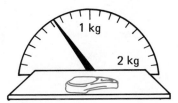

How heavy?

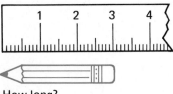

How long?

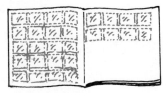

How much?

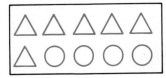

What part of the set?

EXAMPLE 1   How much is shaded?

Think of the whole region as 1 unit.

SOLUTION

Think: The unit is cut into 4 pieces of the same size. 3 of those 4 are shaded.

So, $\frac{3}{4}$ of the region is shaded.

EXAMPLE 2   How much is shaded?

The black lines show the unit.

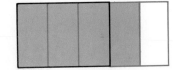

SOLUTION

Think: The unit is cut into 3 pieces of the same size. 4 pieces are shaded.

So, $\frac{4}{3}$, or $1\frac{1}{3}$ is shaded.

How much is shaded? The solid lines show the unit.

1.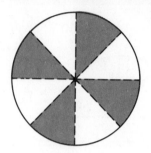

2.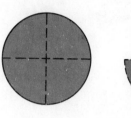

3.

4.

EXAMPLE 3

Think of the whole set as 1 unit.

What part of the set of watch faces reads 9 o'clock?

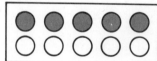

SOLUTION

Think: 2 of the 5 faces read 9 o'clock.

So, $\frac{2}{5}$ of the set reads 9 o'clock.

What part of the set is shaded?

5.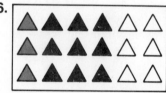

6.

PRACTICE SET 1
How much of each figure is shaded?

1.

2.

3.

PRACTICE SET 2
How much is shaded? The unit is shown by solid lines.

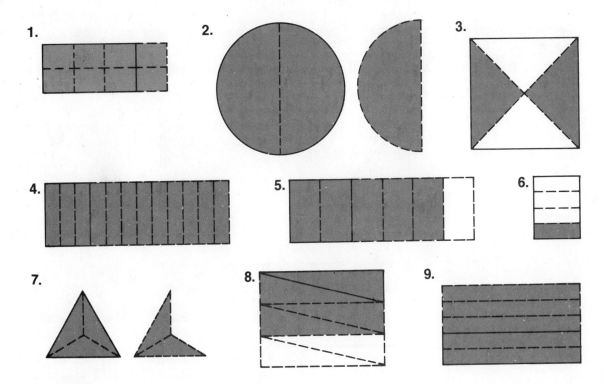

1.

2.

3.

4.

5.

6.

7.

8.

9.

PRACTICE SET 3
What part of each set is described?

1. The cages that have birds in them

2. The glasses that are filled

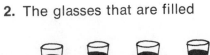

3. The TV sets that have a picture on the screen

4. The apples that have bites out of them

Equivalent Fractions

EXAMPLE 1   What part of each figure is shaded?

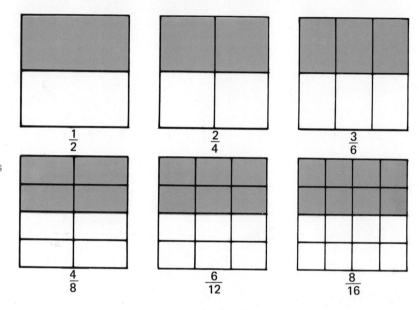

Each figure is the same size. The same portion of each is shaded. But each is divided into a different number of parts.

$$\frac{1}{2} \qquad \frac{2}{4} \qquad \frac{3}{6}$$

$$\frac{4}{8} \qquad \frac{6}{12} \qquad \frac{8}{16}$$

So, $\frac{1}{2}$, $\frac{2}{4}$, $\frac{3}{6}$, $\frac{4}{8}$, $\frac{6}{12}$, and $\frac{8}{16}$ are equivalent fractions.

EXAMPLE 2   Draw a region diagram to show that $\frac{1}{2}$ and $\frac{5}{10}$ are equivalent fractions.

SOLUTION   Draw a diagram showing $\frac{1}{2}$. Then cut the same unit into 10 pieces of the same size.

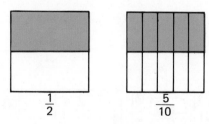

For the same unit, 1 of 2 pieces is the same amount as 5 of 10 pieces.

$$\frac{1}{2} \qquad\qquad \frac{5}{10}$$

So, $\frac{1}{2} = \frac{5}{10}$.

Draw a diagram to show that the fractions in each pair are equivalent.

1. $\frac{1}{3}$ and $\frac{2}{6}$ 2. $\frac{2}{3}$ and $\frac{4}{6}$

3. $\frac{1}{4}$ and $\frac{2}{8}$ 4. $\frac{3}{4}$ and $\frac{6}{8}$

EXAMPLE 3
SOLUTION

Draw a number-line diagram to show that $\frac{5}{3} = \frac{10}{6}$.
Draw a number line and mark it in thirds.

The unit is the segment 0 to 1. It is cut into 3 pieces of the same size.
Now cut the same unit into 6 pieces of the same size.
The dots show that $\frac{5}{3}$ and $\frac{10}{6}$ mark the same point.

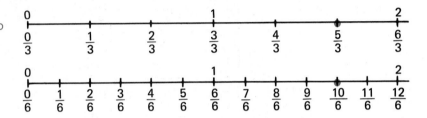

So, $\frac{5}{3} = \frac{10}{6}$.

Draw a number-line diagram to show that each is true.

5. $\frac{1}{2} = \frac{2}{4}$ 6. $\frac{2}{4} = \frac{4}{8}$

7. $\frac{1}{2} = \frac{4}{8}$ 8. $\frac{1}{4} = \frac{2}{8}$

EXAMPLE 4
SOLUTION

Use a set of objects to show that $\frac{2}{3}$ and $\frac{4}{6}$ are the same.

A set of 6 coins is shown in two ways.

4 of the 6 coins are pennies, so $\frac{4}{6}$ of the coins are pennies.

So, $\frac{2}{3} = \frac{4}{6}$.

2 of the 3 groups of coins contain pennies, so $\frac{2}{3}$ of the set are pennies.

- -
Use a set of objects to show each sentence is true.

9. $\frac{1}{2} = \frac{3}{6}$ **10.** $\frac{1}{3} = \frac{2}{6}$

11. $\frac{3}{4} = \frac{6}{8}$ **12.** $\frac{1}{7} = \frac{2}{14}$

EXAMPLE 5 Name the length of the candy bar in three different ways.

The ruler is marked in millimeters.

The length of the candy bar can be named $9\frac{5}{10}$ cm, $9\frac{1}{2}$ cm, or 95 mm.

- -

Name the length of each object in two ways.
Use a ruler marked in millimeters.

13. 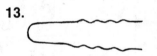 **14.**

PRACTICE SET 4
Draw a diagram to show each sentence is true.

1. $\frac{2}{5} = \frac{4}{10}$ **2.** $\frac{1}{5} = \frac{2}{10}$ **3.** $\frac{3}{5} = \frac{6}{10}$ **4.** $\frac{4}{5} = \frac{8}{10}$

5. $\frac{5}{5} = \frac{10}{10}$ **6.** $\frac{1}{3} = \frac{3}{9}$ **7.** $\frac{2}{3} = \frac{6}{9}$ **8.** $\frac{3}{3} = \frac{9}{9}$

9. $\frac{1}{3} = \frac{4}{12}$ **10.** $\frac{2}{3} = \frac{8}{12}$ **11.** $\frac{3}{3} = \frac{12}{12}$ **12.** $\frac{2}{4} = \frac{4}{8}$

13. $\frac{3}{4} = \frac{9}{12}$ **14.** $\frac{4}{4} = \frac{12}{12}$ **15.** $\frac{5}{10} = \frac{1}{2}$ **16.** $\frac{2}{8} = \frac{1}{4}$

Finding Equivalent Fractions

EXAMPLE 1 Use multiplication to write six fractions equivalent to $\frac{3}{5}$.

SOLUTION

Multiply both numerator and denominator by the same number. Any number except 0 could be used as the multiplier.

So, $\frac{3 \times 2}{5 \times 2} = \frac{6}{10}$ $\frac{3 \times 5}{5 \times 5} = \frac{15}{25}$

$\frac{3 \times 3}{5 \times 3} = \frac{9}{15}$ $\frac{3 \times 6}{5 \times 6} = \frac{18}{30}$

$\frac{3 \times 4}{5 \times 4} = \frac{12}{20}$ $\frac{3 \times 50}{5 \times 50} = \frac{150}{250}$

Use multiplication to write two fractions equivalent to the given fraction.

1. $\frac{1}{5}$ 2. $\frac{4}{5}$ 3. $\frac{5}{6}$ 4. $\frac{7}{8}$

EXAMPLE 2 Use division to find a fraction equivalent to $\frac{8}{10}$.

SOLUTION

Divide both numerator and denominator by the same number, except 0.

Think: Both the numerator, 8, and the denominator, 10, can be divided by 2.

So, $\frac{8 \div 2}{10 \div 2} = \frac{4}{5}$

Use division to write a fraction equivalent to the given fraction.

5. $\frac{6}{10}$ 6. $\frac{6}{8}$ 7. $\frac{14}{20}$ 8. $\frac{15}{25}$

EXAMPLE 3 Find a fraction equivalent to $\frac{3}{8}$ whose denominator is 24.

SOLUTION Think: $\frac{3}{8} = \frac{?}{24}$, and 24 is 8×3.

Multiply both numerator and denominator of $\frac{3}{8}$ by 3.

$\frac{3 \times 3}{8 \times 3} = \frac{9}{24}$

So, $\frac{3}{8} = \frac{9}{24}$

EXAMPLE 4 Find a fraction equivalent to $\frac{15}{20}$ whose denominator is 4.

SOLUTION Think: $\frac{15}{20} = \frac{?}{4}$, and $20 \div 5 = 4$.

Divide both numerator and denominator of $\frac{15}{20}$ by 5.

$$\frac{15 \div 5}{20 \div 5} = \frac{3}{4}$$

So, $\frac{15}{20} = \frac{3}{4}$

- -

Make true sentences.

9. $\frac{3}{4} = \frac{?}{12}$ **10.** $\frac{2}{3} = \frac{?}{15}$ **11.** $\frac{16}{20} = \frac{?}{5}$ **12.** $\frac{18}{24} = \frac{?}{4}$

PRACTICE SET 5
Make true sentences.

1. $\frac{1}{3} = \frac{?}{9}$ **2.** $\frac{2}{3} = \frac{?}{9}$ **3.** $\frac{8}{4} = \frac{?}{12}$ **4.** $\frac{3}{4} = \frac{?}{16}$

5. $\frac{1}{5} = \frac{?}{10}$ **6.** $\frac{2}{5} = \frac{?}{10}$ **7.** $\frac{3}{5} = \frac{?}{10}$ **8.** $\frac{4}{5} = \frac{?}{10}$

9. $\frac{1}{2} = \frac{?}{10}$ **10.** $\frac{1}{2} = \frac{?}{20}$ **11.** $\frac{1}{6} = \frac{?}{12}$ **12.** $\frac{4}{6} = \frac{?}{12}$

13. $\frac{5}{6} = \frac{?}{12}$ **14.** $\frac{1}{8} = \frac{?}{16}$ **15.** $\frac{2}{8} = \frac{?}{16}$ **16.** $\frac{1}{10} = \frac{?}{100}$

PRACTICE SET 6
Make true sentences.

1. $\frac{6}{9} = \frac{?}{3}$ **2.** $\frac{3}{9} = \frac{?}{3}$ **3.** $\frac{9}{12} = \frac{?}{4}$ **4.** $\frac{6}{8} = \frac{?}{4}$

5. $\frac{20}{25} = \frac{?}{5}$ **6.** $\frac{6}{10} = \frac{?}{5}$ **7.** $\frac{8}{10} = \frac{?}{5}$ **8.** $\frac{4}{10} = \frac{?}{5}$

9. $\frac{2}{4} = \frac{?}{2}$ **10.** $\frac{3}{6} = \frac{?}{2}$ **11.** $\frac{6}{12} = \frac{?}{2}$ **12.** $\frac{7}{14} = \frac{?}{2}$

13. $\frac{4}{16} = \frac{?}{4}$ **14.** $\frac{6}{16} = \frac{?}{8}$ **15.** $\frac{10}{16} = \frac{?}{8}$ **16.** $\frac{12}{16} = \frac{?}{4}$

PRACTICE SET 7
Find an equivalent fraction for each one shown with the given denominator.

1. $\frac{1}{2}$, 10   **2.** $\frac{5}{8}$, 24   **3.** $\frac{3}{8}$, 16   **4.** $\frac{6}{7}$, 14

5. $\frac{9}{10}$, 30   **6.** $\frac{7}{8}$, 16   **7.** $\frac{15}{16}$, 32   **8.** $\frac{5}{4}$, 16

Simplifying Fractions

$\frac{1}{2}, \frac{2}{4}, \frac{3}{6}, \frac{4}{8}$, and $\frac{6}{12}$ are equivalent fractions.

$\frac{1}{2}$ is in simplest form.

EXAMPLE 1   Write $\frac{14}{20}$ in simplest form.

SOLUTION   2 divides 14 and 20.

Find the largest number that divides the numerator and denominator.

$$\frac{14 \div 2}{20 \div 2} = \frac{7}{10}$$

So, $\frac{14}{20} = \frac{7}{10}$ in simplest form.

EXAMPLE 2   Simplify $\frac{24}{32}$.

SOLUTION

To simplify means to write in simplest form. 8 is the largest number that divides the numerator and denominator.

2 divides 24 and 32.
4 divides 24 and 32.
8 divides 24 and 32.

$$\frac{24 \div 8}{32 \div 8} = \frac{3}{4}$$

So, $\frac{24}{32} = \frac{3}{4}$ in simplest form.

EXAMPLE 3   Simplify $\frac{12}{6}$.

SOLUTION

The largest number that divides 12 and 6 is 6.

$$\frac{12 \div 6}{6 \div 6} = \frac{2}{1}, \text{ or } 2$$

So, $\frac{12}{6} = 2$ in simplest form.

- -

Simplify each fraction.

1. $\frac{6}{8}$ **2.** $\frac{3}{12}$ **3.** $\frac{6}{27}$

PRACTICE SET 8
Simplify.

1. $\frac{8}{10}$ **2.** $\frac{16}{20}$ **3.** $\frac{9}{15}$ **4.** $\frac{10}{20}$ **5.** $\frac{12}{20}$ **6.** $\frac{8}{12}$

7. $\frac{9}{12}$ **8.** $\frac{6}{9}$ **9.** $\frac{10}{12}$ **10.** $\frac{5}{10}$ **11.** $\frac{12}{10}$ **12.** $\frac{12}{9}$

Comparing Fractions

EXAMPLE 1   Which is greater, $\frac{4}{9}$ or $\frac{7}{9}$?

The two fractions have the same denominator. So, compare numerators.

7 is greater than 4.

So, $\frac{7}{9}$ is greater than $\frac{4}{9}$.

EXAMPLE 2   Which is greater, $\frac{3}{4}$ or $\frac{5}{6}$?

Find equivalent fractions with the same denominator. Compare the numerators of fractions with the same denominator.

$\frac{3}{4} = \frac{18}{24}$ $\frac{5}{6} = \frac{20}{24}$

↑   ↑

Same denominator

20 is greater than 18.

So, $\frac{20}{24}$ is greater than $\frac{18}{24}$

and $\frac{5}{6}$ is greater than $\frac{3}{4}$.

- -

Which fraction in each pair is greater?

1. $\frac{1}{2}, \frac{7}{12}$ 2. $\frac{1}{4}, \frac{1}{3}$ 3. $\frac{5}{8}, \frac{3}{4}$ 4. $\frac{16}{5}, \frac{8}{3}$

PRACTICE SET 9
Which fraction in each pair is greater?

1. $\frac{1}{2}, \frac{2}{5}$ 2. $\frac{1}{2}, \frac{7}{12}$ 3. $\frac{17}{10}, \frac{8}{5}$ 4. $\frac{3}{4}, \frac{9}{12}$

5. $\frac{7}{5}, \frac{3}{2}$ 6. $\frac{19}{20}, \frac{9}{5}$ 7. $\frac{5}{7}, \frac{8}{4}$ 8. $\frac{2}{3}, \frac{6}{9}$

9. $\frac{7}{10}, \frac{67}{100}$ 10. $\frac{3}{10}, \frac{29}{100}$ 11. $\frac{4}{5}, \frac{79}{100}$ 12. $\frac{7}{12}, \frac{13}{24}$

Return to form B on page 196.

Test: Unit 9

How much of each figure is shaded?

1.

2.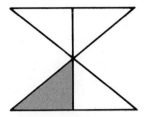

3.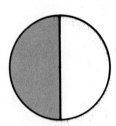

How much is shaded? The solid lines show the unit.

4.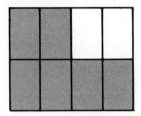

5.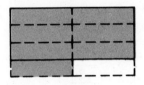

6.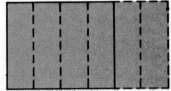

Give two names for the length of each object.

7.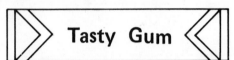
Tasty Gum

8.

Draw a diagram to show each sentence is true.

9. $\frac{2}{8} = \frac{1}{4}$

10. $\frac{2}{5} = \frac{6}{15}$

11. $\frac{3}{7} = \frac{9}{21}$

Make true sentences.

12. $\frac{2}{3} = \frac{?}{12}$

13. $\frac{10}{40} = \frac{?}{8}$

14. $\frac{4}{5} = \frac{?}{100}$

Simplify each fraction.

15. $\frac{9}{24}$

16. $\frac{8}{56}$

17. $\frac{5}{45}$

18. $\frac{28}{7}$

Which fraction in each pair is greater?

19. $\frac{1}{3}, \frac{2}{5}$

20. $\frac{2}{11}, \frac{3}{22}$

21. $\frac{7}{10}, \frac{3}{4}$

Can you complete these patterns? Try.

1.

$$1 \times 1 = 1$$
$$11 \times 11 = 121$$
$$111 \times 111 = 12{,}321$$
$$1{,}111 \times 1{,}111 = 1{,}234{,}321$$
$$11{,}111 \times 11{,}111 = 123{,}454{,}321$$
$$\underline{?} \times \underline{?} = 12{,}345{,}654{,}321$$
$$\underline{?} \times \underline{?} = 1{,}234{,}567{,}654{,}321$$
$$11{,}111{,}111 \times 11{,}111{,}111 = \underline{?}$$

2.

$$1 \times 8 + 1 = 9$$
$$12 \times 8 + 2 = 98$$
$$123 \times 8 + 3 = 987$$
$$1{,}234 \times 8 + 4 = 9{,}876$$
$$\underline{?} \times ? + ? = \underline{?}$$
$$\underline{?} \times ? + ? = \underline{?}$$
$$\underline{?} \times ? + ? = \underline{?}$$
$$\underline{?} \times ? + ? = \underline{?}$$
$$\underline{?} \times ? + ? = \underline{?}$$

Complete this magic square so that the sum of each row, column, and diagonal is 34.

1	12	7	14
8			11
10			5
15	6	9	

UNIT 10

Addition and Subtraction
of Fractions

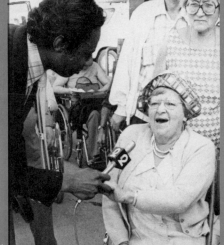

Add.

1. $\dfrac{5}{6}$
   $+\dfrac{1}{6}$

2. $\dfrac{7}{8}$
   $+\dfrac{5}{8}$

3. $\dfrac{7}{16}$
   $+\dfrac{3}{16}$

4. $\dfrac{5}{9}$
   $+\dfrac{4}{9}$

5. $\dfrac{21}{5}$
   $+\dfrac{6}{5}$

6. $\dfrac{11}{16}$
   $+\dfrac{5}{8}$

7. $\dfrac{4}{5}$
   $+\dfrac{1}{2}$

8. $\dfrac{7}{8}$
   $+\dfrac{5}{12}$

9. $\dfrac{12}{7}$
   $+\dfrac{9}{7}$

10. $\dfrac{3}{8}$
    $+\dfrac{3}{4}$

Subtract.

11. $\dfrac{3}{10}$
    $-\dfrac{7}{100}$

12. $\dfrac{11}{100}$
    $-\dfrac{9}{100}$

13. $3\dfrac{3}{4}$
    $-2\dfrac{5}{8}$

14. $13\dfrac{3}{5}$
    $-7\dfrac{7}{10}$

15. $29\dfrac{3}{100}$
    $-12\dfrac{7}{10}$

16. $\dfrac{12}{25}$
    $-\dfrac{7}{25}$

17. $\dfrac{11}{12}$
    $-\dfrac{3}{4}$

18. $2\dfrac{5}{8}$
    $-1\dfrac{1}{2}$

19. $13\dfrac{1}{4}$
    $-4\dfrac{7}{10}$

20. $19\dfrac{1}{10}$
    $-12\dfrac{4}{5}$

Did You Have

More than 10 right? Begin on page 223.	8, 9, or 10 right? Begin on page 215.	Less than 8 right? Begin on page 211.

DIAGNOSTIC TEST: ADDITION AND SUBTRACTION FORM B—30 MINUTES

Add.

1. $\dfrac{3}{8}$
   $+\dfrac{5}{8}$

2. $\dfrac{7}{3}$
   $+\dfrac{4}{3}$

3. $\dfrac{5}{16}$
   $+\dfrac{3}{16}$

4. $\dfrac{8}{7}$
   $+\dfrac{6}{7}$

5. $\dfrac{2}{3}$
   $+\dfrac{5}{6}$

6. $\dfrac{9}{100}$
   $+\dfrac{3}{10}$

7. $\dfrac{11}{100}$
   $+\dfrac{7}{100}$

8. $2\dfrac{3}{8}$
   $+1\dfrac{7}{12}$

9. $8\dfrac{5}{9}$
   $+9\dfrac{7}{9}$

10. $36\dfrac{33}{100}$
    $+18\dfrac{3}{10}$

Subtract.

11. $\dfrac{13}{25}$
    $-\dfrac{8}{25}$

12. $\dfrac{13}{24}$
    $-\dfrac{3}{8}$

13. $13\dfrac{7}{8}$
    $-4\dfrac{3}{4}$

14. $23\dfrac{1}{4}$
    $-5\dfrac{7}{10}$

15. $19\dfrac{3}{10}$
    $-12\dfrac{3}{5}$

More than 8 right? Begin on page 223. Less than 9 right? Consult your teacher.

Adding: Like Fractions

EXAMPLE 1   Draw a diagram to show that this sentence is true.

$$\frac{2}{5} + \frac{1}{5} = \frac{3}{5}$$

SOLUTION

$\frac{2}{5}$ of a unit plus

$\frac{1}{5}$ of the same unit is

$\frac{3}{5}$ of the unit.

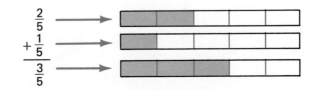

$$\frac{2}{5}$$

$$+\frac{1}{5}$$

$$\frac{3}{5}$$

- -

Draw a diagram to show that each sentence is true.

1. $\frac{3}{8} + \frac{1}{8} = \frac{4}{8}$ **2.** $\frac{4}{7} + \frac{2}{7} = \frac{6}{7}$

3. $\frac{1}{4} + \frac{3}{4} = \frac{4}{4}$, or 1   **4.** $\frac{3}{10} + \frac{1}{10} = \frac{4}{10}$

EXAMPLE 2   Add. $\frac{3}{7} + \frac{2}{7}$

SOLUTION

Since both fractions have
the same denominator, add
the numerators.

$$\frac{3}{7} \longleftarrow$$
$$+\frac{2}{7} \longleftarrow$$
$$\frac{5}{7} \longleftarrow$$

Keep the same

denominator.

So, $\frac{3}{7} + \frac{2}{7} = \frac{5}{7}$.

EXAMPLE 3   Add. $\frac{1}{9}$
$$+\frac{3}{9}$$

SOLUTION

Add the numerators.

Keep the denominator, 9.

$$\frac{1}{9}$$
$$+\frac{3}{9}$$
$$\frac{4}{9}$$

Add.

5. $\frac{4}{7}$
$+\frac{1}{7}$

6. $\frac{1}{8}$
$+\frac{5}{8}$

7. $\frac{3}{10}$
$+\frac{5}{10}$

8. $\frac{3}{100}$
$+\frac{8}{100}$

PRACTICE SET 1
Draw a diagram to show that each sentence is true.

1. $\frac{1}{3}+\frac{1}{3}=\frac{2}{3}$

2. $\frac{2}{7}+\frac{1}{7}=\frac{3}{7}$

3. $\frac{1}{8}+\frac{7}{8}=1$

PRACTICE SET 2
Add.

1. $\frac{1}{5}$
$+\frac{3}{5}$

2. $\frac{2}{5}$
$+\frac{2}{5}$

3. $\frac{1}{4}$
$+\frac{1}{4}$

4. $\frac{2}{3}$
$+\frac{1}{3}$

5. $\frac{2}{7}$
$+\frac{1}{7}$

6. $\frac{6}{7}$
$+\frac{1}{7}$

7. $\frac{3}{10}$
$+\frac{1}{10}$

8. $\frac{7}{10}$
$+\frac{1}{10}$

9. $\frac{3}{100}$
$+\frac{7}{100}$

PRACTICE SET 3
Add.

1. $\frac{7}{10}$
$+\frac{2}{10}$

2. $\frac{3}{10}$
$+\frac{4}{10}$

3. $\frac{5}{7}$
$+\frac{1}{7}$

4. $\frac{5}{6}$
$+\frac{7}{6}$

5. $\frac{3}{20}$
$+\frac{8}{20}$

6. $\frac{13}{20}$
$+\frac{4}{20}$

7. $\frac{5}{3}$
$+\frac{7}{3}$

8. $\frac{5}{8}$
$+\frac{0}{8}$

Simplifying Answers

EXAMPLE 1 How much milk is in both cups together?

SOLUTION

 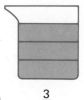  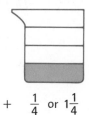

$1\frac{1}{4}$ is a mixed numeral.

$$\frac{2}{4} \quad + \quad \frac{3}{4} \quad = \quad \frac{4}{4} \quad + \quad \frac{1}{4} \text{ or } 1\frac{1}{4}$$

EXAMPLE 2 Add. $\quad \frac{7}{8} + \frac{5}{8}$

SOLUTION

You can think: $12 \div 8 = 1$, remainder 4.
So, $\frac{12}{8} = 1\frac{4}{8}$.

$$\begin{array}{r} \frac{7}{8} \\ +\frac{5}{8} \\ \hline \frac{12}{8} \end{array} = \frac{8}{8} + \frac{4}{8}$$

$\frac{8}{8} + \frac{4}{8} = 1\frac{4}{8}$, or $1\frac{1}{2}$

So, $\frac{7}{8} + \frac{5}{8} = 1\frac{1}{2}$.

- -

Add.

1. $\begin{array}{r} \frac{3}{8} \\ +\frac{5}{8} \\ \hline \end{array}$
2. $\begin{array}{r} \frac{5}{7} \\ +\frac{3}{7} \\ \hline \end{array}$
3. $\begin{array}{r} \frac{4}{5} \\ +\frac{3}{5} \\ \hline \end{array}$
4. $\begin{array}{r} \frac{3}{4} \\ +\frac{7}{4} \\ \hline \end{array}$
5. $\begin{array}{r} \frac{11}{8} \\ \frac{3}{8} \\ +\frac{5}{8} \\ \hline \end{array}$

EXAMPLE 3 Add. $\quad 2\frac{7}{8} + 3\frac{5}{8}$

SOLUTION

Since $\frac{12}{8}$ is $1\frac{1}{2}$,

$5 + 1\frac{1}{2} = 6\frac{1}{2}$.

$$\begin{array}{r} 2\frac{7}{8} \\ +3\frac{5}{8} \\ \hline 5\frac{12}{8} \end{array} \text{, or } 6\frac{1}{2}$$

Add.

6. $2\frac{3}{8}$ **7.** $4\frac{3}{5}$ **8.** $5\frac{7}{10}$ **9.** $8\frac{11}{12}$

   $+3\frac{5}{8}$ $+6\frac{3}{5}$ $+4\frac{9}{10}$ $+5\frac{5}{12}$

PRACTICE SET 4
Make true sentences.

1. $\frac{13}{8} = 1\frac{?}{8}$ **2.** $\frac{7}{4} = 1\frac{?}{4}$ **3.** $\frac{17}{4} = \underline{}\frac{1}{4}$

4. $\frac{24}{5} = \underline{}\frac{4}{5}$ **5.** $\frac{19}{16} = 1\frac{?}{16}$ **6.** $\frac{19}{12} = 1\frac{?}{12}$

7. $\frac{43}{10} = \underline{}\frac{3}{10}$ **8.** $\frac{29}{24} = \underline{}\frac{5}{24}$ **9.** $\frac{11}{3} = \underline{}\frac{2}{3}$

10. $\frac{13}{4} = \underline{}\frac{1}{4}$ **11.** $\frac{36}{5} = \underline{}\frac{1}{5}$ **12.** $\frac{28}{5} = \underline{}\frac{3}{5}$

13. $3\frac{4}{3} = \underline{}\frac{1}{3}$ **14.** $4\frac{15}{8} = \underline{}\frac{7}{8}$ **15.** $5\frac{5}{4} = \underline{}\frac{1}{4}$

16. $6\frac{7}{5} = \underline{}\frac{?}{5}$ **17.** $7\frac{22}{10} = \underline{}\frac{?}{10}$ **18.** $9\frac{11}{8} = \underline{}\frac{?}{8}$

PRACTICE SET 5
Simplify.

1. $\frac{9}{4}$ **2.** $\frac{38}{5}$ **3.** $\frac{29}{14}$ **4.** $\frac{18}{8}$ **5.** $\frac{19}{9}$

6. $\frac{45}{7}$ **7.** $\frac{45}{6}$ **8.** $\frac{3}{9}$ **9.** $\frac{18}{36}$ **10.** $\frac{21}{18}$

11. $\frac{35}{16}$ **12.** $\frac{28}{5}$ **13.** $\frac{19}{4}$ **14.** $\frac{28}{12}$ **15.** $\frac{12}{9}$

16. $2\frac{28}{16}$ **17.** $8\frac{9}{5}$ **18.** $6\frac{29}{4}$ **19.** $5\frac{18}{12}$ **20.** $9\frac{19}{12}$

PRACTICE SET 6
Add.

1. $\frac{5}{7}$ **2.** $\frac{6}{5}$ **3.** $\frac{7}{5}$ **4.** $\frac{4}{10}$ **5.** $\frac{8}{9}$ **6.** $\frac{11}{20}$

  $+\frac{4}{7}$ $+\frac{3}{5}$ $+\frac{4}{5}$ $+\frac{11}{10}$ $+\frac{4}{9}$ $+\frac{13}{20}$

7. $\frac{77}{100}$ **8.** $\frac{53}{100}$ **9.** $\frac{124}{100}$ **10.** $\frac{5}{4}$ **11.** $\frac{2}{3}$ **12.** $\frac{856}{1,000}$

  $+\frac{31}{100}$ $+\frac{54}{100}$ $+\frac{36}{100}$ $+\frac{9}{4}$ $+\frac{5}{3}$ $+\frac{193}{1,000}$

Least Common Denominator

OBJECTIVE To write equivalent fractions with the least common denominator, given two or three fractions

Like fractions have a common denominator.

$$\underbrace{\frac{3}{8}, \frac{5}{8}, \frac{21}{8}}_{}$$ $$\underbrace{\frac{3}{8}, \frac{3}{4}, \frac{23}{6}}_{}$$

Like fractions   Unlike fractions

EXAMPLE 1 Find the least common denominator, LCD, for $\frac{3}{4}$ and $\frac{2}{3}$.

1. Check to see if the larger denominator, 4, is the LCD.
2. If not, multiply the larger denominator, 4, by 2, 3, 4, etc.

4 is not divisible by 3, so 4 is not the LCD.

$4 \times 2 = 8$ 8 is not divisible by 3.
$4 \times 3 = 12$ 12 is divisible by 3.

So, the LCD is 12.

- -

Find the LCD for each pair.

1. $\frac{1}{4}, \frac{2}{5}$ **2.** $\frac{5}{6}, \frac{1}{3}$ **3.** $\frac{1}{8}, \frac{1}{2}$

EXAMPLE 2 Write equivalent fractions with the LCD for $\frac{2}{3}$ and $\frac{2}{5}$.

Find the LCD.

5 is not divisible by 3.
$5 \times 2 = 10$ is not divisible by 3.
$5 \times 3 = 15$ is divisible by 3. 15 is the LCD.

Write equivalent fractions for $\frac{2}{3}$ and $\frac{2}{5}$ with a denominator of 15.

$\frac{2}{3} = \frac{?}{15} \longrightarrow \frac{2 \times 5}{3 \times 5} = \frac{10}{15}$

$\frac{2}{5} = \frac{?}{15} \longrightarrow \frac{2 \times 3}{5 \times 3} = \frac{6}{15}$

- -

Write equivalent fractions with the LCD for each pair.

4. $\frac{1}{6}, \frac{3}{4}$ **5.** $\frac{1}{8}, \frac{5}{6}$ **6.** $\frac{3}{8}, \frac{1}{4}$

EXAMPLE 3 Write equivalent fractions with the LCD for $\frac{3}{4}$, $\frac{1}{2}$, and $\frac{5}{8}$.

SOLUTION 8 is divisible by 2 and by 4.
So, 8 is the LCD.

$$\frac{3}{4} = \frac{?}{8} \longrightarrow \frac{3 \times 2}{4 \times 2} = \frac{6}{8}$$
$$\frac{1}{2} = \frac{?}{8} \longrightarrow \frac{1 \times 4}{2 \times 4} = \frac{4}{8}$$

So, $\frac{6}{8}$, $\frac{4}{8}$, and $\frac{5}{8}$ have the same denominator.

Write equivalent fractions with the LCD for each set of fractions.

7. $\frac{1}{2}, \frac{2}{3}, \frac{5}{6}$ **8.** $\frac{2}{3}, \frac{1}{4}, \frac{3}{8}$ **9.** $\frac{1}{5}, \frac{1}{10}, \frac{3}{4}$

PRACTICE SET 7
Write equivalent fractions with the LCD for each set of fractions.

1. $\frac{3}{8}, \frac{3}{4}$ **2.** $\frac{3}{4}, \frac{5}{8}$ **3.** $\frac{1}{2}, \frac{5}{8}$ **4.** $\frac{5}{16}, \frac{7}{8}$

5. $\frac{1}{2}, \frac{7}{10}$ **6.** $\frac{3}{4}, \frac{7}{20}$ **7.** $\frac{3}{4}, \frac{1}{2}$ **8.** $\frac{3}{4}, \frac{7}{8}$

9. $\frac{3}{5}, \frac{7}{10}$ **10.** $\frac{2}{5}, \frac{9}{20}$ **11.** $\frac{2}{3}, \frac{5}{6}$ **12.** $\frac{3}{4}, \frac{7}{20}, \frac{3}{10}$

13. $\frac{5}{6}, \frac{5}{18}$ **14.** $\frac{1}{6}, \frac{2}{9}$ **15.** $\frac{5}{4}, \frac{5}{6}$ **16.** $\frac{7}{8}, \frac{2}{3}, \frac{1}{4}$

17. $\frac{7}{10}, \frac{3}{100}$ **18.** $\frac{3}{10}, \frac{7}{100}$ **19.** $\frac{1}{2}, \frac{3}{20}$ **20.** $\frac{6}{5}, \frac{1}{2}, \frac{3}{10}$

21. $\frac{3}{5}, \frac{1}{2}, \frac{7}{10}$ **22.** $\frac{1}{3}, \frac{1}{4}, \frac{1}{12}$ **23.** $\frac{9}{10}, \frac{4}{5}, \frac{3}{2}$ **24.** $\frac{13}{10}, \frac{5}{4}, \frac{1}{5}$

25. $\frac{1}{3}, \frac{3}{8}$ **26.** $\frac{3}{10}, \frac{9}{20}$ **27.** $\frac{5}{16}, \frac{3}{4}$ **28.** $\frac{2}{3}, \frac{5}{9}$

29. $\frac{5}{12}, \frac{3}{4}$ **30.** $\frac{1}{2}, \frac{2}{7}$ **31.** $\frac{7}{12}, \frac{5}{8}$ **32.** $\frac{3}{100}, \frac{7}{1,000}$

33. $\frac{4}{5}, \frac{3}{2}, \frac{1}{10}$ **34.** $\frac{1}{4}, \frac{3}{8}, \frac{9}{10}$ **35.** $\frac{1}{7}, \frac{3}{14}, \frac{4}{21}$ **36.** $\frac{9}{100}, \frac{3}{10}, \frac{17}{1,000}$

Adding: Unlike Fractions

EXAMPLE 1   How much sugar is there in the two cups together?

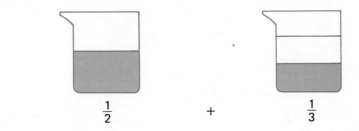

$$\frac{1}{2} \qquad + \qquad \frac{1}{3}$$

SOLUTION

The LCD is 2 × 3, or 6.
So, think of a cup marked
in $\frac{1}{6}$'s.

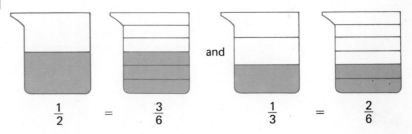

$$\frac{1}{2} \quad = \quad \frac{3}{6} \qquad \text{and} \qquad \frac{1}{3} \quad = \quad \frac{2}{6}$$

Now, add the like fractions,
$\frac{3}{6}$ and $\frac{2}{6}$. The two cups
have $\frac{5}{6}$ cup of sugar.

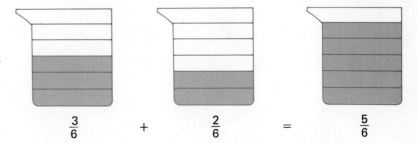

$$\frac{3}{6} \qquad + \qquad \frac{2}{6} \qquad = \qquad \frac{5}{6}$$

EXAMPLE 2   Add. $\frac{2}{5} + \frac{1}{2}$

SOLUTION   The LCD is 10.

1. Find the LCD.
2. Write equivalent
   fraction for each.
3. Add the like fractions.

$$\frac{2}{5} = \frac{2 \times 2}{5 \times 2} = \frac{4}{10}$$
$$+\frac{1}{2} = \frac{1 \times 5}{2 \times 5} = +\frac{5}{10}$$
$$\frac{9}{10}$$

So, $\frac{2}{5} + \frac{1}{2} = \frac{9}{10}$.

Add.

1. $\dfrac{1}{4}$
$+\dfrac{1}{2}$

2. $\dfrac{3}{5}$
$+\dfrac{3}{10}$

3. $\dfrac{2}{3}$
$+\dfrac{1}{6}$

4. $\dfrac{2}{3}$
$+\dfrac{1}{4}$

EXAMPLE 3 Add. $\dfrac{3}{10} + \dfrac{7}{100} + \dfrac{9}{1,000}$

SOLUTION The LCD is 1,000.

$1,000 \div 10 = 100$

$\dfrac{3}{10} \longrightarrow \dfrac{3 \times 100}{10 \times 100} = \dfrac{300}{1,000}$

$\dfrac{7}{100} \longrightarrow \dfrac{7 \times 10}{100 \times 10} = \dfrac{70}{1,000}$

The denominator of $\dfrac{9}{1,000}$ is the LCD.

$\dfrac{9}{1,000} \qquad = \dfrac{9}{1,000}$

$\qquad\qquad\qquad \dfrac{379}{1,000}$

So, $\dfrac{3}{10} + \dfrac{7}{100} + \dfrac{9}{1,000} = \dfrac{379}{1,000}$

Add.

5. $\dfrac{3}{10}$
$+\dfrac{11}{100}$

6. $\dfrac{9}{10}$
$+\dfrac{18}{100}$

7. $\dfrac{17}{100}$
$+\dfrac{81}{1,000}$

8. $\dfrac{7}{10}$
$\dfrac{13}{100}$
$+\dfrac{99}{1,000}$

EXAMPLE 4 Add. $2\dfrac{4}{5} + 3\dfrac{7}{10}$

SOLUTION The LCD is 10.

$\dfrac{15}{10} = 1\dfrac{5}{10}$
So, $5\dfrac{15}{10} = 6\dfrac{5}{10}$

$2\dfrac{4}{5}$
$+3\dfrac{7}{10}$

$\dfrac{4}{5} = \dfrac{4 \times 2}{5 \times 2} = \dfrac{8}{10}$

$2\dfrac{8}{10}$
$+3\dfrac{7}{10}$
$5\dfrac{15}{10} = 6\dfrac{5}{10}$, or $6\dfrac{1}{2}$

So, $2\dfrac{4}{5} + 3\dfrac{7}{10} = 6\dfrac{5}{10}$, or $6\dfrac{1}{2}$

Add.

9. $1\dfrac{3}{8}$
$+2\dfrac{3}{4}$

10. $3\dfrac{3}{4}$
$+2\dfrac{1}{2}$

11. $5\dfrac{7}{8}$
$+2\dfrac{1}{2}$

12. $4\dfrac{7}{10}$
$+5\dfrac{3}{10}$

PRACTICE SET 8

Add.

1. $\dfrac{1}{2}$ $+\dfrac{5}{6}$
2. $\dfrac{1}{2}$ $+\dfrac{2}{3}$
3. $\dfrac{3}{8}$ $+\dfrac{5}{6}$
4. $\dfrac{7}{20}$ $+\dfrac{3}{5}$
5. $\dfrac{3}{5}$ $+\dfrac{1}{2}$
6. $\dfrac{3}{5}$ $+\dfrac{1}{4}$
7. $\dfrac{5}{8}$ $+\dfrac{1}{6}$
8. $\dfrac{4}{4}$ $+\dfrac{1}{6}$

9. $1\dfrac{2}{5}$ $+5\dfrac{1}{2}$
10. $3\dfrac{3}{12}$ $+4\dfrac{1}{4}$
11. $6\dfrac{2}{3}$ $+7\dfrac{3}{5}$
12. $8\dfrac{3}{10}$ $+2\dfrac{3}{5}$
13. $3\dfrac{9}{16}$ $1\dfrac{5}{16}$ $+5\dfrac{3}{8}$
14. $4\dfrac{3}{8}$ $7\dfrac{2}{5}$ $+8\dfrac{1}{2}$
15. $2\dfrac{5}{12}$ $5\dfrac{7}{12}$ $+9\dfrac{3}{4}$
16. $2\dfrac{2}{3}$ $8\dfrac{1}{9}$ $+9\dfrac{5}{9}$

PRACTICE SET 9

Add.

1. $\dfrac{4}{100}$ $+\dfrac{9}{10}$
2. $\dfrac{6}{100}$ $+\dfrac{6}{10}$
3. $\dfrac{7}{100}$ $+\dfrac{6}{10}$
4. $\dfrac{7}{10}$ $+\dfrac{9}{100}$
5. $\dfrac{9}{10}$ $+\dfrac{11}{100}$
6. $\dfrac{18}{100}$ $+\dfrac{8}{10}$

7. $\dfrac{24}{100}$ $+\dfrac{4}{10}$
8. $\dfrac{25}{100}$ $+\dfrac{5}{10}$
9. $\dfrac{8}{100}$ $\dfrac{7}{10}$ $+\dfrac{8}{10}$
10. $\dfrac{8}{100}$ $\dfrac{8}{100}$ $+\dfrac{7}{10}$
11. $\dfrac{7}{100}$ $\dfrac{8}{100}$ $+\dfrac{8}{10}$
12. $\dfrac{5}{100}$ $\dfrac{17}{100}$ $+\dfrac{3}{10}$

13. $4\dfrac{8}{100}$ $+3\dfrac{3}{10}$
14. $2\dfrac{7}{100}$ $+5\dfrac{1}{10}$
15. $3\dfrac{4}{100}$ $+\dfrac{9}{10}$
16. $5\dfrac{6}{100}$ $+5\dfrac{6}{10}$
17. $4\dfrac{7}{100}$ $+3\dfrac{6}{10}$
18. $5\dfrac{9}{100}$ $+3\dfrac{7}{10}$

Solve these problems.

19. Ms. Chan bought drapery material at a sale. She bought $2\dfrac{1}{4}$ meters of white, $2\dfrac{4}{10}$ meters of red, and $4\dfrac{1}{2}$ meters of pink material. How much did she buy in all?

20. Mr. Polk wants to put a fence around his garden. The sides of Mr. Polk's garden measure $1\dfrac{4}{10}$ meters, $2\dfrac{1}{10}$ meters, $\dfrac{3}{4}$ meter, and $1\dfrac{1}{2}$ meters. How much fencing does he need?

21. Desirée worked $7\dfrac{1}{2}$ hours on Monday, $6\dfrac{3}{4}$ hours on Tuesday, $8\dfrac{2}{3}$ hours on Wednesday, $8\dfrac{1}{2}$ hours on Thursday, and $5\dfrac{2}{3}$ hours on Friday. How many hours did she work in all?

22. Fred sold $3\dfrac{3}{4}$ kg of apples, $5\dfrac{3}{10}$ kg of pears, $8\dfrac{9}{10}$ kg of bananas, $4\dfrac{1}{2}$ kg of grapes, and $7\dfrac{3}{4}$ kg of peaches. How much fruit did he sell?

Subtracting

EXAMPLE 1 Subtract. $\frac{5}{8} - \frac{3}{8}$

SOLUTION

Subtract the numerators.

$$\begin{array}{r} \frac{5}{8} \\ -\frac{3}{8} \\ \hline \frac{2}{8} \end{array}$$ ← Keep the same denominator.

$\frac{2 \div 2}{8 \div 2} = \frac{1}{4}$

So, $\frac{5}{8} - \frac{3}{8} = \frac{2}{8}$, or $\frac{1}{4}$

- -

Subtract.

1. $\begin{array}{r} \frac{5}{6} \\ -\frac{1}{6} \\ \hline \end{array}$
2. $\begin{array}{r} \frac{4}{5} \\ -\frac{3}{5} \\ \hline \end{array}$
3. $\begin{array}{r} \frac{7}{10} \\ -\frac{3}{10} \\ \hline \end{array}$
4. $\begin{array}{r} \frac{13}{10} \\ -\frac{7}{10} \\ \hline \end{array}$
5. $\begin{array}{r} \frac{9}{4} \\ -\frac{7}{4} \\ \hline \end{array}$

EXAMPLE 2 Subtract. $\frac{4}{5} - \frac{3}{10}$

SOLUTION The LCD is 10.

To subtract unlike fractions, find the LCD and write equivalent fractions. Then subtract.

$$\begin{array}{r} \frac{4}{5} \\ -\frac{3}{10} \end{array} \longrightarrow \begin{array}{r} \frac{4 \times 2}{5 \times 2} = \frac{8}{10} \\ -\frac{3}{10} \\ \hline \frac{5}{10}, \text{ or } \frac{1}{2} \end{array}$$

So, $\frac{4}{5} - \frac{3}{10} = \frac{5}{10}$, or $\frac{1}{2}$

- -

Subtract.

6. $\begin{array}{r} \frac{3}{5} \\ -\frac{3}{10} \\ \hline \end{array}$
7. $\begin{array}{r} \frac{3}{4} \\ -\frac{5}{8} \\ \hline \end{array}$
8. $\begin{array}{r} \frac{7}{10} \\ -\frac{3}{5} \\ \hline \end{array}$
9. $\begin{array}{r} \frac{3}{2} \\ -\frac{3}{4} \\ \hline \end{array}$
10. $\begin{array}{r} 20\frac{7}{8} \\ -12\frac{1}{4} \\ \hline \end{array}$

EXAMPLE 3 How much milk will be left after $1\frac{3}{4}$ cups are used?

You must subtract,

$$4$$
$$-1\frac{3}{4}$$

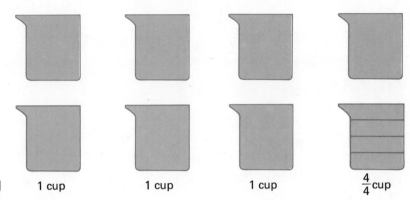

| 1 cup | 1 cup | 1 cup | $\frac{4}{4}$ cup |

SOLUTION

Think of one cup as $\frac{4}{4}$ cup.

$$4 \longrightarrow 3\frac{4}{4}$$
$$-1\frac{3}{4} \longrightarrow -1\frac{3}{4}$$
$$2\frac{1}{4}$$ So, $2\frac{1}{4}$ cups will be left.

- -

Subtract.

11. 3
  $-1\frac{1}{2}$

12. 5
  $-2\frac{1}{4}$

13. 8
  $-3\frac{5}{6}$

14. 15
  $-\;5\frac{7}{8}$

15. 1
  $-\;\frac{3}{5}$

EXAMPLE 4 How much milk will be left after $1\frac{3}{4}$ cups are used?

You must subtract.

$$3\frac{1}{4}$$
$$-1\frac{3}{4}$$

| 1 cup | 1 cup | $\frac{4}{4}$ cup | $\frac{1}{4}$ cup |

SOLUTION

Think of one cup as $\frac{4}{4}$ cup.

$$3\frac{1}{4} \longrightarrow 2\frac{5}{4}$$
$$-1\frac{3}{4} \longrightarrow -1\frac{3}{4}$$
$$1\frac{2}{4}, \text{ or } 1\frac{1}{2}$$ So, $1\frac{1}{2}$ cups will be left.

Subtract.

16. $5\frac{1}{4}$
$-2\frac{3}{4}$

17. $8\frac{1}{5}$
$-3\frac{2}{5}$

18. $10\frac{1}{3}$
$-\ 6\frac{2}{3}$

19. $15\frac{3}{8}$
$-12\frac{1}{2}$

PRACTICE SET 10
Subtract.

1. 16
$-\ 9\frac{3}{5}$

2. 20
$-11\frac{6}{7}$

3. 17
$-12\frac{1}{3}$

4. 6
$-1\frac{2}{5}$

5. 5
$-\ \frac{7}{8}$

6. 11
$-\ 8\frac{1}{4}$

7. 9
$-2\frac{3}{8}$

8. 25
$-17\frac{2}{3}$

9. 32
$-17\frac{5}{8}$

10. 18
$-11\frac{11}{16}$

11. 17
$-\ 8\frac{3}{10}$

12. 19
$-12\frac{2}{7}$

13. 18
$-13\frac{2}{3}$

14. 7
$-2\frac{3}{5}$

15. 4
$-3\frac{5}{6}$

16. 8
$-1\frac{7}{10}$

17. 12
$-\ 3\frac{5}{10}$

18. 9
$-2\frac{8}{100}$

19. 7
$-3\frac{25}{100}$

20. 20
$-\ 5\frac{8}{10}$

PRACTICE SET 11
Subtract.

1. $16\frac{1}{5}$
$-\ 9\frac{3}{5}$

2. $20\frac{2}{7}$
$-11\frac{6}{7}$

3. $20\frac{2}{5}$
$-11\frac{4}{5}$

4. $6\frac{1}{5}$
$-1\frac{2}{5}$

5. $5\frac{3}{8}$
$-4\frac{7}{8}$

6. $11\frac{1}{4}$
$-\ 6\frac{3}{4}$

7. $9\frac{1}{8}$
$-2\frac{3}{8}$

8. $25\frac{1}{3}$
$-17\frac{2}{3}$

9. $32\frac{3}{8}$
$-17\frac{6}{8}$

10. $18\frac{3}{16}$
$-11\frac{11}{16}$

11. $17\frac{1}{10}$
$-\ 8\frac{3}{10}$

12. $19\frac{1}{7}$
$-12\frac{2}{7}$

13. $18\frac{1}{3}$
$-13\frac{2}{3}$

14. $7\frac{2}{5}$
$-2\frac{3}{5}$

15. $4\frac{1}{6}$
$-3\frac{5}{6}$

Solve these problems.

16. Rose had $12\frac{3}{4}$ meters of material. She used $4\frac{2}{3}$ meters to make a dress. How much did she have left?

17. Ricky cut $7\frac{3}{4}$ meters of carpeting from a roll containing $15\frac{1}{2}$ meters of carpeting. How much was left on the roll?

Return to Form B on page 210.

Estimating

EXAMPLE 1 Estimate. $5\frac{1}{4} + 1\frac{3}{8} + 2\frac{1}{2} + 7\frac{3}{4}$

SOLUTION

Add the whole numbers 7, 2, 1, and 5, to get 15. Estimate the sum of the fractions to get 2.

$$5\frac{1}{4}$$
$$1\frac{3}{8} \qquad \frac{3}{4} + \frac{1}{4} = 1$$
$$2\frac{1}{2} \qquad \frac{3}{8} + \frac{1}{2} \text{ is about 1.}$$
$$7\frac{3}{4}$$
$$\overline{15}$$

So, the answer is about 15 and 2, or 17.

EXAMPLE 2 Estimate. $9\frac{1}{2} + 4\frac{1}{20} + 8\frac{3}{100}$

SOLUTION

$$9\frac{1}{2}$$
$$4\frac{1}{20} \qquad \frac{1}{20} \text{ and } \frac{3}{100} \text{ are very small.}$$
$$+8\frac{3}{100} \qquad \text{So, the sum of } \frac{1}{2}, \frac{1}{20}, \text{ and } \frac{3}{100} \text{ is about } \frac{1}{2}.$$
$$\overline{21}$$

The answer is about $21\frac{1}{2}$.

- -

Estimate.

1. $5\frac{6}{7}$
   $8\frac{1}{10}$
   $+9\frac{1}{20}$

2. $\frac{7}{8}$
   $\frac{1}{20}$
   $+\frac{7}{100}$

3. $21\frac{7}{8}$
   $39\frac{1}{20}$
   $+10\frac{7}{100}$

4. $8\frac{93}{100}$
   $9\frac{3}{100}$
   $+1\frac{1}{20}$

EXAMPLE 3 Estimate. $18\frac{1}{5} - 5\frac{3}{10}$

SOLUTION

Estimate the difference between the fractions as 0. Subtract the whole numbers.

$$18\frac{1}{5} \qquad \frac{3}{10} \text{ is close in value to } \frac{1}{5}.$$
$$-5\frac{3}{10} \qquad \text{So, } 18\frac{1}{5} - 5\frac{3}{10} \text{ is about 13.}$$
$$\overline{13}$$

Estimate.

5. $25\frac{2}{5}$ **6.** $45\frac{5}{8}$ **7.** $26\frac{9}{10}$ **8.** $85\frac{1}{8}$

    $-11\frac{3}{10}$ $-13\frac{1}{2}$ $-14\frac{4}{5}$ $-40\frac{1}{4}$

EXERCISES
Estimate.

1. $14\frac{3}{4}$ **2.** $1\frac{1}{2}$ **3.** $5\frac{3}{4}$ **4.** $10\frac{15}{16}$ **5.** $9\frac{1}{16}$

  $8\frac{15}{16}$ $1\frac{1}{2}$ $4\frac{1}{8}$ $8\frac{15}{16}$ $6\frac{1}{16}$

 $+1\frac{1}{4}$ $+10\frac{9}{16}$ $+\frac{5}{16}$ $+\frac{15}{16}$ $+\frac{1}{16}$

6. $9\frac{7}{16}$ **7.** $4\frac{1}{2}$ **8.** $12\frac{1}{2}$ **9.** $6\frac{1}{2}$ **10.** $14\frac{1}{2}$

  $6\frac{7}{16}$ $3\frac{3}{4}$ $2\frac{5}{8}$ $10\frac{1}{5}$ $22\frac{5}{8}$

 $+\frac{3}{16}$ $+2\frac{3}{4}$ $+2\frac{5}{16}$ $2\frac{4}{5}$ $\frac{1}{16}$

                                                 $+\frac{1}{2}$ $+\frac{1}{8}$

11. $21\frac{3}{4}$ **12.** $3\frac{5}{6}$ **13.** $3\frac{1}{2}$ **14.** $10\frac{2}{5}$ **15.** $9\frac{7}{16}$

   $3\frac{3}{8}$ $2\frac{1}{3}$ $20\frac{1}{4}$ $10\frac{3}{10}$ $1\frac{5}{16}$

 $12\frac{3}{8}$ $2\frac{1}{3}$ $1\frac{1}{2}$ $10\frac{1}{2}$ $8\frac{5}{8}$

 $+\ 5$ $+2\frac{1}{3}$ $+4\frac{7}{8}$ $+10\frac{3}{5}$ $+2\frac{3}{8}$

16. $\frac{3}{4}$ **17.** $12\frac{1}{2}$ **18.** $\frac{1}{2}$ **19.** $17\frac{1}{2}$ **20.** $2\frac{1}{4}$

 $6\frac{5}{16}$ $2\frac{3}{8}$ $5\frac{5}{8}$ $10\frac{3}{5}$ $1\frac{9}{16}$

 $+\frac{10}{16}$ $+2\frac{3}{16}$ $+\frac{7}{8}$ $+2\frac{3}{5}$ $+2\frac{7}{16}$

21. $\frac{3}{4}$ **22.** $2\frac{7}{16}$ **23.** $10\frac{2}{5}$ **24.** $3\frac{1}{2}$ **25.** $\frac{5}{6}$

 $5\frac{7}{8}$ $1\frac{5}{16}$ $12\frac{3}{10}$ $10\frac{1}{4}$ $1\frac{1}{3}$

 $1\frac{1}{2}$ $1\frac{5}{8}$ $\frac{1}{2}$ $2\frac{1}{2}$ $5\frac{1}{3}$

 $+1\frac{1}{8}$ $+2\frac{3}{8}$ $+2\frac{3}{5}$ $+5\frac{7}{8}$ $+4\frac{2}{3}$

Estimate.

26. $17\frac{1}{10}$
    $-\ 7\frac{3}{10}$

27. $19\frac{1}{7}$
    $-12\frac{2}{7}$

28. $38\frac{1}{3}$
    $-\ 2\frac{2}{3}$

29. 20
    $-\ 1\frac{3}{4}$

30. 100
    $-\ 12\frac{7}{8}$

31. 10
    $-\ \frac{15}{16}$

32. 36
    $-16\frac{5}{8}$

33. $27\frac{1}{10}$
    $-\ 8\frac{1}{5}$

34. $39\frac{1}{7}$
    $-\ 2\frac{3}{14}$

35. $24\frac{1}{12}$
    $-\ 3\frac{5}{6}$

36. $22\frac{3}{8}$
    $-\ 7\frac{1}{4}$

37. $25\frac{1}{4}$
    $-19\frac{3}{8}$

38. $33\frac{3}{8}$
    $-16\frac{7}{12}$

39. $19\frac{7}{8}$
    $-11\frac{3}{4}$

40. 36
    $-10\frac{1}{2}$

41. $20\frac{6}{7}$
    $-10\frac{2}{7}$

42. $20\frac{1}{3}$
    $-12\frac{2}{3}$

43. $6\frac{1}{5}$
    $-1\frac{2}{5}$

44. $25\frac{3}{8}$
    $-\ \frac{7}{8}$

45. $21\frac{1}{4}$
    $-\ 6\frac{3}{4}$

46. $29\frac{1}{8}$
    $-\ 2\frac{3}{8}$

47. $37\frac{3}{8}$
    $-17\frac{5}{8}$

48. $18\frac{5}{16}$
    $-11\frac{11}{16}$

49. $25\frac{1}{8}$
    $-24\frac{7}{8}$

50. $21\frac{1}{4}$
    $-20\frac{1}{2}$

51. $26\frac{1}{5}$
    $-11\frac{1}{10}$

52. $20\frac{2}{7}$
    $-11\frac{1}{14}$

53. $17\frac{1}{6}$
    $-12\frac{1}{3}$

54. $16\frac{1}{5}$
    $-\ 1\frac{3}{10}$

55. $2\frac{1}{100}$
    $-\ \frac{98}{100}$

Fun Corner

How much money did Tom have before he bought the radio?

I SPENT $\frac{1}{3}$ OF MY MONEY FOR THE RADIO AND I LOST $\frac{2}{3}$ OF WHAT WAS LEFT. I NOW HAVE $12.

Test: Unit 10

Add.

1. $2\frac{2}{8}$
   $7\frac{}{8}$
   $+1\frac{3}{4}$

2. $7\frac{2}{3}$
   $2\frac{1}{3}$
   $+8\frac{1}{4}$

3. $8\frac{2}{5}$
   $4\frac{1}{5}$
   $+3\frac{3}{10}$

4. $4\frac{3}{10}$
   $2\frac{1}{5}$
   $+6\frac{1}{2}$

5. $7\frac{3}{10}$
   $+5\frac{7}{100}$

6. $8\frac{2}{3}$
   $+7\frac{1}{6}$

7. $12\frac{1}{5}$
   $+\ 3\frac{1}{2}$

8. $15\frac{4}{5}$
   $+12\frac{1}{10}$

9. $7\frac{3}{5}$
   $6\frac{1}{3}$
   $+4\frac{4}{5}$

10. $7\frac{3}{10}$
    $8\frac{1}{4}$
    $+5\frac{3}{5}$

Subtract.

11. $\frac{5}{8}$
    $-\frac{3}{8}$

12. $\frac{7}{10}$
    $-\frac{2}{5}$

13. $\frac{15}{16}$
    $-\frac{3}{8}$

14. $8\frac{1}{2}$
    $-2\frac{5}{8}$

15. 7
    $-2\frac{3}{4}$

16. $3\frac{2}{3}$
    $-1\frac{1}{3}$

17. $50\frac{1}{2}$
    $-12\frac{7}{10}$

18. $8\frac{19}{100}$
    $-5\frac{2}{10}$

19. 5
    $-3\frac{2}{3}$

20. $8\frac{2}{3}$
    $-4\frac{1}{4}$

Estimate.

21. $4\frac{1}{2}$
    $2\frac{2}{3}$
    $+3\frac{1}{4}$

22. $\frac{5}{8}$
    $\frac{1}{2}$
    $+\frac{3}{8}$

23. $3\frac{3}{4}$
    $2\frac{1}{2}$
    $+4\frac{3}{4}$

24. $15\frac{1}{4}$
    $-\ 8\frac{1}{2}$

25. 20
    $-10\frac{1}{2}$

Solve these problems.

26. Bart bought $2\frac{3}{4}$ kg of ham, $3\frac{1}{2}$ kg of lamb, and $5\frac{1}{5}$ kg of veal. How much meat did he buy?

27. Yoko's gasoline tank holds 80 L of gas. She used $49\frac{1}{4}$ L on a trip. How much gas did she have left?

UNIT 11

Multiplication and Division of Fractions

DIAGNOSTIC TEST: MULTIPLICATION AND DIVISION FORM A—25 MINUTES

Multiply.

1. $\frac{3}{8} \times \frac{1}{4}$

2. $\frac{3}{5} \times \frac{10}{20}$

3. $4\frac{3}{4} \times 4$

4. $9 \times 6\frac{5}{9}$

5. $\frac{3}{4} \times 22$

6. $2\frac{2}{3} \times \frac{3}{4}$

7. $\frac{1}{2} \times \frac{4}{5}$

8. $5\frac{1}{3} \times 1\frac{1}{2}$

Divide.

9. $\frac{3}{8} \div \frac{1}{4}$

10. $\frac{3}{5} \div \frac{9}{10}$

11. $\frac{7}{8} \div \frac{1}{16}$

12. $8 \div 2\frac{2}{3}$

13. $5\frac{1}{2} \div \frac{3}{4}$

14. $3\frac{5}{10} \div 7$

15. $8\frac{1}{6} \div 7$

16. $\frac{49}{50} \div \frac{7}{10}$

Did You Have

More than 14 right? Begin on page 239.	12, 13, or 14 right? Begin on page 233.	Less than 12 right? Begin on page 229.

DIAGNOSTIC TEST: MULTIPLICATION AND DIVISION FORM B—25 MINUTES

Multiply.

1. $\frac{5}{8} \times \frac{2}{4}$

2. $\frac{2}{5} \times \frac{12}{20}$

3. $2\frac{3}{4} \times 8$

4. $3 \times 4\frac{2}{9}$

5. $14 \times \frac{3}{4}$

6. $3\frac{2}{3} \times \frac{1}{4}$

7. $\frac{3}{5} \times \frac{1}{2}$

8. $4\frac{2}{3} \times 1\frac{5}{6}$

Divide.

9. $\frac{5}{8} \div \frac{3}{4}$

10. $\frac{2}{5} \div \frac{7}{10}$

11. $\frac{5}{8} \div \frac{3}{16}$

12. $12 \div 1\frac{2}{3}$

13. $4\frac{1}{2} \div \frac{3}{4}$

14. $3\frac{9}{10} \div 13$

15. $5\frac{5}{6} \div 7$

16. $\frac{24}{25} \div \frac{3}{10}$

More than 14 right? Begin on page 239. Less than 15 right? Consult your teacher.

Multiplying by a Whole Number

OBJECTIVE   To find the product of a whole number and a fraction

EXAMPLE 1   Multiply. $5 \times \frac{3}{4}$

SOLUTION

Think of a region diagram.
If $\frac{3}{4}$ of each of 5 units is
shaded, then $5 \times \frac{3}{4}$, or
$\frac{15}{4}$ is shaded.

| $\frac{1}{4}$ | $\frac{1}{4}$ | $\frac{1}{4}$ | | $\frac{3}{4}$ |

| $\frac{1}{4}$ | $\frac{1}{4}$ | $\frac{1}{4}$ | | $\frac{3}{4}$ |

| $\frac{1}{4}$ | $\frac{1}{4}$ | $\frac{1}{4}$ | | $\frac{3}{4}$ |

| $\frac{1}{4}$ | $\frac{1}{4}$ | $\frac{1}{4}$ | | $\frac{3}{4}$ |

| $\frac{1}{4}$ | $\frac{1}{4}$ | $\frac{1}{4}$ | | $+\frac{3}{4}$ |

$$\frac{15}{4}$$

So, $5 \times \frac{3}{4} = \frac{15}{4}$, or $3\frac{3}{4}$.

- -

Multiply. Draw a region diagram.

1. $3 \times \frac{3}{4}$ **2.** $4 \times \frac{3}{8}$ **3.** $2 \times \frac{7}{8}$

EXAMPLE 2   Multiply. $4 \times \frac{5}{8}$

SOLUTION

Think of a number line
marked in $\frac{1}{8}$'s.
$\frac{5}{8} = 5 \times \frac{1}{8}$
$4 \times \frac{5}{8}$ is $4 \times 5 \times \frac{1}{8}$, or
$20 \times \frac{1}{8}$

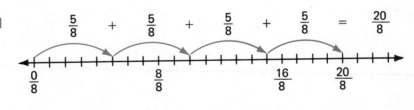

So, $4 \times \frac{5}{8} = \frac{20}{8}$, or $2\frac{1}{2}$.

Multiply. Use a number line.

4. $4 \times \frac{3}{5}$ **5.** $6 \times \frac{2}{3}$ **6.** $4 \times \frac{5}{6}$

EXAMPLE 3   Multiply. $\frac{3}{16} \times 5$

SOLUTION
Multiply the whole number
by the numerator.

$$\frac{3}{16} \times 5 = \frac{3 \times 5}{16}$$

Keep the same denominator.

So, $\frac{3}{16} \times 5 = \frac{15}{16}$.

Multiply.

7. $\frac{1}{10} \times 3$ **8.** $3 \times \frac{3}{8}$ **9.** $\frac{3}{15} \times 2$

PRACTICE SET 1
Multiply. Draw a region diagram.

1. $2 \times \frac{3}{4}$ **2.** $\frac{3}{5} \times 10$ **3.** $\frac{3}{4} \times 6$ **4.** $\frac{2}{3} \times 8$

5. $\frac{1}{2} \times 11$ **6.** $16 \times \frac{1}{8}$ **7.** $\frac{2}{5} \times 13$ **8.** $\frac{3}{5} \times 16$

PRACTICE SET 2
Multiply. Use a number line.

1. $3 \times \frac{3}{4}$ **2.** $\frac{3}{5} \times 8$ **3.** $\frac{3}{10} \times 4$ **4.** $\frac{3}{8} \times 10$

5. $\frac{2}{5} \times 5$ **6.** $\frac{2}{3} \times 9$ **7.** $\frac{1}{7} \times 8$ **8.** $\frac{4}{5} \times 8$

PRACTICE SET 3
Multiply.

1. $4 \times \frac{3}{4}$ **2.** $6 \times \frac{3}{5}$ **3.** $\frac{3}{10} \times 7$ **4.** $\frac{3}{8} \times 20$

5. $\frac{1}{6} \times 5$ **6.** $\frac{5}{6} \times 6$ **7.** $\frac{1}{2} \times 9$ **8.** $\frac{3}{4} \times 8$

9. $\frac{3}{7} \times 21$ **10.** $\frac{5}{13} \times 9$ **11.** $17 \times \frac{3}{9}$ **12.** $19 \times \frac{2}{3}$

13. $17 \times \frac{3}{4}$ **14.** $\frac{2}{12} \times 11$ **15.** $\frac{5}{12} \times 14$ **16.** $\frac{1}{15} \times 12$

17. $\frac{5}{16} \times 13$ **18.** $\frac{7}{12} \times 14$ **19.** $\frac{3}{16} \times 17$ **20.** $\frac{3}{10} \times 20$

Multiplying Fractions

EXAMPLE Multiply. $\frac{2}{3} \times \frac{3}{4}$

SOLUTION Think: $\frac{2}{3}$ of $\frac{3}{4}$ of a unit

Draw a rectangle.

$\frac{2}{3} \times \frac{3}{4}$ means $\frac{2}{3}$ of $\frac{3}{4}$.

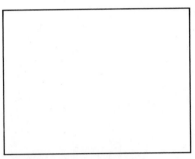

Shade $\frac{3}{4}$ of the unit.

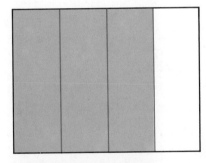

Mark $\frac{2}{3}$ of the unit.

$\frac{2}{3}$ of $\frac{3}{4}$ is $\frac{6}{12}$.

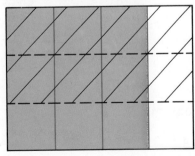

So, $\frac{2}{3} \times \frac{3}{4} = \frac{\overset{1}{2} \times \overset{1}{3}}{\underset{1}{3} \times \underset{2}{4}} = \frac{1}{2}$.

PRACTICE SET 4
Multiply. Draw a region diagram.

1. $\frac{3}{8} \times \frac{3}{4}$ 2. $\frac{5}{8} \times \frac{3}{4}$ 3. $\frac{7}{8} \times \frac{3}{4}$ 4. $\frac{1}{8} \times \frac{3}{4}$

5. $\frac{2}{4} \times \frac{3}{8}$ 6. $\frac{1}{4} \times \frac{3}{8}$ 7. $\frac{1}{4} \times \frac{7}{8}$ 8. $\frac{2}{4} \times \frac{7}{8}$

PRACTICE SET 5

Multiply.

1. $\frac{3}{10} \times \frac{8}{10}$ 2. $\frac{4}{10} \times \frac{7}{10}$ 3. $\frac{1}{10} \times \frac{6}{10}$ 4. $\frac{1}{10} \times \frac{7}{10}$

5. $\frac{7}{16} \times \frac{2}{5}$ 6. $\frac{2}{3} \times \frac{3}{4}$ 7. $\frac{2}{9} \times \frac{3}{5}$ 8. $\frac{1}{11} \times \frac{2}{7}$

9. $\frac{8}{13} \times \frac{2}{11}$ 10. $\frac{1}{4} \times \frac{1}{9}$ 11. $\frac{4}{9} \times \frac{5}{7}$ 12. $\frac{7}{8} \times \frac{5}{6}$

13. $\frac{3}{8} \times \frac{1}{4}$ 14. $\frac{1}{10} \times \frac{1}{10}$ 15. $\frac{8}{10} \times \frac{8}{10}$ 16. $\frac{9}{10} \times \frac{9}{10}$

17. $\frac{5}{10} \times \frac{5}{10}$ 18. $\frac{2}{10} \times \frac{6}{10}$ 19. $\frac{3}{10} \times \frac{2}{5}$ 20. $\frac{1}{10} \times \frac{5}{8}$

21. $\frac{7}{8} \times \frac{1}{16}$ 22. $\frac{1}{8} \times \frac{3}{4}$ 23. $\frac{1}{8} \times \frac{1}{5}$ 24. $\frac{5}{2} \times \frac{3}{4}$

Solve these problems.

25. Mark uses $\frac{3}{8}$ kilogram of butter to make cookies. He uses $\frac{2}{3}$ as much butter to make a cake. How much butter does he use to make the cake?

26. Inez mowed a lawn in $\frac{3}{5}$ of an hour. Maria takes $\frac{2}{3}$ as much time as Inez to mow the same lawn. How long does it take Maria to mow the lawn?

Multiplying with Mixed Numerals

OBJECTIVE To find products such as $\frac{3}{5} \times 3\frac{1}{2}$ and $3\frac{2}{5} \times 4\frac{1}{4}$

EXAMPLE 1 Multiply. $\frac{3}{4} \times 2\frac{1}{2}$

$2\frac{1}{2} = \frac{4}{2} + \frac{1}{2}$

SOLUTION Think: $2\frac{1}{2} = \frac{5}{2}$

So, $\frac{3}{4} \times \frac{5}{2} = \frac{3 \times 5}{4 \times 2} = \frac{15}{8}$, or $1\frac{7}{8}$

- -

Multiply.

1. $\frac{1}{4} \times 2\frac{1}{2}$ **2.** $\frac{3}{8} \times 1\frac{1}{4}$ **3.** $1\frac{2}{3} \times \frac{3}{4}$

EXAMPLE 2 Multiply. $3\frac{1}{2} \times 4\frac{1}{4}$

SOLUTION Think: $3\frac{1}{2} = \frac{7}{2}$ and $4\frac{1}{4} = \frac{17}{4}$

So, $\frac{7}{2} \times \frac{17}{4} = \frac{7 \times 17}{2 \times 4} = \frac{119}{8}$, or $14\frac{7}{8}$

- -

Multiply.

4. $3\frac{1}{2} \times 1\frac{1}{4}$ **5.** $1\frac{1}{2} \times 1\frac{3}{4}$ **6.** $4\frac{1}{2} \times 6\frac{1}{3}$

EXAMPLE 3 Multiply. $12\frac{7}{10} \times \frac{3}{5}$

SOLUTION Think: $12\frac{7}{10} = \frac{127}{10}$

So, $\frac{127}{10} \times \frac{3}{5} = \frac{127 \times 3}{10 \times 5} = \frac{381}{50}$, or $7\frac{31}{50}$

- -

Multiply.

7. $15\frac{3}{8} \times \frac{5}{10}$ **8.** $11\frac{1}{2} \times \frac{3}{12}$ **9.** $12\frac{7}{10} \times \frac{3}{4}$

PRACTICE SET 6
Multiply.

1. $2\frac{3}{8} \times \frac{3}{4}$ 　　　　**2.** $2\frac{5}{8} \times \frac{3}{4}$ 　　　　**3.** $\frac{3}{4} \times 2\frac{7}{8}$ 　　　　**4.** $\frac{3}{4} \times 2\frac{1}{8}$

5. $2\frac{3}{8} \times \frac{1}{4}$ 　　　　**6.** $\frac{3}{8} \times 4\frac{1}{4}$ 　　　　**7.** $\frac{3}{8} \times 6\frac{1}{4}$ 　　　　**8.** $\frac{7}{8} \times 6\frac{1}{4}$

9. $1\frac{1}{2} \times \frac{3}{4}$ 　　　　**10.** $2\frac{2}{5} \times \frac{3}{7}$ 　　　　**11.** $1\frac{2}{7} \times \frac{3}{5}$ 　　　　**12.** $3\frac{1}{4} \times \frac{7}{8}$

13. $\frac{5}{16} \times 2\frac{1}{4}$ 　　　　**14.** $\frac{1}{16} \times 2\frac{3}{4}$ 　　　　**15.** $\frac{3}{16} \times 2\frac{1}{2}$ 　　　　**16.** $\frac{3}{16} \times 3\frac{3}{4}$

PRACTICE SET 7
Multiply.

1. $3\frac{3}{10} \times \frac{8}{10}$ 　　　　**2.** $3\frac{4}{10} \times \frac{7}{10}$ 　　　　**3.** $3\frac{1}{10} \times \frac{6}{10}$ 　　　　**4.** $3\frac{1}{10} \times \frac{7}{10}$

5. $12\frac{5}{10} \times \frac{7}{10}$ 　　　　**6.** $5\frac{8}{10} \times \frac{8}{10}$ 　　　　**7.** $6\frac{9}{10} \times \frac{8}{10}$ 　　　　**8.** $10\frac{5}{10} \times \frac{5}{10}$

9. $3\frac{2}{3} \times \frac{1}{3}$ 　　　　**10.** $\frac{2}{7} \times 3\frac{1}{9}$ 　　　　**11.** $\frac{2}{7} \times 8\frac{2}{5}$ 　　　　**12.** $10\frac{5}{6} \times \frac{9}{10}$

13. $\frac{1}{4} \times 10\frac{1}{3}$ 　　　　**14.** $\frac{1}{10} \times 5\frac{2}{3}$ 　　　　**15.** $\frac{4}{5} \times 20\frac{1}{3}$ 　　　　**16.** $17\frac{3}{10} \times \frac{3}{5}$

PRACTICE SET 8
Multiply.

1. $3\frac{1}{4} \times 2\frac{7}{8}$ 　　　　**2.** $2\frac{2}{5} \times 1\frac{3}{7}$ 　　　　**3.** $1\frac{2}{7} \times 4\frac{3}{5}$ 　　　　**4.** $2\frac{5}{8} \times 2\frac{1}{4}$

5. $4\frac{5}{16} \times 2\frac{1}{4}$ 　　　　**6.** $2\frac{3}{16} \times 2\frac{3}{4}$ 　　　　**7.** $4\frac{1}{16} \times 2\frac{3}{4}$ 　　　　**8.** $1\frac{3}{16} \times 3\frac{3}{4}$

9. $4\frac{3}{5} \times 2\frac{3}{10}$ 　　　　**10.** $2\frac{1}{2} \times 3\frac{2}{3}$ 　　　　**11.** $5\frac{2}{5} \times 7\frac{4}{5}$ 　　　　**12.** $1\frac{1}{2} \times 1\frac{3}{4}$

13. $2\frac{2}{3} \times 3\frac{1}{4}$ 　　　　**14.** $4\frac{3}{8} \times 1\frac{1}{5}$ 　　　　**15.** $1\frac{1}{4} \times 1\frac{1}{4}$ 　　　　**16.** $3\frac{1}{2} \times 2\frac{1}{4}$

Reciprocals

OBJECTIVE   To recognize the reciprocal of a number

Two numbers whose product is 1 are reciprocals of each other.

$$\frac{3}{4} \times \frac{4}{3} = \frac{12}{12}, \text{ or } 1$$

$\frac{3}{4}$ is the reciprocal of $\frac{4}{3}$ and

$\frac{4}{3}$ is the reciprocal of $\frac{3}{4}$

EXAMPLE 1   Find the reciprocal of 9.

SOLUTION   Think: $9 \times \frac{?}{?} = 1$

9 means $\frac{9}{1}$.

$$\overset{1}{\frac{9}{1}} \times \frac{1}{\underset{1}{9}} = \frac{1}{1}, \text{ or } 1$$

So, $\frac{1}{9}$ is the reciprocal of 9.

EXAMPLE 2   Find the reciprocal of $\frac{5}{8}$.

SOLUTION   Think: $\frac{5}{8} \times \frac{?}{?} = 1$

$$\frac{5}{8} \times \frac{8}{5} = \frac{40}{40}, \text{ or } 1$$

So, $\frac{8}{5}$ is the reciprocal of $\frac{5}{8}$.

- -

Make true sentences.

1. $5 \times \frac{?}{?} = 1$ **2.** $\frac{3}{5} \times \frac{?}{?} = 1$ **3.** $6 \times \frac{?}{?} = 1$

EXAMPLE 3 Find the reciprocal of $1\frac{1}{4}$.

SOLUTION Think: $1\frac{1}{4} = \frac{5}{4}$

$$\frac{\overset{1}{\cancel{5}}}{\cancel{4}} \times \frac{\overset{1}{\cancel{4}}}{\cancel{5}} = \frac{1}{1}, \text{ or } 1$$

So, $\frac{4}{5}$ is the reciprocal of $1\frac{1}{4}$.

- -

Find the reciprocal.

4. $1\frac{7}{8}$ **5.** $3\frac{2}{3}$ **6.** $1\frac{2}{5}$

PRACTICE SET 9

Make true sentences.

1. $\frac{2}{3} \times \frac{?}{?} = 1$ **2.** $\frac{7}{8} \times \frac{?}{?} = 1$ **3.** $1\frac{1}{2} \times \frac{?}{?} = 1$

4. $\frac{7}{10} \times \frac{?}{?} = 1$ **5.** $\frac{5}{16} \times \frac{?}{?} = 1$ **6.** $1\frac{5}{8} \times \frac{?}{?} = 1$

7. $\frac{1}{9} \times \frac{?}{?} = 1$ **8.** $8 \times \frac{?}{?} = 1$ **9.** $\frac{2}{9} \times \frac{?}{?} = 1$

PRACTICE SET 10

Find the reciprocal.

1. $\frac{3}{8}$ **2.** $\frac{1}{4}$ **3.** 8 **4.** $\frac{7}{5}$ **5.** $\frac{6}{7}$ **6.** $\frac{7}{10}$

7. $\frac{10}{7}$ **8.** $\frac{4}{5}$ **9.** $\frac{5}{4}$ **10.** 4 **11.** $\frac{2}{3}$ **12.** $\frac{3}{2}$

13. $1\frac{1}{2}$ **14.** $2\frac{3}{8}$ **15.** 6 **16.** 3 **17.** $4\frac{2}{3}$ **18.** $\frac{3}{100}$

19. $4\frac{3}{5}$ **20.** $8\frac{1}{10}$ **21.** 16 **22.** 1 **23.** 100 **24.** $5\frac{5}{9}$

Dividing Fractions

EXAMPLE 1 Divide. $\quad \frac{3}{4} \div \frac{2}{3}$

SOLUTION Think: $\frac{3}{4} \div \frac{2}{3}$ means $\frac{3}{4} \times \frac{3}{2}$.

To divide by any fraction, multiply by the reciprocal of the divisor.
To check, multiply the quotient by the divisor.

$$\frac{3}{4} \div \frac{2}{3} = \frac{3}{4} \times \frac{3}{2} = \frac{9}{8}$$

Check: $\overset{3}{\underset{4}{\cancel{\frac{9}{8}}}} \times \overset{1}{\underset{1}{\cancel{\frac{2}{3}}}} = \frac{3}{4}$

So, $\frac{3}{4} \div \frac{2}{3} = \frac{9}{8}$, or $1\frac{1}{8}$.

- -

Divide.

1. $\frac{2}{3} \div \frac{1}{2}$ 　　　 **2.** $\frac{4}{5} \div \frac{3}{4}$ 　　　 **3.** $\frac{7}{8} \div \frac{2}{9}$

EXAMPLE 2 Divide. $\quad \frac{1}{2} \div 3$

SOLUTION $\frac{1}{2} \div 3 = \frac{1}{2} \times \frac{1}{3} = \frac{1}{6}$

Check: $\frac{1}{6} \times 3 = \frac{3}{6}$, or $\frac{1}{2}$

So, $\frac{1}{2} \div 3 = \frac{1}{6}$.

- -

Divide.

4. $\frac{3}{4} \div 2$ 　　　 **5.** $\frac{1}{6} \div 3$ 　　　 **6.** $\frac{2}{9} \div 4$

EXAMPLE 3 Divide. $\quad 1\frac{1}{4} \div 2\frac{1}{2}$

SOLUTION Think: $1\frac{1}{4}$ is $\frac{5}{4}$ and $2\frac{1}{2}$ is $\frac{5}{2}$.

Multiply $\frac{5}{4}$ by the reciprocal of $\frac{5}{2}$.

$$\frac{5}{4} \times \frac{2}{5} = \frac{10}{20}, \text{ or } \frac{1}{2}$$

So, $1\frac{1}{4} \div 2\frac{1}{2} = \frac{1}{2}$.

- -

Divide.

7. $1\frac{3}{4} \div 2\frac{1}{2}$ 　　　 **8.** $5\frac{1}{2} \div 1\frac{1}{8}$ 　　　 **9.** $2\frac{2}{3} \div 1\frac{1}{5}$

PRACTICE SET 11
Divide.

1. $\frac{5}{8} \div \frac{1}{8}$ **2.** $7\frac{1}{5} \div \frac{1}{6}$ **3.** $10 \div \frac{2}{3}$ **4.** $5\frac{1}{2} \div 3$

5. $\frac{5}{6} \div \frac{2}{5}$ **6.** $10\frac{3}{4} \div 6$ **7.** $5\frac{1}{2} \div 2\frac{3}{8}$ **8.** $5\frac{5}{6} \div 8\frac{3}{4}$

9. $\frac{5}{16} \div \frac{5}{8}$ **10.** $3\frac{1}{2} \div \frac{3}{4}$ **11.** $\frac{5}{8} \div \frac{5}{16}$ **12.** $\frac{3}{4} \div 3\frac{1}{2}$

PRACTICE SET 12
Divide.

1. $\frac{3}{8} \div 4$ **2.** $\frac{3}{4} \div \frac{5}{8}$ **3.** $\frac{1}{2} \div 7\frac{7}{8}$ **4.** $\frac{3}{10} \div \frac{2}{5}$

5. $5\frac{1}{2} \div \frac{3}{8}$ **6.** $\frac{1}{16} \div \frac{1}{8}$ **7.** $8\frac{5}{8} \div 3$ **8.** $\frac{1}{3} \div \frac{1}{6}$

9. $10\frac{1}{5} \div 5\frac{1}{3}$ **10.** $5 \div 6$ **11.** $5\frac{1}{3} \div 10\frac{2}{3}$ **12.** $\frac{1}{6} \div 5$

PRACTICE SET 13
Divide.

1. $\frac{1}{8} \div 3\frac{1}{3}$ **2.** $\frac{1}{10} \div 12$ **3.** $7 \div 6\frac{5}{7}$ **4.** $\frac{7}{8} \div 6$

5. $8\frac{1}{2} \div 3\frac{1}{3}$ **6.** $\frac{7}{8} \div \frac{1}{4}$ **7.** $\frac{5}{6} \div 2\frac{1}{2}$ **8.** $8 \div 9\frac{2}{3}$

9. $\frac{3}{8} \div \frac{4}{5}$ **10.** $4\frac{1}{2} \div 3$ **11.** $\frac{4}{5} \div \frac{3}{8}$ **12.** $3 \div 4\frac{1}{2}$

PRACTICE SET 14
Divide.

1. $\frac{1}{2} \div 5$ **2.** $6 \div \frac{1}{3}$ **3.** $4 \div \frac{3}{5}$ **4.** $\frac{1}{8} \div 7$

5. $3 \div \frac{7}{8}$ **6.** $\frac{1}{4} \div 9$ **7.** $7 \div \frac{6}{7}$ **8.** $\frac{3}{4} \div 4$

9. $8 \div \frac{1}{4}$ **10.** $\frac{1}{5} \div 8$ **11.** $\frac{9}{10} \div 7$ **12.** $5 \div \frac{2}{3}$

13. $10 \div \frac{1}{3}$ **14.** $\frac{1}{7} \div 8$ **15.** $9 \div \frac{5}{6}$ **16.** $6 \div 3\frac{1}{3}$

Return to Form B on page 228.

Finding a Part of a Set

EXAMPLE 1   Find $\frac{1}{6}$ of 24.

SOLUTION

Think of a box containing 24 pieces of candy.

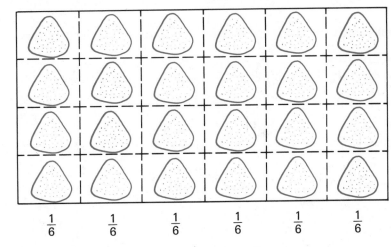

$\frac{1}{6}$ $\frac{1}{6}$ $\frac{1}{6}$ $\frac{1}{6}$ $\frac{1}{6}$ $\frac{1}{6}$

$\frac{1}{6}$ of 24 means $\frac{1}{6} \times 24$.
$\frac{1}{6}$ of 24 is the same as
$24 \div 6$, or 4.

So, $\frac{1}{6}$ of 24 is 4.

- -

Find the answer.

1. $\frac{1}{5}$ of 25   **2.** $\frac{1}{8}$ of 56   **3.** $\frac{1}{4}$ of 24

EXAMPLE 2   Find $\frac{7}{8}$ of 48.

SOLUTION   Think: $\frac{1}{8}$ of 48 is 6.

$\frac{7}{8} = 7 \times \frac{1}{8}$ So, $\frac{7}{8}$ of 48 is 7×6, or 42.

- -

Find the answer.

4. $\frac{3}{4}$ of 12   **5.** $\frac{5}{8}$ of 32   **6.** $\frac{9}{10}$ of 40

7. $\frac{5}{9}$ of 54   **8.** $\frac{2}{7}$ of 56   **9.** $\frac{3}{9}$ of 36

EXAMPLE 3 Find $3\frac{1}{2} \times 20$.

SOLUTION Think: $3\frac{1}{2}$ is $\frac{7}{2}$.

$\frac{1}{2}$ of 20 is 10

$\frac{7}{2} = 7 \times \frac{1}{2}$

$\frac{7}{2}$ of 20 is 7×10, or 70.

So, $3\frac{1}{2} \times 20$ is 70.

- -

Find the answer.

10. $2\frac{1}{4} \times 4$ **11.** $3\frac{1}{6} \times 8$ **12.** $6\frac{1}{2} \times 28$

EXERCISES
Write only the answer.

1. $\frac{1}{5}$ of 35   **2.** $\frac{1}{5}$ of 40   **3.** $\frac{1}{4}$ of 32   **4.** $\frac{1}{6}$ of 42

5. $\frac{1}{3}$ of 27   **6.** $\frac{1}{8}$ of 48   **7.** $\frac{1}{9}$ of 45   **8.** $\frac{1}{3}$ of 18

9. $\frac{1}{6}$ of 54   **10.** $\frac{1}{3}$ of 33   **11.** $\frac{1}{10}$ of 40   **12.** $\frac{1}{8}$ of 64

13. $\frac{1}{6}$ of 660   **14.** $\frac{1}{5}$ of 500   **15.** $\frac{1}{4}$ of 12   **16.** $\frac{1}{9}$ of 144

17. $\frac{2}{3}$ of 27   **18.** $\frac{3}{4}$ of 40   **19.** $\frac{3}{4}$ of 60   **20.** $\frac{5}{8}$ of 48

21. $\frac{3}{5}$ of 35   **22.** $\frac{5}{6}$ of 30   **23.** $\frac{2}{9}$ of 36   **24.** $\frac{7}{8}$ of 32

25. $\frac{3}{4}$ of 88   **26.** $\frac{4}{5}$ of 25   **27.** $\frac{8}{9}$ of 45   **28.** $\frac{3}{7}$ of 112

29. $2\frac{1}{2} \times 10$ **30.** $3\frac{1}{2} \times 20$ **31.** $3\frac{1}{2} \times 8$ **32.** $3\frac{1}{4} \times 12$

33. $2\frac{3}{4} \times 12$ **34.** $2\frac{3}{4} \times 8$ **35.** $2\frac{1}{9} \times 9$ **36.** $5\frac{1}{2} \times 6$

37. $1\frac{1}{6} \times 18$ **38.** $3\frac{1}{3} \times 30$ **39.** $1\frac{3}{4} \times 20$ **40.** $2\frac{1}{3} \times 15$

41. $2\frac{1}{4} \times 8$ **42.** $2\frac{1}{2} \times 60$ **43.** $5\frac{1}{2} \times 20$ **44.** $4\frac{2}{7} \times 49$

45. $3\frac{1}{7} \times 28$ **46.** $8\frac{1}{2} \times 24$ **47.** $9\frac{2}{3} \times 54$ **48.** $12\frac{1}{8} \times 56$

Estimating Products

OBJECTIVE To estimate the product of two fractions

EXAMPLE 1 Estimate. $\frac{3}{4} \times 3\frac{1}{3}$

SOLUTION $0 \times 3 = 0$

$\frac{3}{4}$ is between 0 and 1.

$3\frac{1}{3}$ is between 3 and 4.

$1 \times 4 = 4$ ⟵── $\frac{3}{4} \times 3\frac{1}{3}$ is between 0×3 and 1×4

So, $\frac{3}{4} \times 3\frac{1}{3}$ is between 0 and 4.

EXAMPLE 2 Estimate. $2\frac{1}{2} \times 4\frac{3}{4}$

SOLUTION Think: $2\frac{1}{2}$ is between 2 and 3.

$2 \times 4 = 8$
$3 \times 5 = 15$

$\qquad\qquad 4\frac{3}{4}$ is between 4 and 5.

So, $2\frac{1}{2} \times 4\frac{3}{4}$ is between 8 and 15.

- -

Estimate.

1. $\frac{7}{8} \times 4\frac{1}{2}$ **2.** $\frac{2}{5} \times 2\frac{1}{6}$ **3.** $\frac{2}{3} \times 5\frac{3}{6}$

4. $1\frac{1}{4} \times 2\frac{1}{2}$ **5.** $8\frac{1}{7} \times 9\frac{1}{2}$ **6.** $7\frac{3}{6} \times 10\frac{2}{10}$

EXAMPLE 3 Estimate. $2\frac{2}{3} \times 16$

SOLUTION Think: $2\frac{2}{3}$ is between 2 and 3.

$2 \times 16 = 32$
$3 \times 16 = 48$

So, $2\frac{2}{3} \times 16$ is between 32 and 48.

- -

Estimate.

7. $1\frac{7}{8} \times 24$ **8.** $5\frac{3}{4} \times 16$ **9.** $2\frac{1}{4} \times 48$

EXAMPLE 4 Estimate. $4\frac{1}{2} \times \$2.68$

SOLUTION Think: $4\frac{1}{2}$ is between 4 and 5.

$4 \times \$2 = \$8$
$5 \times \$3 = \$15$

$\$2.68$ is between $2 and $3.

So, $4\frac{1}{2} \times \$2.68$ is between $8 and $15.

- -

Estimate.

10. $2\frac{1}{8} \times \$7.95$ **11.** $6\frac{2}{3} \times \$25$ **12.** $10\frac{1}{4} \times \$.36$

EXERCISES
Estimate.

1. $\frac{7}{8} \times 1\frac{3}{4}$ **2.** $\frac{1}{8} \times 1\frac{3}{4}$ **3.** $\frac{3}{8} \times 1\frac{1}{4}$ **4.** $\frac{1}{4} \times 2\frac{3}{8}$

5. $\frac{1}{5} \times 2\frac{3}{8}$ **6.** $\frac{1}{2} \times 9\frac{3}{4}$ **7.** $\frac{1}{4} \times 2\frac{7}{8}$ **8.** $\frac{2}{10} \times 8\frac{6}{10}$

9. $9\frac{7}{8} \times 6\frac{1}{4}$ **10.** $7\frac{5}{16} \times 2\frac{4}{5}$ **11.** $3\frac{1}{2} \times 2\frac{1}{16}$ **12.** $10\frac{1}{10} \times 16\frac{2}{3}$

13. $8\frac{1}{6} \times 5\frac{1}{5}$ **14.** $\frac{1}{4} \times 3\frac{1}{5}$ **15.** $2\frac{5}{6} \times 7\frac{1}{5}$ **16.** $3\frac{3}{10} \times 2\frac{8}{10}$

17. $3\frac{4}{10} \times 2\frac{8}{10}$ **18.** $3\frac{4}{10} \times 2\frac{7}{10}$ **19.** $3\frac{1}{10} \times 2\frac{6}{10}$ **20.** $3\frac{1}{10} \times 2\frac{7}{10}$

21. $3\frac{1}{10} \times 4\frac{1}{10}$ **22.** $5\frac{8}{10} \times 5\frac{8}{10}$ **23.** $6\frac{9}{10} \times 6\frac{9}{10}$ **24.** $10\frac{5}{10} \times 5\frac{5}{10}$

25. $40\frac{1}{2} \times \$2.00$ **26.** $2\frac{7}{8} \times 24$ **27.** $3\frac{3}{4} \times 16$ **28.** $5\frac{1}{2} \times \$.98$

29. $4\frac{1}{4} \times \$.79$ **30.** $1\frac{3}{4} \times \$.37$ **31.** $2\frac{1}{2} \times \$.73$ **32.** $3\frac{15}{16} \times \$45$

33. $1\frac{1}{2} \times \$49$ **34.** $3\frac{1}{4} \times \$2.98$ **35.** $\frac{1}{3} \times \$23.95$ **36.** $\frac{1}{5} \times \$89.95$

37. $\frac{1}{4} \times \$49.95$ **38.** $\frac{1}{2} \times \$179.50$ **39.** $\frac{1}{10} \times \$224.95$ **40.** $\frac{1}{3} \times \$179.50$

Applying Multiplication and Division

OBJECTIVE   To solve problems containing fractions

Solve these problems.

1. Ms. Lane, the baker, uses $\frac{3}{4}$ kilogram of baking powder a day. How much does she use in 28 days?

2. Miguel worked $6\frac{3}{4}$ hours a day. How many hours did he work in 30 days?

3. Tami rode her bike for $3\frac{1}{4}$ hours. She averaged $9\frac{1}{2}$ kilometers per hour. How far did she ride?

4. The height of a beam is $2\frac{1}{2}$ times its width. The beam is $16\frac{1}{4}$ cm wide. How high is it?

5. Joe drove 397 kilometers. He used $48\frac{1}{2}$ liters of gas. How many kilometers per liter did he average?

6. Jane used $3\frac{3}{4}$ meters of ribbon to tie 5 packages, each the same size. How much ribbon did she need for each package?

7. A bin of candy weighs 34 kilograms. Each piece of candy weighs $\frac{1}{5}$ kilogram. How many pieces of candy are there in the bin?

8. Carlos is packing corn into $\frac{3}{4}$-kilogram packages. How many packages can he get from 75 kilograms of corn?

9. The Johnsons use $\frac{3}{4}$ kilogram of beef per meal. How many meals can they get from a $3\frac{3}{4}$-kilogram roast?

10. The Barkans use $1\frac{1}{2}$ dozen eggs per week. How long will it take them to use $5\frac{1}{4}$ dozen eggs?

Fun Corner

A man wanted to test his son on how well he understood area. He gave him 120 meters of fencing and told him to make a rectangular pen. He told him that he would give him $1 for each square meter in the pen. How should his son make the pen in order to get the greatest amount of money?

Decimals and Fractions

OBJECTIVE To recognize that decimals and fractions can name the same number

You can use a number line to show that a decimal and a fraction can name the same number.

EXAMPLE 1 Write 2 fractions equivalent to .6. Use a number line.

SOLUTION
Draw a number line and label some points.

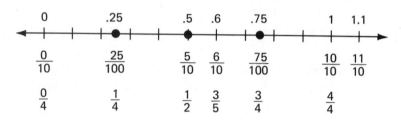

The number line shows $.6 = \frac{6}{10}$ and $\frac{3}{5}$.

- -

Make true sentences. Use the number line.

1. $.1 = \underline{\quad?\quad}$ **2.** $.3 = \underline{\quad?\quad}$ **3.** $0 = \underline{\quad?\quad}$ **4.** $1.25 = \underline{\quad?\quad}$

5. $.75 = \underline{\quad?\quad}$ **6.** $.25 = \underline{\quad?\quad}$ **7.** $1.5 = \underline{\quad?\quad}$ **8.** $.7 = \underline{\quad?\quad}$

EXAMPLE 2 Find an equivalent decimal for $\frac{7}{8}$.

SOLUTION
Divide the numerator by the denominator.

$$8\overline{)7.000} \quad \text{.875}$$

So, $\frac{7}{8} = .875$.

- -

Find an equivalent decimal.

9. $\frac{4}{5}$ **10.** $\frac{5}{8}$ **11.** $\frac{1}{8}$ **12.** $\frac{2}{5}$

EXAMPLE 3 Find an equivalent decimal to the nearest thousandth for $\frac{5}{6}$, for $\frac{11}{12}$.

SOLUTION

Carry the division 4 places.

$$
\begin{array}{r}
.8333 \\
6\overline{)5.0000} \\
\underline{4\,8} \\
20 \\
\underline{18} \\
20 \\
\underline{18} \\
20 \\
\underline{18} \\
2
\end{array}
\qquad
\begin{array}{r}
.9166 \\
12\overline{)11.0000} \\
\underline{10\,8} \\
20 \\
\underline{12} \\
80 \\
\underline{72} \\
80 \\
\underline{72} \\
8
\end{array}
$$

So, $\frac{5}{6} = .833$ to the nearest thousandth and $\frac{11}{12} = .917$ to the nearest thousandth.

- -

Find an equivalent decimal to the nearest thousandth.

13. $\frac{1}{3}$ **14.** $\frac{2}{3}$ **15.** $\frac{1}{6}$ **16.** $\frac{3}{10}$

EXERCISES

Find an equivalent fraction in simplest form.

1. .2   **2.** .7   **3.** .15   **4.** .35   **5.** .45

6. .25   **7.** .5   **8.** .75   **9.** .9   **10.** .8

11. 1.25   **12.** 1.4   **13.** 1.2   **14.** 1.3   **15.** 1.6

16. .6   **17.** .125   **18.** .875   **19.** .625   **20.** .650

Find an equivalent decimal to the nearest thousandth.

21. $\frac{3}{8}$ **22.** $\frac{1}{5}$ **23.** $\frac{1}{12}$ **24.** $\frac{7}{10}$ **25.** $\frac{5}{12}$

26. $\frac{7}{12}$ **27.** $\frac{1}{16}$ **28.** $\frac{3}{16}$ **29.** $\frac{5}{16}$ **30.** $\frac{9}{16}$

31. $\frac{2}{16}$ **32.** $\frac{1}{8}$ **33.** $\frac{10}{16}$ **34.** $\frac{5}{8}$ **35.** $\frac{2}{4}$

36. $\frac{1}{2}$ **37.** $\frac{3}{4}$ **38.** $\frac{6}{8}$ **39.** $\frac{9}{12}$ **40.** $\frac{15}{20}$

Test: Unit 11

Multiply.

1. $5 \times \frac{5}{8}$

2. $\frac{3}{5} \times 21$

3. $\frac{7}{16} \times \frac{4}{7}$

4. $\frac{7}{10} \times \frac{3}{10}$

5. $\frac{4}{5} \times 1\frac{3}{10}$

6. $\frac{4}{5} \times 1\frac{1}{4}$

7. $5\frac{1}{2} \times 2\frac{1}{2}$

8. $2\frac{4}{5} \times 1\frac{1}{10}$

Divide.

9. $\frac{3}{4} \div \frac{3}{8}$

10. $\frac{7}{15} \div \frac{7}{5}$

11. $\frac{1}{2} \div 4$

12. $\frac{2}{3} \div 6$

13. $7 \div \frac{1}{2}$

14. $10 \div \frac{7}{10}$

15. $10\frac{2}{3} \div 5\frac{1}{3}$

16. $5\frac{5}{6} \div \frac{7}{12}$

Find the answer.

17. $\frac{1}{3}$ of 36

18. $\frac{5}{8}$ of 48

19. $3\frac{1}{4} \times 12$

Estimate.

20. $\frac{1}{5} \times 2\frac{3}{8}$

21. $3\frac{3}{4} \times 16$

22. $1\frac{1}{2} \times \$49$

Find an equivalent fraction in simplest form.

23. .125

24. 1.7

Find an equivalent decimal to the nearest thousandth.

25. $\frac{2}{3}$

26. $\frac{3}{8}$

Solve these problems.

27. Lula has $\frac{2}{3}$ meter of material. She needs $4\frac{1}{3}$ times as much to make a coat. How much does she need to make the coat?

28. Akira is packing potatoes into $1\frac{1}{2}$-kilogram packages. How many packages can he get from 170 kilograms of potatoes?

Fun Corner

Here's a quick way for doing some multiplications.

Are the same $\longrightarrow \begin{Bmatrix} 5\frac{1}{4} \\ 5\frac{3}{4} \end{Bmatrix} \longrightarrow$ Sum of 1

$(5 \times 5) + 5 \longrightarrow 30\frac{3}{16} \longleftarrow \frac{3}{4} \times \frac{1}{4} = \frac{3}{16}$

Which multiplications can be done by this method?

1. $3\frac{1}{2}$ 2. $8\frac{1}{4}$ 3. $6\frac{1}{5}$ 4. $10\frac{7}{8}$ 5.   4.6

   $\times 3\frac{1}{2}$ $\times 8\frac{2}{4}$ $\times 6\frac{4}{5}$ $\times 10\frac{1}{8}$ $\times 4.4$

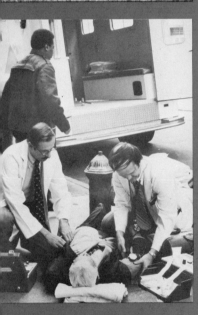

UNIT 12
Equations

Equations: Adding and Subtracting

OBJECTIVE To solve equations such as $x + 7 = 12$, $x + 176 = 200$, $x - 5 = 13$, and $x - 223 = 84$

An equation is a number sentence.

To solve an equation, first think of its English translation.

EXAMPLE 1 Solve. $x + 7 = 12$

SOLUTION

This is the translation.

Think: $\quad x \quad + \quad 7 = 12$ means

a number added to 7 is 12.

To find the number, subtract 7 from 12.

$12 - 7 = 12$

They try 5 in the equation. It works.

$x + 7 = 12$
$5 + 7 = 12$

So, 5 is the number.

EXAMPLE 2 Solve. $x + 176 = 200$

SOLUTION Think: $x + 176 = 200$ means a number added to 176 is 200.

To find the number subtract 176 from 200.

$$\begin{array}{r} \overset{9}{} \\ 1\,\overset{\cancel{10}}{\cancel{0}}\,10 \\ 2\,\cancel{0}\,\cancel{0} \\ -\,1\,7\,6 \\ \hline 2\,4 \end{array}$$

Then try 24 in the equations.

$x + 176 = 200$
$24 + 176 = 200$

$$\begin{array}{r} 24 \\ +\,176 \\ \hline 200 \end{array}$$

So, 24 is the number.

- -

Solve.

1. $x + 8 = 17$ **2.** $x + 6 = 14$ **3.** $x + 105 = 226$

EXAMPLE 3   Solve. $x - 5 = 13$

SOLUTION   Think: $x - 5 = 13$ means

This is the translation.   5 subtracted from a number is 13.

To find the number, add.
$$\begin{array}{r} 13 \\ +\ 5 \\ \hline 18 \end{array}$$

Then try 18 in the
equation. It works.

$x - 5 = 13$ $\begin{array}{r} 18 \\ -\ 5 \\ \hline 13 \end{array}$
$18 - 5 = 13$

So, the number is 18.

EXAMPLE 4   Solve. $x - 223 = 84$

SOLUTION   Think: $x - 223 = 84$ means
223 subtracted from a number is 84.

To find the number, add.
$$\begin{array}{r} 84 \\ +223 \\ \hline 307 \end{array}$$

Then try 307 in the
equation.

$x - 223 = 84$ $\begin{array}{r} 307 \\ -233 \\ \hline 84 \end{array}$
$307 - 223 = 84$

So, the number is 307.

Solve.

4. $x - 7 = 12$ **5.** $x - 9 = 3$ **6.** $x - 116 = 235$

EXERCISES
Solve.

1. $x + 4 = 13$ **2.** $x - 6 = 2$ **3.** $x + 8 = 10$ **4.** $x - 1 = 5$

5. $x - 3 = 7$ **6.** $x + 5 = 8$ **7.** $x + 2 = 11$ **8.** $x - 7 = 3$

9. $x - 9 = 1$ **10.** $x + 3 = 14$ **11.** $x + 8 = 15$ **12.** $x - 15 = 21$

13. $x - 19 = 11$ **14.** $x - 28 = 50$ **15.** $x + 34 = 42$ **16.** $x + 58 = 65$

17. $x - 78 = 31$ **18.** $x + 100 = 113$ **19.** $x + 125 = 232$ **20.** $x - 205 = 146$

Equations: Multiplying and Dividing

EXAMPLE 1   Solve. $2x = 16$

SOLUTION   Think: $2x = 16$ means $2 \cdot x = 16.$

This is the translation.

2 times a number is 16.

To find the number,
divide 16 by 2.

$$2 \overline{)16} \quad \frac{8}{}$$

$$\underline{16}$$

Then try 8 in the
equation. It works.

$2x = 16$
$2(8) = 16$

So, the number is 8.

EXAMPLE 2   Solve. $15x = 90$

SOLUTION   Think: $15x = 90$ means $15 \cdot x = 90.$

This is the translation.   15 times a number is 90.

To find the number,
divide 90 by 15.

$$15 \overline{)90} \quad \frac{6}{}$$

$$\underline{90}$$

They try 6 in the
equation. It works.

$15x = 90$ 15
$15(6) = 90$ $\underline{\times 6}$
               90

So, 6 is the number.

Solve.

1. $6x = 18$ **2.** $9x = 36$

3. $11x = 88$ **4.** $13x = 65$

EXAMPLE 3 Solve. $\frac{x}{2} = 10$

SOLUTION Think: $\frac{x}{2} = 10$ means x ÷ 2 = 10.

This is the translation.   A number divided by 2 is 10.

To find the number, $2 \times 10 = 20$
multiply 10 by 2.

$$\frac{x}{2} = 10 \qquad 2\overline{)20}^{\,10}$$

Then try 20 in the $\frac{20}{2} = 10$
equation. It works. $\underline{20}$

So, the number is 20.

EXAMPLE 4 Solve. $\frac{x}{13} = 13$

SOLUTION Think: $\frac{x}{13} = 13$ means $x \div 13 = 13$.

This is the translation.   A number divided by 13 is 13.

To find the number, $13 \times 13 = 169$
multiply 13 by 13.

Then try 169 in the $\frac{x}{13} = 13$
equation. It works.

$$\frac{169}{13} = 13 \qquad \begin{array}{r} 13 \\ \times 13 \\ \hline 39 \\ 13 \\ \hline 169 \end{array} \qquad \begin{array}{r} 13 \\ 13\overline{)169} \\ \underline{13} \\ 39 \\ \underline{39} \end{array}$$

So, the number is 169.

- -

Solve.

5. $\frac{x}{5} = 3$ **6.** $\frac{x}{3} = 12$ **7.** $\frac{x}{14} = 4$ **8.** $\frac{x}{63} = 17$

EXERCISES
Solve.

1. $3x = 9$ **2.** $5x = 35$ **3.** $8x = 40$ **4.** $7x = 49$

5. $10x = 70$ **6.** $8x = 72$ **7.** $12x = 120$ **8.** $18x = 90$

9. $\frac{x}{4} = 4$ **10.** $\frac{x}{6} = 1$ **11.** $\frac{x}{7} = 2$ **12.** $\frac{x}{2} = 9$

13. $\frac{x}{5} = 5$ **14.** $\frac{x}{12} = 3$ **15.** $\frac{x}{11} = 9$ **16.** $\frac{x}{38} = 12$

Solving Combination Equations

> **OBJECTIVE** To solve equations such as $2x + 7 = 9$, $3x - 4 = 32$, $\frac{x}{2} + 6 = 8$, and $\frac{x}{3} - 2 = 1$

EXAMPLE 1   Solve. $2x + 7 = 9$

SOLUTION   Think: $2x + 7 = 9$ means 2 · x + 7 = 9.

This is the translation.

2 times a number added to 7 is 9.

To find the number, subtract 7 from 9.

$9 - 7 = 2$

Then divide 2 by 2

$$2\overline{\smash)2} \quad \begin{array}{r} 1 \\ \underline{2} \end{array}$$

Try the answer in the equation. It works.

$2x + 7 = 9$
$2 \cdot 1 + 7 = 2 + 7$, or 9

So, the number is 1.

EXAMPLE 2   Solve. $3x - 4 = 32$

SOLUTION   Think: $3x - 4 = 32$ means $3 \cdot x - 4 = 32$.

This is the translation.

4 subtracted from 3 times a number is 32.

To find the number, add 4 to 32. Then divide 36 by 3.

$4 + 32 = 36$

$$3\overline{\smash)36} \quad \begin{array}{r} 12 \\ \underline{3} \\ 6 \\ \underline{6} \end{array}$$

Try the answer in the equation. It works.

$3x - 4 = 32$
$3 \cdot 12 - 4 = 36 - 4$, or 32

$$\begin{array}{r} 12 \\ \times 3 \\ \hline 36 \end{array} \qquad \begin{array}{r} 36 \\ - 4 \\ \hline 32 \end{array}$$

So, the number is 12.

EXAMPLE 3   Solve. $\frac{x}{2} + 6 = 8$

SOLUTION   Think: $\frac{x}{2} + 6 = 8$ means $x \div 2 + 6 = 8$.

This is the translation.   6 added to (a number divided by 2) is 8.

To find the number, $8 - 6 = 2$
subtract 6 from 8.

Then multiply 2 by 2. $2 \times 2 = 4$

$\frac{x}{2} + 6 = 8$

Try the answer in the
equation. It works. $\frac{4}{2} + 6 = 2 + 6$, or 8

So, the number is 4.

EXAMPLE 4   Solve. $\frac{x}{3} - 2 = 1$

SOLUTION   Think: $\frac{x}{3} - 2 = 1$ means $x \div 3 - 2 = 1$.

This is the translation.   2 subtracted from (a number divided by 3) is 1.

To find the number, $1 + 2 = 3$
add 2 to 1. Then multiply $3 \times 3 = 9$
by 3.

$\frac{x}{3} - 2 = 1$

Try the answer in the $\frac{9}{3} - 2 = 3 - 2$, or 1
equation. It works.

So, the number is 9.

Solve.

1. $3x + 7 = 31$ **2.** $10x + 4 = 4$ **3.** $4x - 4 = 12$

4. $\frac{x}{7} + 2 = 4$ **5.** $\frac{x}{4} - 9 = 1$ **6.** $\frac{x}{5} - 2 = 2$

EXERCISES
Solve.

1. $5x + 3 = 18$ **2.** $7x - 6 = 8$ **3.** $6x + 6 = 36$ **4.** $9x - 8 = 46$

5. $\frac{x}{3} + 7 = 10$ **6.** $\frac{x}{8} + 9 = 17$ **7.** $\frac{x}{12} + 5 = 9$ **8.** $\frac{x}{9} - 6 = 2$

9. $16x + 14 = 142$ **10.** $15x - 10 = 125$ **11.** $27x - 3 = 294$ **12.** $23x - 12 = 172$

13. $\frac{x}{6} - 29 = 37$ **14.** $\frac{x}{17} + 14 = 17$ **15.** $\frac{x}{14} - 17 = 9$ **16.** $\frac{x}{25} - 27 = 52$

Choosing the Correct Equation

OBJECTIVE To choose the correct equation for a sentence

EXAMPLE 1 Choose the correct equation for this sentence. If 2 is added to (3 times a number x), the result is the same as 6 minus the number x.
   a. $3x + 2 = 6 - x$ **b.** $3x + 2 = x - 6$ **c.** $2x + 3 = 6 - x$

SOLUTION 2 added to 3 times x is 6 minus x.

$2 + 3 \cdot x = 2 + 3x$,
or $3x + 2$

$$2 \quad + \quad 3 \quad \cdot \quad x = 6 \quad - \quad x$$

So, the correct equation is **a**, or $3x + 2 = 6 - x$.

EXAMPLE 2 Choose the correct equation for this sentence. If 9 is subtracted from a number x, the result is the same as (the number x divided by 2).

   a. $9 - x = \frac{x}{2}$ **b.** $x - 9 = 2x$ **c.** $x - 9 = \frac{x}{2}$

SOLUTION 9 subtracted from x is x divided by 2.

$x \div 2$ means $\frac{x}{2}$

$$x \quad - \quad 9 \quad = x \quad \div \quad 2$$

So, the correct equation is **c**, or $x - 9 = \frac{x}{2}$.

Choose the correct equation.

1. If a number x is multiplied by 4, the result is the same as 6 added to the number x.
   a. $4x + 6 = x$ **b.** $4x = x + 6$ **c.** $4x + x = 6$
2. If 7 is added to a number x, the result is the same as 2 minus (3 times the number x).
   a. $7 + x = 2 + 3x$ **b.** $x + 7 = 3x - 2$ **c.** $x + 7 = 2 - 3x$
3. If 7 is added to (a number x divided by 6), the result is 10.
   a. $6x + 7 = 10$ **b.** $\frac{x}{6} + 7 = 10$ **c.** $\frac{x}{7} + 6 = 10$

4. If 3 is subtracted from (5 times a number x), the result is 37.
   a. $5x + 3 = 37$ **b.** $3 - 5x = 37$ **c.** $5x - 3 = 37$

Using Equations

EXAMPLE 1 If 8 is subtracted from a number, the result is 9. Find the number.

SOLUTION Think: 8 subtracted from a number is 9 means

This is the translation. $x - 8 = 9$.

Now solve the equation. $9 + 8 = 17$
Add 8 to 9.

Try the answer. It works. $17 - 8 = 9$

So, the number is 17.

EXAMPLE 2 If 5 is added to (a number divided by 3), the result is 12. Find the number.

SOLUTION Think: 5 added to a number divided by 3 is 12 means

This is the translation. $\frac{x}{3} + 5 = 12$.

Now solve the equation.
Subtract 5 from 12.
Multiply 7 by 3.

$$\begin{array}{cc} 12 & 7 \\ -\ 5 & \times 3 \\ \hline 7 & 21 \end{array}$$

Try the answer.
It works.

$\frac{21}{3} + 5 = 12$ and $7 + 5 = 12$

So, the number is 21.

Find the number.

1. Two times a number is 12.

2. Six subtracted from a number is 5.

3. A number added to 9 is 20.

4. A number divided by 7 is 7.

5. If 8 is subtracted from (3 times a number), the result is 19.

6. If 6 is added to (a number divided by 10), the result is 10.

7. If 13 is subtracted from (a number divided by 5), the result is 2.

8. If 16 is added to (9 times a number), the result is 79.

The Distance Formula

OBJECTIVE   To use the formula $d = rt$

The dot means times.

The formula $d = rt$ means
distance equals rate · time

Distance is how far a person or a vehicle has gone. Rate is the same as speed. Time means how long a person or a vehicle has been traveling.

EXAMPLE 1   Find d if r is 50 km/h and t is 3 hours.

SOLUTION

Write the formula and plug in the values.

$d = rt$
$d = 50 \cdot 3$
$d = 150$

$$\begin{array}{r} 50 \\ \times 3 \\ \hline 150 \end{array}$$

So, the distance is 150 kilometers.

- -

Find d. Use $d = rt$.
1. r is 60 km/h and t is 5 hours.

2. r is 88 km/h and t is 18 hours.

EXAMPLE 2   Find t if d is 8 km and r is 2 km/h.

SOLUTION

$2 \cdot t$ means 2 times a number.

$d = rt$
$8 = 2 \cdot t$
$4 = t$

$$2\overline{)8}^{4}$$

So, the time is 4 hours.

- -

Find t. Use $d = rt$.
3. d is 54 km and r is 3 km/h.

4. d is 504 km and r is 84 km/h.

EXAMPLE 3 Find *r* if *d* is 880 meters and *t* is 2 minutes.

SOLUTION $d = rt$

r · 2 means 2 times a number.

$880 = r \cdot 2$

$440 = r$

$$
\begin{array}{r}
440 \\
2\overline{)880} \\
\underline{8} \\
8 \\
\underline{8} \\
\end{array}
$$

So, the rate, or speed, is 440 meters per minute.

- -

Find *r*. Use *d* = *rt*.

5. *d* is 1,560 m and *t* is 5 minutes.

6. *d* is 3,264 km and *t* is 24 hours.

EXERCISES

Find *d*. Use *d* = *rt*.

1. *r* is 7 km/h and *t* is 5 hours.

2. *r* is 35 km/h and *t* is 4 hours.

3. *r* is 47 km/h and *t* is 8 hours.

4. *r* is 52 km/h and *t* is 16 hours.

Find *t*. Use *d* = *rt*.

5. *d* is 48 m and *r* is 6 m/min.

6. *d* is 75 km and *r* is 15 km/h.

7. *d* is 132 km and *r* is 12 km/h.

8. *d* is 9,659 m and *r* is 743 m/h.

Find *r*. Use *d* = *rt*.

9. *d* is 63 km and *t* is 7 hours.

10. *d* is 144 m and *t* is 3 hours.

11. *d* is 80 km and *t* is 16 hours.

12. *d* is 252 km and *t* is 21 hours.

Copy and complete.

	d	*r*	*t*
13.		83 km/h	3 h
14.	670 km	134 km/h	
15.	15,840 km		44 h
16.	960 m		16 min

	d	*r*	*t*
17.	1,000 m	25 m/min	
18.		88 km/h	12 h
19.	3,500 m		7 min
20.	1,440 km	720 km/h	

Using the Distance Formula

EXAMPLE A hiker walked 18 kilometers in 3 hours. How fast was she walking?

SOLUTION $d = 18$ and $t = 3$, so $18 = r \cdot 3$.

Remember, $d = rt$.

$$\begin{array}{r} 6 \\ 3\overline{)18} \\ \underline{18} \end{array}$$

So, she was walking at a rate of 6 km/h.

EXERCISES
Solve.

1. A car is traveling at 50 km/h. How far will it go in 7 hours?

2. A boat traveled 75 kilometers in 3 hours. How fast was it going?

3. A train went 960 km at a speed of 80 km/h. How long did it travel?

4. Joan rode her bicycle for 5 hours at 9 km/h. How far did she go?

5. A bus going 37 km/h covered a distance of 481 kilometers. How long did the trip take?

6. It took 9 hours for a motorcycle to go 495 kilometers. What was its speed?

7. A transcontinental jet flew 4,800 kilometers at a speed of 800 km/h. How long did it fly?

8. Chris ran around a 1,640-meter track in 4 minutes. What was his speed?

9. Paulo paddled his canoe for 2 hours at a rate of 7 km/h. How far did he go?

10. Maureen drove 93 kilometers in one and a half hours. How fast was she going?

Test: Unit 12

Solve.

1. $x + 7 = 11$ **2.** $x - 14 = 13$ **3.** $5x = 25$ **4.** $x + 33 = 151$

5. $\frac{x}{2} = 18$ **6.** $\frac{x}{7} - 3 = 4$ **7.** $9x - 2 = 52$ **8.** $4x + 2 = 6$

Choose the correct equation.

9. If 31 is subtracted from (6 times a number x), the result is the same as 4 added to the number x.

   a. $31 - 6x = 4 + x$ **b.** $6x + 31 = x - 4$ **c.** $6x - 31 = x + 4$

10. If 3 is added to (a number x divided by 12), the result is 14.

   a. $12x + 3 = 14$ **b.** $\frac{x}{12} + 3 = 14$ **c.** $\frac{x}{3} + 12 = 14$

Find the number.

11. A number divided by 8 is 7.

12. A number added to 16 is 20.

13. If 26 is added to (11 times a number), the result is 48.

14. If 3 is subtracted from (a number divided by 12), the result is 5.

Use the distance formula $d = rt$.

15. Find d if r is 27 km/h and t is 4 hours.

16. Find r if d is 558 km and t is 9 hours.

17. Find t if d is 95 km and r is 19 km/h.

18. Find r if d is 260 km and t is 20 hours.

Solve. Use $d = rt$.

19. It took a car 4 hours to go 212 kilometers. How fast was the car going?

20. A train traveled for 18 hours at a speed of 170 km/h. How far did it travel?

Fun Corner

Can you complete this pattern? Try.

$$9 \times \quad 9 + \quad 7 = 88$$
$$9 \times \quad 98 + \quad 6 = 888$$
$$9 \times \quad 987 + \underline{\ ?\ } = 8{,}888$$
$$\underline{\ ?\ } \times 9{,}876 + \underline{\ ?\ } = 88{,}888$$
$$\underline{\ ?\ } \times \underline{\ ?\ } + \underline{\ ?\ } = \underline{\ ?\ }$$
$$\underline{\ ?\ } \times \underline{\ ?\ } + \underline{\ ?\ } = \underline{\ ?\ }$$
$$\underline{\ ?\ } \times \underline{\ ?\ } + \underline{\ ?\ } = \underline{\ ?\ }$$
$$\underline{\ ?\ } \times \underline{\ ?\ } + \underline{\ ?\ } = \underline{\ ?\ }$$

UNIT 13
Geometry

Angles

EXAMPLE 1   Measure angle *ABC*.

Angle *ABC* can be written
as $\angle ABC$, or $\angle B$.

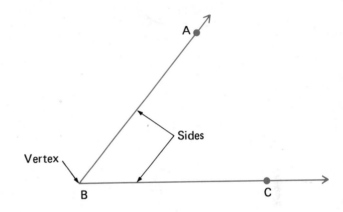

SOLUTION

Use a protractor.

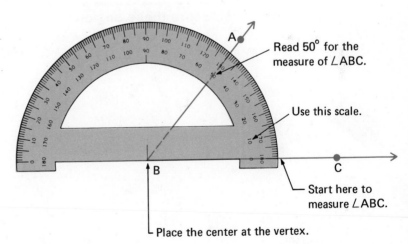

Read 50° for the
measure of $\angle ABC$.

Use this scale.

Start here to
measure $\angle ABC$.

Place the center at the vertex.

$\angle ABC$ measures 50°.

EXAMPLE 2 Measure ∠B.

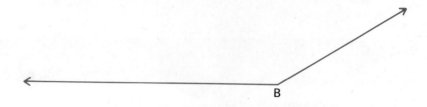

SOLUTION

Use a protractor.

Read 150° for the measure of ∠B.

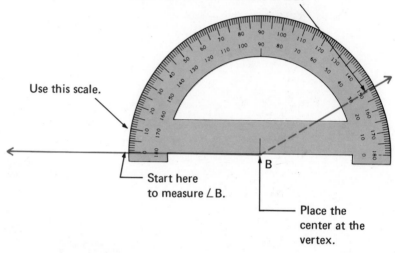

Use this scale.

Start here
to measure ∠B.

B

Place the
center at the
vertex.

∠B measures 150°.

- -

Measure these angles.

1.　　　　　　　　　　　**2.**

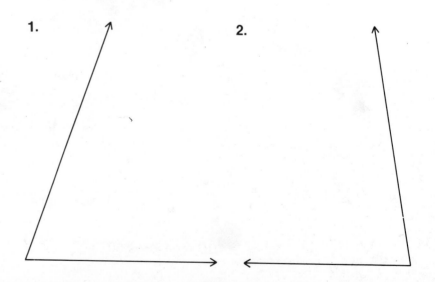

EXERCISES
Measure these angles.

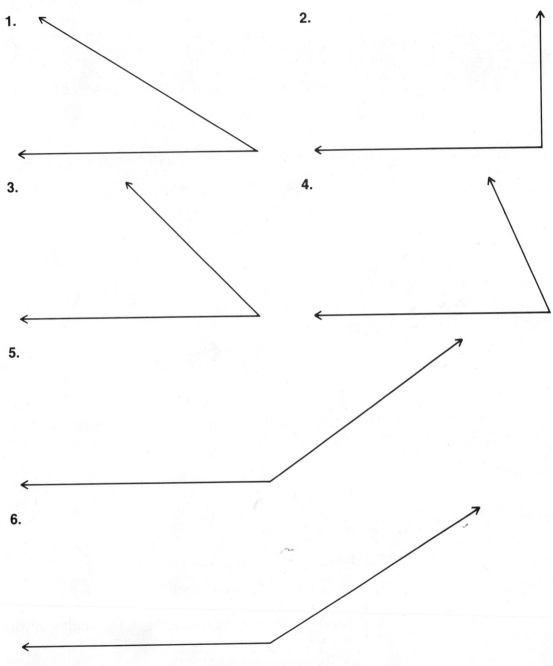

1.

2.

3.

4.

5.

6.

Draw an angle for the given measure. Use your protractor.

7. 60°   **8.** 73°   **9.** 18°   **10.** 45°   **11.** 135°   **12.** 93°

Triangles

EXAMPLE 1 Find the sum of the measures of the angles of △ABC.

read: triangle

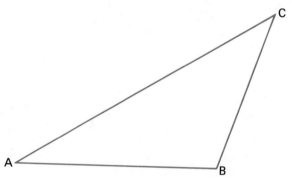

SOLUTION Think: measure of ∠A + measure of ∠B + measure of ∠C
  30°   110°   40°

Use a protractor.

$$\begin{array}{r} 30 \\ 110 \\ +\ 40 \\ \hline 180 \end{array}$$

So, the sum of the measures of the angles of △ABC is 180°.

- -

1. Draw a triangle. Measure each angle.

2. What is the sum of the measures of the angles of your triangle?

The sum of the measures of the angles of a triangle is 180°.

EXAMPLE 2 Find the measure of ∠B in the triangle.

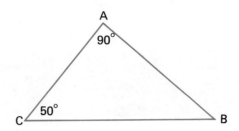

SOLUTION

Find the sum of the measures of ∠A and ∠C. Then subtract the sum from 180°.

90°	180°	←	Sum of the measures of the angles of a triangle
+50°	−140°		
140°	40°		

So, the measure of ∠B is 40°.

- -

Find the measure of ∠B in each triangle.

3.
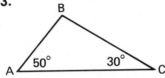

4.
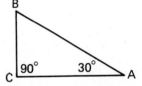

EXERCISES
Find the measure of ∠B in each triangle.

1.
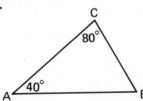

2.
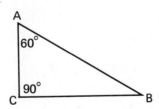

3.
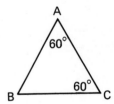

In each triangle, the angles marked x have the same measure. Find the measure of each angle marked x.

4.
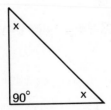

5.
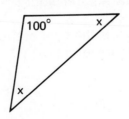

6.
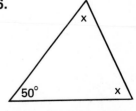

Parallelograms

EXAMPLE 1   Find the sum of the measures of the angles of parallelogram *ABCD*.

A parallelogram is a figure with four sides and with its opposite sides parallel.

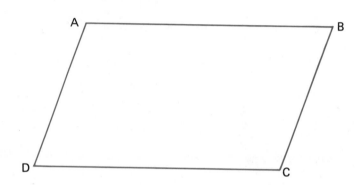

SOLUTION   Measure of ∠*A*:   110°
Use a protractor. Then, add the measures.

Measure of ∠*B*:   70°
Measure of ∠*C*:   110°
Measure of ∠*D*: + 70°
                              360°

So, the sum of the measures of the angles of a parallelogram is 360°.

- -

1. Draw a parallelogram. Measure each angle.

2. What is the sum of the measures of the angles of your parallelogram?

The sum of the measures of the angles of a parallelogram is 360°.

EXAMPLE 2 Find the measure of ∠A in the parallelogram.

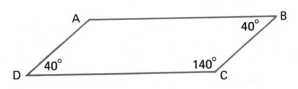

SOLUTION

40°
140°
+ 40°
220°

360° ←————— Sum of the measures of the
−220°   angles of a parallelogram
140°

So, the measure of ∠A is 140°.

——————————————————————————————

Find the measure of ∠A in each parallelogram.

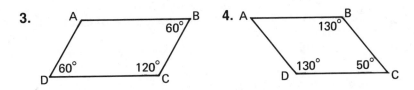

3. ∠A with 60° at B, 60° at D, 120° at C

4. A with 130° at B, 130° at D, 50° at C

EXAMPLE 3 Find the sum of the measures of the angles of each pair of consecutive angles of parallelogram ABCD.

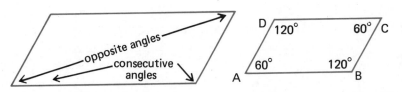

SOLUTION

∠A:	60°	∠B:	120°	∠C:	60°	∠D:	120°
∠B:	+120°	∠C:	+ 60°	∠D:	+120°	∠A:	+ 60°
	180°		180°		180°		180°

So, the sum of the measures of each pair of consecutive angles of a parallelogram is 180°.

EXAMPLE 4 Find the measure of each angle in a pair of opposite angles in the figure in Example 3.

SOLUTION ∠A: 60°   ∠B: 120°
∠C: 60°   ∠D: 120°

So, the opposite angles of a parallelogram have the same measure.

EXAMPLE 5 Find the measure of ∠B and the measure ∠C.

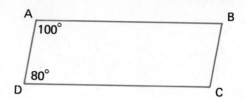

SOLUTION

Consecutive angles of a parallelogram add up to 180°.

∠A + ∠B = 180°	∠A = ∠C
100° + ∠B = 180°	∠A = 100°
∠B = 80°	∠C = 100°

Opposite angles of a parallelogram have the same measure.

So, the measure of ∠B is 80° and the measure of ∠C is 100°.

- -

Find the measure of each angle marked x.

5.
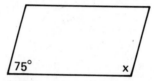

6.
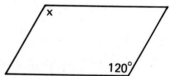

═══

EXERCISES

Find the measure of each angle marked x.

1.
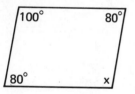

2.
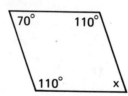

3.

4.

5.
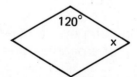

6.
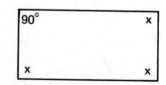

Find the measures of ∠A, ∠B, and ∠C.   **Find the measures of ∠E, ∠F, and ∠G.**

7.
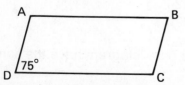

8.
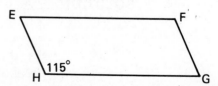

268 PARALLELOGRAMS

Diagonals of Rectangles

OBJECTIVE To discover and use some of the properties of the diagonals of a rectangle

EXAMPLE 1 Find the length of the diagonals of each rectangle. (The diagonals are shown in blue.)

Use a ruler marked in millimeters.

Carefully measure both diagonals in each figure.

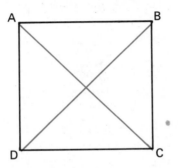

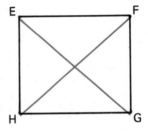

SOLUTION The length of *AC* is 5 cm.
The length of *BD* is 5 cm.

The length of *EG* is 4 cm.
The length of *HF* is 4 cm.

The diagonals of a rectangle are the same length.

- -

Without measuring, find the length of diagonal *AC*.

1.

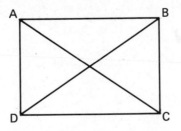

The length of *DB* is 24 cm.

2.

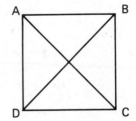

The length of *DB* is 46 cm.

EXAMPLE 2 Is point *O* the midpoint of each diagonal?

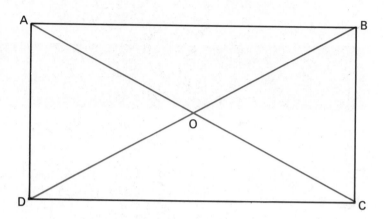

SOLUTION Measure the lengths of *AO* and *OC*.

Use a ruler marked in millimeters.

The length of *AO* is 50 mm. The length of *OC* is 50 mm.

Since the lengths of *AO* and *OC* are the same, point *O* is the midpoint of diagonal *AC*.

Measure the lengths of *DO* and *OB*.

The length of *DO* is 50 mm. The length of *OB* is 50 mm.

Since the lengths of *DO* and *OB* are the same, point *O* is the midpoint of diagonal *DB*.

So, point *O* is the midpoint of each diagonal.

- -

Find the measures.

3.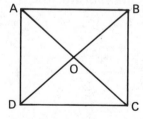

$AO = 6$ cm
$OC = \underline{}$ cm
$BD = \underline{}$ cm
$OB = \underline{}$ cm

4.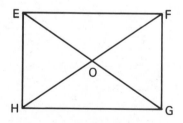

$EG = 30$ mm
$EO = \underline{}$ mm
$OG = \underline{}$ mm
$FH = \underline{}$ mm

EXERCISES
Find the measures.

1.

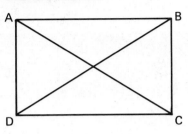

$AC = 17$ cm
$DB = \underline{?}$ cm

2.

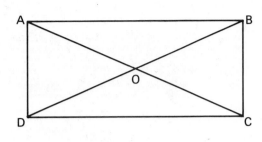

$AC = 72$ cm
$OC = \underline{?}$ cm
$DB = \underline{?}$ cm

3.

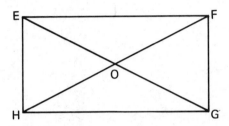

$EO = 40$ cm
$EG = \underline{?}$ cm
$HO = \underline{?}$ cm
$HF = \underline{?}$ cm

4.

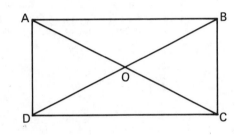

$OB = 12$ cm
$AC = \underline{?}$ cm

5.

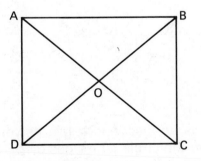

$AO = 15$ cm
$AD = 18$ cm
$OD = \underline{?}$ cm
Perimeter of $\triangle AOD = \underline{?}$ cm

6.

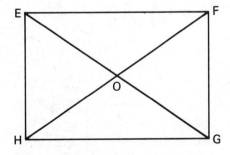

$FH = 52$ mm
$FG = 40$ mm
$FO = \underline{?}$ mm
$OG = \underline{?}$ mm
Perimeter of $\triangle FOG = \underline{?}$ mm

Circles

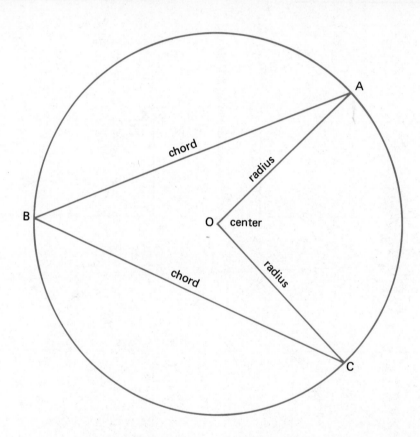

1. ∠AOC is a central angle. Its vertex is the center of the circle. The sides of ∠AOC are radii. ∠AOC cuts off arc AC. Measure ∠AOC.

2. ∠B is an inscribed angle. Its vertex is on the circle. The sides of ∠B are chords. ∠B and ∠AOC cut off the same arc. Measure ∠B.

True or false?

3. The measure of ∠AOC is twice the measure of ∠B.

4. The measure of ∠B is one-half the measure of ∠AOC.

Circles and Their Angles

OBJECTIVE To use the relationship between the measures of an inscribed angle and a central angle of a circle

EXAMPLE 1 Find the measure of the angle marked *x*.

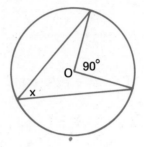

SOLUTION
$$\begin{array}{r} 45 \\ 2\overline{)90} \end{array}$$

The measure of ∠*x* is one-half the measure of ∠*O*.

So, the measure of ∠*x* is 45°.

- -

Find the measure of each angle marked x.

1.
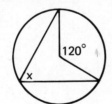

2.
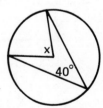

EXERCISES

Find the measure of each angle marked x.

1.
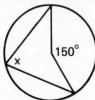

2.
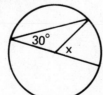

3.
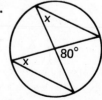

Test: Unit 13

Measure each angle. Use a protractor.

1.

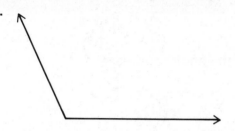

2.

Find the measure of each angle marked x.

3.

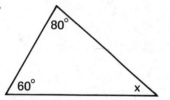

80°

60°   x

4.

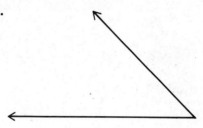

110°   70°

x   110°

5. Find the measures of ∠B, ∠C, and ∠D.

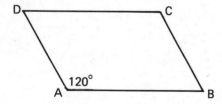

D   C

120°

A   B

6. Find the measures of *OC* and *DB*. *AO* = 14 cm.

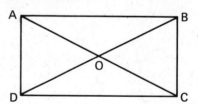

A   B

O

D   C

Find the measure of each angle marked x.

7.

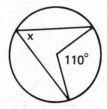

x

110°

8.

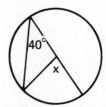

40°

x

UNIT 14

Statistics

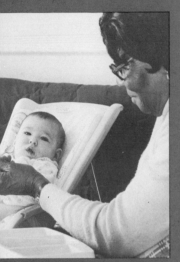

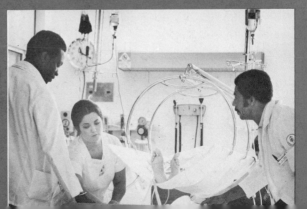

Mode

The mode is the number that occurs most often.

The 84 occurs most often.

95, 95
84, 84, 84 ◀───── MODE
83
81
79, 79
78, 78
71

EXAMPLE   Find the mode for the test scores.

88, 96, 82, 86
96, 70, 72, 82
82, 76, 74, 80

SOLUTION   Put the scores in order.

Arrange them vertically
or horizontally.

96, 96, 88, 86, 82, 82, 82, 80, 76, 74, 72, 70

Select the score that occurs the most.
96, 96, 88, 86, 82, 82, 82, 80, 76, 74, 72, 70

The mode is 82.

EXERCISES
Find the mode.

1. 36, 35, 32, 15, 23, 34
   25, 32, 36, 23, 22, 36

2. 3, 5, 6, 14, 7, 16, 12, 4
   16, 15, 10, 4, 7, 15, 5, 4

3. 42, 47, 46, 42, 42, 43
   43, 41, 46, 44, 40, 44

4. 104, 108, 116, 218, 218
   208, 104, 206, 116, 218

5. 87, 93, 88, 87, 88
   80, 70, 70, 70, 74
   88, 92, 93, 87, 88

6. 220, 215, 210, 215, 210
   225, 235, 200, 210, 235
   215, 240, 270, 215, 215

Median

The median is the number that appears in the middle of a set of data.

83
82
80, 80
The middle score is 79.   79 ←——— MEDIAN
There are four scores   78, 78, 78
above it and four below.   77

EXAMPLE Find the median for the bowling scores.
125, 160, 183
198, 175, 125
156, 160, 190

SOLUTION Put the scores in order.
Arrange them vertically   198
or horizontally.   190
                             183
Count the number of scores, 175
and choose the middle one.   160, 160
                             156
                             125, 125

The median is 160.

EXERCISES
Find the median.

1. 235, 240, 245,
   250, 220, 200,
   260, 250, 240

2. 28, 30, 29, 40, 30,
   36, 42, 44, 50, 49
   29, 37, 39, 40, 33

3. 113, 115, 111
   117, 119, 121
   131, 113, 129

4. 36, 38, 40, 34, 38
   34, 40, 42, 32, 40
   50, 48, 30, 46, 48

Mean

The mean is the average.

40
45
30
35
60
55
50

The average is 45.

$$7\overline{)315}$$

45 ⟵ ——— MEAN
7 scores ⬏   ⬑ Sum of scores

EXAMPLE   Find the mean for the heights in centimeters.

122
120
140
142
130
136
134

SOLUTION   Find the sum.

Add the numbers.   924

Find the number of scores.

Count the numbers.   7

Divide to find the average.

$$7\overline{)924}$$ 132

The mean is 132 centimeters.

EXERCISES
Find the mean.

1. 24, 36, 22, 27, 31

2. 120, 130, 120, 140, 160

3. 213, 315, 205, 300,
   240, 225, 314, 225

4. 7, 8, 15, 12, 19, 23, 11,
   17, 19, 24, 20, 25, 21

Mode, Median, and Mean

OBJECTIVE To find the mode, median, and mean of a set of data

Find the mode, median, and mean for each set of information.

1.

Boys' Squad	
Player	Height in Cm
Amir	185
Guy	190
Dave	175
Isao	178
Bob	180
Jack	178
Pat	195
Jorge	183
Rob	178
Ben	188
Jose	188

2.

Girls' Squad	
Player	Height in Cm
Maria	180
Lea	175
Lu	175
Judy	165
Beth	160
Alicia	168
Reiko	171
Mary	175
Leslie	163
Jill	158
Betty	165

3.

Player	Points Scored
Amir	86
Guy	90
Pat	94
Jose	102
Isao	72
Bob	100
Jorge	72

4.

Player	Points Scored
Maria	102
Lea	89
Beth	87
Alicia	93
Leslie	80
Reiko	102
Judy	70

Reading Bar Graphs

OBJECTIVE To read a bar graph

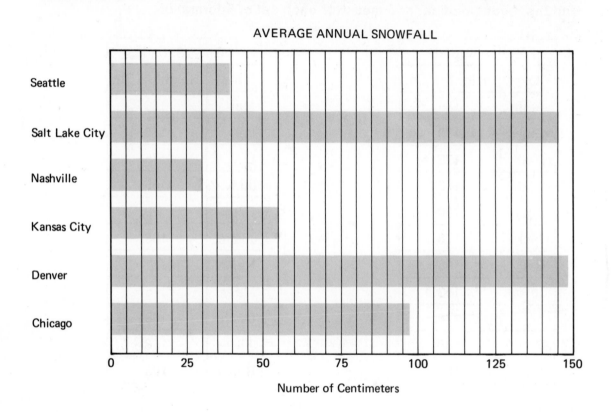

AVERAGE ANNUAL SNOWFALL

Number of Centimeters

Answer each question about the bar graph.

1. What is the title of the bar graph?

2. What is shown on the vertical scale? the horizontal scale?

3. Which city had the most snow? the least?

4. Which cities had more snow than Chicago? less than Chicago?

5. Which two cities together had a total snowfall less than 75 cm?

6. About how much snow fell in each city?

COMMON SURNAMES IN THE U.S.A.

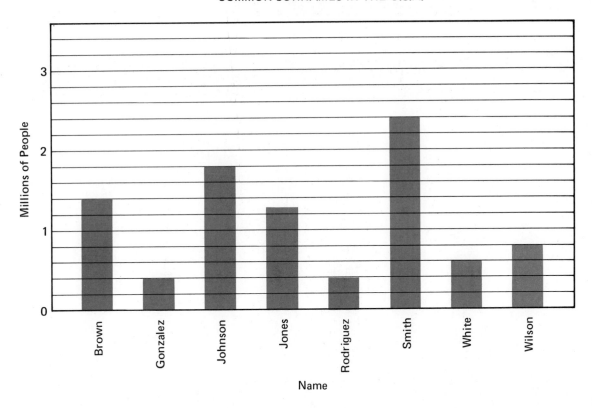

Answer each question about the bar graph.

7. About how many people are named Brown? Rodriguez? Wilson?

8. Which of the names are for more than 1.5 million people? less than 1 million?

9. About how many more Smiths are there than Johnsons?

10. About how many people are named Gonzales or White?

11. Are there more people named Brown than Johnson?

12. Are there more people named Brown than Jones?

Fun Corner

Can you give 3 more numbers in the set? Try it.

1. 1, 5, 9, 13, 17, 21, __?__, __?__, __?__

2. 0, 1, 1, 2, 3, 5, 8, 13, 21, __?__, __?__, __?__

3. 2, 3, 5, 9, 17, 33, 65, __?__, __?__, __?__

Making a Bar Graph

OBJECTIVE   To organize data and make a bar graph to display it

EXAMPLE   Here are the voting results.

VOTES CAST

4	3	4	5	3	1
4	2	2	2	3	2
3	1	4	4	1	5
3	4	2	3	2	4

Organize the voting results and make a bar graph.

SOLUTION

Organize the data in a table.
First tally the votes.
Then count the tallies.

Project	Tally	Votes
Car wash	卌 II	7
Candy sale	卌 I	6
Magazine sale	卌 I	6
Yard work	III	3
Baby-sitting	II	2

Use the table to make a graph.

Label the horizontal and vertical scales.
Give the graph a title.

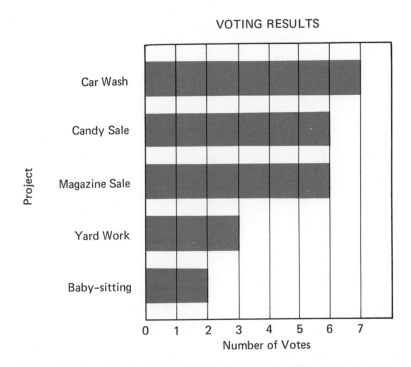

VOTING RESULTS

EXERCISES
Organize the data and make a bar graph.

1. Maximum Temperature in May

Juneau, Alaska	14°C
St. Paul, Minnesota	10°C
Charleston, South Carolina	27°C
Baltimore, Maryland	19°C
Key West, Florida	28°C
Raleigh, North Carolina	23°C
St. Louis, Missouri	18°C

2. Dave's Golf Scores

Game	Score
1	84
2	88
3	86
4	90
5	84
6	88

Reading Broken-line Graphs

OBJECTIVE   To read a broken-line graph

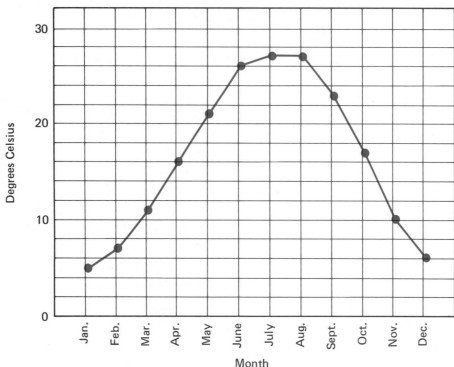

AVERAGE TEMPERATURE FOR MEMPHIS

Answer each question about the broken-line graph.

1. What is the title of the graph?

2. What is shown on each scale?

3. In Memphis, which months have the highest average temperature? the lowest?

4. For which months is the average temperature above 18°C? below 10°C?

5. Between which two months is the change in temperature the greatest? the least?

6. About what is the average temperature for each month?

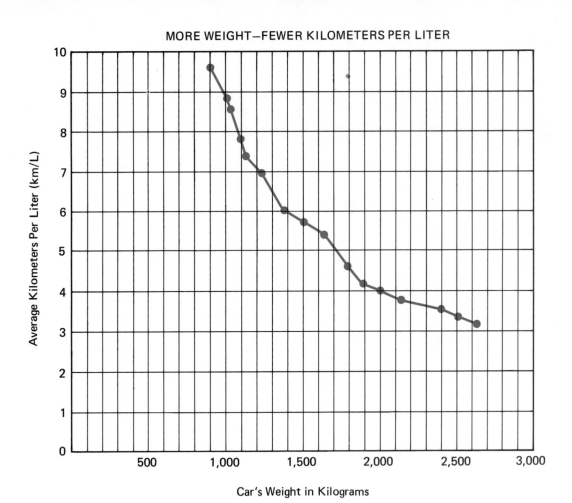

MORE WEIGHT—FEWER KILOMETERS PER LITER

Average Kilometers Per Liter (km/L) (vertical axis)

Car's Weight in Kilograms (horizontal axis)

7. What is shown on the horizontal scale?

8. What is shown on the vertical scale?

9. What weight car averages 5.8 km/L?

10. What weight car averages 4.0 km/L?

11. Estimate the weight of a car that averages 7.8 km/L.

12. Estimate the weight of a car that averages 4.6 km/L.

13. Between which weights is the decrease in km/L the most?

14. Between which weights is the decrease in km/L the least?

15. About how many times as much km/L would you get with a 1,500-kg car than with a 2,000-kg car?

16. About how many times as much km/L would you get with a 1,000-kg car than with a 1,500-kg car?

READING BROKEN-LINE GRAPHS **285**

Making A Broken-line Graph

EXAMPLE Here are Maria's scores on weekly mathematics tests.

80   85   90   75   100   95   70   95   95   70

Make a broken-line graph to show her scores.

SOLUTION

Organize the data
in a table.

Week	Score
1	80
2	85
3	90
4	75
5	100
6	95
7	70
8	95
9	95
10	70

Draw a graph.
Label the horizontal and
vertical scales.
Give the graph a title.

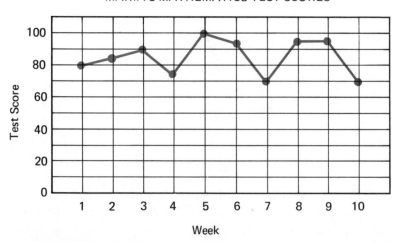

MARIA'S MATHEMATICS TEST SCORES

Make a broken-line graph.

1.

Jack's Sales Record	
Month	Amount
January	$ 950
February	900
March	1,200
April	950
May	1,050
June	1,300
July	1,350
August	1,100
September	1,200
October	800
November	1,150
December	1,500

2.

Tina's Bowling Record	
Game	Score
1	125
2	130
3	140
4	155
5	100
6	160
7	145
8	170
9	185
10	145
11	145
12	165

3. A bus company did a count of passengers during the rush hour on Tuesday. Here is the record.

7:15 am,   5 passengers
7:30 am, 10 passengers
7:50 am, 10 passengers
7:55 am, 50 passengers
8:00 am, 70 passengers
8:05 am, 60 passengers
8:10 am, 80 passengers
8:15 am, 50 passengers
8:20 am, 60 passengers
8:25 am, 90 passengers
8:30 am, 90 passengers
8:35 am, 60 passengers

4. Bill Latham kept a record of the temperature in his home town on Thursday.

7:00 am,   1°C
8:00 am,   2°C
9:00 am,   4°C
10:00 am,   6°C
11:00 am,   7°C
Noon,   8°C
1:00 pm,   9°C
2:00 pm,   11°C
3:00 pm,   13°C
4:00 pm,   12°C
5:00 pm,   10°C
6:00 pm,   8°C

Test: Unit 14

Here are the test scores of 25 students.

95	85	90	85	80
75	70	70	90	85
85	95	85	100	80
80	75	85	65	90
85	80	85	90	80

1. Find the mode.

2. Find the median.

3. Find the mean.

4. Make a bar graph.

5. Make a broken-line graph.

Fun Corner

Some multiplications with mixed numerals can be done mentally.

$12\frac{1}{2} \longrightarrow 12 + \frac{1}{2}$

$\times 10\frac{1}{4} \longrightarrow 10 + \frac{1}{4}$

$120 \longleftarrow 10 \times 12$

$5 \longleftarrow 10 \times \frac{1}{2}$

$3 \longleftarrow \frac{1}{4} \times 12$

$\frac{1}{8} \longleftarrow \frac{1}{4} \times \frac{1}{2}$

$128\frac{1}{8}$

So, $12\frac{1}{2} \times 10\frac{1}{4} = 128\frac{1}{8}$.

Multiply. Use this method.

1. $8\frac{1}{2}$
$\times 4\frac{1}{4}$

2. $8\frac{1}{3}$
$\times 9\frac{1}{4}$

3. $16\frac{1}{5}$
$\times 20\frac{1}{8}$

4. $9\frac{3}{4}$
$\times 8\frac{2}{3}$

UNIT 15
Ratio and Proportion

Ratio

OBJECTIVE   To write a ratio to compare two numbers

EXAMPLE 1

Josh had 22 hits and 10 misses out of 32 tries. Find the ratio, number of hits to number of tries.

SOLUTION   Think: Compare 22 to 32.

Write a fraction.

$\dfrac{22}{32}$ ⟵ Number compared

⟵ Number compared to

So, $\dfrac{22}{32}$ is the ratio.

⌐read: 22 to 32

EXAMPLE 2   Oranges were selling at 3 for 25¢.
Find these ratios: number of oranges to price and price to number of oranges.

SOLUTION   Think: $\dfrac{\text{Number compared}}{\text{Number compared to}}$

$\dfrac{\text{number of oranges}}{\text{price}} = \dfrac{3}{25}$

Notice that the ratios are not the same.

$\dfrac{\text{price}}{\text{number of oranges}} = \dfrac{25}{3}$

- -

Jack traveled 180 km on 30 L of fuel. Find the ratio of the numbers.

1. $\dfrac{\text{kilometers}}{\text{liters of fuel}}$

2. $\dfrac{\text{liters of fuel}}{\text{kilometers}}$

EXERCISES

A math class of 29 students has 15 girls and 14 boys. Find the ratio of the numbers.

1. $\dfrac{girls}{boys}$
2. $\dfrac{boys}{total\ in\ class}$

Tom got 86 votes for president and Meg got 114. Find the ratio of the numbers.

3. $\dfrac{Tom's\ votes}{votes\ cast}$
4. $\dfrac{Meg's\ votes}{Tom's\ votes}$

A punch mixture contained:
4 cups of berries
2 cups of lemonade
3 cups of ginger ale
2 cups of orange juice
Find the ratio of the number of cups.

5. $\dfrac{orange\ juice}{total}$
6. $\dfrac{ginger\ ale}{berries}$

A concrete mixture contained:
1,300 kg of cement
550 kg of water
2,250 kg of sand

Find the ratio of the number of kg.

7. $\dfrac{cement}{sand}$
8. $\dfrac{water}{cement}$

Use the word MISSISSIPPI. Find the ratio.

9. $\dfrac{I}{S}$ 10. $\dfrac{I}{P}$ 11. $\dfrac{P}{I}$ 12. $\dfrac{S}{P}$

A 5-m steel beam weighed 200 kg. Find the ratio.

13. $\dfrac{weight}{length}$
14. $\dfrac{length}{weight}$

Student	Height	Weight
John	175 cm	82 kg
Jane	180 cm	85 kg
Mary	156 cm	50 kg

Find the ratio.

15. $\dfrac{John's\ height}{John's\ weight}$
16. $\dfrac{Jane's\ height}{Jane's\ weight}$
17. $\dfrac{Mary's\ weight}{Mary's\ height}$

Fun Corner

Each letter stands for a digit. Crack the code so the sum will be correct.

```
  F O R T Y
    T E N
    T E N
  S I X T Y
```

Simplifying Ratios

EXAMPLE 1   Cleo got 6 hits out of 10 times at bat.
Write the ratio, number of hits to number of times at bat, in simplest form.

SOLUTION   Think: $\dfrac{\text{number of hits}}{\text{number of times at bat}} = \dfrac{6}{10}$

Change $\frac{6}{10}$ to simplest form. $\dfrac{6}{10} = \dfrac{6 \div 2}{10 \div 2}$, or $\dfrac{3}{5}$
Use division.

The ratio is $\frac{3}{5}$ in simplest form.

EXAMPLE 2   Simplify the ratio $\dfrac{5\frac{1}{2}}{10}$.

SOLUTION   Think of $\dfrac{5\frac{1}{2}}{10}$ as $5\frac{1}{2} \div 10$

$5\frac{1}{2} = 5 + \frac{1}{2}$, or $\frac{10}{2} + \frac{1}{2}$ $5\frac{1}{2} \div 10 = \dfrac{11}{2} \div 10$

Multiply by the reciprocal.   or $\dfrac{11}{2} \times \dfrac{1}{10} = \dfrac{11}{20}$

- -

Simplify the ratio.
1. 15 to 25

2. $7\frac{1}{2}$ to 12

3. $\dfrac{12}{20}$

4. $\dfrac{4\frac{1}{3}}{4}$

EXERCISES
Simplify.
1. 8 to 12

2. 12 to 8

3. 60 to 70

4. 80 to 100

5. $3\frac{1}{2}$ to 8

6. 8 to $3\frac{1}{2}$

7. 9 to $1\frac{1}{3}$

8. $1\frac{1}{3}$ to 9

9. $\dfrac{5\frac{1}{4}}{3}$

10. $\dfrac{2\frac{1}{2}}{1}$

11. $\dfrac{5\frac{1}{2}}{11}$

12. $\dfrac{1\frac{3}{8}}{1}$

Comparing Ratios

OBJECTIVE   To determine which rate from a given set is the best

EXAMPLE   Joe read 55 pages in 22 minutes.
Jill read 70 pages in 25 minutes.
Whose reading rate was better?

SOLUTION   Find the number of pages per minute.
              Joe's Rate   Jill's Rate

Ratio $\dfrac{\text{number pages}}{\text{time}}$ $\dfrac{55}{22}$ $\dfrac{70}{25}$

Write in simplest form. $\dfrac{55 \div 11}{22 \div 11}$ $\dfrac{70 \div 5}{25 \div 5}$

$\dfrac{5}{2} \longrightarrow 2\overline{)5.0}^{\,2.5}$ $\dfrac{5}{2}$ $\dfrac{14}{5}$

$\dfrac{14}{5} \longrightarrow 5\overline{)14.0}^{\,2.8}$

                              2.5   2.8

So, Jill's reading rate was better.

- -

Compare the ratios. Which is the better buy?

1. 6 oranges for 70¢ or 8 apples for $1.10

2. 3 ties for $9.95 or 5 scarves for $14.95

EXERCISES
Solve by comparing the ratios.

1. Which car had the better average?

Car	Distance	Fuel Used
A	150 km	24L
B	176 km	28L

2. Which team had the better record?

Team	Games Won	Games Played
Oak Park	18	25
Novi	19	26

3. Which batter had the better record?

Batter	At Bat	Hits
Cesar	302	97
Joni	239	81

4. Whose painting rate was higher?

Name	Area	Price
Mr. Cato	225 m²	$405
Ms. Day	280 m²	$490

5. Which school had the higher absentee record?

School	Students	Absences
De Kalb	1,282	80
Rushville	3,600	240

6. Who worked faster?

Name	Parts Made	Time
John	1,282	8 h
Joe	1,525	9 h

7. Which driver spent less?

Driver	Distance	Cost
Beth	230 km	$18.40
Lulu	260 km	$23.40

8. Which paint had the better coverage?

Paint	Area	Amount Used
A	1,275 m²	3L
B	1,450 m²	4L

9. Which driver had the fastest driving speed? the slowest?

Driver	Km	Hours
Jim	227	5
Gil	280	6
Lila	180	8

10. Which beam has the highest ratio $\frac{weight}{length}$?

Beam	Length	Weight
A	7 m	200 kg
B	4 m	140 kg
C	6 m	180 kg

Ratios as Decimals

EXAMPLE 1 Write the ratio $\frac{5}{8}$ as a decimal.

SOLUTION

Divide to change
$\frac{5}{8}$ to a decimal.

$$
\begin{array}{r}
.625 \\
8\overline{)5.000} \\
\underline{4\,8} \\
20 \\
\underline{16} \\
40 \\
\underline{40}
\end{array}
$$

So, the ratio $\frac{5}{8}$ = .625.

EXAMPLE 2 Alice had 8 hits out of 15 times at bat.
Write her batting average as a decimal to the
nearest thousandth.

SOLUTION Think: 8 hits out of 15 times at bat = $\frac{8}{15}$.

Carry the division 4
places.

$$
\begin{array}{r}
.5333 \\
15\overline{)8.0000} \\
\underline{7\,5} \\
50 \\
\underline{45} \\
50 \\
\underline{45} \\
50 \\
\underline{45} \\
5
\end{array}
$$

Round to the nearest
thousandth.

So, her batting average is .533.

- -

Write the ratio as a decimal to the nearest thousandth.

1. $\frac{1}{3}$ **2.** $\frac{3}{8}$ **3.** $\frac{5}{16}$ **4.** $\frac{5}{9}$

5. Bill had 7 hits out of 20 times at bat. Find his
batting average to the nearest thousandth.

EXERCISES

Find each player's batting average to the nearest thousandth. Which player had the better record?

1.

Player	At Bat	Hits
Sue	136	37
Betty	223	46

2.

Player	At Bat	Hits
Jon	253	62
Mark	136	44

3.

Player	At Bat	Hits
Chuck	362	97
Ben	413	108

4.

Player	At Bat	Hits
Brenda	406	112
Juma	214	70

5.

Player	At Bat	Hits
Bart	125	32
Sam	53	17

6.

Player	At Bat	Hits
Sally	28	9
Pat	57	19

7.

Player	At Bat	Hits
Marita	75	17
Sandy	82	20

8.

Player	At Bat	Hits
Karl	167	56
Jack	49	16

Fun Corner

The chart shows that 1 twenty-five, 2 fives, 2 ones is 37.

25	5	1	
1	2	2	37
			72
			8
			99

Complete the chart.

Probability

OBJECTIVE To find the probability that an event will occur

EXAMPLE 1 What is the probability of rolling a 5?

SOLUTION Think: There are 6 possible outcomes.

List the possible outcomes.   1, 2, 3, 4, 5, and 6

How many outcomes are 5? 5 is 1 outcome out of 6; 1 to 6 chance of rolling a 5

Write the ratio.   So, $P(5) = \frac{1}{6}$.

└────── read: the probability of rolling 5

EXAMPLE 2 Find the probability of spinning a number less than 3.

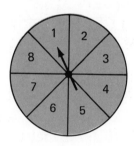

SOLUTION Think: There are 8 possible outcomes.

1 is less than 3 and   1, 2, 3, 4, 5, 6, 7, and 8
2 is less than 3.
2 outcomes out of 8 are less than 3.

So, $P(1 \text{ or } 2) = \frac{2}{8}$, or $\frac{1}{4}$.

- -

Find the probability. Think of rolling a die.

1. $P(6)$ **2.** $P(4)$ **3.** $P(1 \text{ or } 3)$ **4.** $P(3 \text{ or } 4 \text{ or } 5)$

5. $P(5 \text{ or } 6)$ **6.** $P(1 \text{ or } 2 \text{ or } 3 \text{ or } 4 \text{ or } 5 \text{ or } 6)$

EXAMPLE 3 What is the probability of the numbers having a sum of 3?

Spin each one and add
the numbers shown.

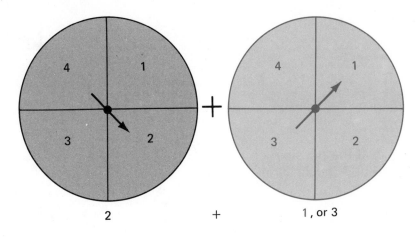

2 + 1, or 3

SOLUTION

Find the possible
outcomes.

1 + 1	2 + 1	3 + 1	4 + 1
1 + 2	2 + 2	3 + 2	4 + 2
1 + 3	2 + 3	3 + 3	4 + 3
1 + 4	2 + 4	3 + 4	4 + 4

Outcomes along the
diagonals have the
same sum.

2 outcomes have a
sum of 3.

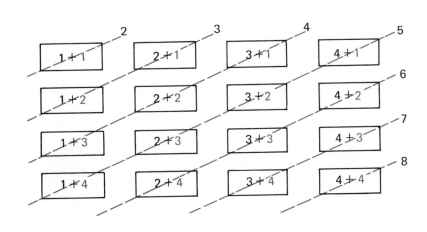

1 to 8 chance of getting
a sum of 3.

So, $P(\text{sum } 3) = \frac{2}{16}$, or $\frac{1}{8}$.

- -

Find the probability. Use the table above.
   7. $P(\text{sum of 2})$ **8.** $P(\text{sum of 8})$ **9.** $P(\text{sum of 5})$

EXERCISES

1. Toss a penny.

List the possible outcomes.
Find *P*(tails). *P*(heads).

2.

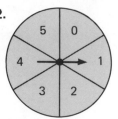

Find *P*(1 or 2). *P*(4 or 5). *P*(3 or 4 or 5).

3.

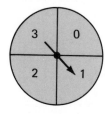

Draw 1 marble.
Find *P*(color). *P*(black).

4.

1,500 gum balls

100 blue gum balls

1 black gum ball

Find *P*(blue gum ball).
P(black gum ball).

5. Roll two dice. List all of the possible outcomes in a table as in Example 3.
Find *P*(sum of 3).
P(sum of 12). *P*(sum of 7).

6. Use your table from Exercise 5.
Find *P*(sum less than 5).
P(sum of 5 or more).
P(sum less than 13).

7. Spin both needles.

List all the possible sums in a table.
Find *P*(sum of 6). *P*(sum of 1).
P(sum of 4).

8. Toss two coins.

List all of the possible outcomes in a table.
Find *P*(heads on both coins).
P(tails on the penny and heads on the quarter).
P(heads on the penny).

Proportion

$\frac{10}{15} = \frac{2}{3}$ $\frac{8}{12} = \frac{2}{3}$

$\frac{10}{15}$ and $\frac{8}{12}$ are equal ratios.

$\frac{10}{15} = \frac{8}{12}$ is a proportion.

In a proportion the cross products are equal.

EXAMPLE 1   Does this box statement show a proportion?

Cupsof sugar	$2\frac{1}{2}$	10
Cookies	20	80

SOLUTION   See if the cross products are equal.

The arrows show the cross products.

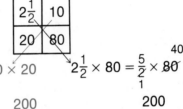

Cups of sugar	$2\frac{1}{2}$	10
Cookies	20	80

10×20

$2\frac{1}{2} \times 80 = \frac{5}{2} \times \overset{40}{\cancel{80}}$
$\qquad\qquad\qquad\quad \underset{1}{}$

The cross products are the same.

200 200

Yes, the box statement shows a proportion.

Does the box statement show a proportion?

1. Hours	10	$2\frac{1}{2}$
Kilometers	16	4

2. Meters	100	50
Hours	125	80

EXAMPLE 2   Write a box statement. Does it show a proportion? Last week, Betty got 10 hits out of 15 times at bat. This week, she got 8 hits out of 12 times at bat.

SOLUTION

Hits	10	8
At bat	15	12

Test the cross products.

$\begin{array}{r} 15 \\ \times\ 8 \\ \hline 120 \end{array}$

$8 \times 15 = 120 \qquad 10 \times 12 = 120$

Yes, the box statement shows a proportion.

Write a box statement. Does it form a proportion?

3. Last week, Willie earned $200 in 40 hours.
This week, he earned $60 in 10 hours.

EXERCISES
Does the box statement show a proportion?

1. Cupcakes

24	32
$1\frac{1}{2}$	2

Cups of sugar

2. Kilometers

80	90
$1\frac{1}{3}$	$1\frac{1}{2}$

Hours

3. Hours

44	30
$55	$45

Pay

4. Meters

5	15
15	25

Centimeters

5. cm

$3\frac{7}{8}$	$2\frac{3}{4}$
31	22

m

6. Tiles

950	300
$171	$54

Cost

7. Ribbons

3	12
$.37	$1.40

Cost

8. Kg

2	6
$1.78	$5.34

Cost

9. m³

2	25
15	180

L

Write a box statement. Then check to see if it shows a proportion.

10. Ellen was paid $2.10 for $5\frac{1}{4}$ hours of baby-sitting. She was paid $1.20 for 3 hours.

11. Gil drove 250 km in $6\frac{1}{4}$ h. Then he drove 200 km in 5 h.

12. One week, Mr. Sense earned $75 on $1,500 in sales. The next week, he made $250 on $5,000 in sales.

13. Sixteen kg of wheat produced 9 kg of flour. 72 kg produced $40\frac{1}{2}$ kg of flour.

14. Sixteen kg of peaches produced 22 L of sliced peaches. $75\frac{1}{2}$ kg produced 55 L of sliced peaches.

15. One week, Sam studied 6 hours and got 82 on a test. The next week he studied 4 hours and got 69 on a test.

16. An LP record provides 18 minutes of music. Five LP records provide 90 minutes of music.

17. One day, a restaurant used 100 kg of meat to serve 220 people. Another day, the restaurant used 125 kg of meat to serve 275 people.

Solving Proportions

OBJECTIVE To find the missing number in a proportion

EXAMPLE 1 What number is missing in the proportion?

Oranges	10	5
Cost	60¢	?

SOLUTION

Write the cross products.
Think: $5 \times 60 = 300$

Check: $10\overline{)300}$ → 30

$10 \times ? = 5 \times 60$
$\underbrace{10 \times ? = 300}$

read: 10 times what number is 300?

$10 \times 30 = 300$

So, the missing number is 30.

EXAMPLE 2 Find the missing number in this proportion.

Kg of meat	13.5	?
People	27	100

SOLUTION

$27 \times ? = 13.5 \times 100$
$27 \times ? = 1,350$

Divide.

$27\overline{)1,350}$ → 50
$\underline{135}$

Check: $\begin{array}{r} 27 \\ \times 50 \\ \hline 1,350 \end{array}$

So, the missing number is 50.

- -

Solve the proportion.

1.

Hits	22	?
Runs	9	54

2.

Meters	100	35
Hours	$2\frac{1}{2}$	?

EXERCISES
Solve the proportion.

1.

Cups of rice	3	?
Portions	8	20

2.

Cans of soup	3	5
Cost	47¢	?

3.

Pages	55	100
Minutes	25	?

4.

Cups of flour	2	$4\frac{1}{2}$
Eggs	3	?

5.

Boys	125	500
Girls	300	?

6.

Kilometers	51.2	?
Liters	8	40

7.

Value	$10,000	?
Taxes	$360	$1,440

8.

Shares of stock	150	500
Cost	$2,250	?

9.

Borrowed	$15,000	$50,000
Interest	$1,200	?

10.

Cups of milk	$2\frac{1}{4}$	?
Cookies	54	36

11.

Hours	12	$3\frac{1}{2}$
Pay	$54	?

12.

Kilometers	155	300
Liters	$10\frac{1}{3}$	?

Fun Corner

How many problems did Camila have right?

CAMILA, YOU GET 16¢ FOR EACH RIGHT ANSWER. YOU LOSE 10¢ FOR EACH WRONG ANSWER. THERE ARE 26 PROBLEMS.

I BROKE EVEN!

Proportions and Problem Solving

OBJECTIVE To solve problems by using proportions

EXAMPLE

120 km

How long to travel 320 kilometers?

SOLUTION Think: The ratio hours to kilometers is $1\frac{1}{2}$ to 120.

A box statement can help you solve the proportion. Show the cross products.

Hours	$1\frac{1}{2}$	?
Kilometers	120	320

$\frac{1}{2} \times 320 = 160;$

$1\frac{1}{2} \times 320 = 480$

To find the time, divide.

$120 \times ? = 1\frac{1}{2} \times 320$

$120 \times ? = 480$

$$\begin{array}{r} 4 \\ 120\overline{)480} \\ \underline{480} \end{array}$$

Check: 120
$\underline{\times 4}$
480

So, it takes 4 hours to travel 320 kilometers.

- -

Solve these problems.

1. Helen paid 80¢ for 48 bolts.
How much would she pay for 21 bolts?

2. Joe's recipe calls for $3\frac{1}{2}$ cups of milk to make 35 brownies. How much milk does he need to make 75 brownies?

EXERCISES
Solve these problems.

1. Ms. Carbone uses 1 kg of sliced turkey for each 8 dinner guests. How much sliced turkey would she use for 220 guests?

2. Rob drove in 64 runs in 256 times at bat. How many times must he bat to drive in 130 runs?

3. Jack mixes 525 kg of sand with each 6 sacks of cement. How much sand would he mix with 20 sacks of cement?

4. Ella earned $15.75 in interest on savings of $300. How much interest would she earn on savings of $550?

5. Alex bought 5 shares of stock for $436.25. How much would he pay for 12 shares of the same stock?

6. Jane paid $16.50 in sales tax on a used car which sold for $550. How much sales tax did she pay on $1?

7. Your town has a property tax of $36.18 per $1,000 value. Your home is valued at $12,200. How much are your taxes?

8. You have a $15,000 life-insurance policy. You pay $18.75 per year for each $1,000 insurance. How much is your annual payment?

9. Miss Gomez borrowed $16,000. The bank charged $960 interest. How much interest would she pay on $20,000?

10. Mike used .5 kg of grass seed to cover 22.5 m^2 of lawn. How much seed would he use to cover 162 m^2 of lawn?

11. A cubic meter of concrete makes 105.3 square meters of sidewalk. How much concrete should Mrs. Greene order for 1,158.3 square meters of sidewalk?

12. Jill's nursery guaranteed a certain evergreen tree would grow .2 meters in 2 years. How tall would the tree be in 7 years?

13. A 36,000-m^2 field produces 15,840 L of potatoes. How many m^2 must be planted to produce 24,640 L?

14. 3,300 kg of sand are needed to make 3 m^3 of concrete. How much concrete can be made with 5,500 kg?

15. Doris bought 8 bags of fertilizer for $15.84. She needs 3 more bags. How much will they cost?

16. Bob bought 4 dozen cupcakes for $5.28. How much did 1 cupcake cost?

17. How much of each ingredient is needed to serve 12 people?

Chicken-Rice: 8 servings

$1\frac{1}{2}$ cups diced chicken
3 cups cooked rice

18. How much of each ingredient is needed to serve 6 people?

Recipe: 8 servings

$\frac{1}{4}$ L creamed soup
2 L sliced potatoes

19. How much of each ingredient is needed to make 5 dozen buns?

Fruit Buns: Makes 18 buns

$\frac{1}{4}$ cup candied cherries
$\frac{1}{4}$ cup chopped nuts
$\frac{1}{4}$ cup shortening
1 egg
$2\frac{1}{4}$ cups flour
$\frac{1}{4}$ cup raisins
$\frac{1}{4}$ cup sugar
$\frac{3}{4}$ cup milk
1 cake of yeast

20. How much of each ingredient is needed to serve 250 people?

Punch: 25 servings

$\frac{2}{3}$ cup pineapple juice

8 lemons
8 oranges
2 cups sugar
6 L ginger ale
$2\frac{1}{2}$ cups strawberries
$5\frac{1}{4}$ cups ice cream
$\frac{3}{4}$ L sherbert

Fun Corner

Arrange the numbers 1 through 9 in the circles so that the sum of the numbers along each side of the triangle is 20. Use each number only once.

Test: Unit 15

Car A traveled 86 km/h. Car B traveled 60 km/h. Write the ratio.

1. $\dfrac{\text{A's speed}}{\text{B's speed}}$

2. $\dfrac{\text{B's speed}}{\text{A's speed}}$

Simplify the ratio.

3. $7\frac{1}{4}$ to 2

4. 75 to 150

5. $\frac{14}{42}$

6. $2\frac{1}{3}$ to 8

7. Which car traveled the greater number of kilometers per liter of fuel?

Car	Fuel	Km
A	25.4 L	370
B	20.4 L	304

8. Find each player's batting average to the nearest thousandth. Who had the better average?

Player	At Bat	Hits
Dave	318	82
Sarah	262	80

9. Find $P(2)$. $P(3$ or $4)$. $P(1$ or 3 or 5 or $7)$.

10. What is the probability of the numbers having a sum of 3?

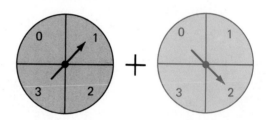

11. Does the box statement show a proportion?

12	18
21	32

12. Jack mixed 151.2 liters of water with 6.3 sacks of cement. How much water should he mix with 1 sack of cement?

Fun Corner

$n = 2 \times 2 \times 3 \times 5 \times 5 \times 7$

Without finding n, make true sentences.

1. $n \div 4 = \underline{\ ?\ }$

2. $n \div 60 = \underline{\ ?\ }$

3. $n \div 12 = \underline{\ ?\ }$

4. $n \div 175 = \underline{\ ?\ }$

UNIT 16
Percent

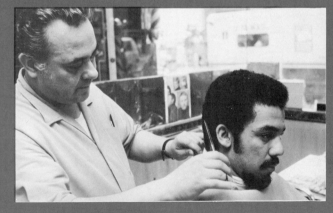

Meaning of Percent

Percent means per hundred, or for each 100.

40% means 40 out of 100, or $\frac{40}{100}$.

└──Read: 40 percent

EXAMPLE 1 Write a ratio with denominator 100.
8% of the students are absent.

SOLUTION Think: 8% means 8 out of 100.

% means for each 100. So, 8% means $\frac{8}{100}$.

EXAMPLE 2 Write a ratio with denominator 100.
Fred spends 150% as much time playing as working.

SOLUTION Think: 150% means 150 out of 100.
So, 150% means $\frac{150}{100}$.

EXAMPLE 3 Write a ratio with denominator 100.

$\frac{1}{2}$% of a cough syrup is alcohol.

SOLUTION Think: $\frac{1}{2}$% means $\frac{1}{2}$ out of 100.

So, $\frac{1}{2}$% means $\frac{\frac{1}{2}}{100}$.

- -

Write a ratio with denominator 100.

1. The sales tax is 3%.

2. The errors were $\frac{1}{4}$% of the total.

3. There was a 200% increase in enrollment.

EXERCISES

Write each as a ratio with denominator 100.

1. Taxes rose $\frac{1}{3}$% in the last year.

2. She saves 10% of her salary.

3. A car radiator contains a mixture which is 25% antifreeze.

4. In a high school 18% of the students are seniors.

5. Jay receives 8% commission on all sales.

6. Of the passes attempted by a quarterback, 42% were completed.

7. Mrs. Santa received a discount of 20% of the regular price.

8. The purchase of an automobile required a down payment of 20%.

9. The cost for masonry was 24% of the cost of the house.

10. A student spends 200% as much time studying as in class.

11. This candy is 40% sugar.

12. Circulation was up 125%.

13. Some wines contain 11% alcohol.

14. A governor received 53% of the votes.

15. Of the passenger planes owned by a company, 30% have jet engines.

16. Mary Ann answered correctly 87% of the questions on a test.

17. Driving a car takes up 40% of a sales rep's working time.

18. The error was less than 1% of the total measurement.

Percents as Decimals

EXAMPLE 1 Change 35% to a decimal.

SOLUTION Think: 35% means $\frac{35}{100}$

Each names 35 hundredths.
$$\frac{35}{100} = .35$$

So, 35% = .35

EXAMPLE 2 Change 250% to a decimal.

SOLUTION

Divide by 100 by "moving" the decimal point 2 places to the left.

$250\% = \frac{250}{100}$

Short Cut
$250\% = 2\,50\% = 2.50$

So, 250% = 2.50

- -

Change to a decimal.

  1. 42%   **2.** 300%   **3.** 50%   **4.** 175%

EXAMPLE 3 Change 7% to a decimal.

SOLUTION $7\% = \frac{7}{100}$ $7\% = \,07\% = .07$

So, 7% = .07

EXAMPLE 4 Change $37\frac{1}{2}\%$ to a decimal.

SOLUTION Think: $37\frac{1}{2}\% = 37.5\%$

$$37.5\% = .375$$

So, $37\frac{1}{2}\% = .375$

- -

Change to a decimal.

  5. 1%   **6.** 9%   **7.** $6\frac{1}{2}\%$ **8.** $13\frac{1}{2}\%$

EXAMPLE 5   Change .5% to a decimal.

SOLUTION   .5% = .005% = .005

So, .5% = .005

EXAMPLE 6   Change $33\frac{1}{3}$% to a decimal.

SOLUTION $33\frac{1}{3}$% = $33\frac{1}{3}$% = $.33\frac{1}{3}$

So, $33\frac{1}{3}$% = $.33\frac{1}{3}$

- -

Change to a decimal.

9. .2%   **10.** $16\frac{2}{3}$%   **11.** .01%   **12.** $5\frac{1}{3}$%

EXERCISES

Change to a decimal.

1. 10%   **2.** $1\frac{1}{2}$%   **3.** 4%   **4.** $12\frac{1}{2}$%   **5.** 125%   **6.** .8%

7. 500%   **8.** 93%   **9.** 2%   **10.** 83.4%   **11.** $5\frac{2}{3}$%   **12.** 375%

13. .9%   **14.** 400%   **15.** $66\frac{2}{3}$%   **16.** .03%   **17.** 8%   **18.** 625%

19. 29%   **20.** 2.9%   **21.** 290%   **22.** $12\frac{1}{3}$%   **23.** $1.2\frac{1}{3}$%   **24.** $123\frac{1}{3}$%

25. 3.5%   **26.** 80%   **27.** .6%   **28.** $41\frac{1}{2}$%   **29.** 325%   **30.** .09%

Fun Corner

Four cats and 3 kittens weigh 18.5 kilograms.
Three cats and 4 kittens weigh 16.5 kilograms.
How much do a cat and a kitten weigh together?

Decimals as Percents

OBJECTIVE To change a decimal to a percent

EXAMPLE 1 Change .25 to percent.

SOLUTION Think: $.25 = \frac{25}{100}$ ⟵——Ratio with denominator 100
So, .25 = 25%.

EXAMPLE 2 Change .7 to percent.

SOLUTION Think: $.7 = \frac{7}{10}$ ——⟶ $\frac{7 \times 10}{10 \times 10} = \frac{70}{100}$.
So, .7 = 70%.

Change to percent.

1. .45	**2.** .9	**3.** .01	**4.** .5

EXAMPLE 3 Change .125 to percent.

SOLUTION $.125 = \frac{125}{1,000}$ Short Cut
$\frac{125}{1,000} = \frac{125 \div 10}{1,000 \div 10} = \frac{12.5}{100}$ $= \frac{12.5}{100}$ .125 = .12ᴧ5 = 12.5%
$12.5 = 12\frac{1}{2}$

So, .125 = 12.5%, or $12\frac{1}{2}$%.

EXAMPLE 4 Change 3.5 to percent.

SOLUTION Think: 3.5 = 3.50ᴧ = 350%

"Move" the decimal point.

So, 3.5 = 350%.

Change to percent.

5. .375	**6.** 2.1	**7.** .085	**8.** 4.8

EXERCISES

Change to percent.

1. .07	**2.** .12	**3.** .38	**4.** .09	**5.** .6	**6.** .4
7. .1	**8.** .02	**9.** .165	**10.** .381	**11.** 1.5	**12.** 4.75

Percents as Fractions

EXAMPLE 1   Write a fraction for 21%.

SOLUTION   Think: 21% means 21 out of 100, or $\frac{21}{100}$.

$\frac{21}{100}$ is in simplest form.   So, $21\% = \frac{21}{100}$.

EXAMPLE 2   Write a fraction in simplest form for 30%.

SOLUTION $30\% = \frac{30}{100}$ ⟵—— Ratio with denominator 100

Divide numerator and denominator by 10. $\frac{30}{100} = \frac{30 \div 10}{100 \div 10}$, or $\frac{3}{10}$

So, $30\% = \frac{3}{10}$ in simplest form.

- -

Write a fraction in simplest form.

1. 3%   **2.** 25%   **3.** 19%   **4.** 10%

EXAMPLE 3   Write a fraction in simplest form for $33\frac{1}{3}\%$.

SOLUTION $33\frac{1}{3}\% = \frac{33\frac{1}{3}}{100}$

$33\frac{1}{3} = \frac{33}{1} + \frac{1}{3} = \frac{99}{3} + \frac{1}{3}$ $\frac{33\frac{1}{3}}{100} \longrightarrow 33\frac{1}{3} \div 100 = \frac{100}{3} \div 100$

Multiply by the reciprocal of 100.   Then, $\frac{100}{3} \div 100 = \frac{100}{3} \times \frac{1}{100}$, or $\frac{1}{3}$

So, $33\frac{1}{3}\% = \frac{1}{3}$ in simplest form.

EXAMPLE 4 Write a fraction in simplest form for $12\frac{1}{2}$%.

SOLUTION $12\frac{1}{2}\% = 12.5\%,$ or $\frac{12.5}{100}$

Multiply numerator and
denominator by 10.

$\begin{array}{r} 8 \\ 125\overline{)1,000} \\ 1,000 \end{array}$

Then, $\frac{12.5}{100} = \frac{12.5 \times 10}{100 \times 10},$ or $\frac{125}{1,000}$

And, $\frac{125}{1,000} = \frac{125 \div 125}{1,000 \div 125},$ or $\frac{1}{8}$

So, $12\frac{1}{2}\% = \frac{1}{8}$ in simplest form.

- -

Write a fraction in simplest form.

5. $37\frac{1}{2}\%$ **6.** $66\frac{2}{3}\%$ **7.** $87\frac{1}{2}\%$ **8.** $8\frac{1}{3}\%$

EXAMPLE 5 Write a mixed numeral in simplest form for 275%.

SOLUTION $275\% = \frac{275}{100}$

$\frac{275}{100} = \frac{200}{100} + \frac{75}{100}$

$\begin{array}{r} 3 \\ 25\overline{)75} \\ 75 \end{array}$ $\begin{array}{r} 4 \\ 25\overline{)100} \\ 100 \end{array}$ $2 + \frac{75 \div 25}{100 \div 25} = 2 + \frac{3}{4},$ or $2\frac{3}{4}$

So, $275\% = 2\frac{3}{4}$ in simplest form.

- -

Write a mixed numeral in simplest form.

9. 130% **10.** 225% **11.** 120% **12.** 300%

EXERCISES
Write a fraction in simplest form.

1. 50% **2.** 75% **3.** $62\frac{1}{2}\%$ **4.** 9% **5.** 60% **6.** 2%

7. 35% **8.** 20% **9.** 40% **10.** 5% **11.** $86\frac{2}{3}\%$ **12.** $6\frac{1}{4}\%$

Write a mixed numeral in simplest form.

13. 125% **14.** 110% **15.** 330% **16.** 250% **17.** 175%

18. 200% **19.** 100% **20.** 140% **21.** 360% **22.** 180%

Fractions as Percents

EXAMPLE 1   Change $\frac{1}{4}$ to percent.

SOLUTION   Think: $\frac{1}{4} = \frac{?}{100}$ ◄——Ratio with denominator 100

A box statement can help
to solve the proportion.

1	?
4	100

Show the cross products.

$$4 \times \underline{} = 1 \times 100$$
$$4 \times \underline{} = 100$$

Divide.

$$\begin{array}{r} 25 \\ 4\overline{)100} \end{array}$$

So, $\frac{1}{4} = \frac{25}{100}$, or 25%.

- -

Change to percent.

1. $\frac{1}{2}$ **2.** $\frac{1}{5}$ **3.** $\frac{1}{10}$ **4.** $\frac{7}{10}$

EXAMPLE 2   Change $\frac{3}{8}$ to percent.

SOLUTION   Think: $\frac{3}{8} = \frac{?}{100}$

Use a box statement to
show the proportion.

3	?
8	100

Show the cross products.

$$8 \times \underline{} = 3 \times 100$$
$$8 \times \underline{} = 300$$

Divide.

$$\begin{array}{r} 37.5 \\ 8\overline{)300.0} \end{array}$$

$37.5 = 37\frac{1}{2}$

So, $\frac{3}{8} = \frac{37\frac{1}{2}}{100}$, or $37\frac{1}{2}$%.

Change to percent.

5. $\frac{5}{8}$ **6.** $\frac{7}{8}$ **7.** $\frac{1}{3}$ **8.** $\frac{5}{6}$

EXAMPLE 3   Change $2\frac{1}{4}$ to percent.

SOLUTION   Think: $2\frac{1}{4} = \frac{9}{4}$;
$$\frac{9}{4} = \frac{?}{100}$$

9	?
4	100

$$4 \times \underline{\quad?\quad} = 9 \times 100$$
$$4 \times \underline{\quad?\quad} = 900$$
$$\overset{225}{4\overline{)900}}$$

Divide.

So, $\frac{9}{4} = \frac{225}{100}$, or 225%

Change to percent.

9. $4\frac{1}{2}$ **10.** $2\frac{1}{5}$ **11.** $1\frac{3}{4}$

EXERCISES

Change to percent.

1. $\frac{2}{5}$ **2.** $\frac{2}{3}$ **3.** $\frac{3}{10}$ **4.** $\frac{3}{4}$ **5.** $\frac{9}{10}$ **6.** $\frac{1}{8}$ **7.** $\frac{49}{100}$

8. $\frac{3}{5}$ **9.** $1\frac{1}{4}$ **10.** $\frac{11}{10}$ **11.** $2\frac{3}{4}$ **12.** $5\frac{1}{2}$ **13.** $3\frac{3}{10}$ **14.** $\frac{4}{3}$

15. $\frac{25}{10}$ **16.** $\frac{325}{100}$ **17.** $\frac{7}{5}$ **18.** $\frac{1}{20}$ **19.** $\frac{2}{25}$ **20.** $\frac{9}{5}$ **21.** $\frac{7}{4}$

Fun Corner

A pipe is 10 meters long. How long will it take to cut the pipe into 10 pieces of equal length? Each cut takes 1 minute.

Percent of a Number

EXAMPLE 1 Mr. Edwards spends 15% of his total receipts for advertising. How much does he spend on advertising out of $940 total receipts?

SOLUTION Think: $15\% = \frac{15}{100}$

Use a box statement
to show the proportion.

15	?
100	940

$$15 \times 940 = 100 \times \underline{\quad ? \quad}$$
$$14{,}100 = 100 \times \underline{\quad ? \quad}$$

$$\begin{array}{r} 940 \\ \times\ 15 \\ \hline 4\ 700 \\ 9\ 40 \\ \hline 14{,}100 \end{array}$$

Divide.

$$\begin{array}{r} 141 \\ 100\overline{)14{,}100} \end{array}$$

So, Mr. Edwards spends $141 on advertising out of $940 total receipts.

EXAMPLE 2 Of the 1,380 Rushville High School seniors, 20% go to college. How many of the seniors go to college?

SOLUTION Think: $20\% = .20$

Change the percent to a
decimal. Then multiply.

$$\begin{array}{r} 1{,}380 \longleftarrow \text{Number of seniors} \\ \times\ .20 \longleftarrow \text{Rate of percent} \\ \hline 276.00 \end{array}$$

So, 276 of the Rushville High School seniors go to college.

- -

Compute.

1. 25% of 200

2. 5% of 1,400

3. 42% of 648

4. 12% of 58

EXAMPLE 3 Find $6\frac{1}{2}\%$ of $3,211.

$$6\frac{1}{2}\% = 6.5\% = .065$$

SOLUTION

$3,211 ⟵——— Amount
  .065 ⟵——— Rate of percent
16 055
192 66

Round to the nearest cent. $208.715, or $208.72

So, $6\frac{1}{2}\%$ of $3,211 is $208.72.

————————————————————————

Compute.

5. 15% of $42.10   **6.** 30% of $158

7. $5\frac{1}{2}\%$ of $326.75   **8.** 4% of $89.20

EXERCISES

Compute.

1. 25% of 96   **2.** $37\frac{1}{2}\%$ of 64   **3.** 80% of 44

4. 15% of $78.30   **5.** 10% of $240   **6.** 60% of $17.50

7. 2% of $345   **8.** 400% of 25   **9.** $5\frac{1}{2}\%$ of $100

Solve these problems.

10. A newspaper contained 1,960 ads. 40% of the ads produced sales. How many sales were produced?

11. Lou saved 10% of $342.50. How much did he save?

12. Lucy gets 3% commission on all sales she makes. She sold $1,800 worth of merchandise. How much did she earn?

13. Henry paid a $1\frac{1}{2}\%$ service charge on his overdue account. He owed $58. How much was his service charge?

14. The Chung family spends 35% of its income on food. The Chungs earned $425 last month. How much did they spend on food?

15. Mr. Martinez earned $8,728 last year. 22% of his income was deducted for taxes. How much was deducted for taxes?

16. A concrete mixture was 30% water. How much water is there in a sidewalk made up of 1,700 kg of concrete?

17. There were 20 questions on a test. Sue got 80% of them right. How many did she get right?

Estimating Percents

EXAMPLE   Estimate 7.8% of $185.

SOLUTION   Think: 7.8% is about 8%.
Round the percent and $185 is about $200.
the number.

8% = .08   Find 8% of 200.   200
                                                 ×.08
                                                 16.00

So, 7.8% of $185 is about $16.

Estimate.
1. 5.1% of $200   2. 9.8% of 50   3. 190% of 12

EXERCISES
Estimate.

1. 8% of $293   2. 11% of $412

3. 6% of $330.11   4. 22% of $259.61

5. 33% of $29.98   6. 89% of $298.65

7. 54% of $156.86   8. 37% of $331.01

9. 26% of $21.86   10. 3% of $318.20

11. 108% of $292   12. 211% of $330

13. 306% of $412   14. 122% of $259

15. 289% of $298.65   16. 6.3% of $293

17. 8.4% of 412   18. 11.5% of 330

19. 6.6% of $259.11   20. 22.2% of $298.65

Finding Percents

EXAMPLE 1   Receipts from the Spring Dance were $280. Expenses were $84. What percent of the receipts were used for expenses?

SOLUTION   Think: $\frac{84}{280} = \frac{?}{100}$ ⟵ Ratio with denominator 100

Use a box statement to help solve the proportion.

Expenses	84	?
Receipts	280	100

$$280 \times \underline{\ ?\ } = 84 \times 100$$
$$280 \times \underline{\ ?\ } = 8{,}400$$

Divide.

$$\begin{array}{r} 30 \\ 280\overline{)8{,}400} \\ 8\,40 \end{array} \longrightarrow \frac{84}{280} = \frac{30}{100}$$

So, 30% of the receipts were used for expenses.

EXAMPLE 2   Teresa had 30 boxes of cookies. She sold 14 boxes. What percent did she sell? Give your answer to the nearest .1%.

SOLUTION

Sold	14	?
Had	30	100

$$30 \times \underline{\ ?\ } = 14 \times 100$$
$$30 \times \underline{\ ?\ } = 1{,}400$$

Carry the division to hundredths. Then round to the nearest tenth.

$$\begin{array}{r} 46.66 \longrightarrow 46.7 \\ 30\overline{)1{,}400.00} \\ 1\,20 \\ \hline 200 \\ 180 \\ \hline 20\,0 \\ 18\,0 \\ \hline 2\,00 \\ 1\,80 \end{array}$$

So, she sold 46.7%.

Find the percent. Round to the nearest .1% where necessary.

1. 150 is what percent of 600?

2. 22 is what percent of 110?

3. 30 is what percent of 70?

4. 55 is what percent of 75?

EXERCISES

Find the percent. Round to the nearest .1% where necessary.

1. 19 is what percent of 38?

2. 91 is what percent of 728?

3. 27 is what percent of 108?

4. 8 is what percent of 32?

5. 48 is what percent of 60?

6. 12 is what percent of 120?

7. 18 is what percent of 72?

8. 60 is what percent of 300?

9. 19 is what percent of 57?

10. 8 is what percent of 12?

11. 27 is what percent of 85?

12. 231 is what percent of 693?

13. 6 is what percent of 21?

14. 18 is what percent of 57?

Solve these problems. Round to the nearest .1% where necessary.

15. Mona saves $10 a week from her salary. Her weekly salary is $250. What percent does she save?

16. Toli borrowed $300 from Fred. Fred charged him $24 interest. What percent interest did Fred charge?

17. Jim was at bat 111 times last season. He had 37 hits. What percent of the times at bat did he get hits?

18. There were 60 items on the bookkeeping test. Christina got 52 right. What percent of the items did Christina get right?

19. Ellen flies a 48,000-kg airplane. 22,000 kg of it is aluminum. What percent of the airplane is made of aluminum?

20. The enrollment at Eastside Senior High School is 1,480. On Tuesday, 105 of the students were absent. What percent were absent?

Finding the Number

EXAMPLE 1   Mr. Edwards spent $78 for ads. This was 15% of his receipts. How much were his receipts?

SOLUTION   Think: $\frac{78}{?} = \frac{15}{100}$

The box statement helps us solve the proportion.
$78 \times 100 = 7,800$

Ads	78	15
Receipts	?	100

$$15 \times \underline{\ ?\ } = 7,800$$

Divide.

$$\begin{array}{r} 520 \\ 15\overline{)7,800} \\ \underline{75} \\ 30 \\ \underline{30} \end{array}$$

So, Mr. Edwards' receipts were $520.

EXAMPLE 2   Judy has a collection of 32 stamps. This is 60% of the number Eva has. How many stamps does Eva have?

SOLUTION

Think: 32 is 60% of what number?

Judy	32	60
Eva	?	100

$$60 \times \underline{\ ?\ } = 3,200 \longleftarrow 32 \times 100$$

Carry the division to tenths.
Then round to the nearest whole number.

$$\begin{array}{r} 53.3 \longrightarrow 53 \\ 60\overline{)3,200.0} \\ \underline{3\ 00} \\ 200 \\ \underline{180} \\ 20\ 0 \\ \underline{18\ 0} \\ 2\ 0 \end{array}$$

So, Eva has 53 stamps.

Find the number. Round to the nearest whole number where necessary.

1. 13 is 25% of what number?

2. 90 is 30% of what number?

3. 6 eggs is 11% of how many eggs?

EXERCISES
Find the number.

1. 16 is 80% of what number?

2. 15 is 5% of what number?

3. 12 is 10% of what number?

4. 3 is 20% of what number?

5. 100 is 50% of what number?

6. 12 is 40% of what number?

7. 15 is 30% of what number?

8. 80 is 40% of what number?

9. 8 is 25% of what number?

10. 16 is 25% of what number?

11. 10 is 40% of what number?

12. 21 is 75% of what number?

Solve these problems. Round to the nearest whole number where necessary.

13. Two years ago, $1,100 in taxes was deducted from Joe's pay. This was 20% of his pay. How much did he earn that year?

14. Ms. Land saves $30 every week. This is 12% of her pay. How much does she earn per week?

15. Debra received a $4.50 dividend for 1 share of stock. The dividend is 4% of the value of the stock. What is the value of the stock?

16. Pete's savings account earned $27.50 interest in 1 year. The interest rate is 5% a year. How much was in Pete's account?

17. All the employees at Trusty, Inc., received a 5% raise. Jane received a $6-a-week increase. What was her weekly pay before that raise?

18. Josh won 57 table tennis games last year. This was 75% of the total number of games he played. How many games did he play?

19. Mike received a commission of $54. This was 3% of his sales. What were his total sales?

20. Maria got 8% interest on her savings. Her interest was $100. How much did she have saved?

Comparisons

EXAMPLE 1   Ms. Jacobs earned $51 interest on $850 in savings.
Mr. Bochenek earned $65 interest on $1,300 in savings.
Who got the higher percent interest? How much higher?

SOLUTION

Use a box statement to help find a percent ratio.

Ms. Jacobs

Interest	51	?
Savings	850	100

Mr. Bochenek

Interest	65	?
Savings	1,300	100

Show the cross products.

$\frac{51}{850} = \frac{6}{100}$

$\frac{1,300}{6,500} = \frac{5}{100}$

$6\% - 5\% = 1\%$

$850 \times \underline{\ ?\ } = 5,100$

$\begin{array}{r} 6 \\ 850\overline{)5,100} \\ \underline{5\ 100} \end{array}$ $\longrightarrow$ 6%

$1,300 \times \underline{\ ?\ } = 6,500$

$\begin{array}{r} 5 \\ 1,300\overline{)6,500} \\ \underline{6\ 500} \end{array}$ $\longrightarrow$ 5%

So, Ms. Jacobs got 1% more interest than Mr. Bochenek.

EXAMPLE 2   The Bears won 21 out of 40 games. The Owls won 23 out of
42 games. Which team won the higher percent of its
games? How much higher?

SOLUTION

Bears

Won	21	?
Played	40	100

Owls

Won	23	?
Played	42	100

Carry each division to hundredths.
Then round to the nearest .1%.

$40 \times \underline{\ ?\ } = 2,100$

$\begin{array}{r} 52.50 \\ 40\overline{)2,100.00} \\ \underline{2\ 00} \\ 100 \\ \underline{80} \\ 20\ 0 \\ \underline{20\ 0} \end{array}$ $\longrightarrow$ 52.5%

$42 \times \underline{\ ?\ } = 2,300$

$\begin{array}{r} 54.76 \\ 42\overline{)2,300.00} \\ \underline{2\ 10} \\ 200 \\ \underline{168} \\ 32\ 0 \\ \underline{29\ 4} \\ 2\ 60 \\ \underline{2\ 52} \end{array}$ $\longrightarrow$ 54.8%

$\begin{array}{r} 54.8\% \\ -52.5\% \\ \hline 2.3\% \end{array}$

So, the Owls won 54.8%−52.5%, or 2.3% more games
than the Bears.

Solve these problems. Round to the nearest .1% where necessary.

1. Jim had 4 out of 5 exercises right. Rose had 17 out of 20 right. Who had the higher percent right? How much higher?

2. Brand A hamburger contained 9 kg of fat in 35 kg of meat. Brand B contained 14 kg of fat in 45 kg of meat. Which had the higher percent of fat? How much higher?

EXERCISES

Solve these problems. Round to the nearest .1% where necessary.

1. Which class completed the higher percent of projects started?

Class	Projects Completed	Projects Started
A	75	110
B	35	40

2. Who had the higher percent of right answers?

	Number Right	Number of Questions
John	36	48
Blanca	32	40

3. Which family saved the higher percent of its earnings? How much higher?

Family	Saved	Earnings
Curci	$12	$400
Owens	$18	$500

4. Who paid the higher percent of interest? How much higher?

Name	Loan	Interest
Vera	$600	$65
Wong	$800	$85

5. Which team had the highest percent of wins? List the teams in order from best to poorest.

Team	Won	Played
Bobcats	22	40
Comets	19	37
Owls	21	39

6. Which company charged the highest percent to deliver? Which company charged the lowest percent?

Company	Value	Delivery Charge
May's	$30	$1.25
Faye's	$50	$2.25
Ray's	$70	$3.25

Percent Change

EXAMPLE 1 Butter increased from $2.40 per kg to $3.00 per kg. What was the percent increase in price?

SOLUTION

Find the amount of the increase.

$3.00 ◄———— New price
−2.40 ◄———— First price
$ .60 ◄———— Increase

$.60 = 60¢
$2.40 = 240¢

Increase	60	?
Price	240	100

$$240 \times \underline{\ ?\ } = 6,000$$

$$
\begin{array}{r}
25 \\
240\overline{)6,000} \\
4\ 80 \\
\overline{1\ 200} \\
1\ 200 \\
\hline
\end{array}
$$

So, the percent increase was 25%.

EXAMPLE 2 A $23 dress was marked down to $18.40. What was the percent decrease in price?

SOLUTION

Find the amount of the decrease.

$23.00 ◄———— First price
−18.40 ◄———— New price
$ 4.60 ◄———— Decrease

Decrease	4.60	?
Price	23	100

4.60 × 100 = 460

$$23 \times \underline{\ ?\ } = 460$$

$$
\begin{array}{r}
20 \\
23\overline{)460} \\
46 \\
\hline
\end{array}
$$

So, the percent decrease was 20%.

Solve these problems. Round to the nearest .1% where necessary.

1. Last year, a tree was 2 m tall. Now, it is 4.5 m tall. What is the percent increase in height?

2. A year ago, Sue weighed 55 kg. Now, she weighs 48 kg. What is the percent decrease in weight?

EXERCISES

Solve these problems. Round to the nearest .1% where necessary.

1. Lisa sold 40 brushes last week. This week, she sold 62 brushes. What was the percent increase in sales?

2. Pete made 15 errors on a typing test. On the next test, he made 9 errors. What was the percent decrease in errors?

3. The cash price of a car is $2,500. The installment price is $3,000. What is the percent increase in price?

4. Last year, Rob averaged 22.5 points per game. This year, he averaged 16 points per game. What was the percent decrease in average?

5. A $120 suit was marked to sell for $145. What was the percent increase in price?

6. Six months ago, Jim weighed 100 kg. He now weighs 80 kg. What is the percent decrease in weight?

7. Beth was earning $3.30 per hour. After her raise, she was earning $3.46 per hour. What was the percent increase in pay?

8. A $96 typewriter was on sale. Judy bought it for $80 at the sale. What was the percent decrease in price?

9. Last year, Iron Welding, Inc., had 600 employees. This year, the company has 800 employees. What is the percent increase in the number of employees?

10. Last year, Red Coat, Inc., had 800 employees. This year, the company has 600 employees. What is the percent decrease in the number of employees?

11. In 1939 a 2-L container of milk could be bought for 20¢. It now costs 90¢. What is the percent increase in price?

12. An $87.50 lawn mower was marked down to sell for $62 at a sale. What was the percent decrease in price?

Test: Unit 16

Change to a decimal.

1. 35%   **2.** $\frac{1}{2}$%   **3.** 160%

Write a fraction in simplest form.

4. 85%   **5.** 4%   **6.** 140%

Change to percent.

7. .01   **8.** 3.25   **9.** $\frac{7}{10}$

Compute.

10. 32% of 6,100

Find the percent.

11. 7 is what percent of 28?

Find the number.

12. 35 is 20% of what number?

Estimate.

13. 22.3% of 798

Solve these problems. Round to the nearest .1% where necessary.

14. David invested $700 in a bank that paid $5\frac{1}{2}$% interest. How much interest did he get for the year?

15. Anna won 32 out of 40 tennis matches. What percent of the matches did she win?

16. The coolant in Barry's car radiator contains 5 liters of antifreeze. This is 20% of the coolant. How much coolant does the radiator hold?

17. Last year, Julia earned $75 per week. This year, she earns $90 per week. What is the percent increase in earnings?

18. Which school had the higher percent on the honor roll? How much higher?

19. A $250 TV set was marked down to sell for $212.50. What was the percent decrease in price?

School	Enrollment	Honor Roll
Bush	640	96
Lake	550	77

Fun Corner

Use four 9's to write 100.

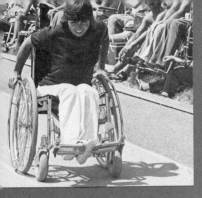

UNIT 17
Earning Money

Business

EXAMPLE 1   Find the selling price.

Profit margin, or profit, is the difference between the selling price and the cost.

SOLUTION   Think: Cost + profit margin = selling price.

Dealer's cost is called cost.

$280 ⟵——— Cost
+ 70 ⟵——— Profit margin
$350 ⟵——— Selling price

— —

Find the selling price.

1. TV set, cost: $169.50
   Profit margin: $85

EXAMPLE 2   Find the selling price.

Profit margin is called margin.

SOLUTION   Think: Cost + margin = selling price.

Find the margin.
40% = .40

$15.00 ⟵——— Cost
× .40 ⟵——— Rate of margin
$6.00 00, or $6.00

The store may mark the shirt to sell for $20.95.

$15.00 ⟵——— Cost
+ 6.00 ⟵——— Margin
$21.00 ⟵——— Selling price

Find the selling price.

2. Pants and shirt, cost: $22.80
Margin: 30%

EXERCISES

Find the selling price.

1. Evening gown, cost: $76
Margin: 40%

2. Couch, cost: $119
Margin: 100%

3. Tire, cost: $18
Margin: 65%

4. Case of soup, cost: $7.60
Margin: 14%

5. Paint, cost: $6
Margin: 30%

6. Camera, cost: $37.50
Margin: 60%

7. Set of dishes, cost $32.50
Margin: 25%

8. Blouse, cost: $12.40
Margin: 25%

9. Dryer, cost: $159
Margin: 60%.

10. Hi-fi, cost: $175
Margin: 40%

11. Hammer, cost: $4.65
Margin: 30%

12. Radio, cost: $37.50
Margin: 45%

13. Dishwasher, cost: $145
Margin: 60%

14. Stove, cost: $179.90
Margin: 30%

15. Ring, cost: $75
Margin: 50%

16. Shaver, cost: $27.25
Margin: 45%

17. Motor, cost: $120
Margin: 55%

18. Shirt, cost: $5.80
Margin: 25%

19. Fur coat, cost: $500
Margin: 75%

20. Battery, cost: $20.50
Margin: 40%

21. Tie, cost: $4.80
Margin: 30%

22. TV set, cost: $145
Margin: 30%

23. Dress, cost: $33.00
Margin: 40%

24. Toaster, cost: $26.20
Margin: 35%

Commission

Salespeople are often paid only a commission on their sales.

EXAMPLE 1 Carl gets a 15% commission on all sales. How much does he earn on sales of $2,500?

SOLUTION

15% = .15

$2,500 ⟵——— Sales
 ×.15 ⟵——— Rate of commission
 125 00
 250 0
$375.00 ⟵——— Commission

So, Carl earns $375 on sales of $2,500.

EXAMPLE 2 Carol's commission is based on this scale.

Sales	Rate
0 – $20,000	8%
over $20,000	12%

How much did she earn on sales of $32,500?

SOLUTION

Find the commission on $20,000.

$20,000 ⟵——— Sales
 ×.08 ⟵——— Rate of commission
$1,600.00 ⟵——— Commission

Find the amount of sales over $20,000.

$32,500 ⟵——— Total sales
−20,000
$12,500 ⟵——— Sales over $20,000

Find the commission on the sales over $20,000.

$12,500
 ×.12
 250 00 $1,600
 1250 0   + 1,500
$1,500.00 $3,100

Add to find the total commission.

So, Carol earned $3,100 on sales of $32,500.

Compute the commission.

1. Sales: $3,900   Rate: 13%

2. Joe's commission is based on this scale.

Sales	Rate
0 – $10,000	8%
over $10,000	10%

How much did he earn on sales of $13,000?

Compute the commission.

1. Sales: $1,250
   Rate: 15%

2. Sales: $2,200
   Rate: 17%

3. Sales: $480
   Rate: 7%

Solve these problems.

4. Manuel's commission is based on this scale.

Sales	Rate
0 – $25,000	6%
over $25,000	9%

How much did he earn on sales of $34,000?

5. Judy's commission is based on this scale.

Sales	Rate
0 – $5,000	7%
over $5,000	10%

How much did she earn on sales of $7,200?

6. Bill's earnings are based on this scale.

Sales	Rate
0 – $1,000	11%
over $1,000	15%

How much did he make on sales of $990?

7. Ms. Sudo's earnings are based on this scale.

Sales	Rate
0 – $500	20%
over $500	25%

How much did she make on sales of $1,000?

8. Your commission for selling magazine subscriptions is 20%. How much do you earn on a $3.50 subscription?

9. A boxer got 40% on gate receipts of $1,000,000. How much did the boxer get?

Payroll

To compute the amount earned for a given number of hours

All businesses covered by the Fair Labor Standards Act must pay time and a half for all hours worked over 40 hours per week.

EXAMPLE 1 How many hours pay is received for 45 hours?

SOLUTION Think: 45 − 40 is 5 hours overtime.

Time and a half means 1.5 hours pay for each hour over 40 hours.

$$\begin{array}{r} 1.5 \\ \times 7 \\ \hline 7.5 \end{array} \qquad \begin{array}{r} 40.0 \\ +\ 7.5 \\ \hline 47.5 \end{array}$$

So, 47.5 hours pay is received for 45 hours.

- -

How many hours pay is received?
1. 46 h   **2.** 50 h   **3.** 41 h   **4.** 38 h

EXAMPLE 2 Robert earns $2.80 per hour at the Go Fast Motor Company. He worked 47 hours last week. How much did he earn?

SOLUTION Think: 47 − 40 is 7 hours overtime.

$$\begin{array}{r} 1.5 \\ \times 7 \\ \hline 10.5 \end{array} \qquad \begin{array}{r} 40.0 \\ +10.5 \\ \hline 50.5 \end{array}$$

So, he must be paid for 50.5 hours.

$$\begin{array}{r} \$2.80 \longleftarrow \text{Rate per hour} \\ \times 50.5 \longleftarrow \text{Number of hours} \\ \hline 1\ 400 \\ 140\ 00 \\ \hline \$141.400 \longleftarrow \text{Amount earned} \end{array}$$

So, Robert earned $141.40 for the week.

- -

Find the amount earned.
5. 44 hours at $3.10 per hour
6. 56 hours at $4.00 per hour

EXAMPLE 3 Find the amount Mr. Dare earned this week from the information on his time sheet.

$3.50/h is read
$3.50 per hour.

Jeffrey Dare	$3.50/h
Mon	10 h
Tues	$11\frac{1}{2}$ h
Wed	12 h
Thurs	10 h
Fri	$9\frac{1}{2}$ h
Sat	8 h

SOLUTION

Add to find the number of hours Mr. Dare worked.

10 h
$11\frac{1}{2}$ h
12 h
10 h
$9\frac{1}{2}$ h
8 h
61 h ⟵ Worked

Then subtract to find the number of overtime hours.

61 h
−40 h
21 h ⟵ Overtime

21 hours overtime is the same as 31.5 hours regular time.

1.5
×21
1 5
30
31.5

40.0 h
+31.5 h
71.5 h ⟵ Paid for

Mr. Dare is paid for 71.5 hours.

$3.50
×71.5
1 750
3 50
245 0
$250.250

So, Mr. Dare earned $250.25 this week.

EXERCISES
How many hours pay is received?

1. 42 h   2. 45 h   3. 51 h   4. 47 h   5. 35 h

6. 43 h   7. 52 h   8. 55 h   9. 49 h   10. 54 h

Find the amount earned. (Time and a half for all hours over 40 hours.)

11. 44 hours at $2.65 per hour

12. 47 hours at $3.50 per hour

13. 52 hours at $3.25 per hour

14. 41 hours at $3.45 per hour

15. 58 hours at $2.875 per hour

16. 53 hours at $4.25 per hour

17. 52 hours at $3.10 per hour

18. 38 hours at $2.72 per hour

19. 49 hours at $4.50 per hour

20. 60 hours at $3.85 per hour

21.

Emma Jackson	$3.25/h
Mon	$8\frac{1}{2}$ h
Tues	10 h
Wed	$10\frac{1}{2}$ h
Thurs	12 h
Fri	9 h

22.

Dave Walters	$2.75/h
Mon	$7\frac{1}{2}$ h
Tues	9 h
Wed	$8\frac{1}{2}$ h
Thurs	10 h
Fri	11 h

23.

Lou Masters	$4.00/h
Mon	9 h
Tues	10 h
Wed	$10\frac{1}{2}$ h
Thurs	$8\frac{1}{2}$ h
Fri	$9\frac{1}{2}$ h

24.

Mary Sanchez	$3.75/h
Mon	$9\frac{1}{2}$ h
Tues	$9\frac{3}{4}$ h
Wed	$10\frac{1}{2}$ h
Thurs	$11\frac{1}{2}$ h
Fri	$8\frac{3}{4}$ h

25.

Laura Schwartz	$5.65/h
Mon	8 h
Tues	$8\frac{1}{2}$ h
Wed	9 h
Thurs	$9\frac{1}{2}$ h
Fri	10 h

26.

Henry Foster	$3.85/h
Mon	12 h
Tues	$8\frac{1}{2}$ h
Wed	8 h
Thurs	$9\frac{1}{2}$ h
Fri	9 h

Interpreting a Paycheck Stub

> **OBJECTIVE**   To interpret the information given on a paycheck stub

ACE HEARING AID COMPANY									Check No. 039885

Social Security No.	Pay End Date	Hourly Rate	Reg. Hours	O.T. Hours	Reg. Earnings	O.T. Earnings	Misc. Earnings	Gross
100 01 1000	6-16-78	4 90	40		196 00			196 00

Deductions

Federal with. Tax	F.I.C.A.	State	City	Retirement	Union Dues	Credit Union		Net
35 42	11 86	6 16		9 77	4 50	25 00		103 29

Employee Name: Eva Black   Employee No: 6948

Year-To-Date Totals

Gross	Federal with. Tax	F.I.C.A.	State	City	Retirement	Union Dues	Credit Union	Date of Check
4704 00	850 08	284 59	147 84		234 48	112 50	600 00	6/20/78

Answer these questions about the paycheck stub.

1. Whose paycheck stub is shown?

2. What is her Social Security Number?

3. How many hours did she work?

4. How much did she earn? (Gross)

5. When did the week end for which she was paid?

6. How much union dues did she pay this week?

7. How much Federal Withholding Tax was deducted?

8. How much State Income Tax was deducted?

9. How much did she pay to the company retirement fund?

10. How much was deducted for Social Security? (F.I.C.A.)

11. What was the amount of her take-home pay? (Net)

12. How much Federal Withholding Tax was deducted so far this year?

13. How much Social Security has been deducted so far this year?

14. How much has she earned so far this year?

Checking a Paycheck

Safety Bank	Seeing Eye Company	No. 42561

Date _April 4, 1978_

Pay to the order of _Dorothy Lynch_

Ninety-seven and 65/100 ___ dollars

David P. Burns
President

Record of Wages and Deductions	
Name: Dorothy Lynch	
Hours worked: 40 Rate: $4.93/h	
Gross Pay	$197.20
Retirement	9.87
Federal Tax	41.18
F.I.C.A.	11.93
State Tax	6.57
Credit Union	30.00
Total Deductions	99.55
Net Pay	$97.65

EXAMPLE Check to see if Ms. Lynch's paycheck is correct.

SOLUTION Check the gross pay.

Notice that she did not work overtime. Gross pay checks.

$4.93 ⟵ Hourly rate
×40 ⟵ Number of hours
$197.20 ⟵ Gross pay

Check the total deductions.

$ 9.87

Add the deductions listed on the stub.

41.18
11.93
6.57
30.00

Total deductions check.

$99.55

Check the net pay.

$197.20 ⟵ Gross pay
−99.55 ⟵ Total deductions
$97.65 ⟵ Net pay

Net pay checks. Everything checks.

So, Ms. Lynch's paycheck is correct.

Three of the pay records contain errors. Find the errors.

1.

Record of Wages and Deductions

Name: Manuel Gomez

Hours worked: 40   Rate: $5.46/h

Gross Pay	$218.40
Retirement	10.92
Federal Tax	43.42
F.I.C.A.	13.21
State Tax	7.23
Credit Union	50.00
Total Deductions	124.78
Net Pay	$93.62

2.

Record of Wages and Deductions

Name: Tina Bronson

Hours worked: 40   Rate: $4.14/h

Gross Pay	$164.71
Retirement	8.29
Federal Tax	32.92
F.I.C.A.	10.02
State Tax	6.47
Credit Union	46.00
Total Deductions	103.70
Net Pay	$61.01

3.

Record of Wages and Deductions

Name: Susan Farrell

Hours worked: 40   Rate: $4.55/h

Gross Pay	$181.99
Retirement	9.10
Federal Tax	34.54
F.I.C.A.	11.01
State Tax	7.10
Credit Union	25.00
Total Deductions	86.75
Net Pay	$95.24

4.

Record of Wages and Deductions

Name: Anthony Ottilio

Hours worked: 40   Rate: $3.98/h

Gross Pay	$159.20
Retirement	7.90
Federal Tax	28.38
F.I.C.A.	9.63
State Tax	6.20
Credit Union	32.00
Total Deductions	84.11
Net Pay	$74.09

5.

Record of Wages and Deductions

Name: James Stein

Hours worked: 40   Rate: $5.17/h

Gross Pay	$206.80
Retirement	10.35
Federal Tax	41.42
F.I.C.A.	12.51
State Tax	6.95
Credit Union	33.50
Total Deductions	104.73
Net Pay	$102.07

6.

Record of Wages and Deductions

Name: Leslie Marlowe

Hours worked: 40   Rate: $4.72/h

Gross Pay	$188.80
Retirement	8.62
Federal Tax	33.88
F.I.C.A.	11.42
State Tax	7.23
Credit Union	30.00
Total Deductions	91.15
Net Pay	$97.65

Making Out Bills

OBJECTIVE   To make out a bill accurately and legibly

For accurate record keeping, every bill should be neat and clear. All important information should be included. @ $.85/kg is read at $.85 per kilogram.

	Leon's Service Center	958-6120
Customer	Mr. Bates	
Sold by	Jeff	Date 3/3/79

2	kg grease @ $.85/kg	$	1	70
2	tubes		5	50
			7	20
	Tax			22
		$	7	42

Answer these questions about the bill.

1. On what date was the bill made out?

2. Who made out the bill?

3. What is the customer's name?

4. For what was the customer charged?

5. How much sales tax did he pay?

6. Is the arithmetic correct?

Find the errors, if any, in these bills.

7.

	Clara's Dress Shop			
Customer	Amy Walsh			
Date	May 2, 1979			

2	skirts @ $7.00	$	14	00
3	pr. stockings @ $1.20		3	80
		$	17	80

8.

Fresh Fish Market		548-5000
Customer	Mr. Rodriguez	
Date	9/10/79	

3kg	Cod @ $1.60/kg	$4	80
2kg	Shrimp @ $7.60/kg	$15	20
		$20	00

Prepare a bill. Use today's date.

9. At Novack's Dept. Store, Warren Davis bought:

   3 shirts at $5.95 each
   4 pairs of socks at $.89 a pair
   A pair of shoes for $18.50
   A hat for $10.95

   The sales tax was $1.53

10. At Ace Drug Store, Jean Rising Sun bought:

    2 boxes of stationery at $3.20 each
    A package of razor blades for $.98
    A toy for $3.98
    Prescription medicine for $5.85

    The sales tax was $.86.

11. Mr. Crown bought the following from Commercial Fabrics, Inc.

    80 m of cloth @ $3.85/m
    60 m of cloth @ $4.50/m
    50 m of lining @ $1.19/m

    The sales tax was $33.13.

12. At Durable Appliances, Inc., the Jenkins family bought:

    A garbage disposal unit for $109.95
    A television set for $189.95
    A dishwasher for $287.50

    The sales tax was $29.37.

13. At Annamaria's Boutique, Pamela Brown bought:

    2 dresses at $41.95 each
    A pair of shoes for $23.50
    2 blouses at $13.50 each
    A handbag for $18.00

    The sales tax was $8.42.

14. At the Acme Furniture Company, Mr. and Mrs. Gomez bought:

    A bedroom suite for $499.50
    2 lamps at $28.50 each
    A rug for $159.50

    The sales tax was $35.80.

15. At Edith's Auto Supply Store, Bill Condon bought:

    5 tires at $21.95 each
    A can of car polish for $2.25
    A fog light for $10.50
    15 liters of oil at $.79 per liter

    The sales tax was $6.72.

16. At Ken's Hardware Store, Ms. White bought:

    8 L wall paint at $1.65/L
    1 L of enamel for $2.39
    A brush for $1.85
    4 L of thinner for $1.08

    The sales tax was $.94.

Fun Corner

1. Write 100 in three different ways, using only 4 fives.

2. A chicken weighs 2 kg plus .5 of its own weight. How much does the chicken weigh?

Test: Unit 17

Solve these problems.

1. The dealer's cost of a 1979 Tagmy is $4,855. The profit margin is 30%. Find the selling price.

2. Mr. O'Dwyer earns 9% commission on all sales. How much does he earn on total sales of $11,200?

3. Margaret's commission is based on this scale.

Sales	Rate
0 – $5,000	7%
over $5,000	10%

How much does she earn on $7,800 in sales?

4. Lucy worked 48 hours one week. She is paid $3.50 per hour and gets time and a half for all hours over 40 hours per week. How much did she earn?

5. How much did Joe earn this week? He gets time and a half for all hours over 40 hours per week.

Joe Young $4.20/h	
Mon	$11\frac{1}{2}$ h
Tues	$11\frac{1}{2}$ h
Wed	$12\frac{1}{2}$ h
Thurs	$13\frac{1}{2}$ h
Fri	10 h

6. Find the error on Ellen's pay record.

Record of Wages and Deductions	
Name: ELLEN SMITH	
Hours worked: 40 Rate: $4.50 / h	
Gross Pay	$180.00
Retirement	10.93
Federal Tax	38.06
F.I.C.A.	10.89
State Tax	6.60
Total Deductions	66.48
Net Pay	$114.48

Prepare a bill. Use today's date.

7. At Cameo Boutique and Beauty Salon, Ruby Scudder bought:

   2 scarves at $3.98 each
   A lipstick refill for $2.50
   A bottle of nail polish for $1.75
   A can of hair spray for $1.65

   The sales tax was $.70.

UNIT 18
Managing Money

Budgeting

A budget is a plan for using money.

EXAMPLE Ellen receives an allowance of $10.00 per week. She earns $15.00 per week as a nurse's aide.

Here are some budgets she made for herself.

Ellen can make several budgets, but she cannot spend more than $25.00 per week.

Bus fare, $.80 daily	$4.00
Lunch, $1.30 daily	6.50
School supplies	2.50
Recreation	6.00
Savings	6.00
Total	$25.00

(Ride bike to school)	
Lunch, $1.30 daily	$6.50
School supplies	4.00
Recreation	7.00
Savings	7.50
Total	$25.00

Bus fare, $.80 daily	$4.00
Milk, 15¢ daily	.75
(Bring lunch)	
School supplies	3.00
Recreation	7.25
Savings	10.00
Total	$25.00

(Ride bike to school)	
Milk, 15¢ daily	$.75
(Bring lunch)	
School supplies	3.00
Recreation	8.25
Savings	13.00
Total	$25.00

EXERCISES

Prepare two different budgets for each person.

1. David has an allowance of $6.00 per week. He can ride his bike to school or spend 80¢ per day for bus fare. He can bring his lunch and spend 15¢ per day for milk or spend 65¢ per day for lunch in the school cafeteria.

2. Mildred has an allowance of $5.00 per week. She earns $3.50 per week delivering newspapers and averages $2.40 per week at other jobs. She buys her own clothes and cosmetics and pays her school expenses. Mildred and David go to the same school.

3. Allen has an allowance of $5.00 per week and earns $7.50 per week as a stock boy. He goes to the same school as David and Mildred. Allen's hobby is building model rockets.

4. Sally has an allowance of $3.50 per week and earns $5.00 per week as a baby-sitter. She goes to the same school as David, Mildred, and Allen.

5. Stanley is a high-school senior. He has a part-time job and earns $30 per week. He is interested in buying a car which will require payments of $70 per month. He pays his own school expenses and likes to date once a week. Show one budget in which Stanley cannot make the car payments.

6. You are married and have two children, ages 3 and 8. Your take-home income is $750 a month. Your rent is $190 a month, and you must pay all utilities: gas, electricity, water, and heat. Your family expenses include food, housing, clothing, transportation, household goods, such as furniture and appliances, savings, insurance, medical bills, and recreation. (Hospital insurance is part of payroll deductions.)

Fun Corner

The chart shows that 1 eight, 0 four's, 1 two, and 0 one's is 10. Complete the chart.

8	4	2	1	
1	0	1	0	10
				5
				13
				15

Personal Accounts

To plan to use your money in the best way, it is necessary to know exactly how you earn and spend money.

EXAMPLE This record was prepared by a high-school student.

Personal Cash Account — *Mary Burns*									
		Received					Paid		
Apr	4	Balance on hand	1	13					
		Received allowance	7	50					
					Apr	5	Lunch	1	25
							Busfare		40
							Notebook	1	00
					Apr	6	Make-up	1	98
							Lunch	1	00
Apr	7	Baby-sitting fee	5	25					
					Apr	8	Lunch	1	15
							Magazine	1	25
					Apr	9	Lunch	1	00
							Malt		75
					Apr	10	Lunch		95
							Movie	2	50
		TOTAL	13	88			Church donation		50
			13	73			TOTAL	13	73
Apr	11	Balance on hand		15					

EXERCISES
Prepare a personal cash account.

1. Carla Gonzalez recorded these items in her personal account: March 4, cash on hand, $2.92; received allowance, $5.00; bought lunch, $.92; bought paper and pencils, $.34. March 5, bought lunch, $.98; bought lipstick, $1.50. March 6, bought lunch, $.95. March 7, bought lunch, $.98; bought birthday gift, $2.87. March 8, received $5.40 for selling magazines. March 9, gave church donation, $.50; spent $2.50 for movies.

2. Don Higgins records the following: September 8, cash on hand, $18. September 9, bought 2 school books, $7.13; bought other school supplies, $1.84; carfare, $.40. September 10, carfare, $.40. September 11, carfare, $.40; chemistry laboratory fee, $2.00. September 12, carfare, $.40; bought ice-cream, $.75. September 13, bought 2 ball-point pens, $.50; bought parts for bike, $3.78. September 14, earned $4.50 cutting grass.

3. Robert Wake made the following entries: May 4, cash on hand, $.34; received pay, $32.18. May 5, bought gasoline, $3.25; bought lunch, $.95. May 6, bought carburetor kit for car, $6.25; bought brake cylinder kit, $3.80. May 7, bought school supplies $1.05; bought lunch $.85; bought ice-cream, $.65. May 8, bought school yearbook, $6.00; bought gasoline and oil, $4.85. May 9, borrowed from brother, $5.00; spent on date, $7.80.

4. Coleen O'Hara made the following entries: June 15, cash on hand, $18.40; received allowance, $4.00; received gift, $5.00; bought home-permanent kit, $2.53; bought lunch, $.45; carfare, $.40. June 16, cap and gown fee, $8.00; bought school yearbook, $6.00; carfare, $.40; bought lunch, $.85. June 17, bought lipstick, $1.50, bought school supplies, $.83; bought lunch, $.85; carfare, $.40. June 18, bought lunch, $1.00; carfare, $.40; bought dance ticket, $2.50.

Fun Corner

Solve.

1. A pencil and an eraser cost $1.50. The pencil costs $1.00 more than the eraser. How much does the eraser cost?

2. A pair of shoes and a pair of socks cost $10.80. The shoes cost $10.00 more than the socks. How much did the socks cost?

Monthly Payments

OBJECTIVE To compute total cost of an item to be paid for in monthly payments, without interest

EXAMPLE 1 How much is each monthly payment?

$50 down, 12 months to pay!

$199.95

SOLUTION

$199.95 ⟵——— Cash price
− 50.00 ⟵——— Down payment
$149.95 ⟵——— To be paid in monthly payments

Keep in mind that no interest has been added.
Round to the nearest cent.

```
      12.495, or $12.50
12) 149.950
    12
    29
    24
     5 9
     4 8
     1 15
     1 08
        70
        60
        10
```

So, each monthly payment is $12.50.

- -

How much is each monthly payment?

1. The cost of the washing machine is $237.50. This is to be paid in 15 monthly payments with $50 down.

EXAMPLE 2   Jean can buy a fur coat for $10 down and 24 monthly payments of $37.50 each. What is the total cost?

SOLUTION

$37.50 ⟵ Monthly payment
×24 ⟵ Number of months
150 00
750 0
$900.00

Add the down payment to the amount paid in 24 mo.

+ 10.00 ⟵ Down payment
$910.00
So, the coat costs $910.

2. Dave put $520 down on a used car. He must make 24 monthly payments of $59.50 each. How much is the car?

EXERCISES

Find the monthly payment.

	Item	Price	Down Payment	Months
1.	TV set	$279.95	$55	12
2.	Boat	$210	$30	12
3.	Used car	$850	$185	12
4.	Truck	$2,347.87	$850	24
5.	Used car	$1,095	$195	10

Solve these problems.

6. Mr. Day made a $6,000 down payment on a house. He must pay $115 a month for the next 20 years. How much did the house cost?

7. Ms. Harris put $10 down on a vacuum cleaner. She must now make 18 monthly payments of $9.88 each. How much did it cost?

8. To have his house landscaped, Joe has to pay $18.90 a month for 36 months. He did not have to make any down payment. How much did the landscaping cost?

9. Joanna was given a trade-in allowance of $1,680 on a new car. She must make 28 monthly payments of $98.72 each. How much did the new car cost?

10. Steve put $5 down on a new coat. He must pay $6.85 for 15 months. How much did the coat cost?

11. The Delgatos made a $4,500 down payment on a new house. For 20 years, they must pay $129.50 per month. How much did the house cost?

Installment Buying

OBJECTIVE   To compute the charges added when merchandise is bought on the installment plan

When you buy on the installment plan, you pay more for an item than you would if you paid cash.

EXAMPLE 1   Find the additional charge if the TV is bought on the installment plan.

$199.95   *or* $50 down
$13.75 a month
(for 12 months)

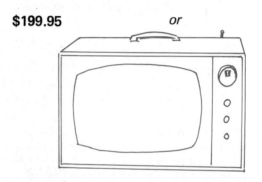

SOLUTION

Multiply to find how much is paid in monthly payments. Add the down payment.

Subtract the cash price.

$13.75 ←——— Monthly payment
×12 ←——— Number of months
27 50
137 5
$165.00
+ 50.00 ←——— Down payment
$215.00 ←——— Total price
−199.95
$ 15.05 ←——— Installment charge

So, the additional charge is $15.05.

- -

Find the charge for buying on the installment plan.

REFRIGERATOR, double door,
frost free.   **$345.**
$45 down. $17 per month.
2 years to pay

EXAMPLE 2 From the advertisement, compute the installment charge.

> **PIANO,** spinet, excellent condition, w/bench
>
> **$510 FULL PRICE**
>
> $20 DOWN $6 PER WEEK
>
> 2 years to pay

SOLUTION

There are 52 weeks in 1 year; 104 weeks in 2 years.

$6.00 ⟵ Weekly payment
  1 04 ⟵ Number of weeks
 24 00
 600 0
$624.00
+ 20.00 ⟵ Down payment
$644.00 ⟵ Installment price

Subtract the cash price.

−510.00 ⟵ Cash price
$134.00 ⟵ Installment charge
So, the installment charge is $134.

EXERCISES

Find the charge for buying on the installment plan. The time for which the payments are made is written under each ad.

1.

> **$114.99**
>
> Occasional chair
>
> $10 down $10 monthly

12 monthly payments

2.

> **MINK COAT**
>
> $1,350
>
> $149 down
>
> $79 monthly

18 months to pay

3.

> **SWIVEL TV**
>
> Swivels to face any part of the room! A sleek modern cabinet with 21″ diagonal measure screen, "duo-cone" speaker.
>
> **$238**
>
> *$27 down, $16 monthly*

2 years to pay

4.

> Sofa
>
> **$209**
>
> $22 down $37.50 monthly

1 year to pay

Comparing Prices

EXAMPLE 1   Kent's Jewelers is offering 10% off on a wrist watch it usually sells for $42.50. Central Department Store is offering 20% off on a watch it usually sells for $46.95. The watches are equal in quality. Which is the better deal?

SOLUTION

Find the discount price for each.

Kent		Central	
$42.50	$42.50	$46.95	$46.95
×.10	− 4.25	×.20	− 9.39
4.2500	$38.25	9.3900	$37.56

So, Central Department Store's price is the better deal.

EXAMPLE 2   At Ann's Supermarket, 2 sizes of a certain soap powder are sold. The regular size weighs 600 g and costs $.66. The large size weighs 1 kg 400 g and costs $1.26. Which is the better buy?

SOLUTION

Regular Size

Find the price per gram for each size. Divide to find the price per gram.

$$\begin{array}{r} .11 \\ 600\overline{)66.00} \\ \underline{60\ 0} \\ 6\ 00 \\ \underline{6\ 00} \end{array}$$

So, the regular size costs .11 cents per gram.

Large Size

Think: There are 1,000 grams in 1 kilogram.
So, 1 kg 400 g is 1,000 g and 400 g, or 1,400 g.

Divide to find the cost per gram.

$$\begin{array}{r} .09 \\ 1,400\overline{)126.00} \\ \underline{126\ 00} \end{array}$$

So, the large size costs .09 cents per gram.

In this case, the large size is the better buy.

Which is the better buy?

1. Store A is selling a barbecue grill for $44.95 with 10% off. Store B sells the same grill for $38.95.

2. A 2-kg package of sugar costs $.96. A 4-kg package of the same sugar costs $1.90.

EXERCISES

Compare the offers in each case and decide which is the better buy. Assume that the articles are equal in quality.

	Item	Store A	Store B
1.	Lounge chair	$139.95 with 20% off	$132.95
2.	Man's suit	$75 with $\frac{1}{3}$ off	$55.95 with 10% off
3.	Turntable	$62.50 with $\frac{1}{4}$ off	$52.00 with 5% off
4.	Washing machine	$229.50 with $\frac{1}{3}$ off	$229.95 with 10% off
5.	Wrist watch	$42.50 with 10% off	$46.95 with 20% off
6.	Outboard motor	$229.50 with 10% off	$204.95

Which size of each item offers the better buy?

7. Cooking oil:
   .7-L bottle for $.81
   1.1-L bottle for $1.14

8. Pancake syrup:
   .5-L bottle for $.51
   1-L bottle for $.72

9. Rice cereal:
   280-g package for $.72
   370-g package for $.77

10. Oat cereal:
    196-g package for $.56
    420-g package for $.66

11. Bread:
    .5-kg loaf for $.59
    .7-kg loaf for $.72

12. Liquid starch:
    1-L bottle for $.45
    2-L bottle for $.84

13. Aluminum foil:
    6-m roll for $.24
    18-m roll for $.63

14. Canned pears:
    .5-kg can for $.44
    .8-kg can for $.98

Making Out Deposit Slips

ACCT. NO. _910683_

DEPOSITED IN

THE YOURTOWN SAVINGS BANK

DATE _April 3_ 19 _79_

FOR CREDIT ACCOUNT OF

NAME _Lula Schwartz_

Please advise any change of address.

	Dollars	Cents
BILLS	125	00
COIN	5	50
CHECKS	20	40
PLEASE LIST EACH CHECK	7	89
CHECKS ARE CREDITED SUBJECT TO COLLECTION	10	98
TOTAL	169	77

For Credit to the Account of

SPENCER'S TV SERVICE

Acct. No. ‖⁰005‴559308‖⁰

DATE _April 4_ 19 _79_

ALLTOWN BANK

Checking Account
Deposit Ticket

Bank Use Only

Units

		DOLLARS	CENTS
Cash Include Coupons		83	00
Checks List Separately	1	21	15
	2	52	40
	3		
	4		
	5		
	6		
	7		
	8		
Total		156	55

Answer these questions about the deposit slips.

1. In which bank was the savings account? the checking account?

2. Who made the savings deposit? the checking account deposit?

3. How much of Lula's deposit was in bills? in coins?

4. How much of Spencer's deposit was in bills and coins?

5. How much did Lula deposit in checks?

6. How much did Spencer deposit in checks?

Make out a deposit slip.

7. June 1: Cash $ 90.00
         Checks   29.58
               222.61
               43.51

8. June 5: Checks $ 82.50
               123.16
               36.14
               50.88

9. June 6: Cash $ 75.00
         Checks   47.18
               521.63
               64.31
               62.61

10. June 7: Cash $ 70.00
         Checks   129.11
               49.61
               23.43
               17.95

11. June 8: Cash $130.00
         Checks   81.62
               72.11
               52.86
               36.96
               17.00

12. June 12: Checks $ 22.61
               19.28
               21.00
               66.12
               36.11
               65.62

13. June 13: Cash $ 35.00
         Checks 310.33
               100.33
               103.76
               29.71
               38.61
               48.10

14. June 14: Cash $105.00
         Checks   49.00
               18.60
               13.12
               21.11
               18.52
               20.01

15. June 15: Cash $ 60.00
         Checks   47.18
               510.52
               53.20
               92.51
               16.68

16. June 19: Cash $120.00
         Checks   70.50
               61.00
               41.75
               25.85
               21.86

Using a Checking Account

```
National Bank of Yourtown                      No. 285

                                   March 27      19 79

Pay to the
order of    Spencer's T.V. Service          $ 38.20

Thirty-eight and 20/100 _____ Dollars

                                   John Williams
```

Answer these questions about the check.

1. To whom is the check made out?

2. What is the date on the check?

3. Who made out the check?

4. What is the amount of the check?

The check stub lists the balance in the account after the last check was written. It also lists deposits made since that time.

```
No. 285            Date 3/27/79
To  Spencer's
For Repair         Amt. $38.20
```

DOLLARS	CENTS	
425	15	Bal. Forward
49	50	Deposit
474	65	Total
38	20	This Check
	15	Charge
436	30	New Balance

Answer these questions about the check stub.

5. How much money did Mr. Williams have in his account before writing this check?

6. What was the charge for writing this check?

7. How much is left in his account after writing this check?

8. What was the purpose of this check?

Make out a check and stub. Use the current year and a check charge of 15¢. Change any Sunday deposit date to Friday.

9. Balance: $328.15
   March 1: Check to J. L. Pope Company for $19.25

10. March 2: Check to J. A. Johnson for $64.50

11. March 3: Check to Michigan Consolidated Gas Co. for $18.53

12. March 4: Deposited $187.60; check to Cash for $80.00

13. March 7: Check to James Carpet Company for $83.50

14. March 8: Check to Dr. A. J. Holmes for $18.00

15. March 10: Check to City of Detroit Traffic Court for $4

16. March 12: Deposited $20; check to Bank of the Commonwealth for $88.12

17. March 13: Deposited $50; check to All City Insurance for $32.18

18. March 14: Check to Weekly Magazine for $9.13

19. March 15: Deposited $100.00; check to Acme Department Store for $75.00

20. March 25: Check to Beth's Answering Service for $22.50

Make out a check and stub. Use the current year and a check charge of 15¢. Change any Sunday deposit date to Monday.

21. Balance: $216.83
    April 1: Check to Able TV Company for $37.60

22. April 2: Check to the J. L. Hudson Company for $51.17

23. April 3: Check to the Board of Water Commissioners for $4.85

24. April 4: Check to cash for $60; deposited $118

25. April 5: Check to Acme Furniture Co. for $18.50

26. April 6: Check to Detroit Edison Co. for $12.32

27. April 7: Check to Michigan Bell Telephone Co. for $6.95

28. April 8: Check to Northland Clothing Co. for $51.50

29. April 9: Check to Ray's Service Station for $18.75

30. April 10: Check to The American Red Cross for $5.00

31. April 13: Deposited $500.00; check to Linda's Dry Cleaning Co. for $7.98; check to Kay's Salon for $22.75

32. April 14: Check to Internal Revenue Service for $223.98; check to Maria's Boutique for $57.90

Test: Unit 18

Prepare a personal cash account.

1. Ines Gomez recorded these items.
   June 15 Cash on hand $22.50
   - Allowance   3.50
   - Lunch   .85
   - Hair kit   1.50
   - June 19 Supplies   1.10
   - Lunch   1.00
   - June 20 Carfare   .40
   - Lunch   .80
   - Movies   1.50
   - Baby-sitting   3.00
   - Magazine   .75

3. The cost of a motorcycle is $895. Ed wants to put $200 down and pay the rest over the next 24 months. How much will he have to pay each month? There is no interest charge.

5. A jacket is selling for $79.00. Jeff can pay cash for the jacket, or he can put $2.00 down and pay $1.75 per week for 1 year. What is the additional charge for buying the jacket on the installment plan?

7. Make out a deposit slip. Use your name and today's date.
   Bills: $138.00
   Coin: $4.50
   Checks: $3.54
     $24.86
     $75.89
     $168.91
     $278.11

Prepare a budget.

2. Kevin receives an allowance of $3.00 per week. He earns $13.00 per week as a stock boy. He can bring his lunch and spend 15¢ per day for milk, or spend 60¢ per day for lunch in the school cafeteria. He can ride his bike to school or spend $1.00 per day for bus fare. He wants to save for a car.

4. Lynne put $25 down on a lawn mower. She paid $10.50 per month for 12 months. How much did the lawn mower cost?

6. A certain detergent comes in two sizes. The regular size weighs 680 g and sells for $.84. The large size weighs 1 kg 540 g and sells for $1.62. Which is the better buy?

8. Make out a check and stub. Use the current year and a check charge of 15¢.
   April 10: Balance, $27.22; deposited $53.78; check to Thrifty Butcher Shop for $35.49

UNIT 19

Insurance

Insurance Policies

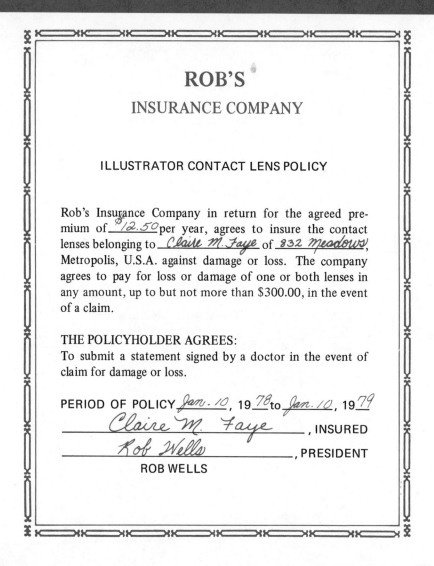

ROB'S

INSURANCE COMPANY

ILLUSTRATOR CONTACT LENS POLICY

Rob's Insurance Company in return for the agreed premium of *$12.50* per year, agrees to insure the contact lenses belonging to *Claire M. Faye* of *832 Meadows*, Metropolis, U.S.A. against damage or loss. The company agrees to pay for loss or damage of one or both lenses in any amount, up to but not more than $300.00, in the event of a claim.

THE POLICYHOLDER AGREES:
To submit a statement signed by a doctor in the event of claim for damage or loss.

PERIOD OF POLICY *Jan. 10*, 19*78* to *Jan. 10*, 19*79*

___*Claire M. Faye*___ , INSURED

___*Rob Wells*___ , PRESIDENT
ROB WELLS

Answer these questions. A premium is the amount paid for insurance.

1. What does the policy cover?

2. What is the annual premium?

3. What does the insurance company agree to do?

4. What does the policyholder agree to do?

SARA'S
INSURANCE COMPANY
ILLUSTRATOR BICYCLE POLICY

Sara's Insurance Company, in return for the agreed premium of _$4.00_ per year, agrees to insure a _Granada_ bicycle, Model _B-7470_, License No. _RY 283_ belonging to _Tony Zally_ of _115 45 Chicago_, Metropolis, U.S.A., against theft or damage from accident or fire. The company agrees to pay repair bills, up to but not more than $70, in the event of a claim. In the event of damage beyond repair or unrecovered theft, the company agrees to replace the bicycle with one of equivalent value.

THE POLICYHOLDER AGREES:
(a) A company representative must examine the bicycle in the event of a claim.
(b) The policy does not cover normal wear and tear, such as worn brakes, parts, or tires.
(c) The policy does not cover loss through theft.

Inspection statement: I have examined the _Granada_ Bicycle, Model _B-7470_, License No. _RY 283_ and found it in good condition.

Mary Roe INSPECTOR, SARA'S INSURANCE CO.

PERIOD OF POLICY _Jan. 20_, 19_78_ to _Jan. 20_, 19_79_

Tony Zally , OWNER

Sara Nelson , PRESIDENT
SARA NELSON

---

5. What does the policy cover?

6. What is the annual premium?

7. What does the insurance company agree to do?

8. What does the policyholder agree to do?

Make up an insurance policy for any two of these.

9. TV set repair

10. Loss of jewelry by theft

11. Damage to parcel sent through the mail

12. Injury to a high-school athlete during practice or competition

Profit and Insurance

Premiums are based on an estimate of the number of claims.

EXAMPLE 1   How much gross profit did Sam's company earn?

Sam's Insurance Co.
Number of bicycles insured: 1,000 Premium: $4 per year Paid: 50 claims, averaging $45 each

SOLUTION

Salesmen's commissions and other operating expenses must be paid from the gross profit.

Income	Claims Paid	Gross Profit
1,000	$45	$4,000
×$4	×50	−2,250
$4,000	$2,250	$1,750

So, Sam's company earned $1,750 gross profit.

EXAMPLE 2   Suppose the company wants to make a gross profit of $5 per policy. What should the premium be on each policy?

U & C Boat Insurance
Number of boats insured: 2,000 Amount paid in damage claims: $40,000

SOLUTION

2,000 ←——— Number of policies
×$5 ←——— Profit per policy
$10,000 ←——— Profit on 2,000 policies

$40,000 ←——— Amount paid in claims
+10,000 ←——— Profit
$50,000 ←——— Total income needed by company

Divide to find how much to charge per policy.

$$\begin{array}{r} 25 \\ 2{,}000\overline{)50{,}000} \\ \underline{40\ 00} \\ 10\ 000 \\ \underline{10\ 000} \end{array}$$

The premium should be $25 on each boat policy.

EXERCISES

1.

Jody's Insurance Co.
Number of dogs insured: 5,000
Premium: $2 per year
Paid: 400 claims, averaging $22.15 each

How much gross profit did the company make on its dog health and accident policies?

2.

Jones' Insurance Co.
Number of dogs insured: 2,000
Premium: $3 per year
Paid: 150 claims, averaging $29.50 each

How much gross profit, or loss, did the company have for the year?

3.

Athletic League Insurance
Number of players insured: 1,200
Amount paid in injury claims: $1,800

Suppose the company wants to make $50 gross profit per policy. What should the premium be on each policy?

4.

Trail Bike Insurance Co.
Number of bikes insured: 500
Amount paid in damage claims: $15,000

Suppose the company wants to make $4 gross profit per policy. What should the premium be on each policy?

5.

Gabbert TV Insurance Co.
Number of sets insured: 1,500
Premium: $30 per year
Amount paid in service claims: $30,630

How much gross profit did the company make? What was the average profit per set?

6.

Elaine's Insurance Co.
Number of diamond rings insured: 2,000
Premium: $15 per year
Amount paid in claims: $22,500

How much gross profit did the company make? What was the average profit per ring?

Fire Insurance

It is only necessary to insure the value of the house or property that can be destroyed by fire.

EXAMPLE 1   How much fire insurance is needed to protect the investment in the house?

Purchase price	$22,000
Value of lot	$3,500

SOLUTION

Fire cannot usually destroy a lot.

$22,000 ⟵——Purchase price
− 3,500 ⟵——Lot value
$18,500 ⟵——Value of the house

So, the home should be insured for $18,500.

EXAMPLE 2

A homeowner should always increase his insurance as the value of his home increases.

Mr. Scantland bought his home 4 years ago for $20,000. He has it insured for $16,000. The value of the house has increased 30%. The lot is now valued at $4,500. How much more insurance does he need?

SOLUTION

Find the increase in value.

$20,000 ⟵——Purchase price
   ×.30 ⟵——30% increase
$6,000.00 ⟵——Amount of increase

Add to find the present value.

$20,000 ⟵——Value 4 years ago
+ 6,000 ⟵——Amount of increase
$26,000 ⟵——Present value

Subtract the value of the lot.

$26,000 ⟵——Total value
− 4,500 ⟵——Value of the lot
$21,500 ⟵——Value of the house

$21,500 ⟵——Amount of insurance needed
−16,000 ⟵——Amount of insurance owned
$ 5,500 ⟵——Additional insurance needed

So, Mr. Scantland needs $5,500 more insurance.

EXAMPLE 3 What is the annual premium for fire insurance?

Purchase price	$25,000
Value of lot	$5,000
Premium $4.25 per $1,000	

SOLUTION

$25,000
$- \underline{5,000}$
$20,000$ ◄──────── Amount insured

$20,000 \div 1,000 = 20$

4.25 ◄──────── Rate per $1,000
$\underline{\times 20}$ ◄──────── Number of $1,000 insured
85.00 ◄──────── Premium

So, the annual premium is $85.

EXERCISES

1.

Purchase price	$28,000
Value of lot	$5,000

How much insurance is needed to protect the house?

2. Mrs. Jones bought her home for $30,000. She has it insured for $25,000. The value of the house has increased 25%. The lot is now worth $5,700. How much more insurance does she need?

3.

Purchase price	$32,500
Value of lot	$8,000
Monthly premium	$3.80

What is the annual premium per $1,000 insurance?

4.

Purchase price	$27,000
Value of lot	$4,000
Premium	$4.25 per $1,000

What is the annual premium for fire insurance?

5.

Purchase price	$40,000
Lot value	$6,700
Premium	$4.10 per $1,000

The premium for 3 years is 2.7 times the annual premium. What is the 3-year premium?

6.

Annual fire insurance premium	$37.40
Rate	$4.00 per $1,000

For what amount is the property insured?

Automobile Insurance

OBJECTIVE   To be aware of the elements of automobile insurance

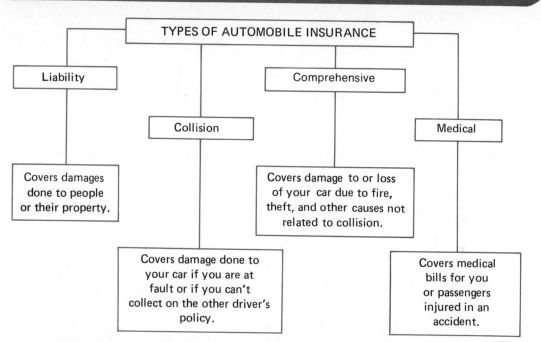

EXAMPLE 1

$20,000/$40,000 liability means that the liability of the company is limited to $20,000 per person and $40,000 per accident.

Anita Fontanez carries $20,000/$40,000 liability insurance. She caused an accident in which Mr. and Mrs. Cooper were injured. Mr. Cooper claimed $22,000 and Mrs. Cooper claimed $18,000. How much must Ms. Fontanez pay? How much must the insurance company pay?

SOLUTION

The insurance company will pay a limit of $20,000 per person and up to $40,000 per accident.
Ms. Fontanez must pay the rest.

	Fontanez pays	Insurance pays
Mr. Cooper	$22,000 −20,000 2,000	$20,000
Mrs. Cooper	0	$18,000
Total	$2,000	$38,000

So, Ms. Fontanez must pay $2,000 and the insurance company must pay $38,000.

EXAMPLE 2　Mr. McGlome did not stop at a red light and caused an accident. The damage to his car was $320. The damage to the other car was $1,050. The driver was injured and claimed $18,000. Mr. McGlome has a $20,000/$40,000 liability policy and a $100 deductible collision policy.

$100 deductible means that the policyholder pays the first $100 damage to his or her car.

How much did Mr. McGlome pay? How much did the insurance company pay?

SOLUTION

Mr. McGlome pays $100 of the $320 damage to his car.

	Mr. McGlome pays	Insurance pays
Other driver	0	$18,000
Mr. McGlome's car	$100	$320 −100 $220
Other car	0	$1,050
Total	$100	$19,270

Mr. McGlome pays $100 and the insurance company pays $19,270.

EXERCISES

1. Bill Johnson caused an accident. The damage to his car was $510. The other car, worth $3,150, was completely wrecked. Bill was covered by a $20,000/$40,000 liability policy, but no collision policy. Who will pay for the damage and how much?

2. Jan Heyse had an accident which resulted in $45 damage to her car and $95 in damage to the other car. Both drivers were at fault. Jan is covered by a $20,000/$40,000 liability and a $50 deductible collision policies. The other driver was not insured. How much did Jan pay?

3. A driver of a car injured a pedestrian and was found at fault. The person injured had medical bills of $1,250 and was awarded $20,000 additionally by the court. The driver was covered by a $20,000/$40,000 liability policy. How much did the insurance company pay? How much did the driver pay?

4. George Brooks caused an accident in which Mrs. Greene and her daughter were injured. Mrs. Greene was awarded $25,000 and her daughter was awarded $20,000. The damage to Mr. Brooks' car was $500. He is covered by a $20,000/$40,000 liability policy and a $100 deductible collision policy. How much must Mr. Brooks pay?

Health Insurance

To recognize and use the elements of health insurance

Use this policy for the Example and all Exercises.

This policy covers only employees of the Acme Oil Co. Premiums are deducted from the employees' salaries.

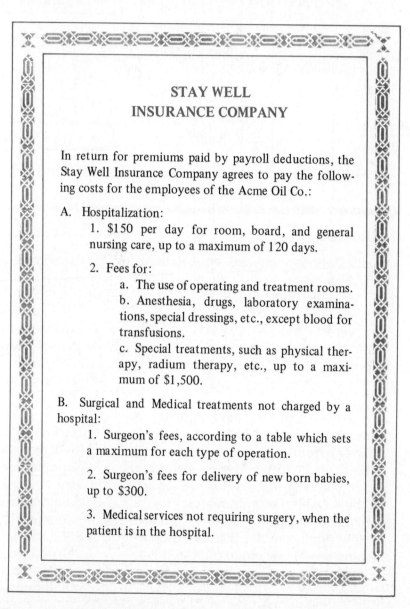

**STAY WELL
INSURANCE COMPANY**

In return for premiums paid by payroll deductions, the Stay Well Insurance Company agrees to pay the following costs for the employees of the Acme Oil Co.:

A. Hospitalization:

1. $150 per day for room, board, and general nursing care, up to a maximum of 120 days.

2. Fees for:
a. The use of operating and treatment rooms.
b. Anesthesia, drugs, laboratory examinations, special dressings, etc., except blood for transfusions.
c. Special treatments, such as physical therapy, radium therapy, etc., up to a maximum of $1,500.

B. Surgical and Medical treatments not charged by a hospital:

1. Surgeon's fees, according to a table which sets a maximum for each type of operation.

2. Surgeon's fees for delivery of new born babies, up to $300.

3. Medical services not requiring surgery, when the patient is in the hospital.

EXAMPLE   Beth Wells had her appendix removed.

City Hospital Statement	
Item	Cost
7 days @ $131	$917
Operating room	$75
Surgeon	$275
Telephone and TV	$21

How much did her father have to pay?

SOLUTION

Check the policy to
see which items are
covered.

Item	Cost	Ins. Co. Pays
7 days @ $131	$917	$917
Operating room	$75	$75
Surgeon	$275	$275
Telephone and TV	$21	$0

The policy does not cover the telephone and TV.
So, Mr. Wells had to pay $21.

EXERCISES

**How much did the insurance company pay? How much did the
policyholder pay?**

1. Mrs. Kain went to the hospital for
an operation. The policy's surgical
table allowed $285 for this type of
operation.

Mrs. Kain's Statement	
Item	Cost
28 days @ $140	$3,920
Blood	$70
Operating room	$100
X-rays	$45
Special drugs	$40
Surgeon's fee	$425

2. Mr. Gold was seriously hurt in an
accident. The surgical table allowed
$275 for this type of operation.

Hospital Statement	
Item	Cost
30 days @ $145	$4,350
Operating room	$75
Special drugs	$55
Blood	$70
Special nurse	$120
Physical therapy	$200
Surgeon's fee	$450

Test: Unit 19

1.

Purchase price	$31,000
Value of lot	$6,000

How much fire insurance does the owner need to be fully protected?

2.

Purchase price	$18,500
Value of lot	$3,500
Premium	$6.15 per $1,000

What will it cost to insure this house?

3.

Go Wrong TV Insurance
Number of sets insured: 2,500
Premium: $48 per year
Paid out in claims: $71,635

Did the company show a profit? How much was it?

4.

Sue's Dog Insurance
Number of dogs insured: 1,500
Premium: $5 per year
Paid: 40 claims, averaging $25 each

Did Sue's company show a profit? How much was it?

5. Ms. Hart has a $20,000/$40,000 liability policy and a $100 deductible collision policy. She caused an accident. The settlement was as follows:

Damage to her car: $585
Damage to the other car: $670
Ms. Hart's medical bills: $384
Other person's medical bills: $580
Damages to other person: $4,000

How much did Ms. Hart pay?

How much did the insurance company pay?

6. Mr. Washington received this bill for a recent operation. His health insurance policy pays $135 a day for room, board, etc., and up to $400 for the surgeon's fees. The policy also pays for all other expenses from an operation. How much will his insurance company pay?

Hospital Statement	
Item	Cost
10 days @ $135	$1,350
Operating room	$90
Surgeon's fee	$550
X-rays	$65
Drugs	$50

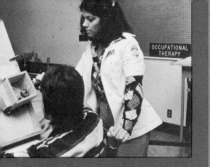

UNIT 20

Taxes

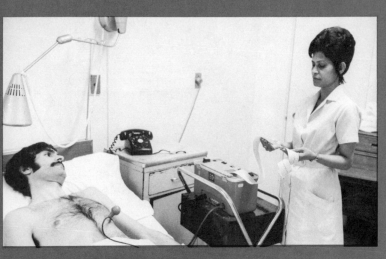

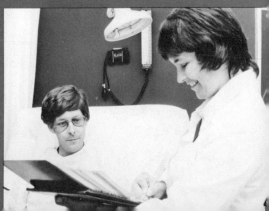

Sales Tax

EXAMPLE How much tax must be paid on the car? What is the total cost?

SOLUTION

4% sales tax is 4¢ on each $1.

$2,150	⟵ Price of car
×.04	⟵ Sales tax rate
$86.00	⟵ Sales tax

The total cost is the price of the car plus sales tax.

$2,150	⟵ Price of car
+ 86	⟵ Sales tax
$2,236	⟵ Total cost

So, the sales tax is $86, and the total cost is $2,236.

EXERCISES

Compute the sales tax.

1. Suit: $58.50
   Rate: 5%

2. Furniture: $87.95
   Rate: 4%

3. Books: $10.80
   Rate: 5%

4. Lumber: $74.62
   Rate: 6%

5. Toaster: $29.95
   Rate: 3%

6. Magazines: $5.85
   Rate: 4%

7. Tires: $43.80
   Rate: 4%

8. Car: $3,495
   Rate: 6%

9. TV set: $385
   Rate: 4%

10. Chair: $43.80
    Rate: 5%

11. TV tubes: $25.68
    Rate: 4%

12. Records: $5.98
    Rate: 7%

Add the sales tax to each bill. Then find the total cost.

13. Mary's Drug Co.
   Prescription $4.25 (no tax)
   Razor blades   .51 (no tax)
   Toothpaste   .79
   Ice cream   1.29
   Magazine   .25
   Rate: 3%

14. Bill's Grocery
   Eggs $.95 (no tax)
   Bread   .61 (no tax)
   Milk   .72 (no tax)
   Soap powder .79
   Paper towels .37
   Rate: 5%

15. Mike's TV Service
   TV tube $ 2.80
   Picture tube 18.50
   Condensers   3.85
   Labor   8.00 (no tax)
   Rate: 6%

16. June's Carpets Inc.
   Carpeting $159.00
   Padding   17.00
   Installation 30.00 (no tax)
   Rate: $5\frac{1}{2}$%

17. City Garage
   Parts $28.00
   Labor 22.00 (no tax)
   Gas   5.70
   Oil   2.25
   Rate: 7%

18. B and B Department Store
   Chair $25.99
   Pajamas   7.95 (no tax)
   Stationery   3.15
   Candy   2.25
   Rate: 4%

19. Dr. Gomez, Podiatrist
   Treatment $15.00 (no tax)
   Foot pads   1.75
   Rate: 3%

20. Ace Refrigeration Service
   Parts $81.00
   Labor 18.00
   Rate: 7%

Fun Corner

Make true sentences. Use only 2, 3, 5, and 7.

1. $\underline{\ ?\ } \times \underline{\ ?\ } = 6$

2. $\underline{\ ?\ } \times \underline{\ ?\ } \times \underline{\ ?\ } = 8$

3. $\underline{\ ?\ } \times \underline{\ ?\ } \times \underline{\ ?\ } = 20$

4. $\underline{\ ?\ } \times \underline{\ ?\ } \times \underline{\ ?\ } = 30$

5. $\underline{\ ?\ } \times \underline{\ ?\ } \times \underline{\ ?\ } = 45$

6. $\underline{\ ?\ } \times \underline{\ ?\ } \times \underline{\ ?\ } = 98$

Property Tax

EXAMPLE 1

OAKLAND COUNTY

Tax rate: $37 per $1,000 value

How much property tax does Ms. Pine pay on her $21,500 home?

SOLUTION

Multiply to find the taxes.

21,500 ÷ 1,000 ⟶ 21,500 = 21.5

```
   21.5
  ×$37  ⟵───── Tax rate
  150 5
  645
 $795.5, or $795.50 ⟵───── Taxes
```

So, Ms. Pine pays a property tax of $795.50.

EXAMPLE 2

1 mill = .1¢, or $.001

CAMP BELL

Tax rate: 34 mills per $1

How much property tax does Mr. Campbell pay on his $27,000 home? Mr. Campbell pays his taxes monthly. How much is each monthly payment?

SOLUTION

Multiply the value of the home by the tax rate. To find the monthly payment, divide by 12.

Think: 1 mill = .$.001, so 34 mills = $.034

```
$ 27,000
  ×.034  ⟵───── Tax rate
 108 000
 810 00
$918.000, or $918
```

```
         $ 76.50
      12)$918.00
          84
          78
          72
           6 0
           6 0
```

So, Mr. Campbell pays a property tax of $918, and each monthly payment is $76.50.

EXERCISES

Town	Tax Rate
Rushville	$39.20 per $1,000
Pontiac	42 mills per $1
Bloomville	$4.20 per $100
Pine Valley	$5.80 per $1,000
Coopertown	44 mills per $1
Green Oaks	3.7%

Solve these problems. Use the table. Round to the nearest cent.

1. Steve Butler owns an $18,750 home in Rushville. How much property tax does he pay each year?

2. Mr. Butler pays his taxes monthly. How much is each payment?

3. Melba Outler has a $37,200 home in Pontiac. How much property tax does she pay each year?

4. Miss Outler pays her taxes monthly. How much is each payment?

5. Pat Sarcuni has a $65,300 home in Bloomville. How much property tax does he pay each year?

6. Mr. Sarcuni pays his taxes monthly. How much is each payment?

7. Mrs. Garcia has a $50,000 home in Pine Valley. How much property tax does she pay each year?

8. Mrs. Garcia pays her taxes monthly. How much is each payment?

9. Mr. Wells has a $29,500 home in Coopertown. He pays his property taxes monthly. How much is each payment?

10. Ms. Blake has a $35,000 home in Green Oaks. She pays her property taxes monthly. How much is each payment?

Solve these problems. Round to the nearest cent.

11. Ms. Miles pays a city tax of $31.50 per $1,000. She also pays a county tax of $4.25 per $1,000. She has a $40,000 home. How much property tax does Ms. Miles pay each year?

12. Ms. Miles has a fire insurance policy which costs $40 per year. How much per month does it cost Ms. Miles for property tax and fire insurance?

Assessed Value

A house has two values: the market value for sales purposes and the assessed value for tax purposes.

Market value: $37,600
Assessed value: 50% of market value
Tax rate: 31 mills per $1

EXAMPLE Find the annual property tax on Mr. Bear's home.

SOLUTION Think: The tax is figured on assessed value.

Find the assessed value.
50% = .50

$37,600 ⟵——— Market value
× .50 ⟵——— Percent of market value
$18,800.00 ⟵——— Assessed value

31 mills = $.031

$18,800 ⟵——— Assessed value
× .031 ⟵——— Tax rate
18800
56400
$582.800, or $582.80 ⟵——— Tax

So, the annual property tax on Mr. Bear's home is $582.80.

EXERCISES
Find the annual property tax. Round to the nearest cent.

1. Ms. Red E. Mix's Home

Market value: $26,300

Assessed value: 80% of market value

Tax rate: $4.25 per $100

2. John Dean's Lot

Market value: $10,000

Assessed value: 75% of market value

Tax rate: 18 mills per $1

3. Mrs. K. Day's Home

Market value: $41,850

Assessed value: 50% of market value

Tax rate: 3.4%

4. Mr. B. Stone's Home

Market value: $38,100

Assessed value: 100% of market value

Tax rate: $31.75 per $1,000

5. Miss Loida Garcia's Home

Market value: $64,000

Assessed value: 65% of market value

Tax rate: $34.85 per $1,000

6. Mrs. Grace Bell's Home

Market value: $56,700

Assessed value: 70% of market value

Tax rate: $2.85 per $100

7. Mr. R. Hay's Home

Market value: $48,300

Assessed value: 85% of market value

Tax rate: 3.5%

8. Ms. L. Chan's Home

Market value: $60,000

Assessed value: 60% of market value

Tax rate: 4.25%

9. Mr. J. Spence's Home

Market value: $65,500

Assessed value: 80% of market value

Tax rate: $4.90 per $100

10. Miss A. Rand's Home

Market value: $52,000

Assessed value: 75% of market value

Tax rate: 33 mills per $1

Federal Income Tax

Sandra Motz is a clerk. Here's a copy of her W-2 statement.

	Wage and Tax Statement 1977	
Bates Drugs 1060 Telegraph Rd. Metropolis, U.S.A. 48522 734-3933	Type or print EMPLOYER'S name, address, ZIP code and Federal identifying number.	**Copy B To be filed with employee's FEDERAL tax return** Employer's State identifying number 734-3933

Employee's social security number	1 Federal income tax withheld	2 Wages, tips, and other compensation	3 FICA employee tax withheld	4 Total FICA wages
100-01-0023	$478.00	$6,182.50	$361.68	$6,182.50

Type or print Employee's name, address, and ZIP code below.	5 Was employee covered by a qualified pension plan, etc.?	6	7
Sandra Motz 18046 Grand Ave. Metropolis, U.S.A. 48522	8 State or local tax withheld	9 State or local wages	10 State or locality
	11 State or local tax withheld	12 State or local wages	13 State or locality

Form **W-2**   This information is being furnished to the Internal Revenue Service.   Department of the Treasury—Internal Revenue Service
☆ GPO : 1976—O-218-028EI 362441915

Sandra also earned $34.50 interest on savings.

Answer these questions. Use the tax form that follows.

1. On what line did she enter her wages? her interest?

2. What were her total earnings? On what line is the total entered?

3. How does the line in the table (page 383) in which she found her tax read? How much is her tax? On what line did she enter her tax?

4. How much tax was withheld from her pay? On what line was this tax entered? Does she owe more tax, or does she get a refund? How much?

Form
1040A
Department of the Treasury—Internal Revenue Service
U.S. Individual Income Tax Return
1977

Use IRS label. Otherwise, print or type.	First name and initial (if joint return, give first names and initials of both) SANDRA K. — Last name MOTZ — Your social security number 100 01 0023
	Present home address (Number and street, including apartment number, or rural route) 18046 GRAND AVE. — For Privacy Act Notice, see page 9 of Instructions. — Spouse's social security no.
	City, town or post office, State and ZIP code METROPOLIS, U.S.A. 48522 — Occupation Yours ▶ CLERK — Spouse's ▶

Presidential Election Campaign Fund
Do you want $1 to go to this fund? . . . . [X] Yes [ ] No
If joint return, does your spouse want $1 to go to this fund? [ ] Yes [ ] No

Note: Checking "Yes" will not increase your tax or reduce your refund.

Filing Status
Check Only One Box

1 [X] Single
2 [ ] Married filing joint return (even if only one had income)
3 [ ] Married filing separately. If spouse is also filing, give spouse's social security number in the space above and enter full name here ▶ ....
4 [ ] Unmarried Head of Household. Enter qualifying name ▶ .... See page 6 of Instructions.

Exemptions
Always check the "Yourself" box. Check other boxes if they apply.

5a [X] Yourself   [ ] 65 or over   [ ] Blind
b [ ] Spouse   [ ] 65 or over   [ ] Blind

Enter number of boxes checked on 5a and b ▶ [1]

c First names of your dependent children who lived with you ▶ ....
Enter number of children listed ▶ [ ]

d Other dependents:

(1) Name	(2) Relationship	(3) Number of months lived in your home.	(4) Did dependent have income of $750 or more?	(5) Did you provide more than one-half of dependent's support?

Enter number of other dependents ▶ [ ]

6 Total number of exemptions claimed . . . .
Add numbers entered in boxes above ▶ [1]

7	Wages, salaries, tips, and other employee compensation. (Attach Forms W–2. If unavailable, see page 11 of Instructions)	7	6,182 50
8	Interest income (see page 4 of Instructions)	8	34 50
9a	Dividends............. 9b Less exclusion .... Balance ▶	9c	
	(See pages 4 and 11 of Instructions)		
10	Adjusted gross income (add lines 7, 8, and 9c). If under $8,000, see page 2 of Instructions on "Earned Income Credit." If eligible, enter child's name	10	6,217 00

11a Credit for contributions to candidates for public office. Enter one-half of amount paid but do not enter more than $25 ($50 if joint return) . . . . | 11a | 478 00 |

IF YOU WANT IRS TO FIGURE YOUR TAX, PLEASE STOP HERE AND SIGN BELOW.

b Total Federal income tax withheld (if line 7 is larger than $16,500, see page 12 of Instructions) . . . . | 11b | |

c Earned income credit (from page 2 of Instructions) . . . . . | 11c | |

12	Total (add lines 11a, b, and c)	12	478 00
13	Tax on the amount on line 10. (See Instructions for line 13 on page 12, then find your tax in Tax Tables on pages 14–25.)	13	487 00
14	If line 12 is larger than line 13, enter amount to be **REFUNDED TO YOU** . . . . ▶	14	
15	If line 13 is larger than line 12, enter **BALANCE DUE.** Attach check or money order for full amount payable to "Internal Revenue Service." Write social security number on check or money order . . ▶	15	9 00

Under penalties of perjury, I declare that I have examined this return, including accompanying schedules and statements, and to the best of my knowledge and belief, it is true, correct, and complete. Declaration of preparer (other than taxpayer) is based on all information of which preparer has any knowledge.

Please Sign
Your signature *Sandra K. Motz* Date 2/17/78

Spouse's signature (if filing jointly, BOTH must sign even if only one had income)

Paid preparer's signature and identifying number (see Instructions)

Paid preparer's address (or employer's name, address, and identifying number)

☆ U.S. GOVERNMENT PRINTING OFFICE : 1977—O-235-254   23-0916750

1977 Tax Table A—SINGLE (BOX 1)

(For single persons with Adjusted Gross Income of $20,000 or less who claim fewer than 4 exemptions)

To find your tax: Read down the left income column until you find your income as shown on line 10 of Form 1040A. Read across to the column headed by the total number of exemptions claimed on line 6 of Form 1040A. The amount shown at the point where the two lines meet is your tax. Enter on Form 1040A, line 13.

The $2,200 zero bracket amount, your deduction for exemptions, and the general tax credit have been taken into account in figuring the tax shown in this table. Do not take a separate deduction for them.

Caution. *If you can be claimed as a dependent on your parent's return AND you have unearned income (interest, dividends) of $750 or more AND your earned income is less than $2,200, you must use Form 1040.*

If line 10, Form 1040A is— Over	But not over	And the total number of exemptions claimed on line 6 is— 1	2	3
		Your tax is—		

If $3,200 or less your tax is 0

Over	But not over	1	2	3
3,200	3,250	4	0	0
3,250	3,300	11	0	0
3,300	3,350	18	0	0
3,350	3,400	25	0	0
3,400	3,450	32	0	0
3,450	3,500	39	0	0
3,500	3,550	46	0	0
3,550	3,600	54	0	0
3,600	3,650	61	0	0
3,650	3,700	69	0	0
3,700	3,750	76	0	0
3,750	3,800	84	0	0
3,800	3,850	91	0	0
3,850	3,900	99	0	0
3,900	3,950	106	0	0
3,950	4,000	114	0	0
4,000	4,050	122	0	0
4,050	4,100	130	0	0
4,100	4,150	138	0	0
4,150	4,200	146	0	0
4,200	4,250	154	4	0
4,250	4,300	162	11	0
4,300	4,350	170	19	0
4,350	4,400	178	26	0
4,400	4,450	186	34	0
4,450	4,500	194	41	0
4,500	4,550	203	49	0
4,550	4,600	211	56	0
4,600	4,650	220	64	0
4,650	4,700	228	71	0
4,700	4,750	236	79	0
4,750	4,800	244	87	0
4,800	4,850	251	95	0
4,850	4,900	259	103	0
4,900	4,950	266	111	0
4,950	5,000	274	119	0
5,000	5,050	283	127	0
5,050	5,100	291	135	0
5,100	5,150	300	143	0
5,150	5,200	308	151	0
5,200	5,250	317	159	6
5,250	5,300	325	168	14
5,300	5,350	334	176	21
5,350	5,400	342	185	29
5,400	5,450	351	193	36
5,450	5,500	359	202	44
5,500	5,550	368	210	52
5,550	5,600	376	219	60
5,600	5,650	385	227	68
5,650	5,700	393	236	76
5,700	5,750	402	245	84
5,750	5,800	410	254	92

Continued next column

Over	But not over	1	2	3
5,800	5,850	419	264	100
5,850	5,900	427	273	108
5,900	5,950	436	283	116
5,950	6,000	444	292	124
6,000	6,050	453	302	133
6,050	6,100	461	311	141
6,100	6,150	470	321	150
6,150	6,200	478	330	158
6,200	6,250	487	340	167
6,250	6,300	495	349	175
6,300	6,350	504	359	184
6,350	6,400	512	368	192
6,400	6,450	521	378	201
6,450	6,500	529	387	210
6,500	6,550	538	397	219
6,550	6,600	546	406	229
6,600	6,650	555	416	238
6,650	6,700	563	425	248
6,700	6,750	572	435	257
6,750	6,800	580	444	267
6,800	6,850	589	454	276
6,850	6,900	597	463	286
6,900	6,950	606	473	295
6,950	7,000	615	482	305
7,000	7,050	624	492	314
7,050	7,100	634	501	324
7,100	7,150	643	511	333
7,150	7,200	653	520	343
7,200	7,250	662	529	352
7,250	7,300	672	538	362
7,300	7,350	681	546	371
7,350	7,400	691	555	381
7,400	7,450	700	563	390
7,450	7,500	710	572	400
7,500	7,550	719	580	409
7,550	7,600	729	589	419
7,600	7,650	738	597	428
7,650	7,700	748	606	438
7,700	7,750	757	615	447
7,750	7,800	767	624	457
7,800	7,850	776	634	466
7,850	7,900	786	643	476
7,900	7,950	795	653	485
7,950	8,000	805	662	495
8,000	8,050	814	672	504
8,050	8,100	824	681	514
8,100	8,150	833	691	523
8,150	8,200	843	700	533
8,200	8,250	852	710	542
8,250	8,300	862	719	552
8,300	8,350	871	729	561
8,350	8,400	881	738	571

Continued next column

Over	But not over	1	2	3
8,400	8,450	890	748	580
8,450	8,500	900	757	590
8,500	8,550	909	767	601
8,550	8,600	919	776	611
8,600	8,650	928	786	622
8,650	8,700	938	795	632
8,700	8,750	947	805	643
8,750	8,800	957	814	653
8,800	8,850	966	824	664
8,850	8,900	976	833	674
8,900	8,950	985	843	685
8,950	9,000	996	852	695
9,000	9,050	1,007	862	706
9,050	9,100	1,018	871	716
9,100	9,150	1,029	881	727
9,150	9,200	1,040	890	737
9,200	9,250	1,051	900	748
9,250	9,300	1,062	909	758
9,300	9,350	1,073	919	769
9,350	9,400	1,084	928	779
9,400	9,450	1,095	938	790
9,450	9,500	1,106	947	800
9,500	9,550	1,117	957	811
9,550	9,600	1,128	966	821
9,600	9,650	1,139	976	832
9,650	9,700	1,150	985	842
9,700	9,750	1,161	996	852
9,750	9,800	1,172	1,007	862
9,800	9,850	1,183	1,018	871
9,850	9,900	1,194	1,029	881
9,900	9,950	1,205	1,040	890
9,950	10,000	1,216	1,051	900
10,000	10,050	1,227	1,062	909
10,050	10,100	1,238	1,073	919
10,100	10,150	1,249	1,084	928
10,150	10,200	1,260	1,095	938
10,200	10,250	1,271	1,106	947
10,250	10,300	1,282	1,117	957
10,300	10,350	1,293	1,128	966
10,350	10,400	1,304	1,139	976
10,400	10,450	1,315	1,150	985
10,450	10,500	1,326	1,161	996
10,500	10,550	1,337	1,172	1,007
10,550	10,600	1,348	1,183	1,018
10,600	10,650	1,359	1,194	1,029
10,650	10,700	1,370	1,205	1,040
10,700	10,750	1,381	1,216	1,051
10,750	10,800	1,392	1,227	1,062
10,800	10,850	1,403	1,238	1,073
10,850	10,900	1,414	1,249	1,084
10,900	10,950	1,425	1,260	1,095
10,950	11,000	1,436	1,271	1,106

Continued on next page

Prepare U.S. Form 1040A. Use the table at the left.

5. Employee: Sue Moore
         909 Michigan Ave.
         Metropolis, U.S.A. 48522
  Social security number: 201-18-7192
  Total F.I.C.A. wages paid: $5,800
  F.I.C.A. employee tax withheld: $339.30
  Total wages paid: $5,800
  Federal income tax withheld: $415.50
  Sue is a cashier at Fluffy Bakery.

6. Employee: Bill Allen
         15 W. Lawrence St.
         Metropolis, U.S.A. 48522
  Social security number: 201-19-6668
  Total F.I.C.A. wages paid: $6,000
  F.I.C.A. employee tax withheld: $351
  Total wages paid: $6,000
  Federal income tax withheld: $676
  Bill is an attendant at Ron's Service Station.
  He earned $60 interest.

7. Employee: Rose White Feather
         28 Main Street
         Metropolis, U.S.A. 48522
  Social security number: 145-17-1134
  Total F.I.C.A. wages paid: $7,475.50
  F.I.C.A. employee tax withheld: $437.32
  Total wages paid: $7,475.50
  Federal income tax withheld: $710
  Rose is a bookkeeper at Bud's Garage.
  She earned $100 interest.

8. Employee: John Carson
         957 State St.
         Metropolis, U.S.A. 48522
  Social security number: 104-16-2181
  Total F.I.C.A. wages paid: $6,150
  F.I.C.A. employee tax withheld: $359.78
  Total wages paid: $6,150
  Federal income tax withheld: $480
  John is a baker at Sweet's Bakery.

Test: Unit 20

Add the sales tax to the bill. Then find the total cost.

1. Josie's Market
   Eggs $ .93 (no tax)
   Bacon   1.59 (no tax)
   Detergent   .87
   Paper products   3.58
   Rate: 5%

Solve the problem. Round to the nearest cent.

2.
   | Mr. S. Bruno's Home |

   Property value: $75,000

   Tax rate: 34 mills per $1

   Mr. Bruno pays his taxes monthly. How much is each payment?

Find the annual property tax. Round to the nearest cent.

3. Ms. L. Bonk's Home

   Market value: $40,000

   Assessed value: 80% of market value

   Tax rate: $34.50 per $1,000

4. The Kerr's Home

   Market value: $30,000

   Assessed value: 75% of market value

   Tax rate: 4.3%

Prepare U.S. Form 1040A. Use the table on page 383.

5. Employee: Don Hansen
   870 Grand Ave.
   Metropolis, U.S.A. 48522

   Social security number: 201-16-2197
   Total F.I.C.A. wages paid: $5,850
   F.I.C.A. employee tax withheld: $342.23
   Total wages paid: $5,850
   Federal income tax withheld: $600

   Don is a service station attendant at Auto Garage.

Photo Credits

Credits read clockwise starting with upper-left photo.

Page 2—Editorial Photocolor Archives. Taurus Photos © Jack Kroll. HRW Photo by Russell Dian. HRW Photo by Russell Dian. Stock, Boston. HRW Photo by Russell Dian.

Page 97—Taurus Photos © Mike L. Wannemacher. Editorial Photocolor Archives. National Wheelchair Athletic Association. Vivian Fenster. Taurus Photos. Monkmeyer Press Photo Service. Editorial Photocolor Archives. *Center*, Black Star.

Page 98—Salvation Army. HRW Photo by Russell Dian. Editorial Photocolor Archives. Colonial Penn Group, Inc. ICD Rehabilitation and Research Center. HRW Photo by Russell Dian.

Page 115—HRW Photo by Lois Ciesla-Safrani. Stock, Boston. HRW Photo by Charles Biasiny. Stock, Boston. HRW Photo by Russell Dian. HRW Photo by Russell Dian. Long Island Railroad. *Center*, HRW Photo by Russell Dian.

Page 129—Al Green Studio. HRW Photo by Vivian Fenster. Editorial Photocolor Archives. Editorial Photocolor Archives. Taurus Photos © Jack Kroll. Editorial Photocolor Archives. Al Green Studio. Photo © Betty Medsger.

Page 147—HRW Photo by Russell Dian. ICD Rehabilitation and Research Center. HRW Photo by Russell Dian. HRW Photo by R. H. Goff. AT&T Co. Photo Center. HRW Photo by Russell Dian. HRW Photo by Russell Dian. Stock, Boston.

Page 193—HRW Photo by Russell Dian. Irene Fertik. HRW Photo by Russell Dian. HRW Photo by E. Reichmann. HRW Photo by Russell Dian. HRW Photo by Russell Dian. HRW Photo by Russell Dian. Editorial Photocolor Archives.

Page 194—Stock, Boston. Douglas Spillane. HRW Photo by R. H. Goff. Stock, Boston. HRW Photo by Michal Heron. Taurus Photos © Mike L. Wannemacher.

Page 209—Editorial Photocolor Archives. Vivian Fenster. Andy Mercado/Jeroboam. HRW Photo by Russell Dian. ICD Rehabilitation and Research Center. HRW Photo by Russell Dian. HRW Photo by Russell Dian. Editorial Photocolor Archives.

Page 227—Editorial Photocolor Archives. Vivian Fenster. HRW Photo by Russell Dian. HRW Photo by Russell Dian. HRW Photo by Russell Dian. HRW Photo by Russell Dian. Bowerman-Camelback Inn, Scottsdale, Arizona. *Center*, Focus on Sports.

Page 247—HRW Photo by Lonny Kalfus. Photo © Betty Medsger. Taurus Photos. HRW Photo by Lois Ciesla-Safrani. HRW Photo by Russell Dian. HRW Photo by Russell Dian. Grumman Corporation. *Center*, Editorial Photocolor Archives.

Page 260—Taurus Photos © Eric Kroll. Bethlehem Steel. Jeroboam. Webb Ag Photos. Alcan Aluminum Corporation. ILGWU. Argonne National Laboratory Photo. *Center*, HRW Photo by Michal Heron.

Page 275—Taurus Photos. Food and Drug Administration. HRW Photo by Russell Dian. HRW Photo by Russell Dian. Peter Arnold Photo Archives. HRW Photo by Russell Dian. HRW Photo by Russell Dian. HRW Photo by Vivian Fenster.

Page 289—Colonial Penn Group, Inc. HRW Photo by Vivian Fenster. Taurus Photos © R. D. Ullmann. HRW Photo by John Running. HRW Photo by Russell Dian. HRW Photo by Russell Dian. Jeroboam. HRW Photo by Russell Dian.

Page 290—Taurus Photos. Stock, Boston. HRW Photo by Russell Dian. HRW Photo by Russell Dian. Taurus Photos. HRW Photo by Russell Dian.

Page 309—HRW Photo by Russell Dian. HRW Photo by Russell Dian. HRW Photo by Russell Dian. Taurus Photos. HRW Photo by Russell Dian. Editorial Photocolor Archives. HRW Photo by Russell Dian. AT&T Co. Photo Center.

Page 331—National Wheelchair Athletic Association. Vivian Fenster. National Wheelchair Athletic Association. Al Green Studio. Taurus Photos. HRW Photo by Lois Ciesla-Safrani. Taurus Photos © Eric Kroll. Al Green Studio.

Page 345—HRW Photo by Russell Dian. Al Green Studio. HRW Photo by Lois Ciesla-Safrani. HRW Photo by Russell Dian. HRW Photo by Russell Dian. HRW Photo by Russell Dian. HRW Photo by Helena Kolda. *Center*, HRW Photo by Russell Dian.

Page 361—HRW Photo by Russell Dian. Taurus Photos © R. D. Ullmann. HRW Photo by Russell Dian. HRW Photo by Russell Dian. HRW Photo by Russell Dian. Travelers Insurance Co., Hartford, Conn. Al Green Studio. *Center*, HRW Photo by Russell Dian.

Page 373—HRW Photo by Russell Dian. Instrument Society of America. HRW Photo by Russell Dian. Al Green Studio. HRW Photo by Russell Dian. Taurus Photos. DPI, Inc. Photo © Betty Medsger.

Index

Facts tests
addition, 3
division, 74
multiplication, 50
subtraction, 28

Federal income tax, 380–383

Fire insurance, 366–367

Form 1040 A, 381

Formula(s)
distance, 256–258

Fraction(s)
addition of, 211–214, 217–219
addition with mixed numerals, 213–214, 217–219
comparing, 206
division of, 237–238
division with mixed numerals, 237–238
equivalent, 200–204
estimating differences, 223–225
estimating products, 241–242
estimating sums, 223–224
least common denominator of, 215–216
meaning of, 197–199
mixed numerals for, 213–214
multiplication of, 229–232
multiplication with mixed numerals, 233–234
as names for decimals, 244–245
as percents, 317–318
percents as, 315–316
simplifying, 205, 213–214
subtraction of, 220–222
subtraction with mixed numerals, 220–222
using to find parts of sets, 239–240

Fun Corners, 19, 46, 48, 69, 70, 72, 91, 95, 96, 114, 128, 139, 141, 145, 146, 155, 165, 181, 186, 190, 192, 208, 225, 243, 246, 259, 281, 288, 292, 297, 304, 307, 308, 313, 318, 330, 343, 347, 349, 375

Gram, 182

Graph
bar, 280–283
broken-line, 284–287

Health insurance, 370–371

Hectometer, 185

Installment buying, 352–353

Insurance
automobile, 368–369
fire, 366–367
health, 370–371
interpreting policies, 362–363
liability, 368
premium, 362
profit and, 364–365

Japanese method of addition, 165

Kilogram, 182

Kilometer, 152

Kilowatt, 126

Kilowatt-hours, 126

Least common denominator, 215–216

Liter, 179

Numeral(s)
expanded form, 12
for fractions, 197–199
mixed numerals, 213–214
periods, 100
place value, 100–101

Parallelogram(s)
consecutive angles of, 267–268
opposite angles of, 267–268
sum of the measures of the angles of, 266–268

Paycheck, 339–341

Payroll, 336–338

Percent(s)
comparing, 326–327
as decimals, 312–313
decimals as, 314
estimating, 321
finding, 322–323
finding the number, 324–325
as fractions, 315–316
fractions as, 317–318
increase or decrease, 328–329
of a number, 319–320
as ratios, 310–311

Perimeter, 156–159, 175, 271

Personal accounts, 348–349

Place value, 100–101

Premium, 362

Probability, 298–300

Problem solving
amount of information, 124
area, 170–171
averages, 86–87, 93, 111
better buy, 354–355
capacity, 181
choosing the correct operation, 47
coins in, 24–25
cost of electricity, 126
decimals, 109, 121, 137, 142
distance formula, 258
fractions, 243
interpreting charts, data, graphs, tables, diagrams, 39, 68–69, 71, 85, 144–145
making change, 40–41
making up problems, 112
mean, mode, median, 279
multi-step problems, 42–43
not enough information, 17
number problems, 62, 255
odometer readings, 109
perimeter, 159
pony express, 111
proportions, 305–307
rare coins, 113
record sales, 93
rewriting problems, 94–95
size records, 88
speed records, 127
temperature, 190
too much information, 110
using money, 90–91
volume, 178
women in sports, 142

Profit, 332–333

Profit margin, 332–333

Property tax, 376–379

Answers

Unit 1

Pages 4–5 *1.* 13 *2.* 14 *3.* 12 *4.* 12 *5.* 17 *6.* 11 *7.* 13 *8.* 14 *9.* 17 *10.* 21 *11.* 15 *12.* 15 *13.* 17 *14.* 13 *15.* 14

Pages 6–7 *1.* 36; 46 *2.* 42; 72 *3.* 57; 97 *4.* 83; 93 *5.* 33; 73 *6.* 83; 53
Practice Set 2 *2.* 52 *4.* 57 *6.* 87 *8.* 54 *10.* 101 *12.* 61 *14.* 33 *16.* 93 *18.* 63 *20.* 64 *22.* 75 *24.* 35
Practice Set 3 *2.* 84 *4.* 79 *6.* 58 *8.* 60 *10.* 71 *12.* 102 *14.* 101 *16.* 30 *18.* 62 *20.* 41 *22.* 50 *24.* 57
Practice Set 4 *2.* 100 *4.* 23 *6.* 56 *8.* 83 *10.* 71 *12.* 43 *14.* 71 *16.* 67 *18.* 23 *20.* 45 *22.* 56 *24.* 71

Page 8 *1.* 110 *2.* 1,100 *3.* 11,000
Practice Set 5 *2.* 170 *4.* 90 *6.* 100 *8.* 160 *10.* 60 *12.* 140 *14.* 130 *16.* 90 *18.* 130
Practice Set 6 *2.* 1,000 *4.* 900 *6.* 1,500 *8.* 1,400 *10.* 1,100 *12.* 1,700 *14.* 1,300 *16.* 7,000 *18.* 3,700 *20.* 6,300

Pages 10–11 *1.* 30 *2.* 30 *3.* 30 *4.* 27 *5.* 31
Practice Set 7 *2.* 53 *4.* 45 *6.* 64 *8.* 54
Practice Set 8 *2.* 45 *4.* 44 *6.* 38 *8.* 37 *10.* 40 *12.* 43 *14.* 40 *16.* 42 *18.* 49
Practice Set 9 *2.* 48 *4.* 50 *6.* 46 *8.* 52 *10.* 43 *12.* 45 *14.* 47 *16.* 49 *18.* 41

Pages 12–14 *1.* 133 *2.* 135 *3.* 192 *4.* 777 *5.* 1,296 *6.* 1,745 *7.* 160; 15; 175 *8.* 61; 86; 62; 85; 147
Practice Set 10 *2.* 214 *4.* 185 *6.* 171 *8.* 111 *10.* 68 *12.* 814 *14.* 1,185 *16.* 1,671 *18.* 1,811 *20.* 1,468
Practice Set 11 *2.* 138 *4.* 146 *6.* 146 *8.* 148 *10.* 164 *12.* 164 *14.* 197 *16.* 1,130 *18.* 1,130

Pages 12–14 continued
Practice Set 12 *2.* 48; 51; 90, 9, 99 *4.* 36; 87; 110, 13, 123 *6.* 56; 76; 120, 12, 132 *8.* 83; 88; 160, 11, 171 *10.* 52; 41; 81, 12, 93 *12.* 92; 76; 76, 92, 168 *14.* 3; 30; 50, 9, 59 *16.* 4; 70; 77; 11, 121 *18.* 87; 50; 58; 130, 15 *20.* 8, 58; 101; 110; 151

Pages 15–16 *1.* 2,473 *2.* 4,049 *3.* 6,179
Practice Set 13 *2.* 246 *4.* 3,812 *6.* 2,645 *8.* 449 *10.* 5,354 *12.* 4,962
Practice Set 14 *2.* 324 *4.* 4,373 *6.* 289 *8.* 294 *10.* 3,480

Page 17 *2.* how much per car *4.* number of meters of material *6.* kilometers traveled *8.* the amount used for payment

Pages 18–19 *1.* 40 *2.* 80 *3.* 90 *4.* 130 *5.* 160 *6.* 500 *7.* 800 *8.* 1,000 *9.* 800 *10.* 200
Exercises *2.* 70 *4.* 360 *6.* 180 *8.* 990 *10.* 900 *12.* 400 *14.* 200 *16.* 600 *18.* 700 *20.* 700 *22.* 500 *24.* 600 *26.* 1,400

Pages 20–22 *1.* 170 *2.* 190 *3.* 140 *4.* 420 *5.* 800 *6.* 1,700 *7.* 1,600 *8.* 2,000 *9.* $22.30 *10.* $17.60
Exercises *2.* 290 *4.* 190 *6.* 790 *8.* 280 *10.* 2,150 *12.* 1,960 *14.* 1,800 *16.* 3,200 *18.* 3,000 *20.* 2,400 *22.* 3,300 *24.* 900 *26.* $11.50 *28.* $44.70 *30.* 4,200 *32.* 620 m²

Page 23 *1.* $3.91 *2.* $3.75 *3.* $9.70 *4.* $6.70
Exercises *2.* $4.83 *4.* $5.91 *6.* $10.70 *8.* $8.57 *10.* $6.81

Pages 24–25 *2.* 6 dimes, 6 nickels *4.* 6 quarters, 8 dimes *6.* 5 half dollars, 1 quarter, 1 dime *8.*–*10.* Answers may vary.

Unit 2

Page 29 *1.* 2 *2.* 7 *3.* 8 *4.* 4 *5.* 7 *6.* 7 *7.* 6
8. 8

Pages 30–31 *1.* 57; 87 *2.* 19; 29
Practice Set 2 *2.* 34 *4.* 54 *6.* 67 *8.* 86 *10.* 46
12. 26 *14.* 28 *16.* 44 *18.* 74
Practice Set 3 *2.* 27 *4.* 19 *6.* 77 *8.* 29
10. 16 *12.* 36 *14.* 47 *16.* 39 *18.* 67
20. 16 *22.* 74 *24.* 37
Practice Set 4 *2.* 39 *4.* 27 *6.* 49 *8.* 38
10. 72 *12.* 87 *14.* 67 *16.* 44 *18.* 28
20. 98 *22.* 98 *24.* 98
Practice Set 5 *2.* 34 *4.* 25 *6.* 93 *8.* 39 *10.* 95
12. 74 *14.* 119 *16.* 126 *18.* 106 *20.* 424
22. 980 *24.* 203

Pages 32–33 *1.* 8 *2.* 80 *3.* 800 *4.* 8,000
5. 1,200 *6.* 15,000 *7.* 15,000
Practice Set 6 *2.* 10 *4.* 80 *6.* 90 *8.* 40 *10.* 70
12. 80 *14.* 50 *16.* 50 *18.* 60
Practice Set 7 *2.* 60 *4.* 60 *6.* 60 *8.* 60 *10.* 90
12. 90 *14.* 80 *16.* 70 *18.* 80
Practice Set 8 *2.* 600 *4.* 600 *6.* 800 *8.* 500
10. 0 *12.* 300 *14.* 600 *16.* 200 *18.* 6,000
20. 2,000 *22.* 9,000 *24.* 6,000
Practice Set 9 *2.* 1,100 *4.* 1,200 *6.* 100
8. 120 *10.* 13,000 *12.* 12,000 *14.* 8,000

Pages 35–36 *1.* 769 *2.* 5,209 *3.* 80,798
4. 443 *5.* 4,721 *6.* 19,147
Practice Set 10 *2.* 479 *4.* 838 *6.* 657 *8.* 693
10. 145 *12.* 6 *14.* 3,737
Practice Set 11 *2.* 26,881 *4.* 20,627
6. 58,095 *8.* 81,228 *10.* 43,630 *12.* 5,537
Practice Set 12 *2.* $59.92 *4.* $89.35 *6.* 89,935
8. 7,616 *10.* 39,063 *12.* 3,990,630

Pages 37–38 *1.* 5,206 *2.* 9,186 *3.* 8,911
4. 18,899
Practice Set 13 *2.* 43,320 *4.* 24,723
6. 82,541 *8.* 40,267 *10.* 18,464 *12.* 14,195

Pages 37–38 continued
Practice Set 14 *2.* 16,836 *4.* 71,749
6. 43,667 *8.* 14,748 *10.* 33,519
12. 71,149
Practice Set 15 *2.* 26,881 *4.* 20,627
6. 58,095 *8.* 81,228 *10.* 43,630
12. 5,537
Practice Set 16 *2.* 49,920 *4.* 42,000 *6.* 49,167
8. 49,197 *10.* 46,992 *12.* 43,000
14. 49,212 *16.* 57,431 *18.* 60,894
20. 80,399

Page 39 *2.* Mercury *4.* Jupiter, 773 million;
Saturn, 1,418 million; Uranus, 2,852
million; Neptune, 4,468 million; Earth,
149 million; Venus, 108 million; Mars,
227 million; Pluto, 5,875 million;
Mercury, 58 million *6.* Jupiter, 773 h;
Saturn, 1,418 h; Uranus, 2,852 h;
Neptune, 4,468 h; Earth, 149 h; Venus,
108 h; Mars, 227 h; Pluto, 5,875 h;
Mercury, 58 h

Pages 40–41 *1.* $2.50 *2.* $6.85 *3.* $11.73
4. $9.00 *5.* $6.60
Exercises *2.* $1.51 *4.* $4.11 *6.* $1.15
8. $6.55 *10.* $10.05 *12.* $.65 *14.* $7.00
16. $7.90 *18.* $15.75 *20.* $3.75 *22.* $.15

Pages 42–43 *2.* She has enough money.
4. $185.60 *6.* 2 half dollars, 1 quarter,
1 dime, 1 nickel

Pages 44–46 *1.* 200 *2.* 1,700 *3.* 1,000
4. $119 *5.* $814 *6.* $84 *7.* 56,000
8. 23,000 *9.* 9,000
Exercises *2.* 200 *4.* 7,000 *6.* $10 *8.* $11
10. $5 *12.* $29 *14.* 6,000 *16.* 26,000
18. 79,000 *20.* 5,000 *22.* $25 *24.* $2,505
26. 10,000 L *28.* 800 *30.* 400 km
32. $133 *34.* $667

Page 47 *2.* Add. *4.* Subtract. *6.* Divide.

Unit 3

Pages 51–53 *1.* 10 rows of 2 each *2.* 10 rows of 3 each *3.* 10 rows of 4 each *4.* 10 rows of 6 each *5.* 10 rows of 7 each *6.* 10 rows of 8 each *7.* 10 rows of 9 each *8.* 10 rows of 10 each *9.* 42 *10.* 20 *11.* 64 *12.* 81 *13.* 21 *14.* 36 *15.* 36 *16.* 56 *17.* 45 *18.* 54 *19.* 81 *20.* 63

Page 54 *1.* 180 *2.* 18,000 *3.* 200 *4.* 2,000
Practice Set 2 *2.* 2,400 *4.* 280 *6.* 320 *8.* 32,000 *10.* 40,000 *12.* 5,600 *14.* 630 *16.* 40 *18.* 4,000 *20.* 6,000 *22.* 3,000 *24.* 1,800

Pages 55–56 *1.* 318 *2.* 410 *3.* 288 *4.* 592 *5.* 855 *6.* 1,648 *7.* 2,805 *8.* 5,004 *9.* 4,935 *10.* 7,023 *11.* 18,092 *12.* 28,615 *13.* 8,844
Practice Set 3 *2.* 185 *4.* 456 *6.* 540 *8.* 1,404 *10.* 1,830 *12.* 3,542 *14.* 984 *16.* 17,284 *18.* 25,926 *20.* 45,801 *22.* 58,887 *24.* 61,074 *26.* 63,120 *28.* 63,056 *30.* 27,228 *32.* 10,218 *34.* 26,991

Pages 58–59 *1.* 816 *2.* 988 *3.* 1,824 *4.* 3,696 *5.* 9,648 *6.* 24,605 *7.* 21,708 *8.* 29,304 *9.* 38,254 *10.* 64,168 *11.* 231,552 *12.* 399,570
Practice Set 4 *2.* 7,448 *4.* 2,301 *6.* 546 *8.* 3,360 *10.* 3,280 *12.* 3,080 *14.* 6,786 *16.* 3,627 *18.* 240
Practice Set 5 *2.* 17,472 *4.* 14,586 *6.* 57,226 *8.* 21,672 *10.* 49,200 *12.* 91,374 *14.* 41,958 *16.* 64,640 *18.* 72,160
Practice Set 6 *2.* 72,576 *4.* 558,144 *6.* 542,974 *8.* 30,512 *10.* 465,311

Pages 60–61 *1.* 377,004 *2.* 191,444 *3.* 472,082 *4.* 208,131 *5.* 2,276,092 *6.* 1,099,875 *7.* 1,445,793
Practice Set 7 *2.* 80,256 *4.* 76,518 *6.* 447,832 *8.* 289,732 *10.* 213,108 *12.* 438,984 *14.* 146,672
Practice Set 8 *2.* 828,144 *4.* 2,423,520 *6.* 2,702,040 *8.* 4,834,836 *10.* 5,361,525 *12.* 4,270,098 *14.* 2,027,040

Pages 60–61 continued
Practice Set 9 *2.* 466,929 *4.* 518,924 *6.* 7,902 *8.* 1,032,216 *10.* 208,740 *12.* 1,609,186 *14.* 214,963 *16.* 25,506 *18.* 1,505,290 *20.* 272,690 *22.* 136,853 *24.* 425,211

Page 62 *2.* 10, 5 *4.* 10, 10 *6.* 9, 8 *8.* 15, 5 *10.* 10, 9 *12.* 70, 10

Pages 63–64 *1.* 600 *2.* 900 *3.* 1,000 *4.* 600 *5.* 3,200 *6.* 12,000 *7.* 35,000 *8.* 30,000 *9.* 72,000 *10.* 140,000 *11.* 240,000 *12.* 360,000 *13.* 540,000
Exercises *2.* 600 *4.* 1,400 *6.* 2,800 *8.* 1,200 *10.* 2,000 *12.* 3,200 *14.* 7,200 *16.* 4,000 *18.* 8,000 *20.* 28,000 *22.* 32,000 *24.* 20,000 *26.* 12,000 *28.* 30,000 *30.* 63,000 *32.* 420,000 *34.* 210,000 *36.* 480,000 *38.* 140,000 *40.* 420,000 *42.* 300,000 *44.* 810,000 *46.* 60,000 *48.* 6,000,000 *50.* 2,700,000 *52.* 300,000 *54.* 30,000,000 *56.* 4,900,000 *58.* 720,000 *60.* 72,000,000

Page 65 *1.* 8,000 *2.* 10,000 *3.* 5,000 *4.* 900 *5.* 24,000 *6.* 10,000
Exercises *2.* 1,200 *4.* 3,000 *6.* 2,800 *8.* 3,000 *10.* 300 *12.* 1,800 *14.* 3,600 *16.* 6,000 *18.* 40,000 *20.* 30,000

Pages 66–67 *1.* $9 to the nearest dollar *2.* $30 *3.* $7.20 *4.* $5 to the nearest dollar
Exercises *2.* $120 to the nearest dollar *4.* $2,500 to the nearest hundred dollars *6.* $136 *8.* $2.70 *10.* $41 *12.* $324

Pages 68–69 *2.* $16.50 *4.* 10 rows *6.* 1,365 cm² *8.* 32

Page 70 *1.* 880 *2.* 88,000 *3.* 9,400 *4.* 76,400 *5.* 90,000 *6.* 546,000
Exercises *2.* 5,200 *4.* 27,300 *6.* 676,000 *8.* 325,000 *10.* 5,980 *12.* 487,900 *14.* 81,000 *16.* 2,400 *18.* 740,000 *20.* 4,600

Page 71 *2.* T *4.* T *6.* T *8.* F

Page 75 *1.* 4 *2.* 4 *3.* 5 *4.* 7 *5.* 8 *6.* 9 *7.* 6

Pages 76–77 *1.* 30 *2.* 300 *3.* 6 *4.* 10
    5. 1,000 *6.* 3
Practice Set 2 *2.* 100 *4.* 10 *6.* 100 *8.* 100
    10. 20 *12.* 300 *14.* 70 *16.* 80 *18.* 80 *20.* 90
    22. 800 *24.* 9 *26.* 70 *28.* 30 *30.* 300
    32. 40 *34.* 50 *36.* 7
Practice Set 3 *2.* 3 *4.* 2 *6.* 9 *8.* 3 *10.* 9
    12. 7
Practice Set 4 *2.* 50 *4.* 6 *6.* 90 *8.* 900

Page 79 *1.* 9r1 *2.* 1r1 *3.* 14r2 *4.* 2r4 *5.* 2
    6. 1r1 *7.* 8r6 *8.* 1r3
Practice Set 5 *2.* 6r2 *4.* 8r3 *6.* 5r4 *8.* 5r4
    10. 2r7 *12.* 2r2 *14.* 6r6 *16.* 8r7 *18.* 5r3
    20. 4r2 *22.* 4r1 *24.* 7r7 *26.* 6r4 *28.* 7r1
    30. 2 *32.* 4r4 *34.* 7 *36.* 6r2 *38.* 4r2
    40. 2r5

Pages 80–81 *1.* 72 *2.* 322 *3.* 343r6
    4. 80r1 *5.* 256r2 *6.* 513r2
Practice Set 6 *2.* 333 *4.* 419r5 *6.* 611
    8. 501 *10.* 301 *12.* 53r1 *14.* 30 *16.* 622
    18. 432 *20.* 1,211 *22.* 1,532 *24.* 1,023
    26. 1,472 *28.* 1,633 *30.* 142r5 *32.* 771r3
    34. 623r3 *36.* 975 *38.* 766r1 *40.* 587r5
    42. 2,954r6 *44.* 3,379r3

Pages 82–83 *1.* 322r10 *2.* 4,261r6
    3. 629r44
Practice Set 7 *2.* 507 *4.* 3,058 *6.* 7,013
    8. 302 *10.* 307 *12.* 280
Practice Set 8 *2.* 2,205 *4.* 2,609 *6.* 505
    8. 703 *10.* 1,333r12 *12.* 247r2

e 84 Practice Set 9 *2.* 263 *4.* 39 *6.* 710
    8. 125 *10.* 98 *12.* 189 *14.* 310r8 *16.* 257

Page 85 *2.* 48

Pages 86–87 *1.* 50 *2.* 99 *3.* 16 *4.* 27
Exercises *2.* 55 sec *4.* $1.05 *6.* 1,173

Page 88 *2.* about 167 times *4.* about $55. 56
    6. about 1,928 m *8.* about 1,213,000 g

Page 89 *1.* 100 *2.* 8 *3.* 4 *4.* 360
Exercises *2.* 325 *4.* 613 *6.* 1,360 *8.* 1,000
    10. 1,333 *12.* 7 *14.* 500 *16.* 50 *18.* 5
    20. 140 *22.* $2.46 *24.* $7.33 *26.* $1.17

Pages 90–91 *2.* 29 km *4.* about 64L
    6. about 24, 232 L *8.* $3,392.48 *10.* No,
    total expense is $126.25 *12.* $1,910.50

Page 92 *1.* 211 *2.* 31 *3.* 53 *4.* 5,000
Exercises *2.* 143 *4.* 131 *6.* 195 *8.* 923
    10. 822 *12.* 304 *14.* 6 km/L *16.* 12

Page 93 *2.* $27,250,000 *4.* about 202,128
    6. $1,083,333.33

Pages 94–95 *2.–10.* Answers may vary.

Pages 100–101 1. Seventy-eight a pag̲ tenths 2. Seven and eighty-three hundredths 3. Seven hundred eighty-three thousandths 4. One and seventy-eight thousandths 5. 846.78 6. 574.15

Practice Set 1 2. Three and four thousand two hundred sixty-three ten thousandths 4. One thousand seven hundred eighty-nine and forty-three hundredths 6. Seventeen thousand eight hundred ninety-four and three hundred seventy-one thousandths 8. Sixty-four thousand two hundred forty-three and one hundred seven thousandths

Practice Set 2 2. 743.44 4. 999.99 6. 134.2 8. 693.551

Pages 102–103 1. 277.43 2. 506.561 3. 450.79 4. 1.2

Practice Set 3 2. 43.72 4. 11.03 6. 1,232 8. 1.437 10. 7.47 12. 14 14. 4.979 16. 7,484.4 18. 4.725 20. 30.081 22. 95.75 24. 607.228 26. .163 28. 1,131.4

Pages 104–106 1. 420.54 2. 2,096.95 3. 653.8235

Practice Set 4 2. 100.6747 4. 990.0051 6. 128.29 8. 29.247 10. 102.35 12. 162.75

Pages 104–106 continued
Practice Set 5 2. 434.0813 4. 89.2808 6. 126.125 8. 3,512.689 10. 643.82 12. 8.96757

Practice Set 6 2. 32.2 sec 4. 53 min 6. $16,908.94 8. 481.4 km

Pages 107–108 1. 887.12 2. 2.6 3. 598.923 4. 1,924.9 5. 2,268.91

Practice Set 7 2. $11.02 4. 547.144 6. 985.35 8. 508.16 10. $749.25 12. 8,920.42

Practice Set 8 2. 46.884 4. 21.9215 6. 4,107.34 8. 78.083 10. 41,073.4 12. 49,107.34

Practice Set 9 2. 5.5 m 4. $5.50 6. 2.7 kg

Page 109 194.1 km
Exercises 2. 948 km 4. 240.5 km 6. 741.8 km

Page 110 2. the average speed at which he traveled 4. heights of Amir and Bill 6. his commuting expenses

Page 111 2. 9 to 10 days 4. 12 hours 6. 18 to 19 days 8. 1,280 km 10. 18 months 21 days

Page 112 2.–12. Answers may vary.

Page 113 2. $6,700 4. $3,350 6. $555,500 8. 7 silver dollars 10. $57,200

Unit 6

Pages 117–118 *1.* 49.538 *2.* 1,337.625
    3. 8,762.8778
Practice Set 1 *2.* 64.2108 *4.* 7.1262
    6. 273.5271 *8.* 841.4604 *10.* 2,506.212
    12. 17,049.03 *14.* 849.409 *16.* 3,929.42
    18. 39.2942 *20.* 11.9184 *22.* 38.9464
    24. 36,194.99

Pages 119–121 *1.* 22.6352 *2.* 5.6808
    3. 335.8
Practice Set 2 *2.* 39.60 *4.* 2.016 *6.* .4565
    8. .00069 *10.* 8.184 *12.* 195.16
    14. 959.79 *16.* 51.975
Practice Set 3 *2.* 456.61 *4.* 12.22 *6.* .00595
    8. 6.909 *10.* .2875 *12.* 56.34 *14.* 4.51904
    16. 451.904 *18.* 451.904 *20.* 5,599.692
    22. 559.9692 *24.* .045024 *26.* 505.707
    28. 24.91776 *30.* 229.032 *32.* .647901
    34. 4,389.12 *36.* 318.6544 *38.* 4.51904
    40. 559.9692 *42.* 14.4130989
    44. 4,974.16

Pages 119–121 continued
Practice Set 4 *2.* $96.95 *4.* $4.80 *6.* $800
Practice Set 5 *2.* $22.80 *4.* $11.10 *6.* $3.52
    8. $9.80 *10.* $3.20 *12.* $5.52 *14.* $1.96

Pages 122–123 *1.* 24,776 *2.* 37.5 *3.* 147
    4. 16
Exercises *2.* 617.5 *4.* 648 *6.* 4,730 *8.* 6,690
    10. 3,780 *12.* .64 *14.* 810.8 *16.* 28,010
    18. .064 *20.* 642.5

Page 124 *2.* Not enough *4.* Too much
    6. Too much *8.* Enough

Page 125 *2.* 108.7 *4.* 7,473.0 *6.* .4 *8.* .99

Page 126 *2.* 28.05¢ or 28¢ *4.* .2601¢ or .26 ¢
    6. $139.6125 or $139.61 *8.* 291

Page 127 *2.* 393.6 km *4.* 1,335.9 km
    6. 5,863.785 km

Unit 7

Page 131 *1.* 6.0 *2.* 5.80 *3.* 21.0
Practice Set 1 *2.* 2.4648 *4.* 8.72 *6.* 16.602

Pages 132–133 *1.* 1.44 *2.* .144 *3.* 330.3
Practice Set 2 *2.* 7.51 *4.* .147 *6.* .195 *8.* 6.51
  10. .00259 *12.* .6071
Practice Set 3 *2.* 2.1 *4.* .4 *6.* 1.25 *8.* 1.9
  10. .3 *12.* .06 *14.* 1.5 *16.* .5
Practice Set 4 *2.* $52.70 *4.* 129

Page 134 *1.* 88 *2.* 506 *3.* 57 *4.* 43
Practice Set 5 *2.* 577 *4.* 603 *6.* 6,812
  8. 89 *10.* 4 *12.* 3 *14.* 765 *16.* 690

Page 135 *1.* 18 *2.* 1.2 *3.* .12
Practice Set 6 *2.* 2 *4.* .3 *6.* 4 *8.* 10 *10.* 10
  12. 10 *14.* 8.5

Pages 136–137 *1.* 288 *2.* 1.9 *3.* 16
Practice Set 7 *2.* 25,300 *4.* 29 *6.* 24.3
  8. 3.25 *10.* 10.1 *12.* 16,110 *14.* 26.4
  16. 20

Pages 136–137 continued
Practice Set 8 *2.* 6 *4.* 40 *6.* 3 *8.* 70 *10.* 50
  12. 500
Practice Set 9 *2.* 124 *4.* 42 *6.* 58 *8.* 312

Pages 138–139 *1.* 8.49 *2.* .00765 *3.* 4.56
Exercises *2.* .0865 *4.* .583 *6.* .368 *8.* .00902
  10. .057 *12.* .408 *14.* .01768 *16.* .64
  18. .00658 *20.* $.35 *22.* .04006 *24.* 6
  26. 28.48 *28.* 24.24 *30.* .064

Pages 140–141 *1.* 17.6 *2.* 8.75
Exercises *2.* 40 *4.* 371.6 *6.* .853 *8.* 7.68
  10. 13.5 *12.* 2,000 *14.* 70 *16.* 435.2
  18. 545

Page 142 *2.* 7.77 *4.* 127.46 kg/m *6.* $20.68
  8. .5865 km/min

Page 143 *2.* 2.5 *4.* 39.7 *6.* .1 *8.* 562.18

Pages 144–145 *2.–6.* Answers may vary.

Unit 8

Pages 148–149 *1.* 10 cm *2.* 8 cm *3.* 1 cm *4.* 1 cm *5.* 3 cm

Exercises *2.* 13 cm *4.* 10 cm *6.* 7 cm *8.* 6 cm *10.* 12 cm *12.* 14 cm *14.* 11 cm *16.* 6 cm *18.* 10 cm *20.* 14 cm

Page 150 *1.* 40 mm *2.* 25 mm *3.* 47 mm *4.* 38 mm

Exercises *2.* 29 mm *4.* 58 mm *6.* 32 mm *8.* 122 mm

Pages 151–153 *1.* 7.6 cm; 76 mm *2.* 8.9 cm; 89 mm *3.* 9.5 cm; 95 mm *4.* 450 cm *5.* 50 cm *6.* 24 cm *7.* 56 cm *8.* .6 m *9.* 1.2 m *10.* 1.85 km *11.* 3,600 mm

Exercises *2.* 36 mm; 3.6 cm *4.* 48 mm; 4.8 cm *6.* 59 mm; 5.9 cm *8.* 80 mm; 8 cm *10.* 71 mm; 7.1 cm *12.* 2,000 m *14.* 9,600 m *16.* 2.5 km *18.* 1 m *20.* 5 m *22.* .1 m *24.* 870 cm *26.* 90 cm *28.* .8 m *30.* .008 m *32.* 7.8 cm *34.* .2 cm *36.* 76 mm *38.* .3 cm

Pages 154–155 *1.–6.* Answers may vary.
Exercises *2.–18.* Answers may vary.

Pages 156–159 *1.* 14 cm *2.* 12.5 cm *3.* 12 cm *4.* 11.4 cm

Exercises *2.* 10.2 cm *4.* 14.6 cm *6.* 23.1 cm *8.* 19.8 cm *10.* 3.8 m *12.* $549 *14.* $1.62 *16.* 82.4 m

Pages 160–162 *1.* 7 cm² *2.* 4.5 cm²
Exercises *2.* 11 cm² *4.* 3 cm² *6.* 3 cm² *8.* 12 cm² *10.* 8.5 cm² *12.* 9.5 cm² *14.* 4.5 cm²

Pages 163–165 *1.* 598 cm² *2.* 410 cm² *3.* 408 mm² *4.* 44.8 m² *5.* 52 cm² *6.* 120 mm²

Exercises *2.* 912 cm² *4.* 124.02 cm² *6.* 1,302.4 cm² *8.* 7,300 mm² *10.* 153.7 m² *12.* 28 km² *14.* 798 cm² *16.* 10 mm² *18.* 612 mm² *20.* 10,812 m² *22.* 24 cm² *24.* 21.35 cm²

Pages 166–169 *1.* 8.5 cm² *2.* 9 cm² *3.* 48 cm² *4.* 36 cm²
Exercises *2.* 42 cm² *4.* 32 cm²

Pages 170–171 $132.00
Exercises *2.* 684 *4.* 25 mm *6.* 31.28 m² *8.* 3 L

Pages 172–173 *2.* 36.1 cm²

Page 174 *1.* Answers may vary. *2.* A 4-cm by 4-cm square

Exercises *2.* 10-cm by 10-cm sq *4.* 9-cm by 9-cm sq *6.* 7-cm by 7-cm sq *8.* 1-cm by 1-cm sq

Page 175 *1.* Answers may vary. *2.* 6-cm by 6-cm sq

Exercises *2.* 3-cm by 3-cm sq *4.* 10-cm by 10-cm sq *6.* 8-cm by 8-cm sq *8.* 20-cm by 20-cm sq

Pages 176–178 *1.* 12 cm³ *2.* 80 cm³
Exercises *2.* 300 cm³ *4.* 49 cm³ *6.* 1,260 cm³ *8.* 595.32 m³ *10.* 73,500 cm³ *12.* 6 cm

Pages 179–181 *1.* 2,450 mL *2.* 760 mL *3.* .007256 L *4.* .825 L *5.* 5 L or 5,000 mL *6.* 13.44 L or 13,440 mL

Exercises *2.* 8,000 mL *4.* 12,500 mL *6.* 470 mL *8.* 2.45 L *10.* .373 L *12.* .088 L *14.* 3.81 L *16.* 946 cm³ *18.* $4.25

Pages 182–184 *1.* .566 kg *2.* 1,200 g
Exercises *2.* .240 kg *4.* .1 kg *6.* 1,000 kg *8.* .475 kg *10.* 23,000 g *12.* 3,400 g *14.* 4,100 g *16.* .810 g *18.* 28.4 g *20.* 2,000 g *22.* 6,200 g *24.* 2,260,000 g *26.* 1 g *28.* 1 kg *30.* .1 kg *32.* .001 kg *34.* 1.742 kg *36.* 1.543 g *38.* .028 g

Pages 185–186 *1.* 15 dam; 1.5 hm *2.* 12 hg; 120 dag *3.* 34.5 dL; .345 daL

Exercises *2.* 2.06 dam *4.* .842 km *6.* .842 dam *8.* 8.80 hg *10.* .165 kL *12.* 16.5 daL

Pages 188–190 *1.* too cold *2.* too hot *3.* comfortable *4.* too cold *5.* 10° *6.* 20° *7.* −10°C

Exercises *2.* hot *4.* cold *6.* cold *8.* cold *10.* comfortable *12.* 50°C *14.* 20° *16.* 10° *18.* −5°C *20.* 30°C

Unit 9

Pages 197–199 *1.* $\frac{5}{6}$ *2.* 1 *3.* $\frac{4}{8}$ *4.* $\frac{5}{4}$, or $1\frac{1}{4}$ *5.* $\frac{5}{10}$ *6.* $\frac{12}{18}$
Practice Set 1 *2.* $\frac{2}{10}$
Practice Set 2 *2.* $\frac{3}{2}$ *4.* $\frac{12}{3}$, or 4 *6.* $\frac{1}{4}$ *8.* 4
Practice Set 3 *2.* $\frac{7}{10}$ *4.* $\frac{10}{24}$

Pages 200–202 *1.–8.* **Check drawings.**
9.–12. **Answers may vary.** *13.* **32 mm,**
$3\frac{2}{10}$ **cm** *14.* **47 mm, 4$\frac{7}{10}$ cm**
Practice Set 4 *2.–16.* **Check drawings.**

Pages 203–204 *1.–4.* **Answers may vary.**
5. $\frac{3}{5}$ *6.* $\frac{3}{4}$ *7.* $\frac{7}{10}$ *8.* $\frac{3}{5}$ *9.* 9 *10.* 10 *11.* 4
12. 3

Pages 203–204 continued
Practice Set 5 *2.* 6 *4.* 12 *6.* 4 *8.* 8 *10.* 10
12. 8 *14.* 2 *16.* 10
Practice Set 6 *2.* 1 *4.* 3 *6.* 3 *8.* 2 *10.* 1
12. 1 *14.* 3 *16.* 3
Practice Set 7 *2.* $\frac{15}{24}$ *4.* $\frac{12}{14}$ *6.* $\frac{14}{16}$ *8.* $\frac{20}{16}$

Page 205 *1.* $\frac{3}{4}$ *2.* $\frac{1}{4}$ *3.* $\frac{2}{9}$
Practice Set 8 *2.* $\frac{4}{5}$ *4.* $\frac{1}{2}$ *6.* $\frac{2}{3}$ *8.* $\frac{2}{3}$ *10.* $\frac{1}{2}$ *12.* $\frac{4}{3}$

Page 206 *1.* $\frac{7}{12}$ *2.* $\frac{1}{3}$ *3.* $\frac{3}{4}$ *4.* $\frac{16}{5}$
Practice Set 9 *2.* $\frac{7}{12}$ *4.* **equal** *6.* $\frac{9}{5}$ *8.* **equal**
10. $\frac{3}{10}$ *12.* $\frac{7}{12}$

Unit 10

Pages 211–212 *1.–4.* Check drawings.
  5. $\frac{5}{7}$ *6.* $\frac{3}{4}$ *7.* $\frac{4}{5}$ *8.* $\frac{11}{100}$
Practice Set 1 *2.* Check drawings.
Practice Set 2 *2.* $\frac{4}{5}$ *4.* 1 *6.* 1 *8.* $\frac{4}{5}$
Practice Set 3 *2.* $\frac{7}{10}$ *4.* 2 *6.* $\frac{17}{20}$ *8.* $\frac{5}{8}$

Pages 213–214 *1.* 1 *2.* $1\frac{1}{7}$ *3.* $1\frac{2}{5}$ *4.* $2\frac{1}{2}$ *5.* $2\frac{3}{8}$
  6. 6 *7.* $11\frac{1}{5}$ *8.* $10\frac{3}{5}$ *9.* $14\frac{1}{3}$
Practice Set 4 *2.* 3 *4.* 4 *6.* 7 *8.* 1 *10.* 3 *12.* 5
  14. 5 *16.* 7; 2 *18.* 10; 3
Practice Set 5 *2.* $7\frac{3}{5}$ *4.* $2\frac{1}{4}$ *6.* $6\frac{3}{7}$ *8.* $\frac{1}{3}$ *10.* $1\frac{1}{6}$
  12. $5\frac{3}{5}$ *14.* $2\frac{1}{3}$ *16.* $3\frac{3}{4}$ *18.* $13\frac{1}{4}$ *20.* $10\frac{7}{12}$
Practice Set 6 *2.* $1\frac{4}{5}$ *4.* $1\frac{1}{2}$ *6.* $1\frac{1}{5}$ *8.* $1\frac{7}{100}$
  10. $3\frac{1}{2}$ *12.* $1\frac{49}{1,000}$

Pages 215–216 *1.* 20 *2.* 6 *3.* 8 *4.* $\frac{2}{12}$, $\frac{9}{12}$
  5. $\frac{3}{24}$, $\frac{20}{24}$ *6.* $\frac{3}{8}$, $\frac{2}{8}$ *7.* $\frac{3}{6}$, $\frac{4}{6}$, $\frac{5}{6}$ *8.* $\frac{16}{24}$, $\frac{6}{24}$, $\frac{9}{24}$
  9. $\frac{4}{20}$, $\frac{2}{20}$, $\frac{15}{20}$
Practice Set 7 *2.* $\frac{6}{8}$, $\frac{5}{8}$ *4.* $\frac{5}{16}$, $\frac{14}{16}$ *6.* $\frac{15}{20}$, $\frac{7}{20}$
  8. $\frac{6}{8}$, $\frac{7}{8}$ *10.* $\frac{8}{20}$, $\frac{9}{20}$ *12.* $\frac{15}{20}$, $\frac{7}{20}$, $\frac{6}{20}$ *14.* $\frac{3}{18}$, $\frac{4}{18}$
  16. $\frac{21}{24}$, $\frac{16}{24}$, $\frac{6}{24}$ *18.* $\frac{30}{100}$, $\frac{7}{100}$ *20.* $\frac{12}{10}$, $\frac{5}{10}$, $\frac{3}{10}$
  22. $\frac{4}{12}$, $\frac{3}{12}$, $\frac{1}{12}$ *24.* $\frac{26}{20}$, $\frac{25}{20}$, $\frac{6}{20}$ *26.* $\frac{6}{20}$, $\frac{9}{20}$
  28. $\frac{6}{9}$, $\frac{5}{9}$ *30.* $\frac{7}{14}$, $\frac{4}{14}$ *32.* $\frac{30}{1,000}$, $\frac{7}{1,000}$
  34. $\frac{10}{40}$, $\frac{15}{40}$, $\frac{36}{40}$ *36.* $\frac{90}{1,000}$, $\frac{300}{1,000}$, $\frac{17}{1,000}$

Pages 217–219 *1.* $\frac{3}{4}$ *2.* $\frac{9}{10}$ *3.* $\frac{5}{6}$ *4.* $\frac{11}{12}$ *5.* $\frac{41}{100}$
  6. $1\frac{2}{25}$ *7.* $\frac{251}{1,000}$ *8.* $\frac{929}{1,000}$ *9.* $4\frac{1}{8}$ *10.* $6\frac{1}{4}$
  11. $8\frac{3}{8}$ *12.* 10
Practice Set 8 *2.* $1\frac{1}{6}$ *4.* $\frac{19}{20}$ *6.* $\frac{17}{20}$ *8.* $1\frac{1}{6}$ *10.* $7\frac{1}{2}$
  12. $10\frac{9}{10}$ *14.* $20\frac{11}{40}$ *16.* $20\frac{1}{3}$
Practice Set 9 *2.* $\frac{33}{50}$ *4.* $\frac{79}{100}$ *6.* $\frac{49}{50}$ *8.* $\frac{3}{4}$ *10.* $\frac{43}{50}$
  12. $\frac{13}{25}$ *14.* $7\frac{17}{100}$ *16.* $10\frac{33}{50}$ *18.* $8\frac{79}{100}$
  20. $5\frac{3}{4}$ m *22.* $30\frac{1}{5}$ kg

Pages 220–222 *1.* $\frac{2}{3}$ *2.* $\frac{1}{5}$ *3.* $\frac{2}{5}$ *4.* $\frac{3}{5}$ *5.* $\frac{1}{2}$ *6.* $\frac{3}{10}$
  7. $\frac{1}{8}$ *8.* $\frac{1}{10}$ *9.* $\frac{3}{4}$ *10.* $8\frac{5}{8}$ *11.* $1\frac{1}{2}$ *12.* $2\frac{3}{4}$ *13.* $4\frac{1}{2}$
  14. $9\frac{1}{8}$ *15.* $\frac{2}{5}$ *16.* $2\frac{1}{2}$ *17.* $4\frac{4}{5}$ *18.* $3\frac{2}{3}$ *19.* $2\frac{7}{8}$
Practice Set 10 *2.* $8\frac{1}{7}$ *4.* $4\frac{3}{5}$ *6.* $2\frac{3}{4}$ *8.* $7\frac{1}{3}$
  10. $6\frac{5}{16}$ *12.* $6\frac{5}{7}$ *14.* $4\frac{3}{5}$ *16.* $6\frac{3}{10}$ *18.* $6\frac{23}{25}$
  20. $14\frac{1}{5}$
Practice Set 11 *2.* $8\frac{3}{7}$ *4.* $4\frac{4}{5}$ *6.* $4\frac{1}{2}$ *8.* $7\frac{2}{3}$ *10.* $6\frac{1}{2}$
  12. $6\frac{6}{7}$ *14.* $4\frac{4}{5}$ *16.* $8\frac{1}{12}$ m

Pages 223–225 *1.* $22\frac{6}{7}$, or 23 *2.* $\frac{7}{8}$, or 1
  3. $70\frac{7}{8}$, or 71 *4.* $18\frac{96}{100}$, or 19 *5.* 14
  6. 32 *7.* 12 *8.* 45
Exercises *2.* $12\frac{9}{16}$, or 13 *4.* 21 *6.* 16
  8. $17\frac{5}{16}$ *10.* 37 *12.* 11 *14.* 42 *16.* 8 *18.* 2
  20. $6\frac{1}{4}$ *22.* 8 *24.* 22 *26.* 10 *28.* 36 *30.* 87
  32. 19 *34.* 37 *36.* 15 *38.* 17 *40.* 25
  42. 8 *44.* 24 *46.* 26 *48.* 6 *50.* $\frac{1}{4}$ *52.* 9
  54. 15

Unit 11

Pages 229–230 1. $2\frac{1}{4}$ 2. $1\frac{1}{2}$ 3. $1\frac{3}{4}$ 4. $2\frac{2}{5}$ 5. 4
6. $3\frac{1}{3}$ 7. $\frac{3}{10}$ 8. $1\frac{1}{8}$ 9. $\frac{6}{15}$
Practice Set 1 2. 6 4. $5\frac{1}{3}$ 6. 2 8. $9\frac{3}{5}$
Practice Set 2 2. $4\frac{4}{5}$ 4. $3\frac{3}{4}$ 6. 6 8. $6\frac{2}{5}$
Practice Set 3 2. $3\frac{3}{5}$ 4. $7\frac{1}{2}$ 6. 5 8. 6 10. $3\frac{6}{13}$
12. $12\frac{2}{3}$ 14. $1\frac{5}{6}$ 16. $\frac{4}{5}$ 18. $8\frac{1}{6}$ 20. 6

Pages 231–232 1. $\frac{3}{8}$ 2. $\frac{9}{16}$ 3. $1\frac{1}{8}$
Practice Set 4 2. $\frac{15}{32}$ 4. $\frac{3}{32}$ 6. $\frac{3}{32}$ 8. $\frac{7}{16}$
Practice Set 5 2. $\frac{7}{25}$ 4. $\frac{7}{100}$ 6. $\frac{1}{2}$ 8. $\frac{2}{77}$ 10. $\frac{1}{36}$
12. $\frac{35}{48}$ 14. $\frac{1}{100}$ 16. $\frac{81}{100}$ 18. $\frac{3}{25}$ 20. $\frac{1}{16}$
22. $\frac{3}{32}$ 24. $1\frac{1}{8}$ 26. $\frac{2}{5}$ h

Pages 233–234 1. $\frac{5}{8}$ 2. $\frac{15}{32}$ 3. $1\frac{1}{4}$ 4. $4\frac{3}{8}$ 5. $2\frac{5}{8}$
6. $28\frac{1}{2}$ 7. $7\frac{11}{16}$ 8. $2\frac{7}{8}$ 9. $9\frac{21}{40}$
Practice Set 6 2. $1\frac{31}{32}$ 4. $1\frac{19}{32}$ 6. $1\frac{19}{32}$ 8. $5\frac{15}{32}$
10. $1\frac{1}{35}$ 12. $2\frac{27}{32}$ 14. $\frac{11}{64}$ 16. $\frac{45}{64}$
Practice Set 7 2. $2\frac{19}{50}$ 4. $2\frac{17}{100}$ 6. $4\frac{16}{25}$ 8. $5\frac{1}{4}$
10. $\frac{8}{9}$ 12. $9\frac{3}{4}$ 14. $\frac{17}{30}$ 16. $10\frac{19}{50}$
Practice Set 8 2. $3\frac{3}{7}$ 4. $5\frac{29}{32}$ 6. $6\frac{1}{64}$ 8. $4\frac{29}{64}$
10. $9\frac{1}{6}$ 12. $2\frac{5}{8}$ 14. $5\frac{1}{4}$ 16. $7\frac{7}{8}$

Pages 235–236 1. $\frac{1}{5}$ 2. $\frac{5}{3}$ 3. $\frac{1}{6}$ 4. $\frac{8}{15}$ 5. $\frac{3}{11}$
6. $\frac{5}{7}$
Practice Set 9 2. $\frac{8}{7}$ 4. $\frac{10}{7}$ 6. $\frac{8}{13}$ 8. $\frac{1}{8}$
Practice Set 10 2. 4 4. $\frac{5}{7}$ 6. $\frac{10}{7}$ 8. $\frac{5}{4}$ 10. $\frac{1}{4}$
12. $\frac{2}{3}$ 14. $\frac{8}{19}$ 16. $\frac{1}{3}$ 18. $\frac{100}{3}$ 20. $\frac{10}{81}$ 22. 1
24. $\frac{9}{50}$

Pages 237–238 1. $1\frac{1}{3}$ 2. $1\frac{1}{15}$ 3. $3\frac{15}{16}$ 4. $\frac{3}{8}$
5. $\frac{1}{18}$ 6. $\frac{1}{18}$ 7. $\frac{7}{10}$ 8. $4\frac{8}{9}$ 9. $2\frac{2}{9}$
Practice Set 11 2. $43\frac{1}{5}$ 4. $1\frac{5}{6}$ 6. $1\frac{19}{24}$ 8. $\frac{2}{3}$
10. $4\frac{2}{3}$ 12. $\frac{3}{14}$
Practice Set 12 2. $1\frac{1}{5}$ 4. $\frac{3}{4}$ 6. $\frac{1}{2}$ 8. '2 10. $\frac{5}{6}$
12. $\frac{1}{30}$
Practice Set 13 2. $\frac{1}{120}$ 4. $\frac{7}{48}$ 6. $3\frac{1}{2}$ 8. $\frac{24}{29}$
10. $1\frac{1}{2}$ 12. $\frac{2}{3}$
Practice Set 14 2. 18 4. $\frac{1}{56}$ 6. $\frac{1}{36}$ 8. $\frac{3}{16}$
10. $\frac{1}{40}$ 12. $7\frac{1}{2}$ 14. $\frac{1}{56}$ 16. $1\frac{4}{5}$

Pages 239–240 1. 5 2. 7 3. 6 4. 9 5. 20
6. 36 7. 30 8. 16 9. 12 10. 9 11. $25\frac{1}{3}$
12. 182
Exercises 2. 8 4. 7 6. 6 8. 6 10. 11 12. 8
14. 100 16. 16 18. 30 20. 30 22. 25
24. 28 26. 20 28. 48 30. 70 32. 39
34. 22 36. 33 38. 100 40. 35 42. 150
44. 210 46. 204 48. 679

Pages 241–242 1. between 0 and 5
2. between 0 and 3 3. between 0 and
6 4. between 2 and 6 5. between 72
and 90 6. between 70 and 88 7. between
24 and 48 8. between 80 and 96
9. between 96 and 144 10. between
$14 and $24 11. between $150 and
$175 12. between $3.60 and $3.96
Exercises 2. between 0 and 2 4. between
0 and 3 6. between 0 and 10
8. between 0 and 9 10. between 14
and 24 12. between 160 and 187
14. between 0 and 4 16. between 6
and 12 18. between 6 and 12
20. between 6 and 12 22. between 25
and 36 24. between 50 and 66
26. between 48 and 72 28. between $0
and $6 30. between $0 and $2
32. between $135 and $180
34. between $6 and $12 36. between
$0 and $90 38. between $0 and
$180 40. between $0 and $180

Page 243 2. $202\frac{1}{2}$ hr 4. $40\frac{5}{8}$ cm 6. $\frac{3}{4}$ m
8. 100 10. $3\frac{1}{2}$ weeks

Pages 244–245 1. $\frac{1}{10}$ 2. $\frac{3}{10}$ 3. $\frac{0}{10}$ 4. $1\frac{1}{4}$ 5. $\frac{3}{4}$
6. $\frac{1}{4}$ 7. $1\frac{1}{2}$ 8. $\frac{7}{10}$ 9. .800 10. .625 11. .125
12. .400 13. .333 14. .667 15. .167
16. .300
Exercises 2. $\frac{7}{10}$ 4. $\frac{7}{20}$ 6. $\frac{1}{4}$ 8. $\frac{3}{4}$ 10. $\frac{4}{5}$ 12. $1\frac{2}{5}$
14. $1\frac{3}{10}$ 16. $\frac{3}{5}$ 18. $\frac{7}{8}$ 20. $\frac{13}{20}$ 22. .200
24. .700 26. .583 28. .188 30. .563
32. .125 34. .625 36. .500 38. .750
40. .750

Unit 12

Pages 248–249 *1.* 9 *2.* 8 *3.* 121 *4.* 19 *5.* 12 *6.* 351

Exercises *2.* 8 *4.* 6 *6.* 3 *8.* 10 *10.* 11 *12.* 36 *14.* 78 *16.* 7 *18.* 13 *20.* 351

Pages 250–251 *1.* 3 *2.* 4 *3.* 8 *4.* 5 *5.* 15 *6.* 36 *7.* 56 *8.* 1,071

Exercises *2.* 7 *4.* 7 *6.* 9 *8.* 5 *10.* 6 *12.* 18 *14.* 36 *16.* 456

Pages 252–253 *1.* 8 *2.* 0 *3.* 4 *4.* 14 *5.* 40 *6.* 20

Exercises *2.* 2 *4.* 6 *6.* 64 *8.* 72 *10.* 9 *12.* 8 *14.* 51 *16.* 1,975

Page 254 *2.* c *4.* c

Page 255 *2.* 11 *4.* 49 *6.* 40 *8.* 7

Pages 256–257 *1.* 300 km *2.* 1,584 km *3.* 18 h *4.* 6 h *5.* 312 m/min *6.* 136 km/h

Exercises *2.* 140 km *4.* 832 km *6.* 5 h *8.* 13 h *10.* 48 m/h *12.* 12 km/h *14.* 5 h *16.* 60 m/min *18.* 1,056 km *20.* 2 h

Page 258 *2.* 25 km/h *4.* 45 km *6.* 55 km/h *8.* 410 m/min *10.* 62 km/h

Unit 13

Pages 261–263 *1.* 70° *2.* 80°

Exercises *2.* 90° *4.* 65° *6.* 149° *8.–12.* Check drawings.

Pages 264–265 *1.* Answers may vary. *2.* 180° *3.* 100° *4.* 60°

Exercises *2.* 30° *4.* 45° *6.* 65°

Pages 266–268 *1.* Answers may vary. *2.* 360° *3.* 120° *4.* 50° *5.* 105° *6.* 120°

Exercises *2.* 70° *4.* 90° *6.* 90° *8.* $\angle E = 65°$, $\angle F = 115°$, $\angle G = 65°$

Pages 269–271 *1.* 24 cm *2.* 46 cm *3.* OC = 6 cm, BD = 12 cm, OB = 6 cm *4.* EO = 15mm, OG = 15 mm, FH = 30 mm

Exercises *2.* OC = 36 cm, DB = 72 cm *4.* 24 cm *6.* FO = 26 mm, OG = 26 mm, perimeter of $\triangle$ FOG = 92 mm

Page 272 *2.* 45° *4.* T

Page 273 *1.* 60° *2.* 80°

Exercises *2.* 60°

Unit 14

Page 276 *2.* 4 *4.* 218 *6.* 215

Page 277 *2.* 37 *4.* 40

Page 278 *2.* 134 *4.* 17

Page 279 *2.* mode 175; median 168; mean 168.6 cm *4.* mode 102; median 89; mean 89

Pages 280–281 *2.* Cities, Centimeters of snow *4.* More: Salt Lake City, Denver; Less: Seattle, Nashville, Kansas City *6.* Seattle, 39 cm; Salt Lake City, 145 cm; Nashville, 30 cm; Kansas City, 55 cm; Denver, 148 cm; Chicago, 97 cm *8.* Johnson, Smith; Gonzalez, Rodriguez, White, Wilson *10.* 1 million *12.* yes

Pages 282–283 *2.* Answers may vary.

Pages 284–285 *2.* degrees Celsius and months of the year *4.* May, June, July, Aug., Sept.; Jan., Feb., Dec. *6.* Jan. 5; Feb. 7; March 11; April 16; May 21; June 26; July 27, Aug. 27; Sept. 23; Oct. 17, Nov. 10; Dec. 6 *8.* Average kilometers per liter *10.* 2,000 kg *12.* 1,800 kg *14.* 2,150; 2,400 *16.* about 1.5 times as much

Pages 286–287 *2.–4.* Answers may vary.

Unit 15

Pages 291–292 1. $\frac{180}{30}$ 2. $\frac{30}{180}$
Exercises 2. $\frac{14}{29}$ 4. $\frac{114}{86}$ 6. $\frac{3}{4}$ 8. $\frac{550}{1,300}$ 10. $\frac{4}{2}$
12. $\frac{4}{2}$ 14. $\frac{5 \text{ m}}{200 \text{ kg}}$ 16. $\frac{180 \text{ cm}}{85 \text{ kg}}$

Page 293 1. $\frac{3}{5}$ 2. $\frac{5}{8}$ 3. $\frac{3}{5}$ 4. $\frac{13}{12}$
Exercises 2. $\frac{3}{2}$ 4. $\frac{4}{5}$ 6. $\frac{16}{7}$ 8. $\frac{4}{27}$ 10. $\frac{5}{2}$ 12. $\frac{11}{8}$

Pages 294–295 1. 8 apples for $1.10
2. 3 ties for $9.95
Exercises 2. Novi 4. Mr. Cato 6. Joe
8. Paint A 10. B

Pages 296–297 1. .333 2. .375 3. .313
4. .556 5. .350
Exercises 2. .245; .324; Mark 4. .276; .327;
Juma 6. .321; .333; Pat 8. .335; .327;
Karl

Pages 298–300 1. $\frac{1}{6}$ 2. $\frac{1}{6}$ 3. $\frac{1}{3}$ 4. $\frac{1}{2}$ 5. $\frac{1}{3}$ 6. 1
7. $\frac{1}{16}$ 8. $\frac{1}{16}$ 9. $\frac{1}{4}$
Exercises 2. $\frac{1}{3}, \frac{1}{3}, \frac{1}{2}$ 4. $\frac{1}{15}, \frac{1}{1,500}$ 6. $\frac{1}{6}, \frac{5}{6}$, 1
8. 4 possible outcomes; $\frac{1}{4}, \frac{1}{4}, \frac{1}{2}$

Pages 301–302 1. yes 2. no 3. no
Exercises 1. yes 2. yes 3. no 4. no 5. yes
6. yes 7. no 8. yes 9. no 10. yes 11. yes
12. yes 13. yes 14. no 15. no 16. yes
17. yes

Pages 303–304 1. 132 2. $\frac{7}{8}$
Exercises 2. $78\frac{1}{3}$¢ 4. $6\frac{3}{4}$ 6. 256 8. $7,500
10. $1\frac{1}{2}$ 12. 20

Pages 305–307 1. 35¢ 2. $7\frac{1}{2}$ cups
Exercises 2. 520 4. $28.88 6. $.03
8. $281.25 10. 3.6 kg 12. .7 m 14. 5 m³
16. $.11 18. $\frac{3}{16}$ L; $1\frac{1}{2}$ L 20. $6\frac{2}{3}$ cups; 80
lemons; 80 oranges; 20 cups; 60 L;
25 cups; $52\frac{1}{2}$ cups; $7\frac{1}{2}$ L

Unit 16

Pages 310–311 *1.* $\frac{3}{100}$ *2.* $\frac{1}{4}$ *3.* $\frac{200}{100}$
Exercises *2.* $\frac{10}{100}$ *4.* $\frac{18}{100}$ *6.* $\frac{42}{100}$ *8.* $\frac{20}{100}$
10. $\frac{200}{100}$ *12.* $\frac{125}{100}$ *14.* $\frac{53}{100}$ *16.* $\frac{87}{100}$ *18.* $\frac{1}{100}$

Pages 312–313 *1.* .42 *2.* 3 *3.* .5 *4.* 1.75
5. .01 *6.* .09 *7.* .065 *8.* .135 *9.* .002
10. .16$\frac{2}{3}$ *11.* .0001 *12.* .05$\frac{1}{3}$
Exercises *2.* .015 *4.* .125 *6.* .008 *8.* .93
10. .834 *12.* 3.75 *14.* 4 *16.* .0003
18. 6.25 *20.* .029 *22.* .12$\frac{1}{3}$ *24.* 1.23$\frac{1}{3}$
26. .8 *28.* .415 *30.* .0009

Page 314 *1.* 45% *2.* 90% *3.* 1% *4.* 50%
5. 37.5% *6.* 210% *7.* 8.5% *8.* 480%
Exercises *2.* 12% *4.* 9% *6.* 40% *8.* 2%
10. 38.1% *12.* 475%

Pages 315–316 *1.* $\frac{3}{100}$ *2.* $\frac{1}{4}$ *3.* $\frac{19}{100}$ *4.* $\frac{1}{10}$ *5.* $\frac{3}{8}$
6. $\frac{2}{3}$ *7.* $\frac{7}{8}$ *8.* $\frac{1}{12}$ *9.* 1$\frac{3}{10}$ *10.* 2$\frac{1}{4}$ *11.* 1$\frac{1}{5}$ *12.* 3
Exercises *2.* $\frac{3}{4}$ *4.* $\frac{9}{100}$ *6.* $\frac{1}{50}$ *8.* $\frac{1}{5}$ *10.* $\frac{1}{20}$ *12.* $\frac{1}{16}$
14. 1$\frac{1}{10}$ *16.* 2$\frac{1}{2}$ *18.* 2 *20.* 1$\frac{2}{5}$ *22.* 1$\frac{4}{5}$

Pages 317–318 *1.* 50% *2.* 20% *3.* 10%
4. 70% *5.* 62$\frac{1}{2}$% *6.* 87$\frac{1}{2}$% *7.* 33$\frac{1}{3}$%
8. 83$\frac{1}{3}$% *9.* 450% *10.* 220% *11.* 175%
Exercises *2.* 66$\frac{2}{3}$% *4.* 75% *6.* 12$\frac{1}{2}$% *8.* 60%
10. 110% *12.* 550% *14.* 133$\frac{1}{3}$%
16. 325% *18.* 5% *20.* 180%

Pages 319–320 *1.* 50 *2.* 70 *3.* 272.16
4. 6.96 *5.* $6.32 *6.* $47.40 *7.* $17.97
8. $3.57
Exercises *2.* 24 *4.* $11.75 *6.* $10.50 *8.* 100
10. 784 *12.* $54 *14.* $148.75 *16.* 510 kg

Page 321 *1.* $10 *2.* 5 *3.* 24
Exercises—Answers may vary. *2.* $40
4. $52 *6.* $270 *8.* $120 *10.* $9 *12.* $660
14. $300 *16.* $18 *18.* 36 *20.* $60

Pages 322–323 *1.* 25% *2.* 20% *3.* 42.9%
4. 73.3%
Exercises *2.* 12.5% *4.* 25% *6.* 10% *8.* 20%
10. 66.7% *12.* 33.3% *14.* 31.6% *16.* 8%
18. 86.7% *20.* 7.1%

Pages 324–325 *1.* 52 *2.* 300 *3.* 55 eggs
Exercises *2.* 300 *4.* 15 *6.* 30 *8.* 200 *10.* 64
12. 28 *14.* $250 *16.* $550 *18.* 76
20. $1,250

Pages 326–327 *1.* Rose; 5% *2.* Brand B;
5.4%
Exercises *2.* Blanca *4.* Vera; .2% *6.* Ray's;
May's

Pages 328–329 *1.* 125% *2.* 12.7%
Exercises *2.* 40% *4.* 28.9% *6.* 20%
8. 16.7% *10.* 25% *12.* 29.1%

Unit 17

Pages 332–333 *1.* $254.50 *2.* $29.64
Exercises *2.* $238 *4.* $8.66 *6.* $60 *8.* $15.50
   10. $245 *12.* $54.38 *14.* $233.87
   16. $39.51 *18.* $7.25 *20.* $28.70
   22. $188.50 *24.* $35.37

Pages 334–335 *1.* $507 *2.* $1,100
Exercises *2.* $374 *4.* $2,310 *6.* $108.90
   8. 70¢

Pages 336–338 *1.* 49 *2.* 55 *3.* 41.5 *4.* 38
   5. $142.60 *6.* $256
Exercises *2.* 47.5 *4.* 50.5 *6.* 44.5 *8.* 62.5
   10. 61 Rounded to the nearest cent
   12. $176.75 *14.* $143.18 *16.* $252.88
   18. $103.36 *20.* $269.50 *22.* $134.75
   24. $206.25 *26.* $194.43

Page 339 *2.* 100-01-1000 *4.* $196 *6.* $4.50
   8. $6.16 *10.* $11.86 *12.* $850.08
   14. $4,704

Pages 340–341 *2.* Gross pay should be
   $165.60. *4.* Net pay $75.09 *6.* O.K.

Pages 342–343 *2.* Jeff *4.* 2 kg grease and
   2 tubes *6.* yes *8.* O.K. *10.* $18.07
   12. $616.77 *14.* $751.80 *16.* $19.46

Unit 18

Pages 346–347 *2.–6.* Answers may vary.

Pages 348–349 *2.* Balance on hand: $4.90
   4. Balance on hand; $1.29

Pages 350–351 *1.* $12.50 *2.* $1,948
Exercises *2.* $15 *4.* $62.41 *6.* $33,600
   8. $680.40 *10.* $107.75

Pages 352–353 $108
Exercises *2.* $221 *4.* $63

Pages 354–355 *1.* Store B *2.* larger pkg
Exercises *2.* Store A *4.* Store A *6.* Store B
   8. larger *10.* larger *12.* larger
   14. smaller

Pages 356–357 *2.* Lula Schwartz;
   Spencer's TV Service *4.* $83 *6.* $73.55
   8.–16. Total deposit for each is given.
   8. $292.68 *10.* $290.10 *12.* $230.74
   14. $245.36 *16.* $340.96

Pages 358–359 *2.* 3/27/79 *4.* $38.20
   6. $.15 *8.* Repair work *10.–32.* New
   balance is given. Answer based on
   15¢ check charge. *10.* $244.10
   12. $332.87 *14.* $231.07 *16.* $158.65
   18. $167.04 *20.* $169.24 *22.* $127.76
   24. $180.61 *26.* $149.49 *28.* $90.74
   30. $255.69 *32.* $253.48

Unit 19

Pages 362–363 *2.* $12.50 *4.* To submit a statement signed by a doctor in the event of making a claim *6.* $4 *8.* To let a company representative examine the bicycle in the event of a claim *10.–12.* Answers may vary.

Pages 364–365 *2.* $1,575 profit *4.* $34 *6.* $7,500; $3.75

Pages 366–367 *2.* $6,800 *4.* $97.75 *6.* $9,350

Pages 368–369 *2.* $45 *4.* Mr. Brooks: $5,100

Pages 370–371 *2.* Insurance: $4,955; Mr. Gold: $365

Unit 20

Pages 374–375 *2.* $3.52 *4.* $4.48 *6.* $.23 *8.* $209.70 *10.* $2.19 *12.* $.42 *14.* $3.50 *16.* $215.68 *18.* $40.60 *20.* $105.93

Pages 376–377 *2.* $61.25 *4.* $130.20 *6.* $228.55 *8.* $24.17 *10.* $107.92 *12.* $122.50

Pages 378–379 *2.* $135 *4.* $1,209.68 *6.* $1,131.17 *8.* $1,530 *10.* $1,287

Pages 380–383 *2.* $6,217; 10 *4.* $478: 11b; owes $9 *6.* refund:$215 *8.* refund: $10